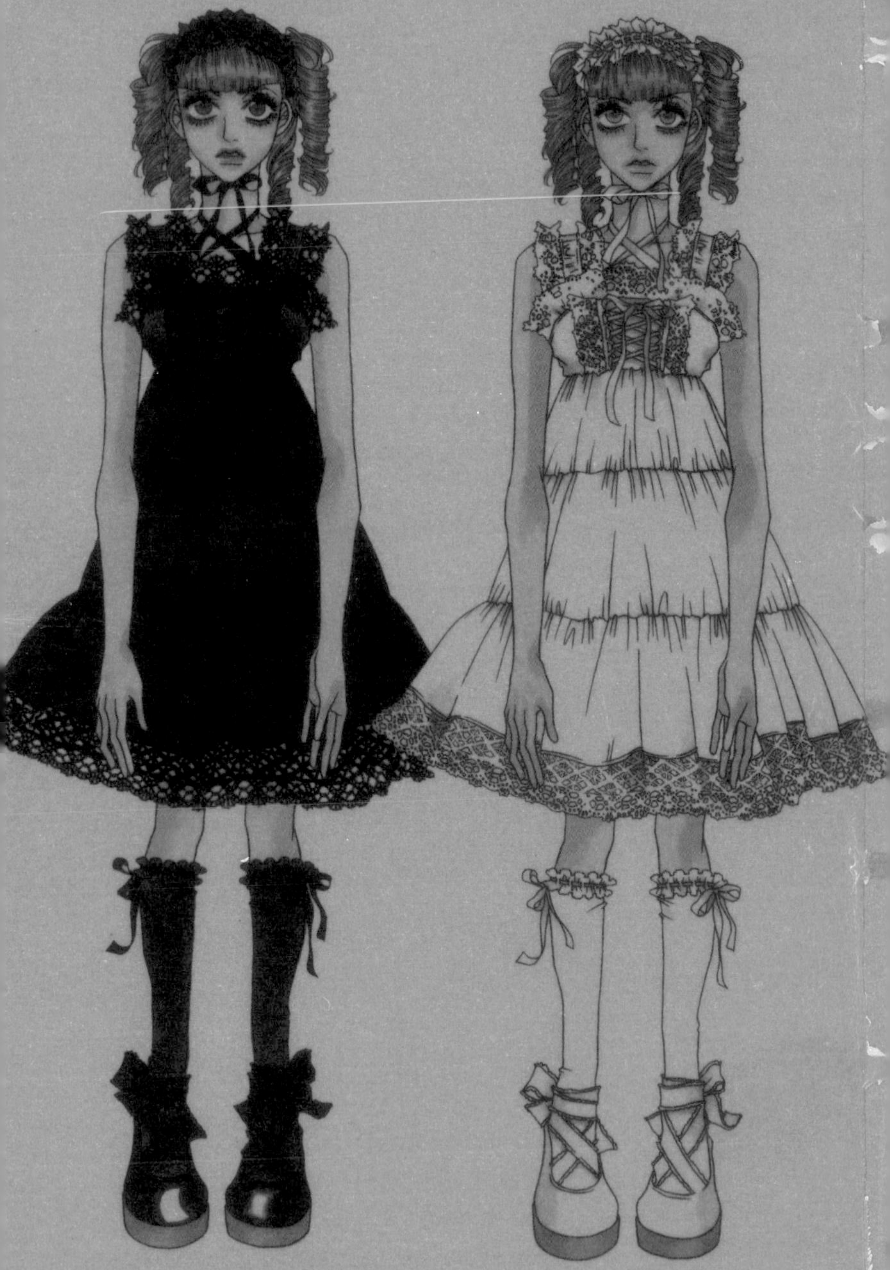

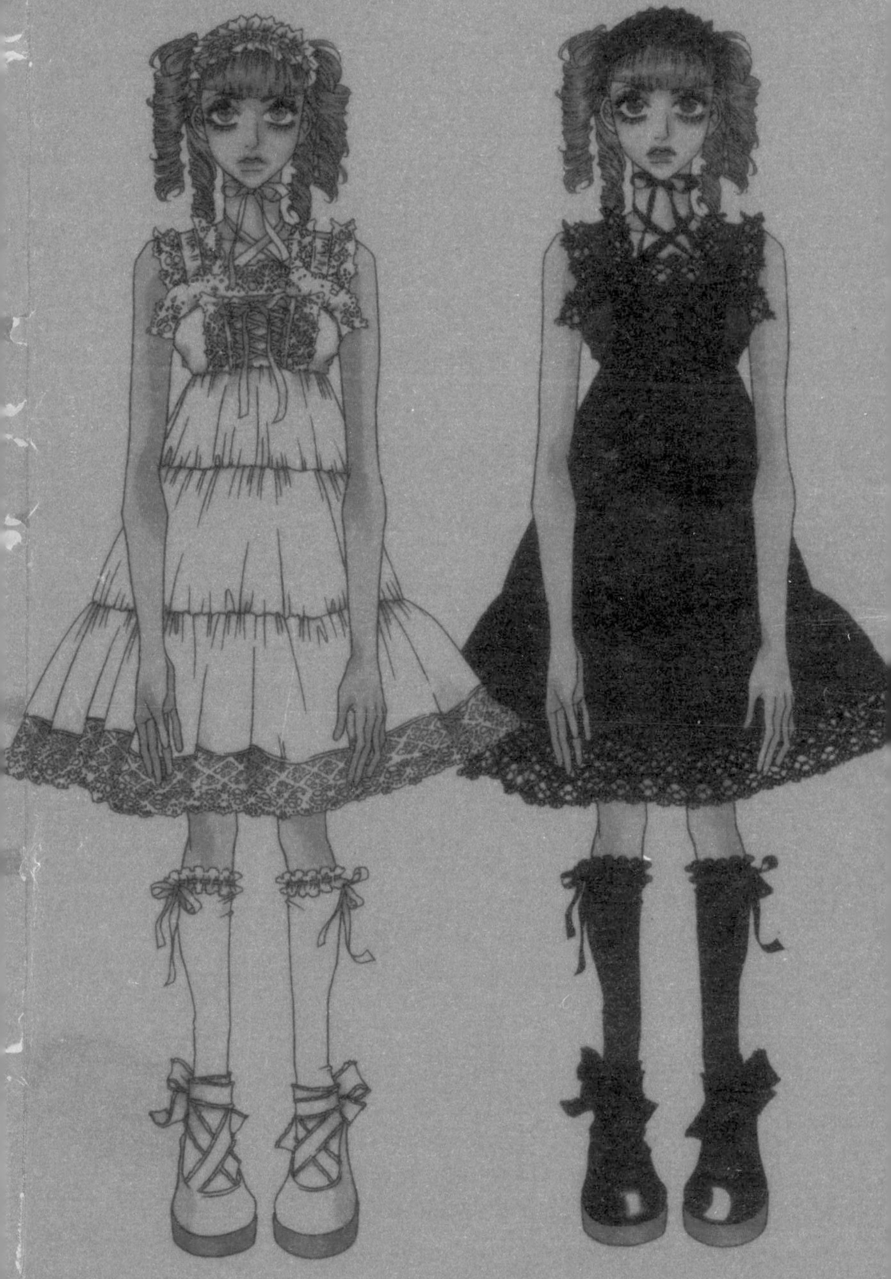

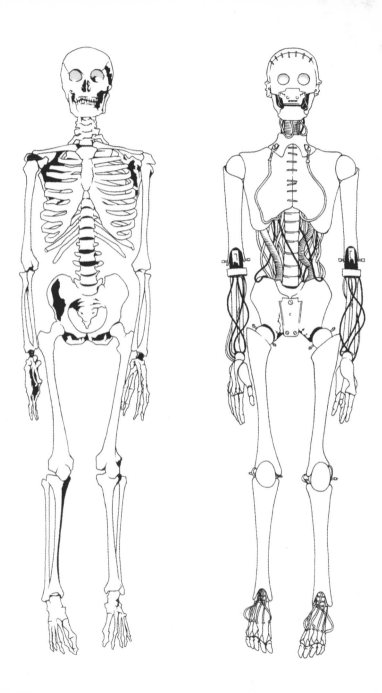

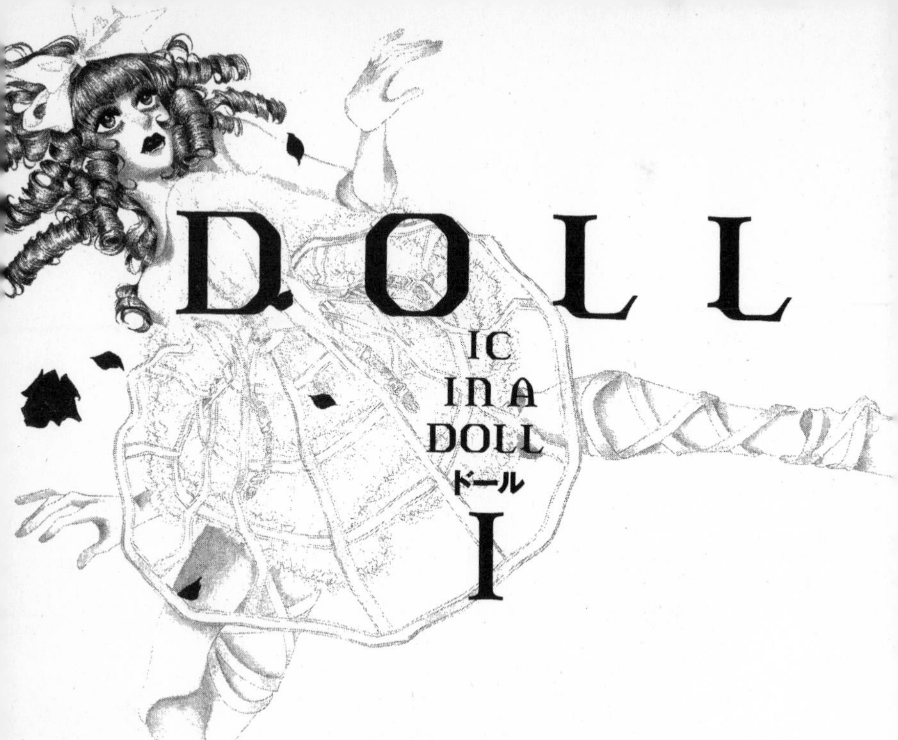

DOLL

IC IN A DOLL

ドール

I

MITSUKAZU MIHARA

三原ミツカズ

Translator - Yuki N. Johnson
English Adaptation - Simon Furman
Retouch & Lettering - Yoohae Yang
Cover Layout -Harlan Harris

Editor - Rob Tokar
Managing Editor - Jill Freshney
Production Coordinator - Antonio DePietro
Production Managers - Jennifer Miller & Mutsumi Miyazaki
Art Director - Matthew Alford
Editorial Director - Jeremy Ross
VP of Production - Ron Klamert
President & C.O.O. - John Parker
Publisher & C.E.O. - Stuart Levy

Email: info@TOKYOPOP.com
Come visit us online at www.TOKYOPOP.com

A  Manga

TOKYOPOP Inc.
5900 Wilshire Blvd. Suite 2000
Los Angeles, CA 90036

Doll Volume 1

ISBN: 1-59182-709-4

First TOKYOPOP® printing: May 2004

10 9 8 7 6 5 4 3 2 1

Printed in the USA

DOLL

VOLUME 1

BY
MITSUKAZU MIHARA

LOS ANGELES • TOKYO • LONDON

DOLL I

CONTENTS

LIST 1   a nameless doll

LIST 2   MARIA

LIST 3   AI

LIST 4   KAORU

LIST 5   AYAKO

LIST 6   a maid servant

L I S T I

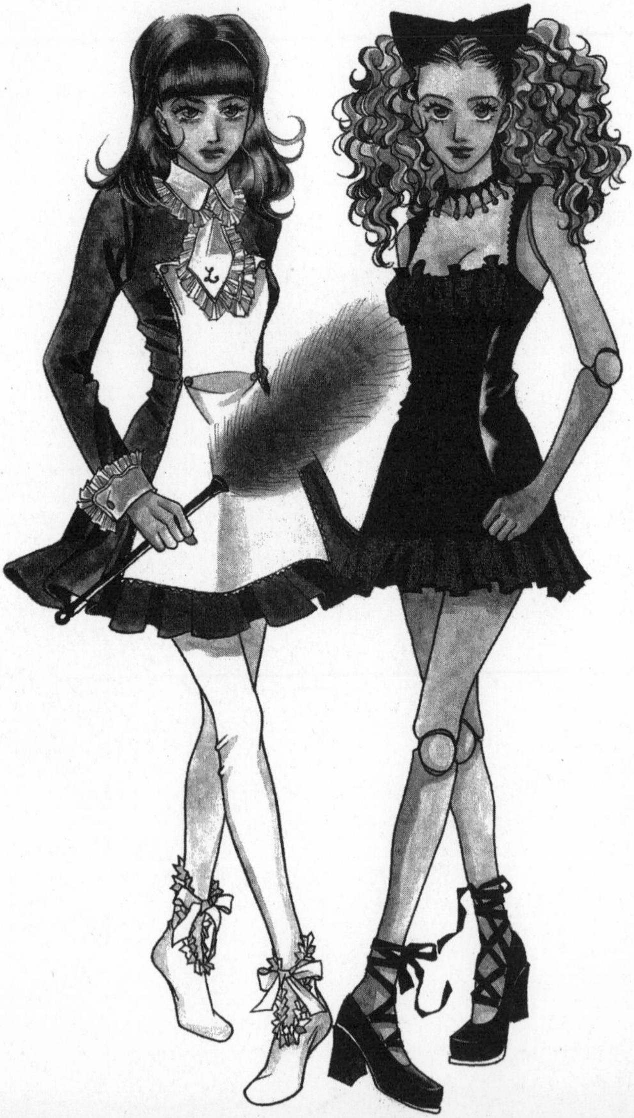

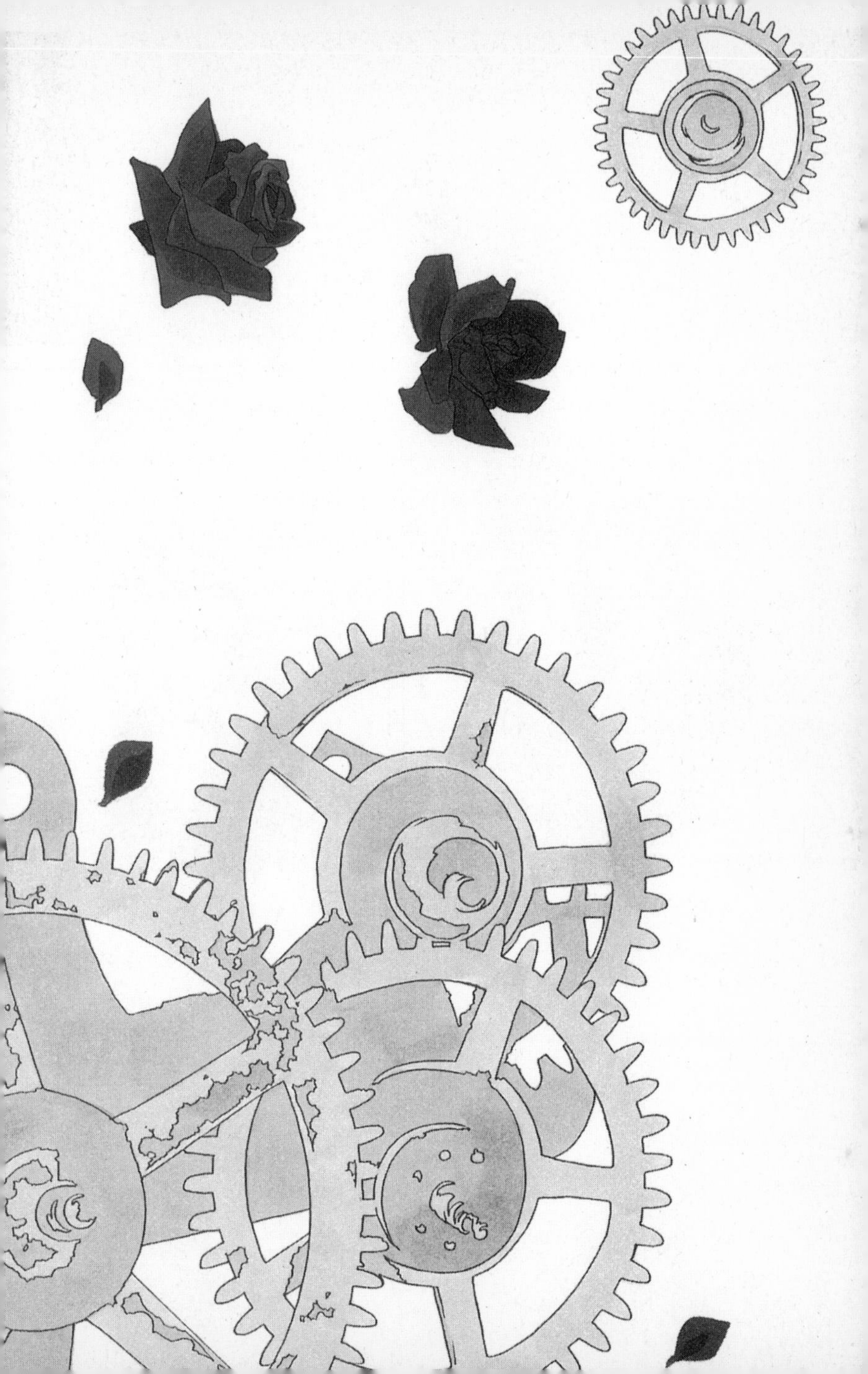

1. a nameless doll

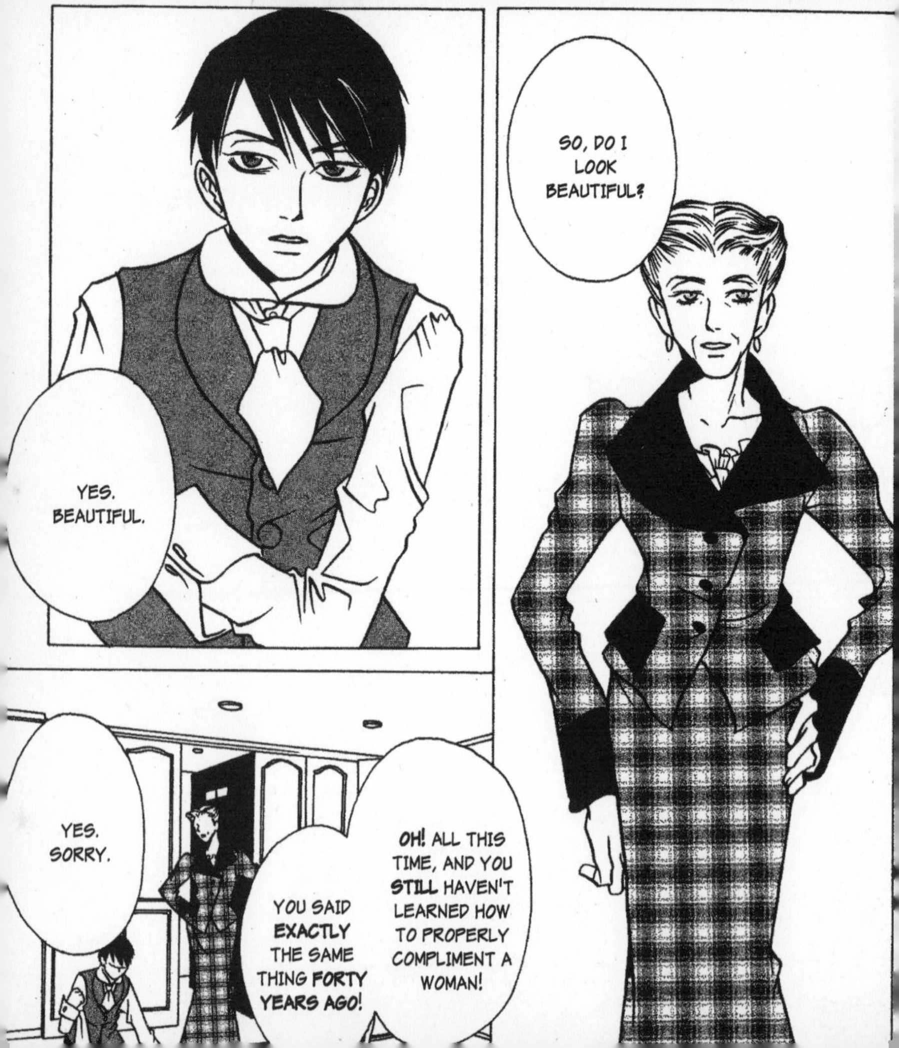
SO, DO I LOOK BEAUTIFUL?
YES. BEAUTIFUL.
OH! ALL THIS TIME, AND YOU STILL HAVEN'T LEARNED HOW TO PROPERLY COMPLIMENT A WOMAN!
YOU SAID EXACTLY THE SAME THING FORTY YEARS AGO!
YES. SORRY.

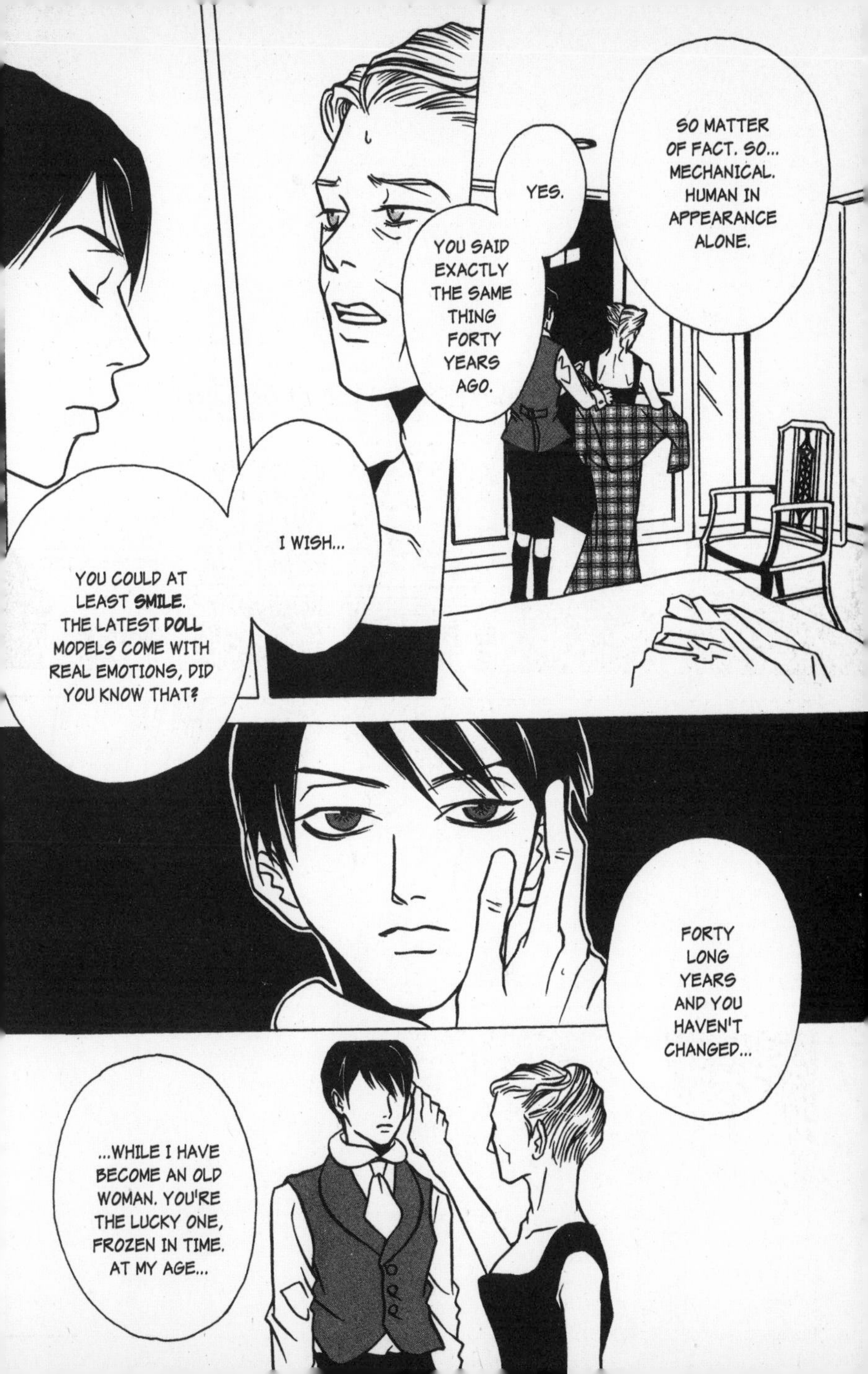
SO MATTER OF FACT. SO... MECHANICAL. HUMAN IN APPEARANCE ALONE.
YES.
YOU SAID EXACTLY THE SAME THING FORTY YEARS AGO.
I WISH...
YOU COULD AT LEAST SMILE. THE LATEST DOLL MODELS COME WITH REAL EMOTIONS, DID YOU KNOW THAT?
FORTY LONG YEARS AND YOU HAVEN'T CHANGED...
...WHILE I HAVE BECOME AN OLD WOMAN. YOU'RE THE LUCKY ONE, FROZEN IN TIME. AT MY AGE...

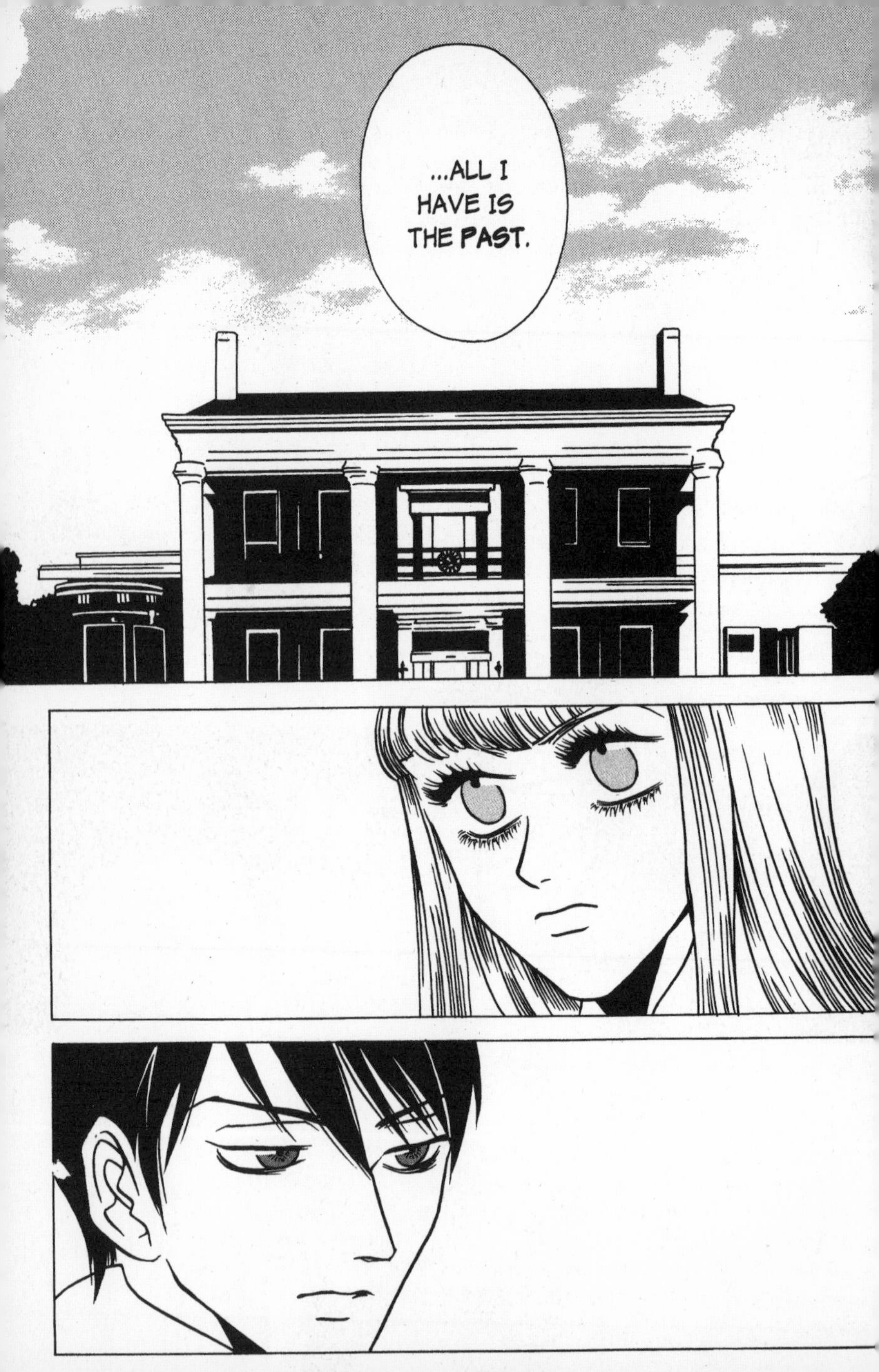
...ALL I HAVE IS THE PAST.

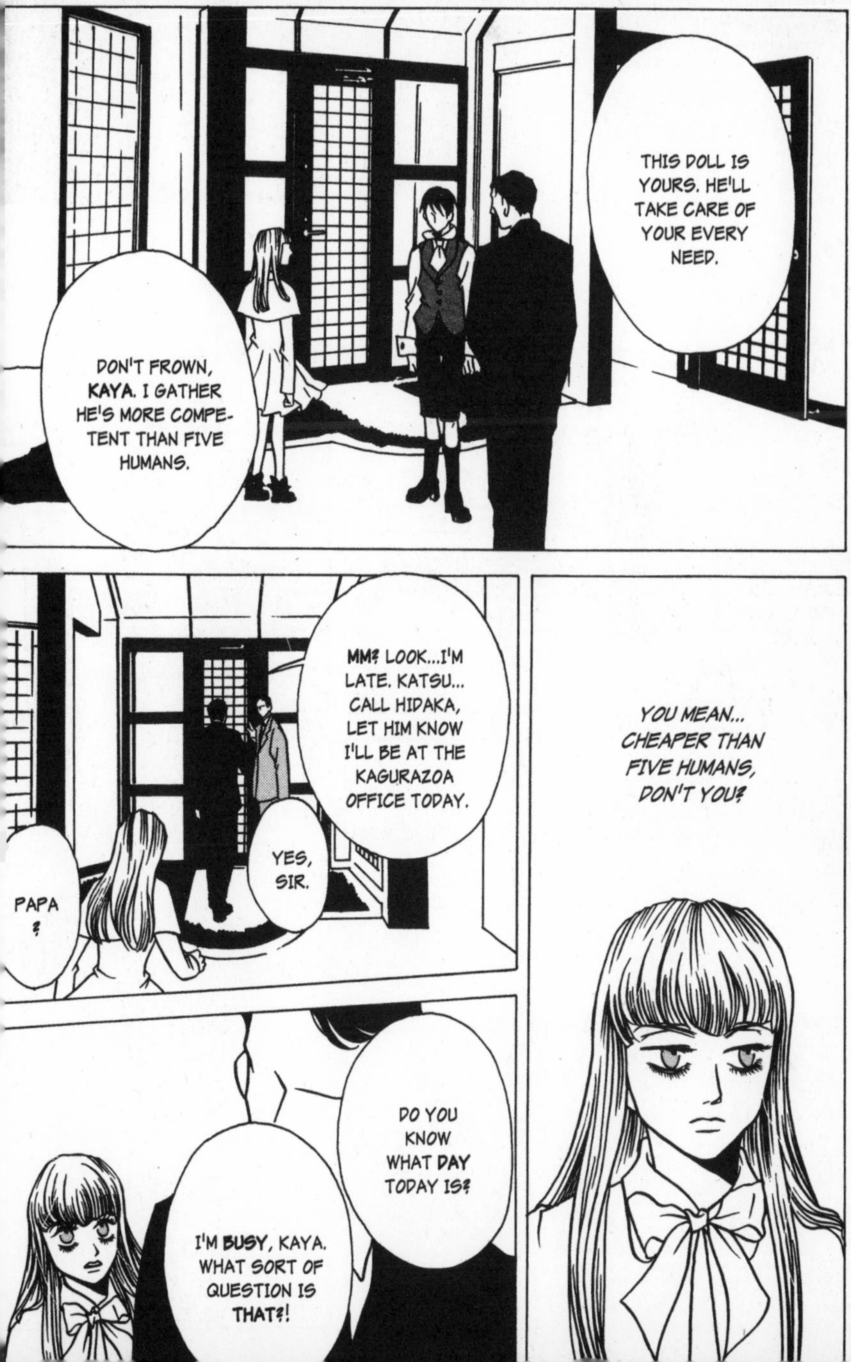
THIS DOLL IS YOURS. HE'LL TAKE CARE OF YOUR EVERY NEED.
DON'T FROWN, **KAYA**. I GATHER HE'S MORE COMPETENT THAN FIVE HUMANS.
YOU MEAN... CHEAPER THAN FIVE HUMANS, DON'T YOU?
MM? LOOK...I'M LATE. KATSU... CALL HIDAKA, LET HIM KNOW I'LL BE AT THE KAGURAZOA OFFICE TODAY.
YES, SIR.
PAPA?
DO YOU KNOW WHAT **DAY** TODAY IS?
I'M **BUSY**, KAYA. WHAT SORT OF QUESTION IS **THAT?!**

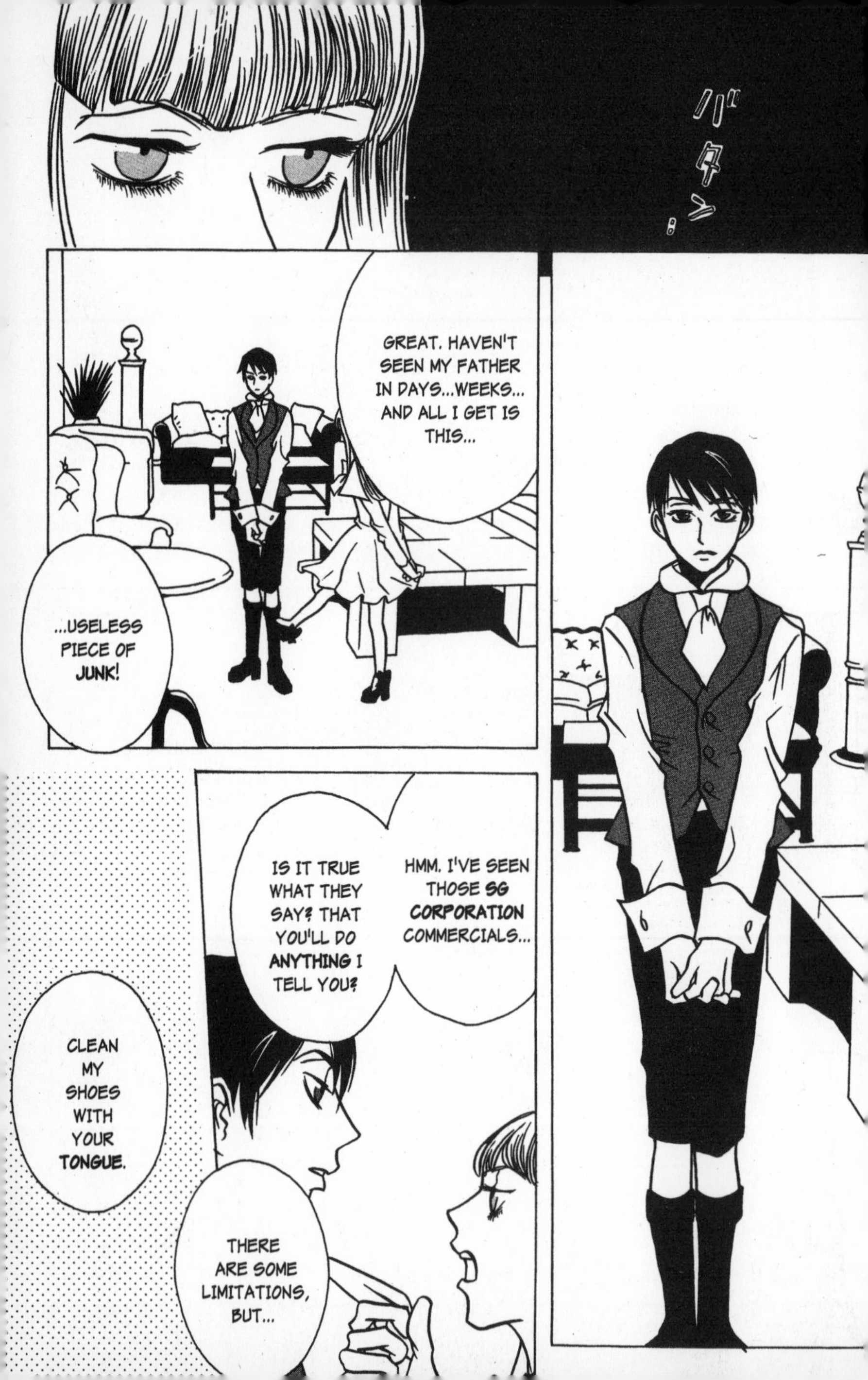
バタン
GREAT. HAVEN'T SEEN MY FATHER IN DAYS...WEEKS... AND ALL I GET IS THIS...
...USELESS PIECE OF JUNK!
HMM. I'VE SEEN THOSE SG CORPORATION COMMERCIALS...
IS IT TRUE WHAT THEY SAY? THAT YOU'LL DO ANYTHING I TELL YOU?
CLEAN MY SHOES WITH YOUR TONGUE.
THERE ARE SOME LIMITATIONS, BUT...

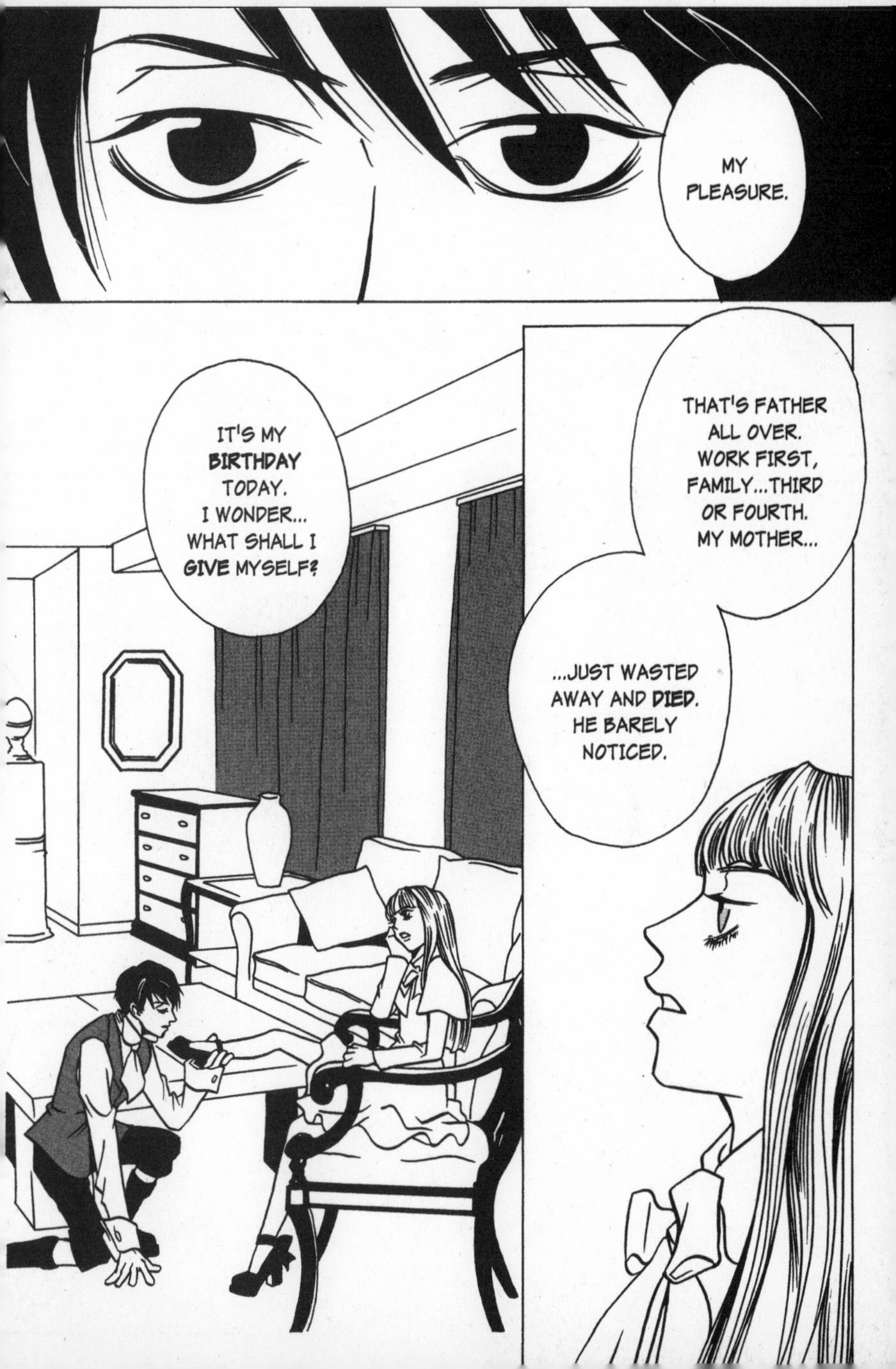
MY PLEASURE.
THAT'S FATHER ALL OVER. WORK FIRST, FAMILY...THIRD OR FOURTH. MY MOTHER...
...JUST WASTED AWAY AND DIED. HE BARELY NOTICED.
IT'S MY BIRTHDAY TODAY. I WONDER... WHAT SHALL I GIVE MYSELF?

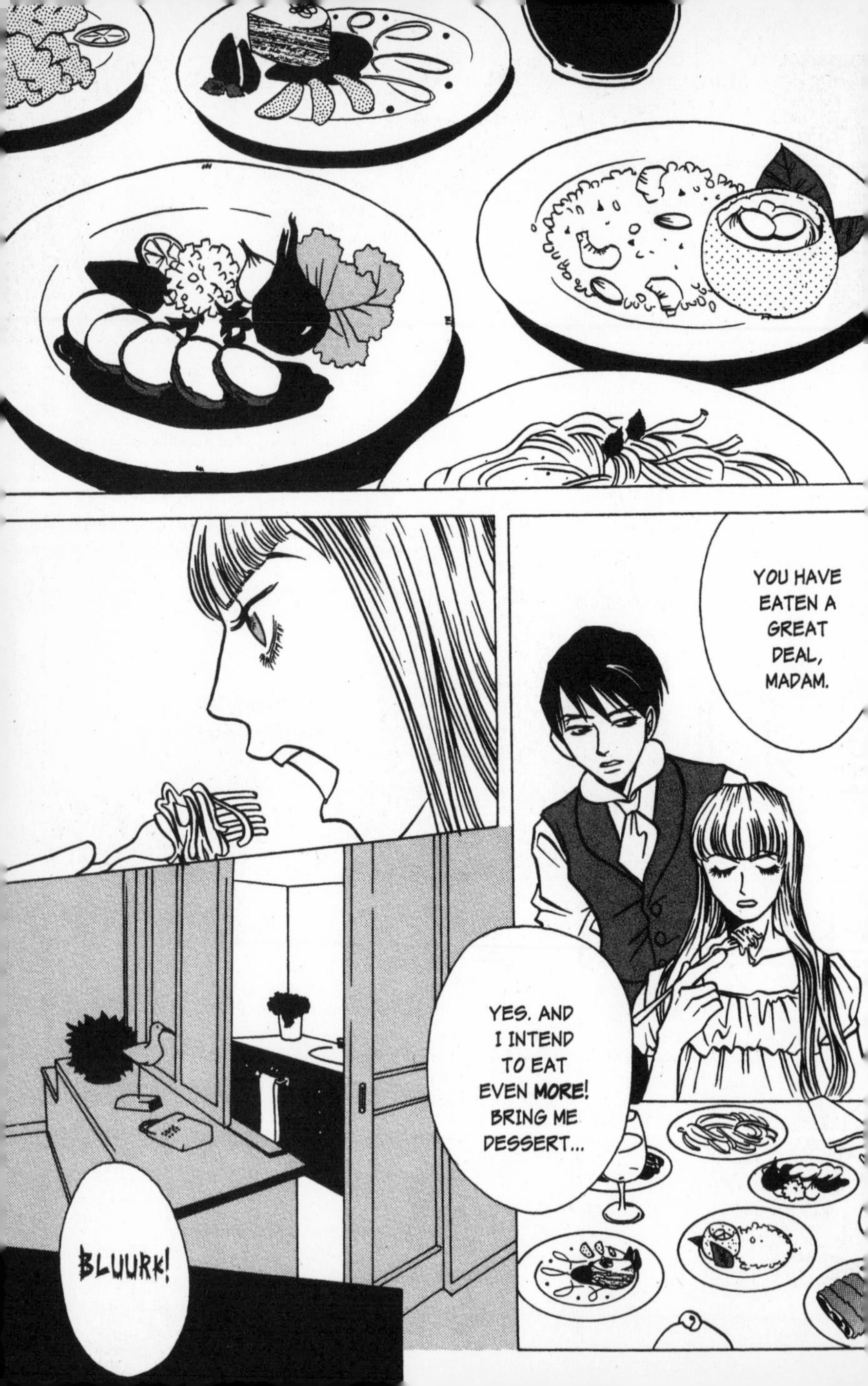
YOU HAVE EATEN A GREAT DEAL, MADAM.
YES. AND I INTEND TO EAT EVEN **MORE!** BRING ME DESSERT...
BLUURK!

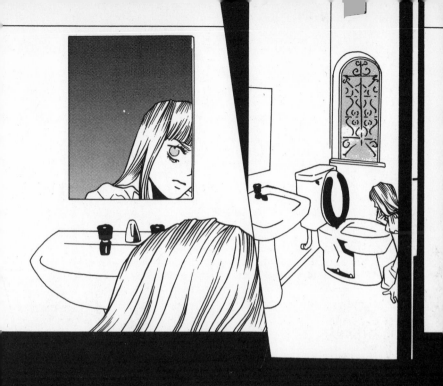

I WAS THE GIRL WITH EVERYTHING...AND NOTHING.

HELLO. I'M **TAKANORI IMAZU**. YOU MUST BE KAYA.

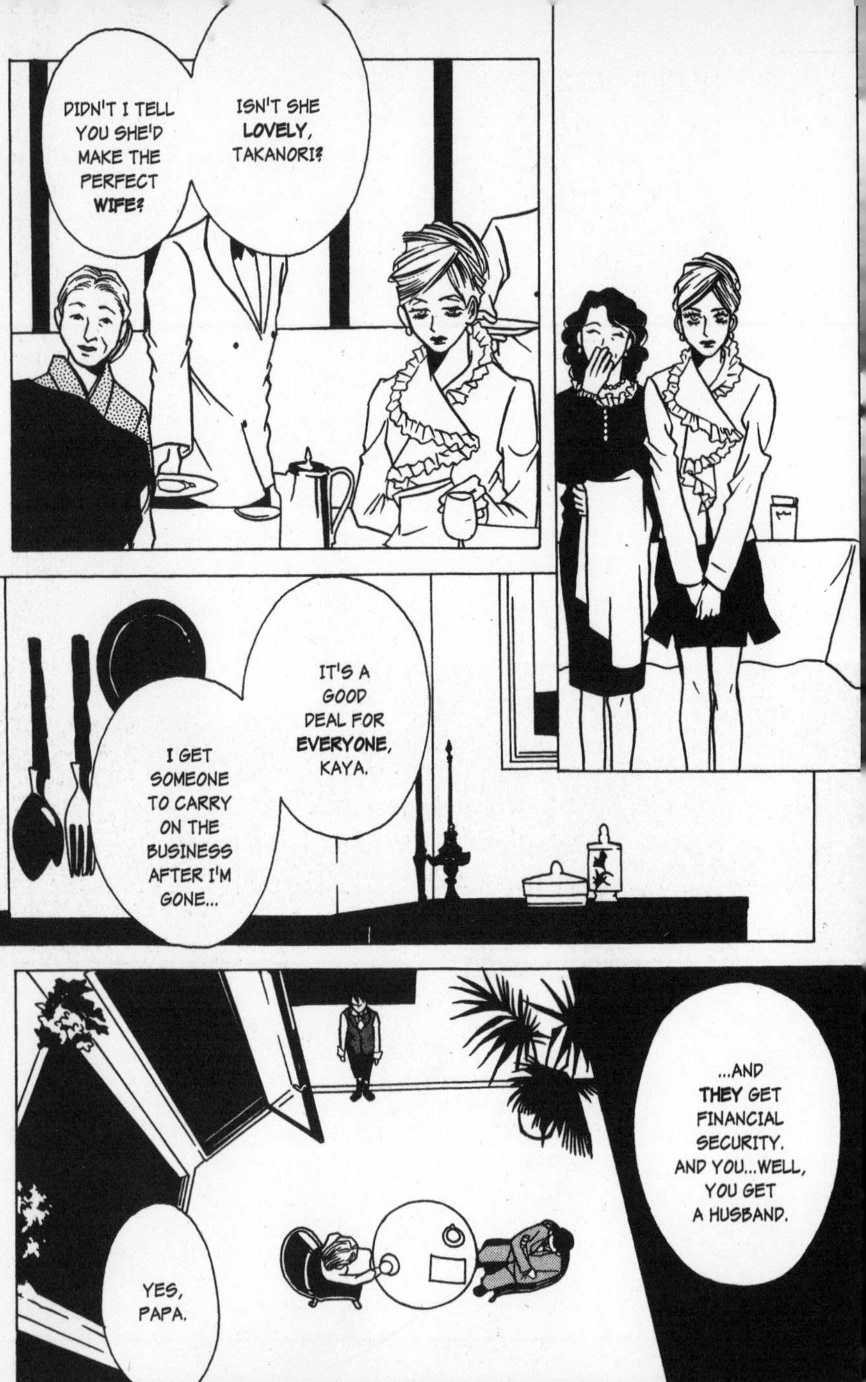
ISN'T SHE **LOVELY**, TAKANORI?
DIDN'T I TELL YOU SHE'D MAKE THE PERFECT **WIFE**?
IT'S A GOOD DEAL FOR **EVERYONE**, KAYA.
I GET SOMEONE TO CARRY ON THE BUSINESS AFTER I'M GONE...
...AND **THEY** GET FINANCIAL SECURITY. AND YOU...WELL, YOU GET A HUSBAND.
YES, PAPA.

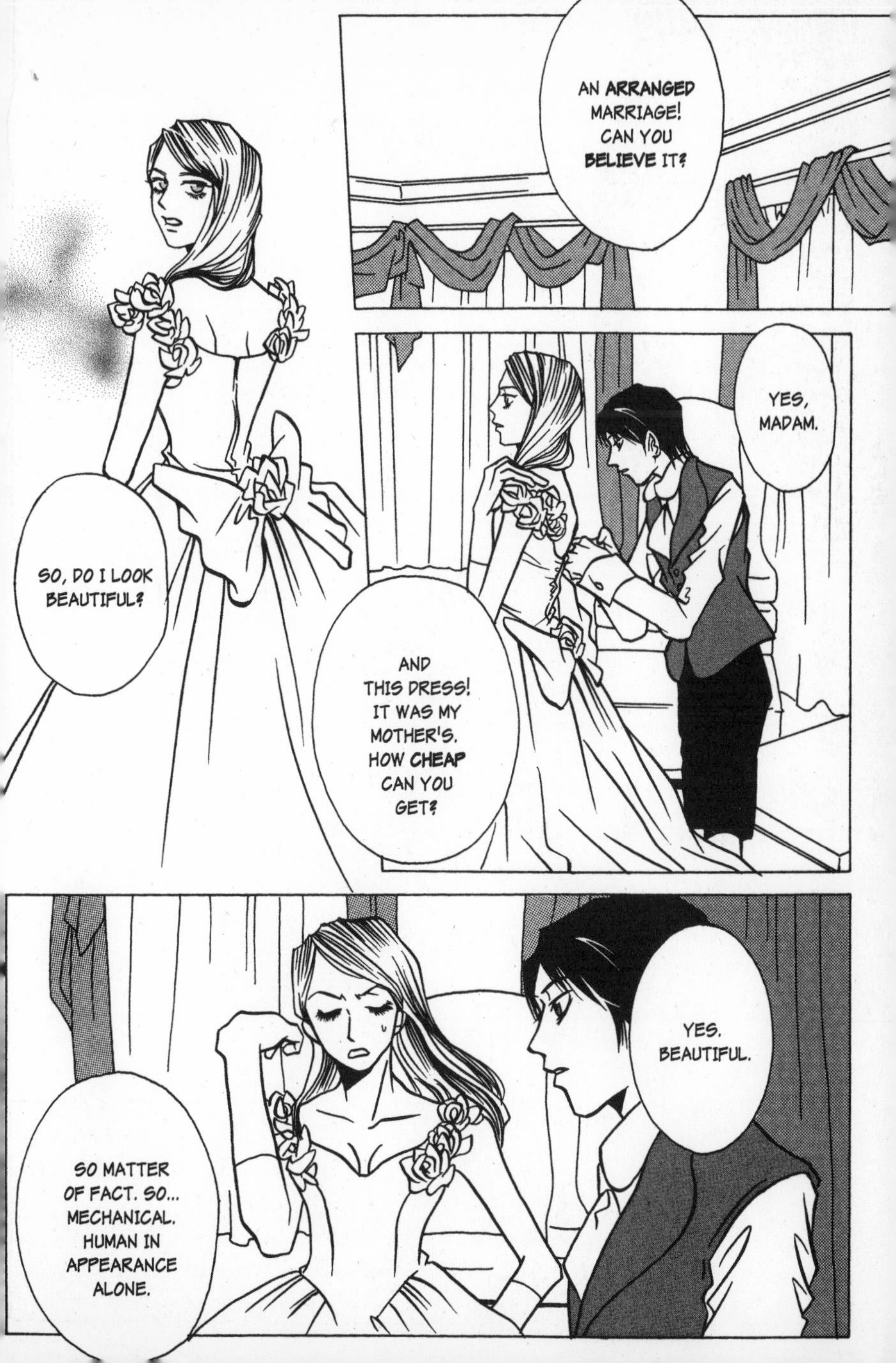
AN ARRANGED MARRIAGE! CAN YOU BELIEVE IT?
YES, MADAM.
AND THIS DRESS! IT WAS MY MOTHER'S. HOW CHEAP CAN YOU GET?
SO, DO I LOOK BEAUTIFUL?
YES. BEAUTIFUL.
SO MATTER OF FACT. SO... MECHANICAL. HUMAN IN APPEARANCE ALONE.

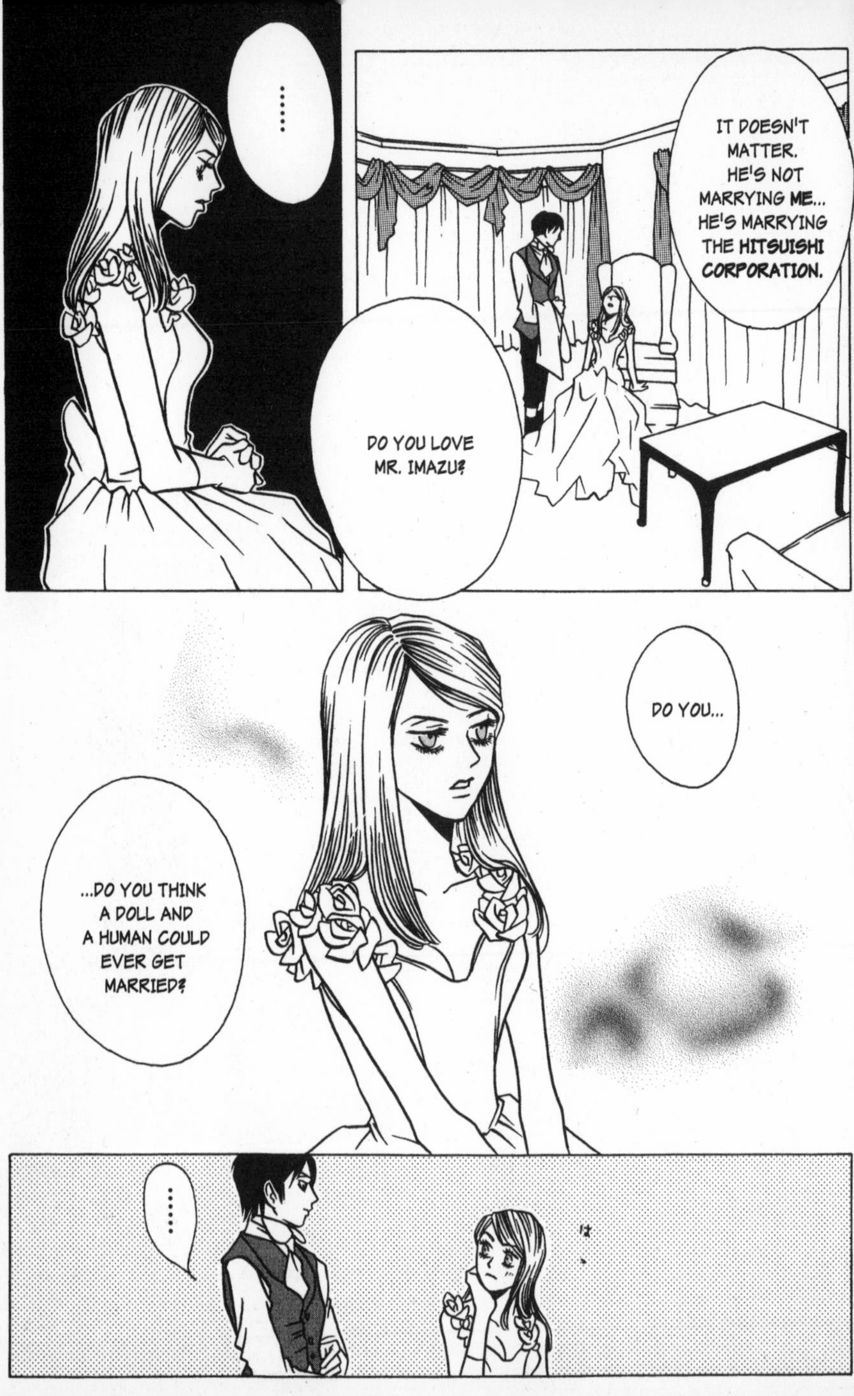
IT DOESN'T MATTER. HE'S NOT MARRYING **ME**... HE'S MARRYING THE **HITSUISHI CORPORATION.**
DO YOU LOVE MR. IMAZU?
......
DO YOU...
...DO YOU THINK A DOLL AND A HUMAN COULD EVER GET MARRIED?
......

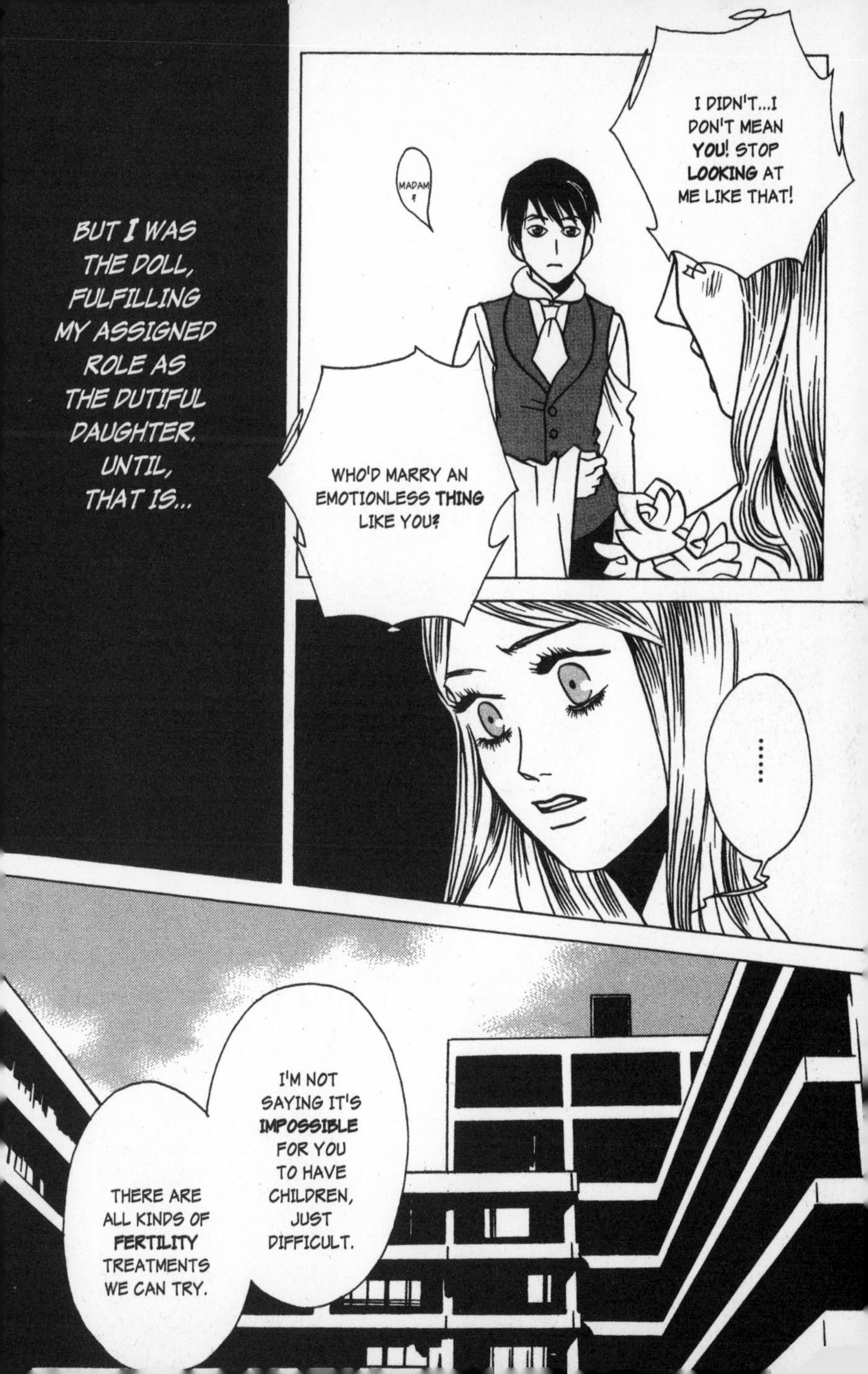
I DIDN'T...I DON'T MEAN YOU! STOP LOOKING AT ME LIKE THAT!
MADAM?
WHO'D MARRY AN EMOTIONLESS THING LIKE YOU?
......
BUT I WAS THE DOLL, FULFILLING MY ASSIGNED ROLE AS THE DUTIFUL DAUGHTER. UNTIL, THAT IS...
I'M NOT SAYING IT'S IMPOSSIBLE FOR YOU TO HAVE CHILDREN, JUST DIFFICULT.
THERE ARE ALL KINDS OF FERTILITY TREATMENTS WE CAN TRY.

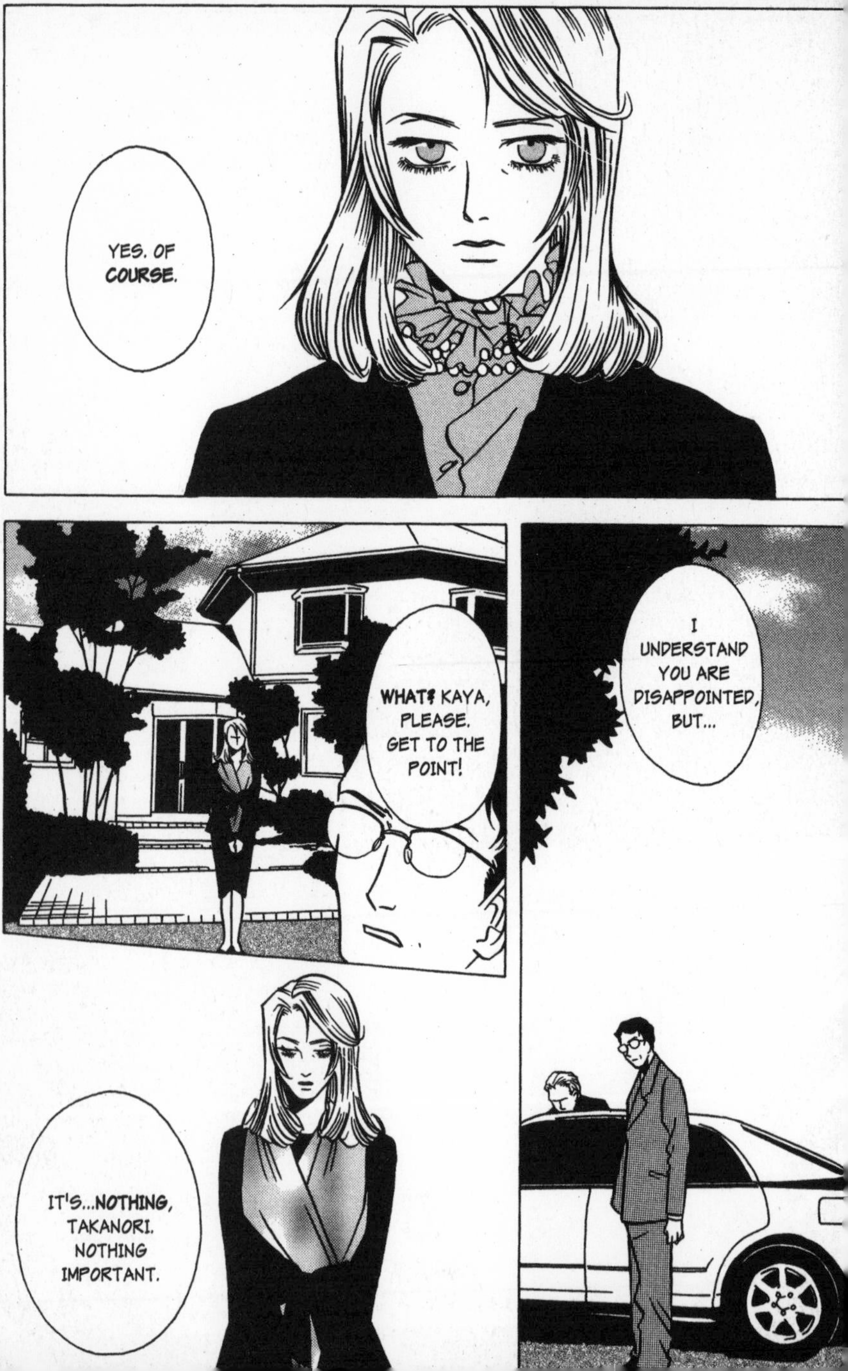
YES. OF COURSE.
I UNDERSTAND YOU ARE DISAPPOINTED, BUT...
WHAT? KAYA, PLEASE. GET TO THE POINT!
IT'S...NOTHING, TAKANORI. NOTHING IMPORTANT.

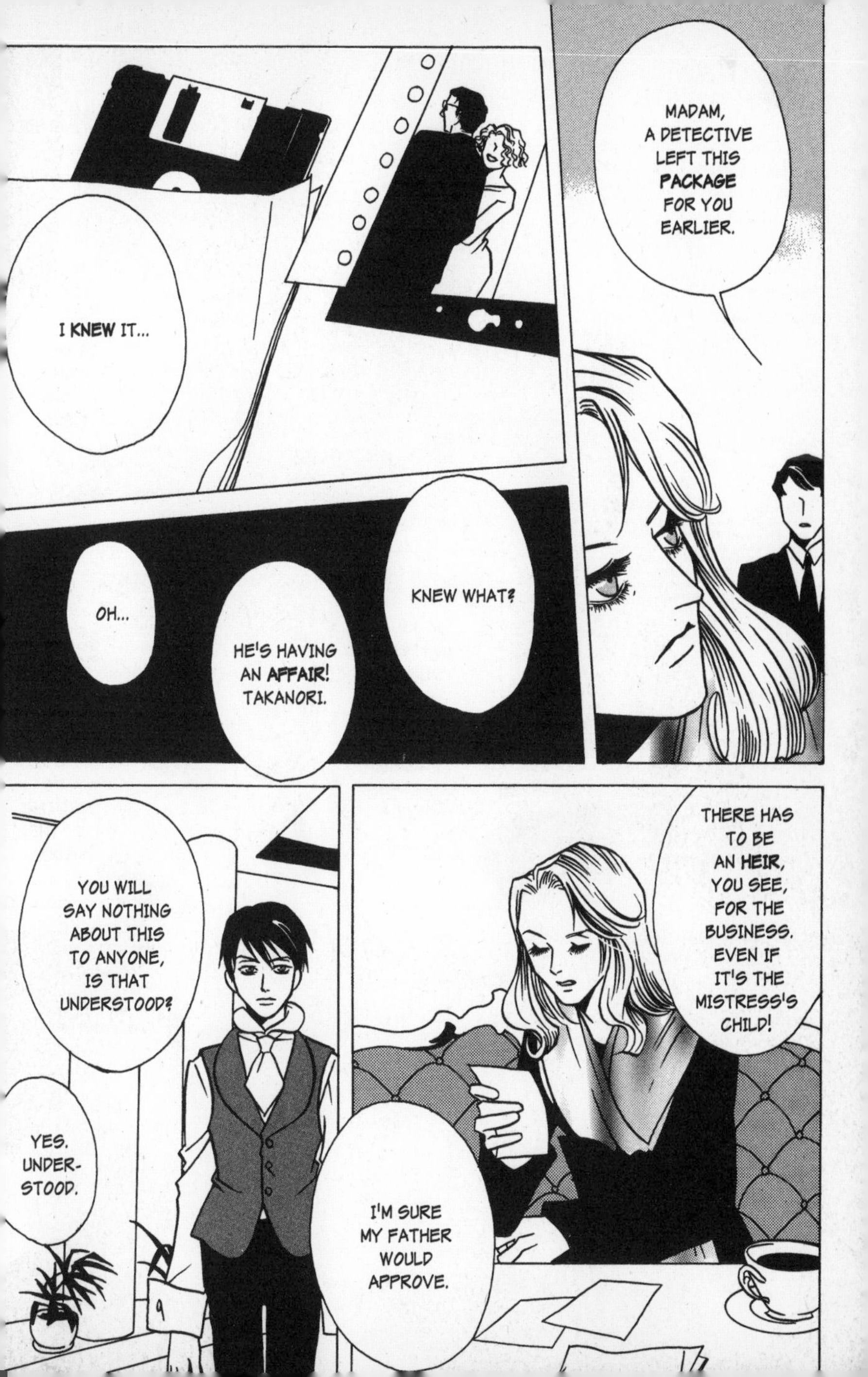
MADAM, A DETECTIVE LEFT THIS PACKAGE FOR YOU EARLIER.
I KNEW IT...
KNEW WHAT?
HE'S HAVING AN AFFAIR! TAKANORI.
OH...
THERE HAS TO BE AN HEIR, YOU SEE, FOR THE BUSINESS. EVEN IF IT'S THE MISTRESS'S CHILD!
I'M SURE MY FATHER WOULD APPROVE.
YOU WILL SAY NOTHING ABOUT THIS TO ANYONE, IS THAT UNDERSTOOD?
YES. UNDER-STOOD.

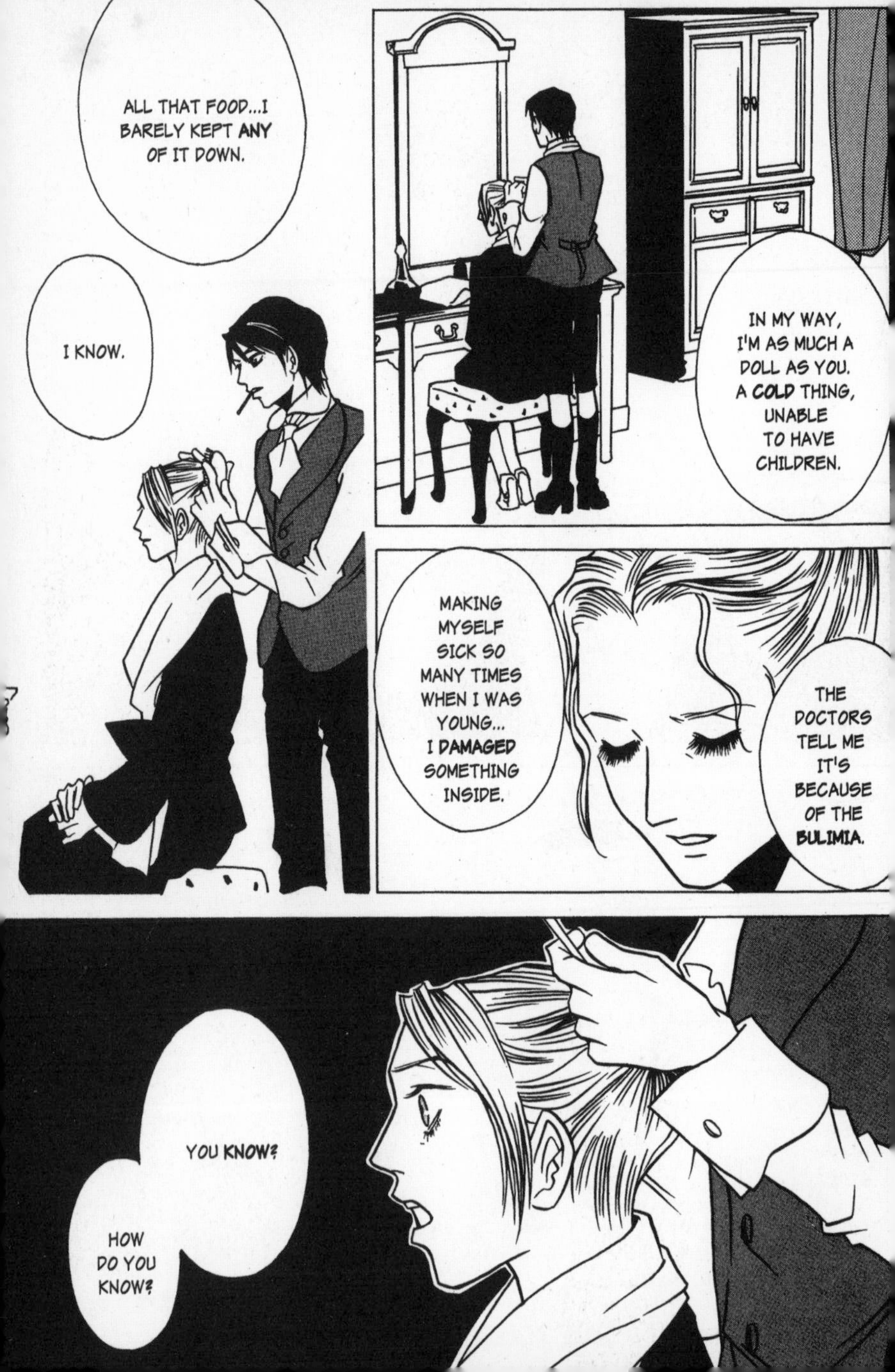
IN MY WAY, I'M AS MUCH A DOLL AS YOU. A **COLD** THING, UNABLE TO HAVE CHILDREN.
THE DOCTORS TELL ME IT'S BECAUSE OF THE **BULIMIA.**
MAKING MYSELF SICK SO MANY TIMES WHEN I WAS YOUNG... I **DAMAGED** SOMETHING INSIDE.
ALL THAT FOOD...I BARELY KEPT **ANY** OF IT DOWN.
I KNOW.
YOU **KNOW?**
HOW DO YOU KNOW?

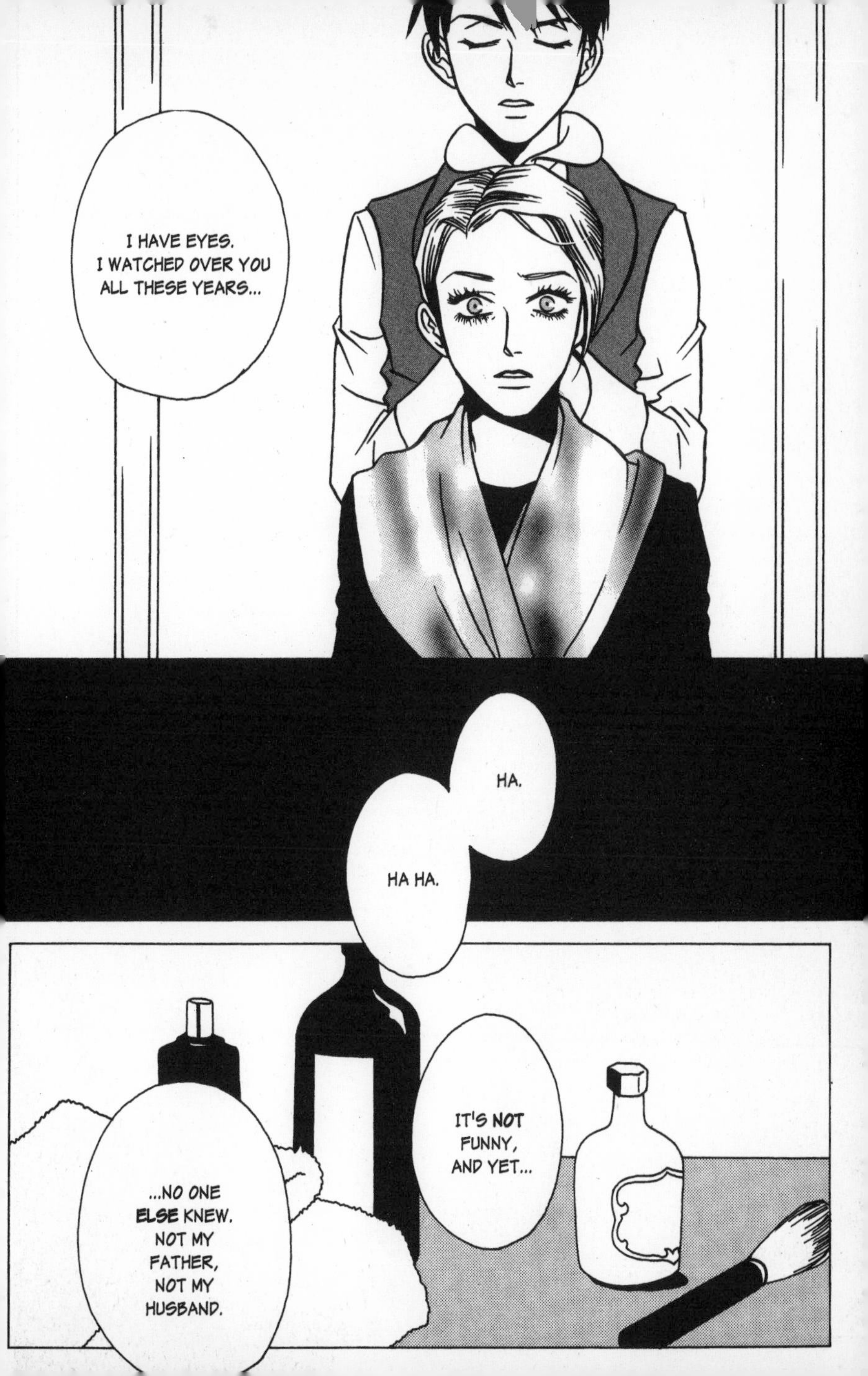
I HAVE EYES. I WATCHED OVER YOU ALL THESE YEARS...
HA.
HA HA.
IT'S NOT FUNNY, AND YET...
...NO ONE ELSE KNEW. NOT MY FATHER, NOT MY HUSBAND.

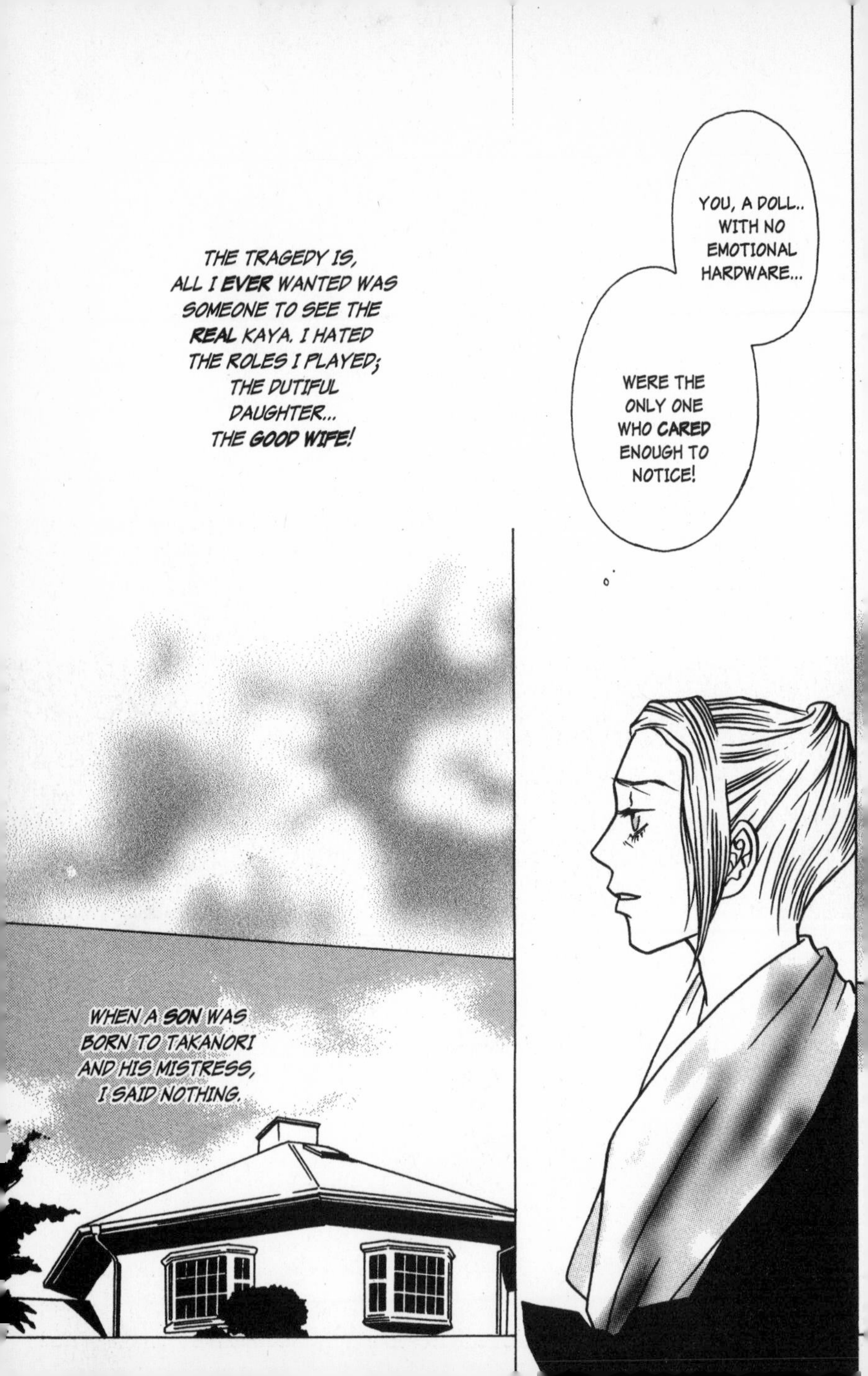
YOU, A DOLL.. WITH NO EMOTIONAL HARDWARE...
WERE THE ONLY ONE WHO CARED ENOUGH TO NOTICE!
THE TRAGEDY IS, ALL I EVER WANTED WAS SOMEONE TO SEE THE REAL KAYA. I HATED THE ROLES I PLAYED; THE DUTIFUL DAUGHTER... THE GOOD WIFE!
WHEN A SON WAS BORN TO TAKANORI AND HIS MISTRESS, I SAID NOTHING.

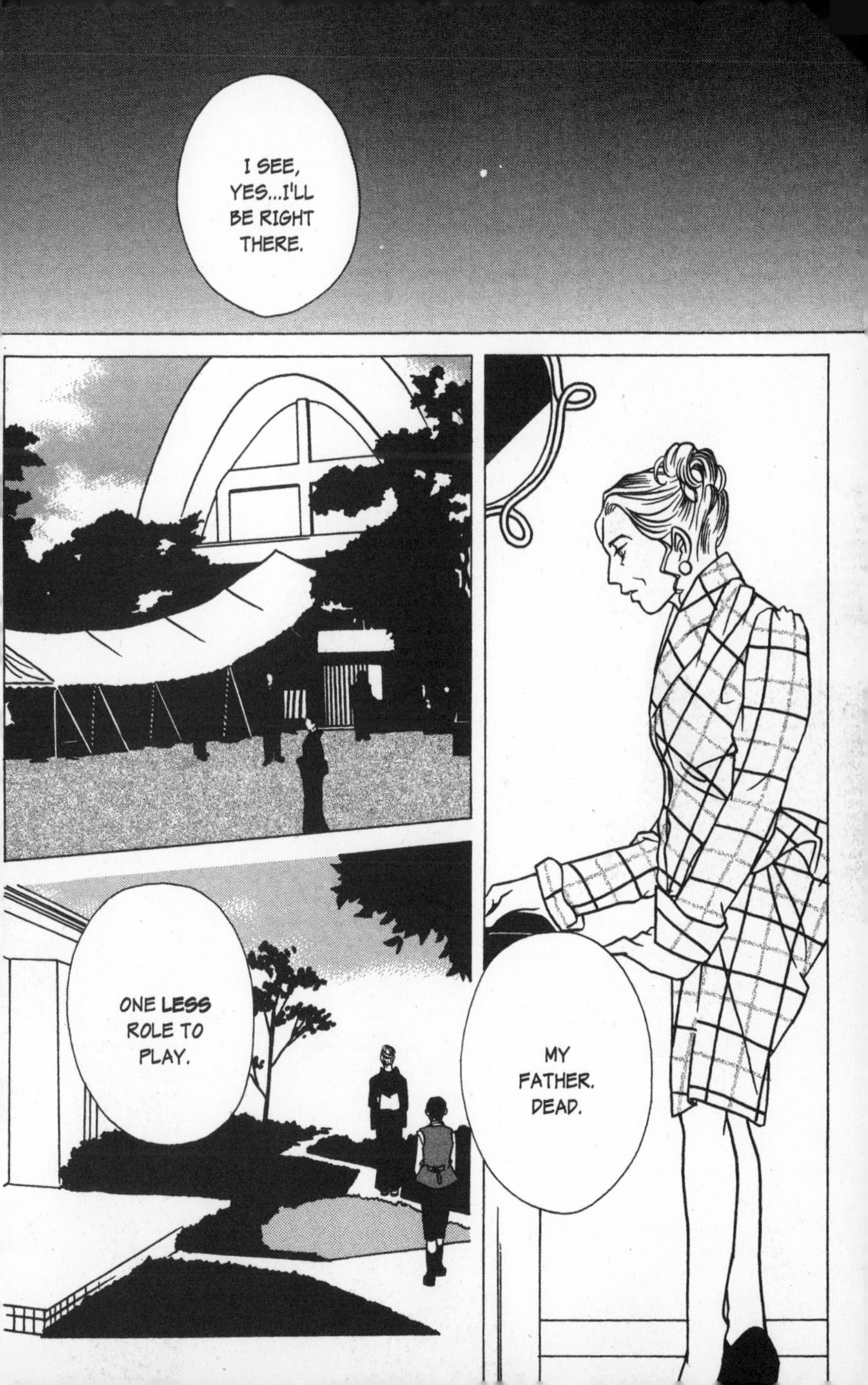
I SEE, YES...I'LL BE RIGHT THERE.
MY FATHER. DEAD.
ONE LESS ROLE TO PLAY.

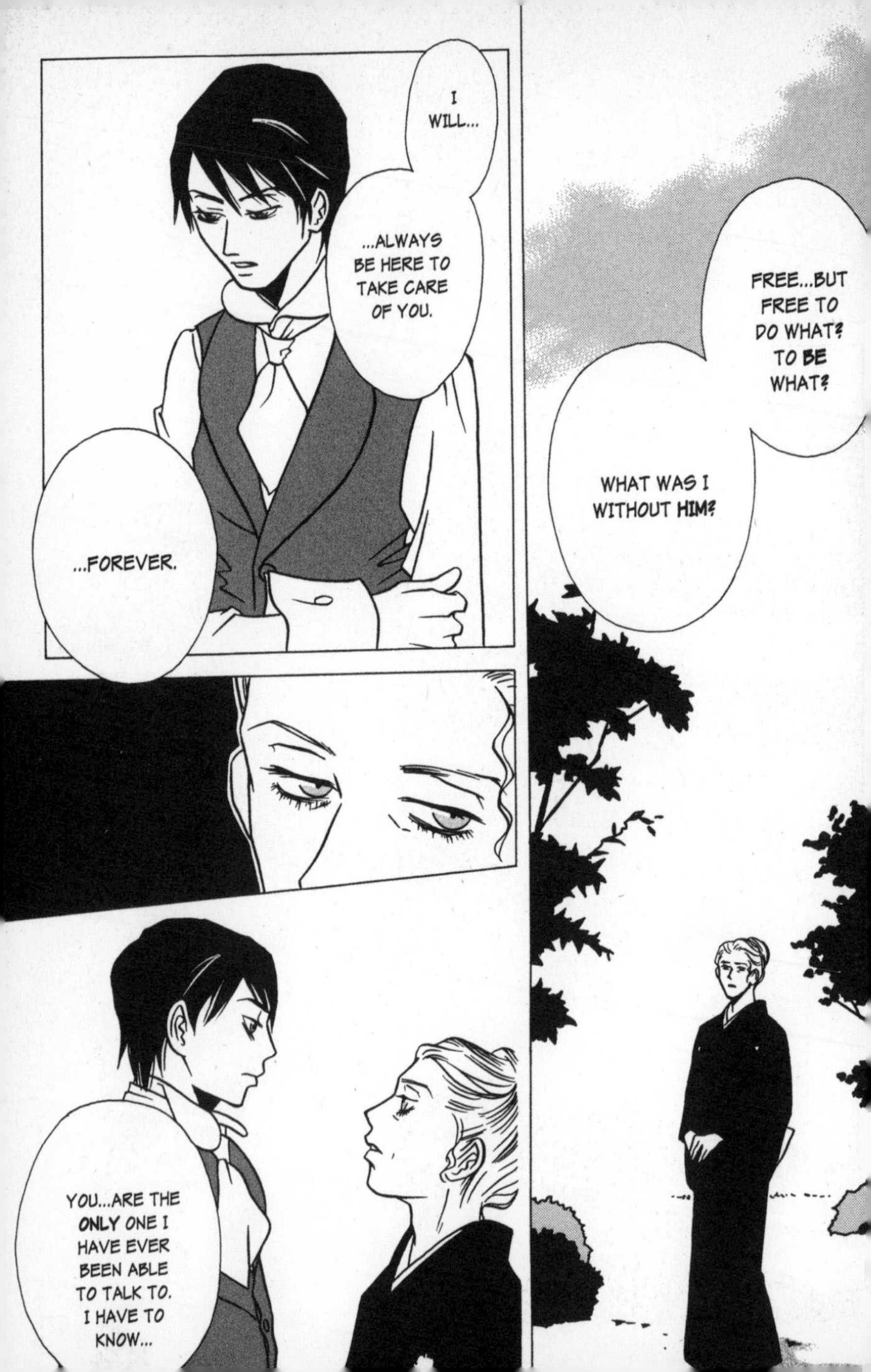
FREE...BUT FREE TO DO WHAT? TO BE WHAT?
WHAT WAS I WITHOUT HIM?
I WILL...
...ALWAYS BE HERE TO TAKE CARE OF YOU.
...FOREVER.
YOU...ARE THE ONLY ONE I HAVE EVER BEEN ABLE TO TALK TO. I HAVE TO KNOW...

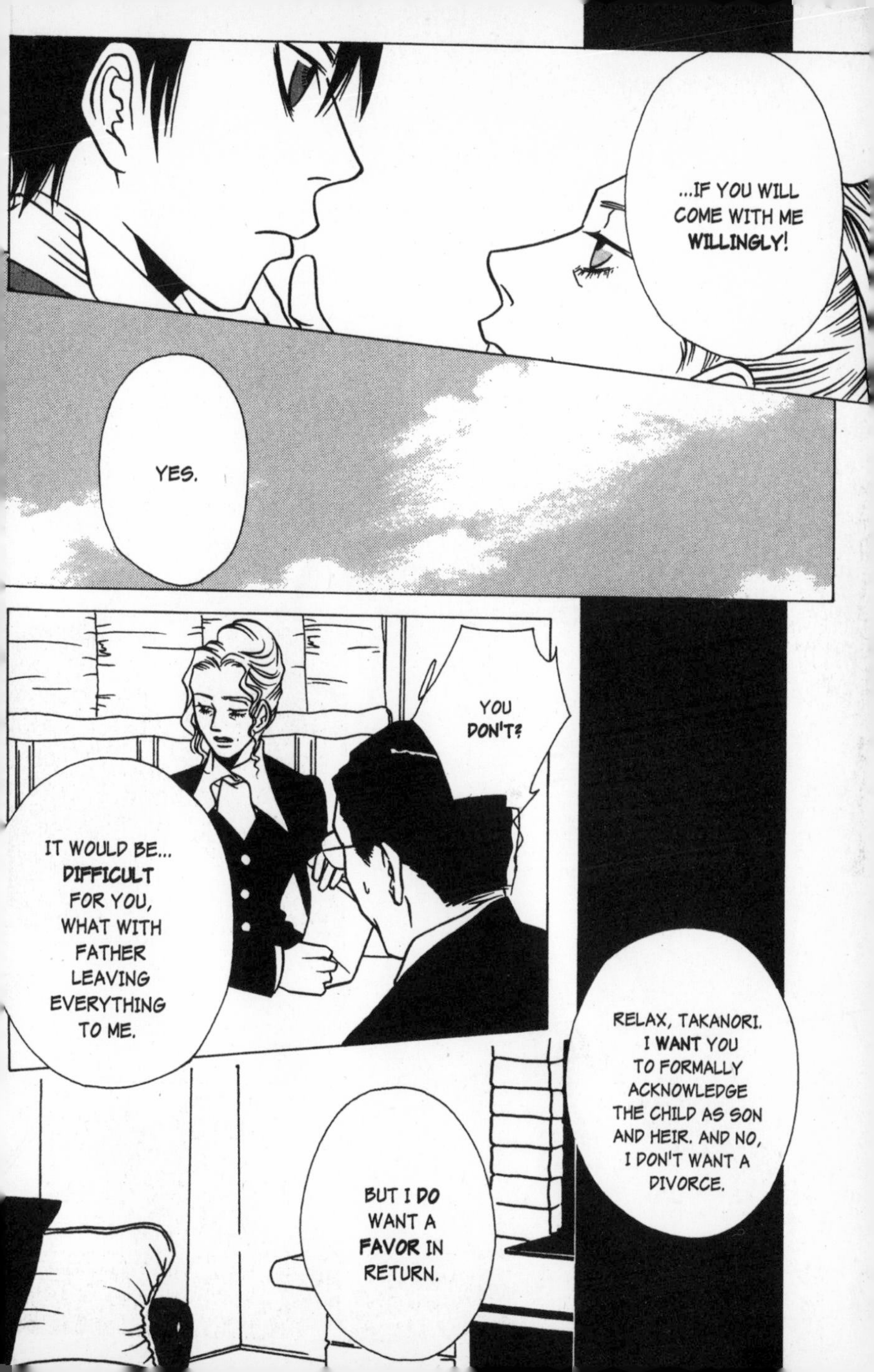
...IF YOU WILL COME WITH ME WILLINGLY!
YES.
YOU DON'T?
IT WOULD BE... DIFFICULT FOR YOU, WHAT WITH FATHER LEAVING EVERYTHING TO ME.
RELAX, TAKANORI. I WANT YOU TO FORMALLY ACKNOWLEDGE THE CHILD AS SON AND HEIR. AND NO, I DON'T WANT A DIVORCE.
BUT I DO WANT A FAVOR IN RETURN.

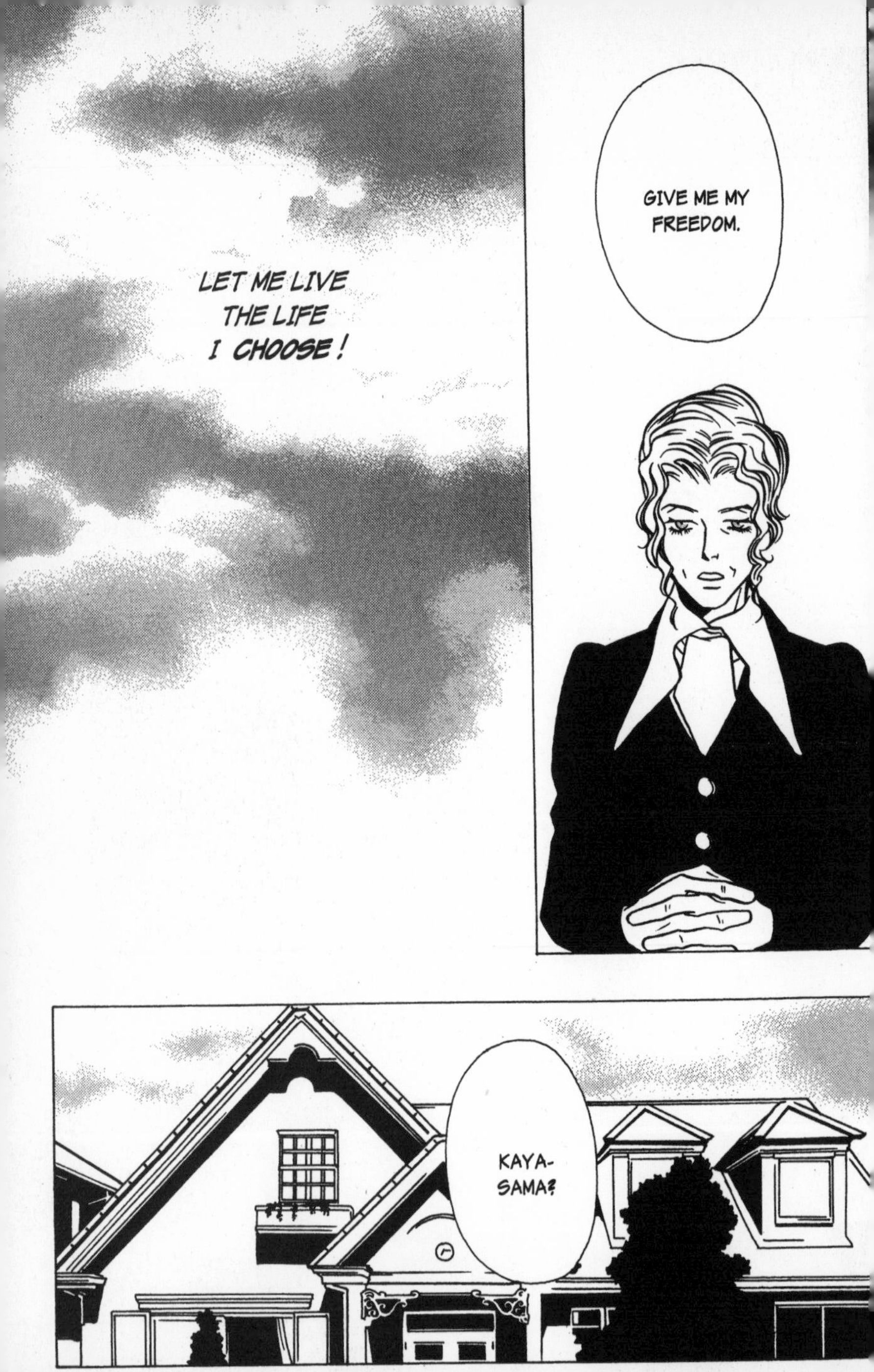
GIVE ME MY FREEDOM.
LET ME LIVE THE LIFE I CHOOSE!
KAYA-SAMA?

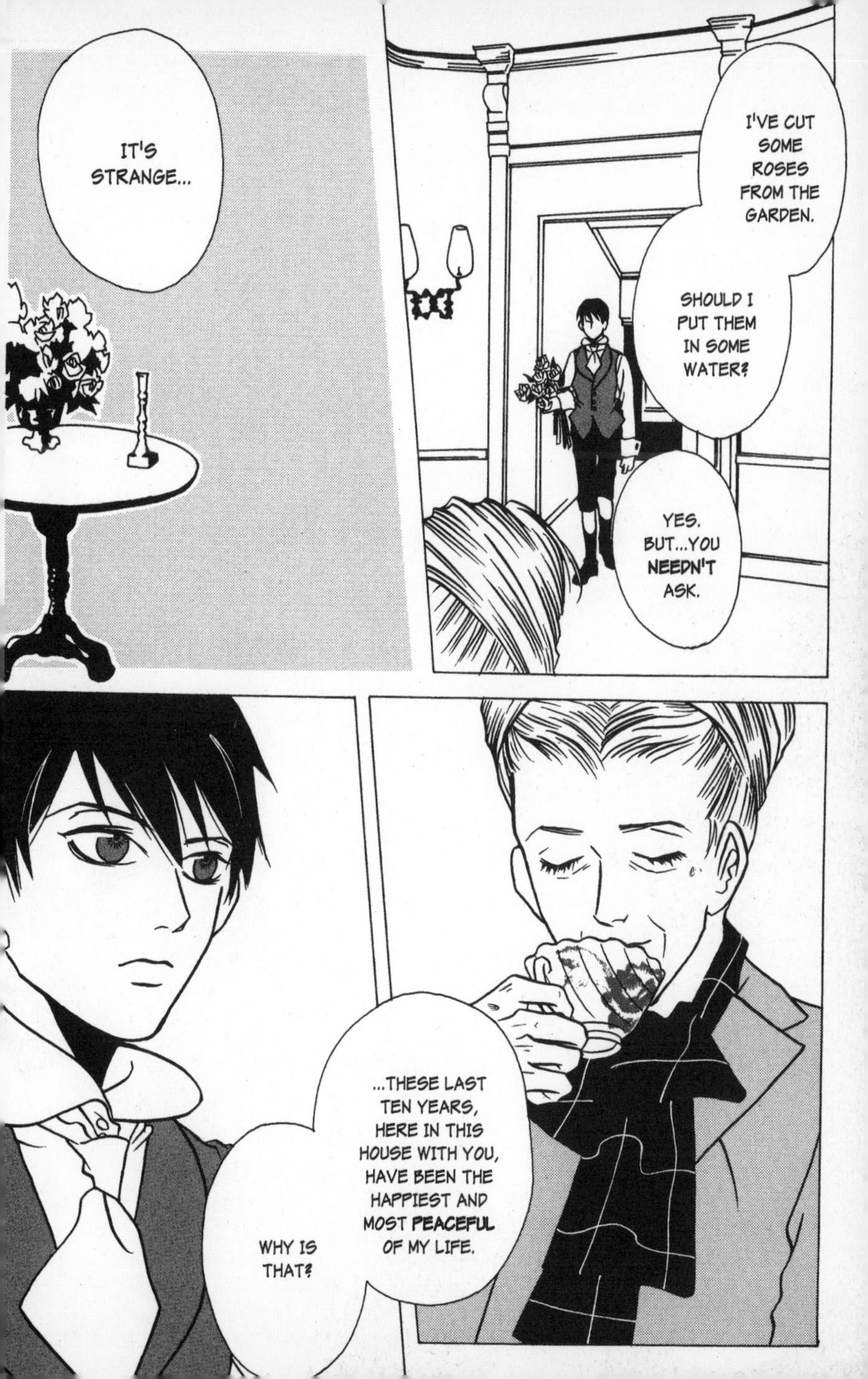
I'VE CUT SOME ROSES FROM THE GARDEN.
SHOULD I PUT THEM IN SOME WATER?
YES. BUT...YOU NEEDN'T ASK.
IT'S STRANGE...
...THESE LAST TEN YEARS, HERE IN THIS HOUSE WITH YOU, HAVE BEEN THE HAPPIEST AND MOST PEACEFUL OF MY LIFE.
WHY IS THAT?

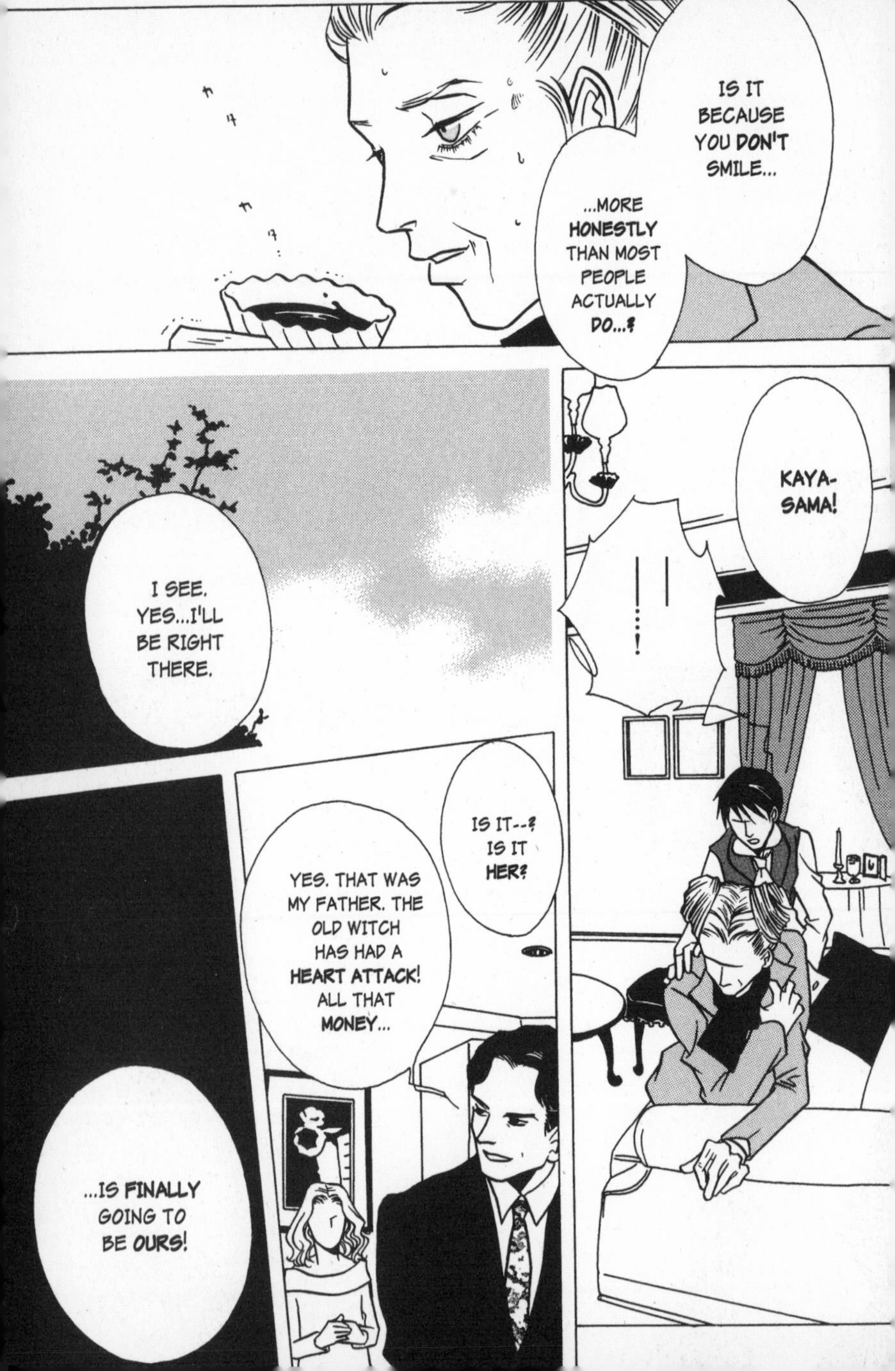
IS IT BECAUSE YOU DON'T SMILE...
...MORE HONESTLY THAN MOST PEOPLE ACTUALLY DO...?
KAYA-SAMA!
I SEE. YES...I'LL BE RIGHT THERE.
IS IT--? IS IT HER?
YES. THAT WAS MY FATHER. THE OLD WITCH HAS HAD A HEART ATTACK! ALL THAT MONEY...
...IS FINALLY GOING TO BE OURS!

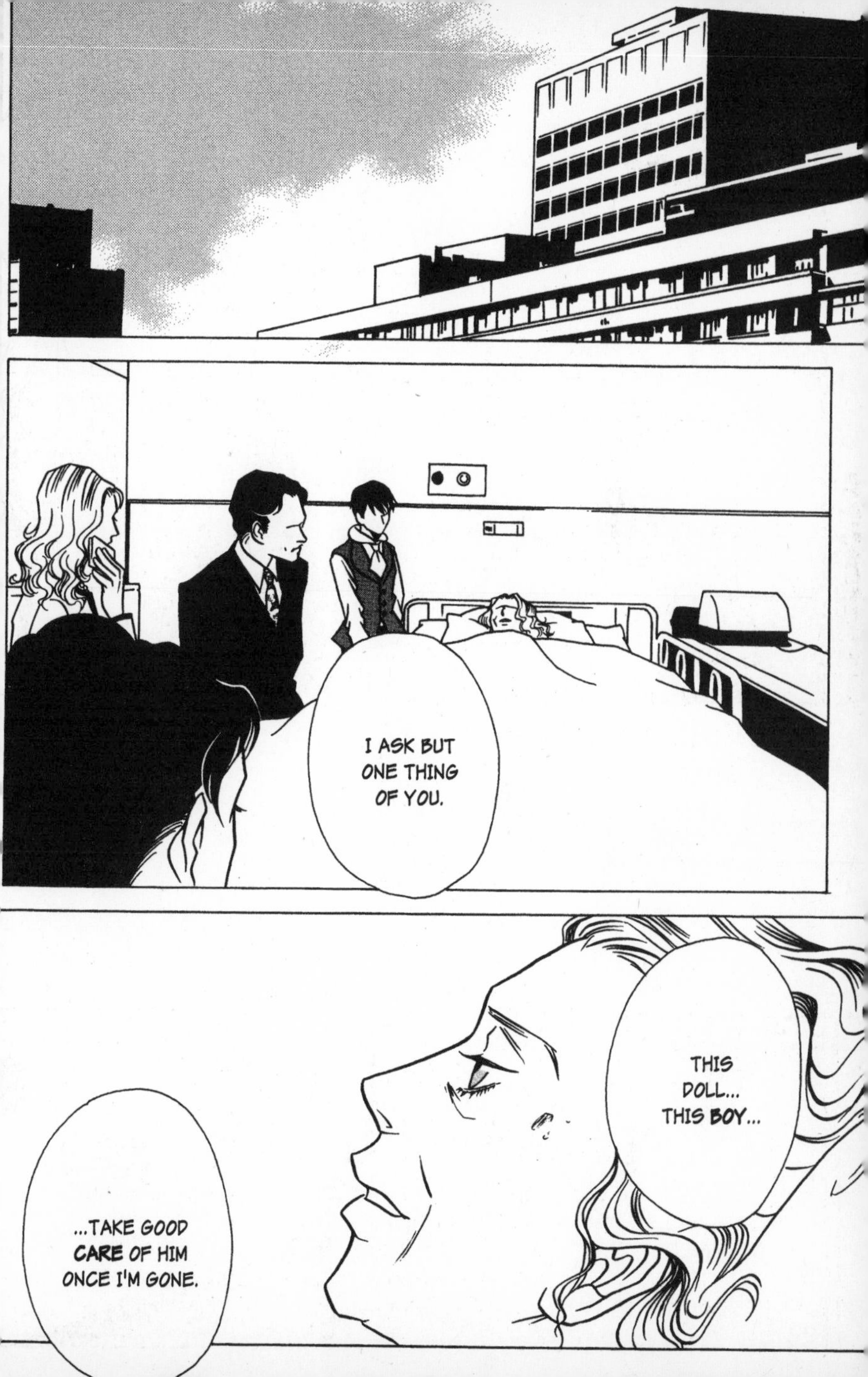
I ASK BUT ONE THING OF YOU.
THIS DOLL... THIS BOY...
...TAKE GOOD CARE OF HIM ONCE I'M GONE.

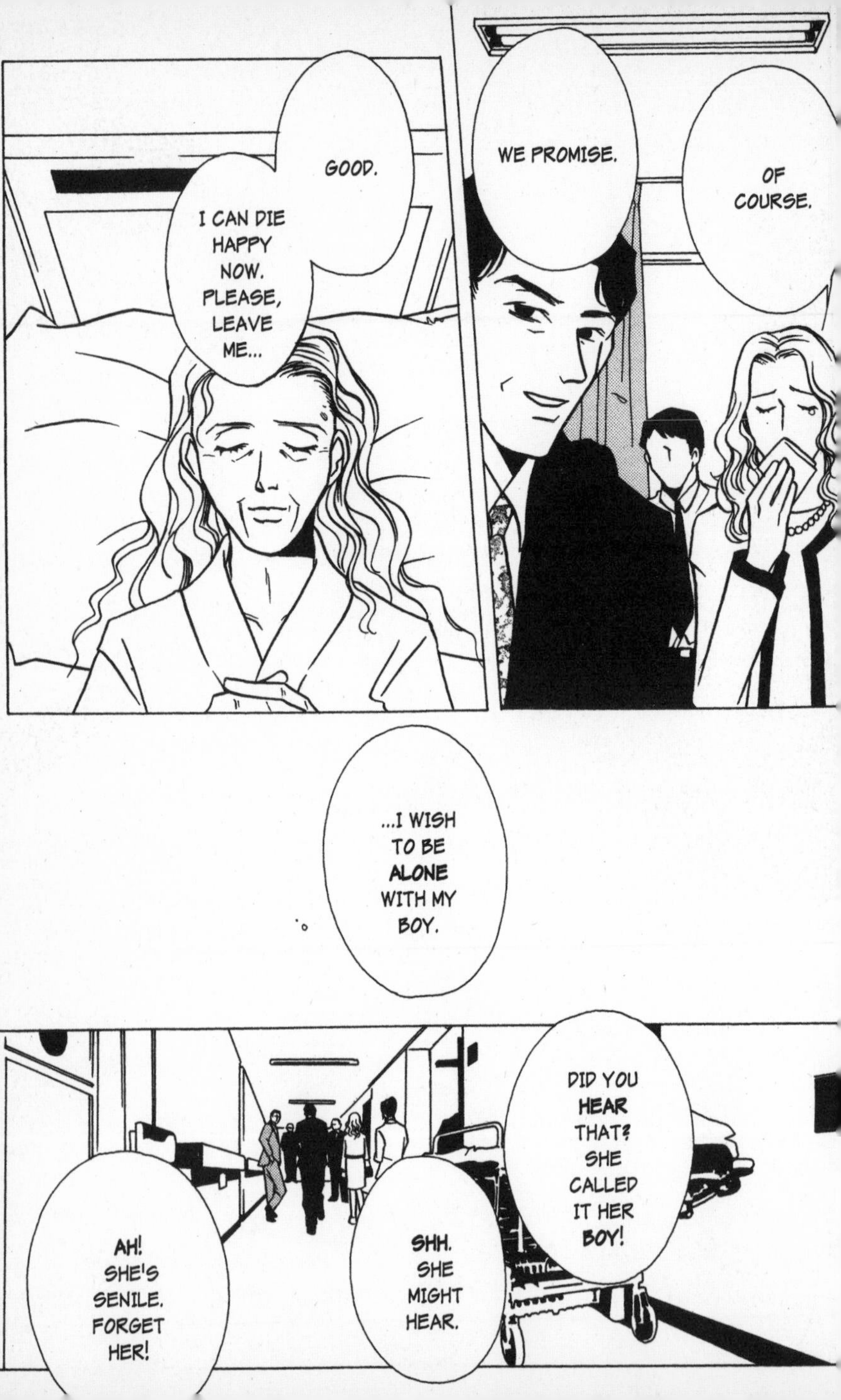
OF COURSE.
WE PROMISE.
GOOD.
I CAN DIE HAPPY NOW. PLEASE, LEAVE ME...
...I WISH TO BE ALONE WITH MY BOY.
DID YOU HEAR THAT? SHE CALLED IT HER BOY!
SHH. SHE MIGHT HEAR.
AH! SHE'S SENILE. FORGET HER!

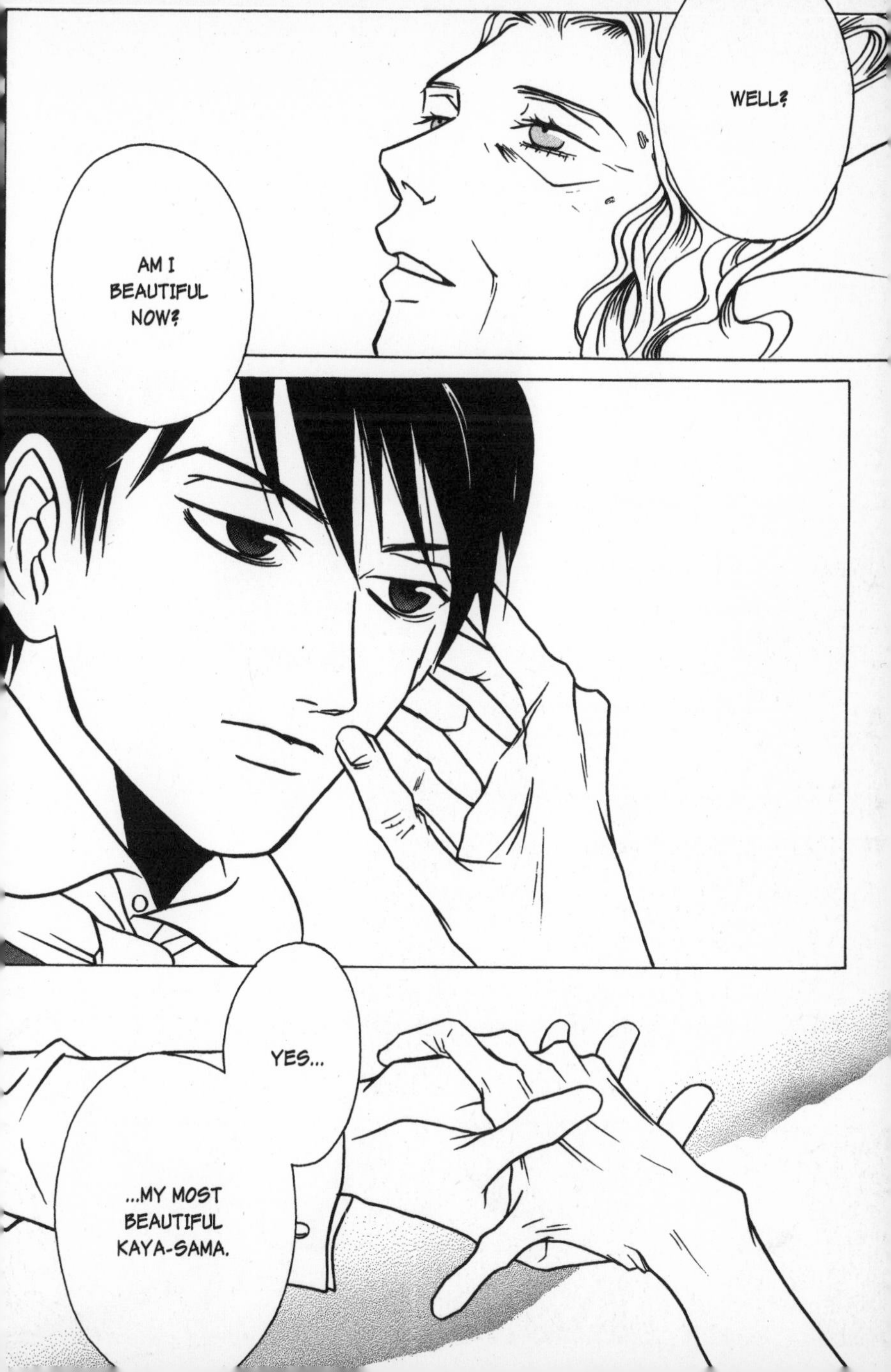
WELL?
AM I BEAUTIFUL NOW?
YES...
...MY MOST BEAUTIFUL KAYA-SAMA.

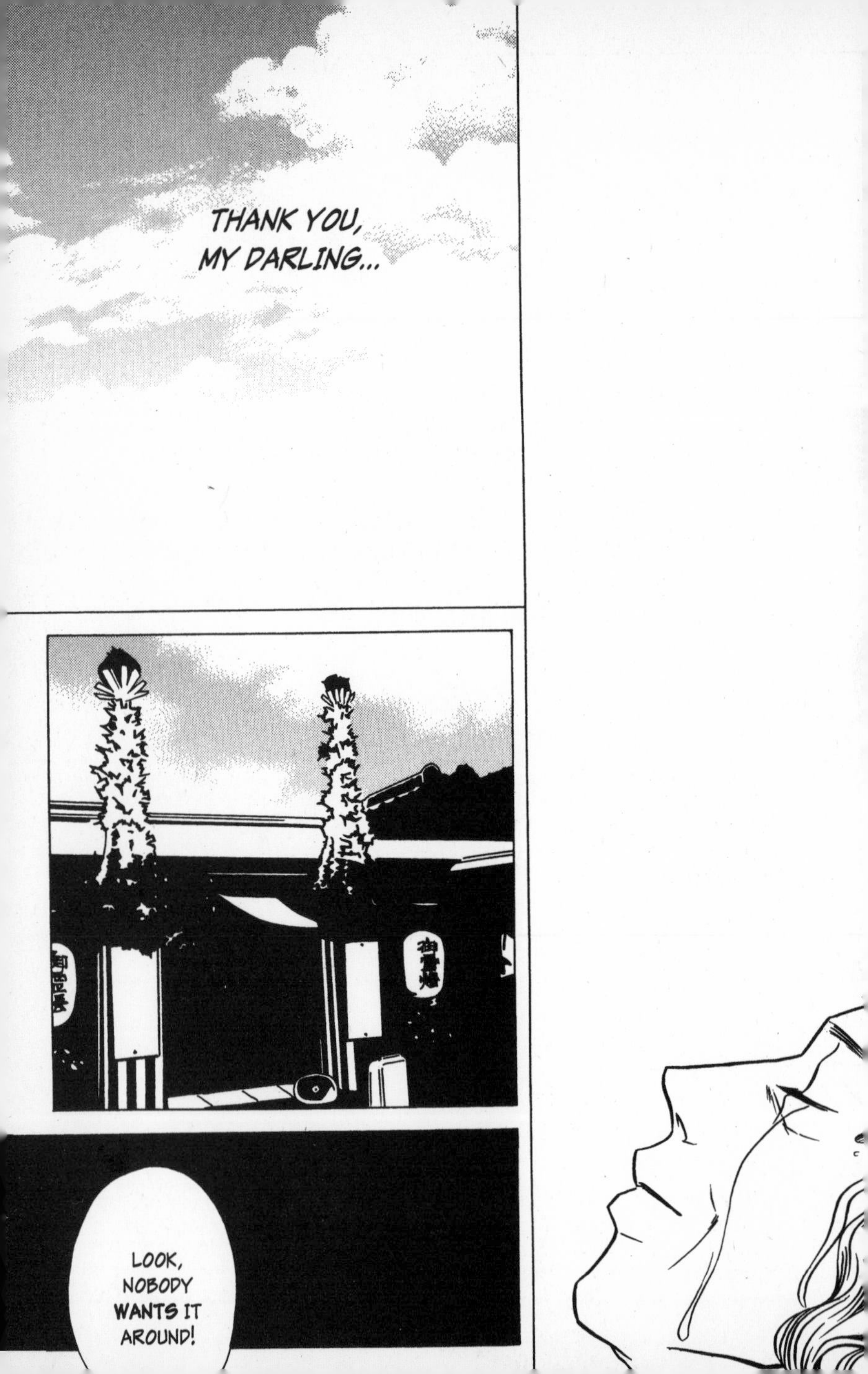
THANK YOU, MY DARLING...
LOOK, NOBODY WANTS IT AROUND!

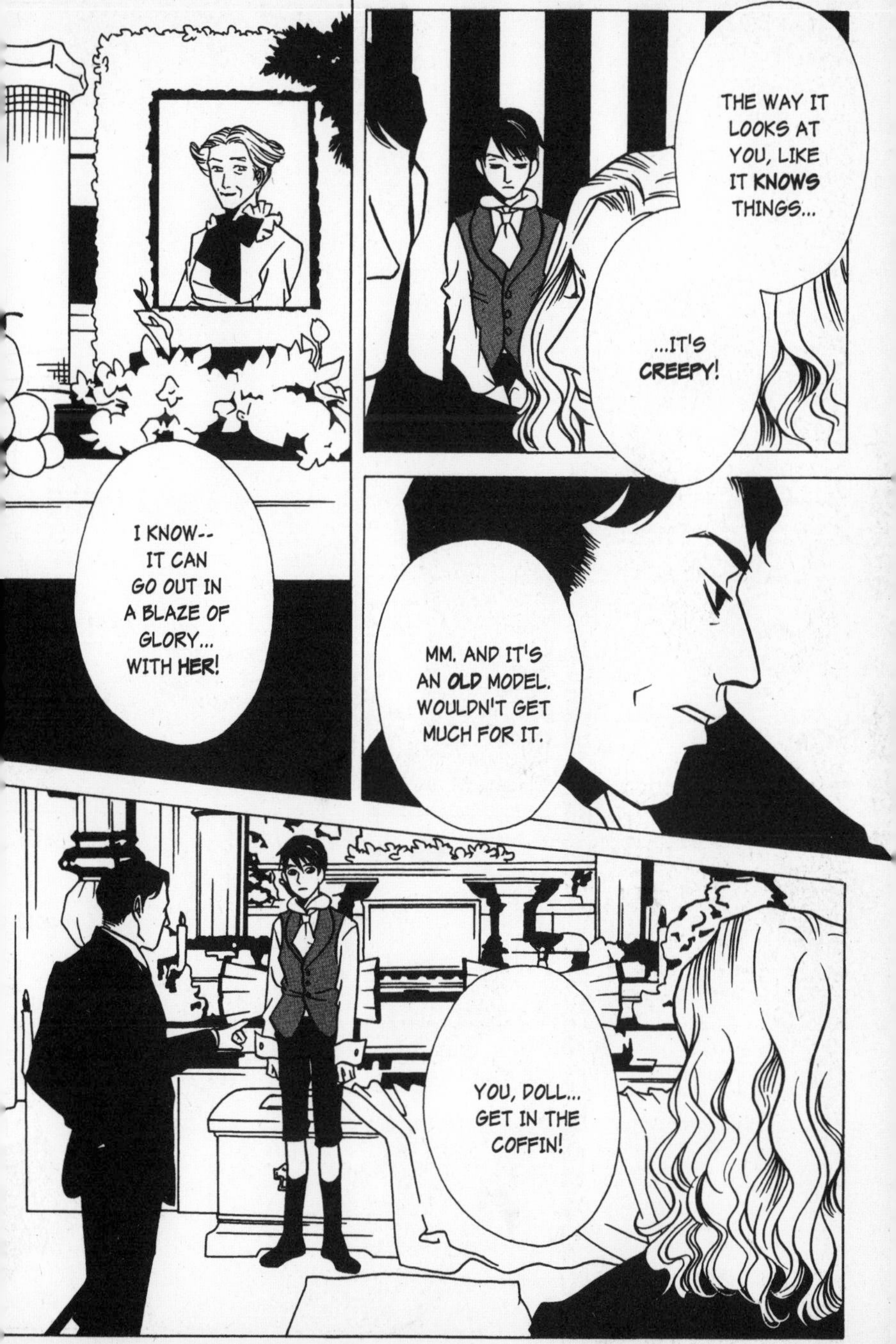
THE WAY IT LOOKS AT YOU, LIKE IT KNOWS THINGS...
...IT'S CREEPY!
MM. AND IT'S AN OLD MODEL. WOULDN'T GET MUCH FOR IT.
I KNOW-- IT CAN GO OUT IN A BLAZE OF GLORY... WITH HER!
YOU, DOLL... GET IN THE COFFIN!

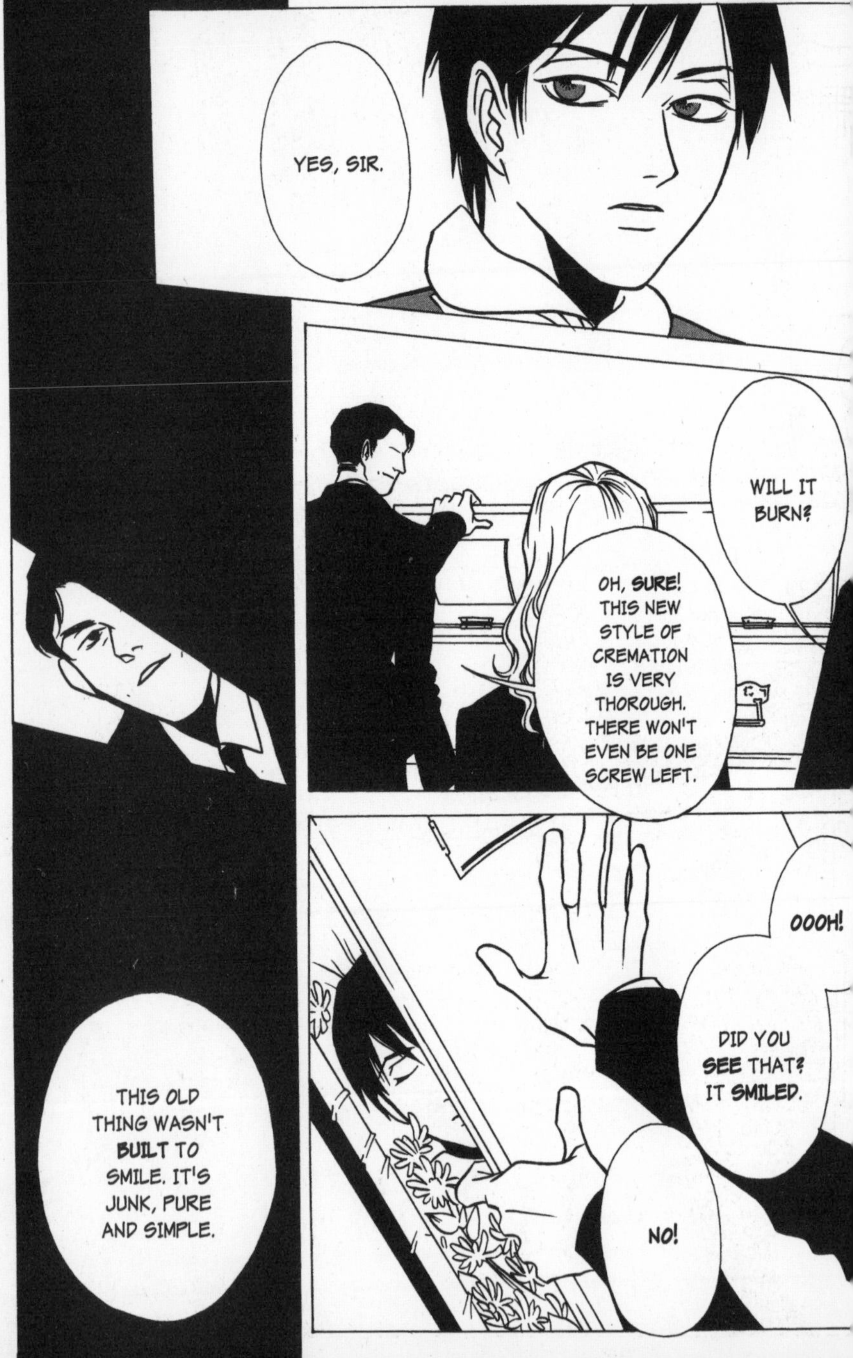
YES, SIR.
WILL IT BURN?
OH, SURE! THIS NEW STYLE OF CREMATION IS VERY THOROUGH. THERE WON'T EVEN BE ONE SCREW LEFT.
OOOH!
DID YOU SEE THAT? IT SMILED.
NO!
THIS OLD THING WASN'T BUILT TO SMILE. IT'S JUNK, PURE AND SIMPLE.

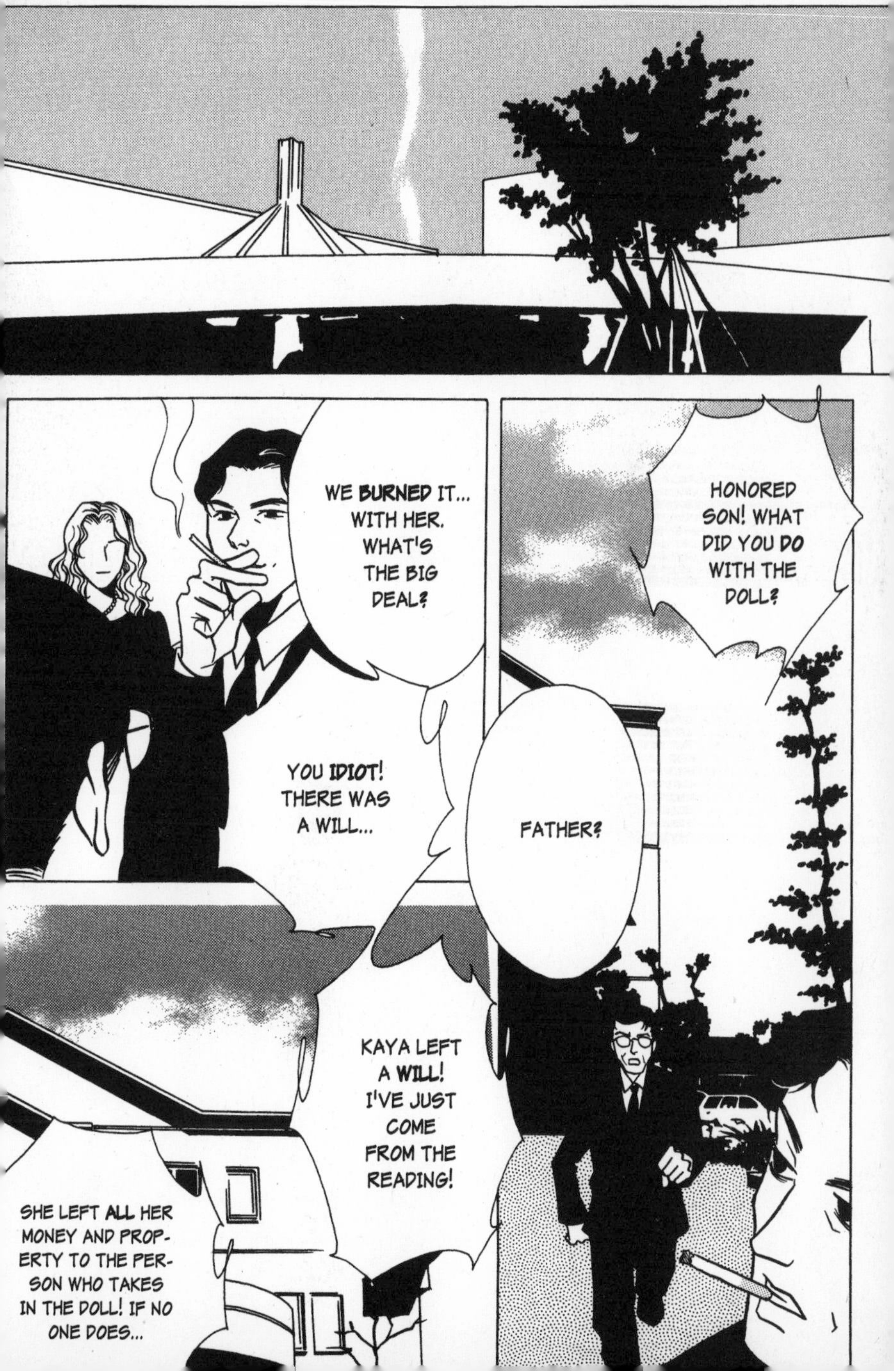
HONORED SON! WHAT DID YOU DO WITH THE DOLL?
FATHER?
WE BURNED IT... WITH HER. WHAT'S THE BIG DEAL?
YOU IDIOT! THERE WAS A WILL...
KAYA LEFT A WILL! I'VE JUST COME FROM THE READING!
SHE LEFT ALL HER MONEY AND PROPERTY TO THE PERSON WHO TAKES IN THE DOLL! IF NO ONE DOES...

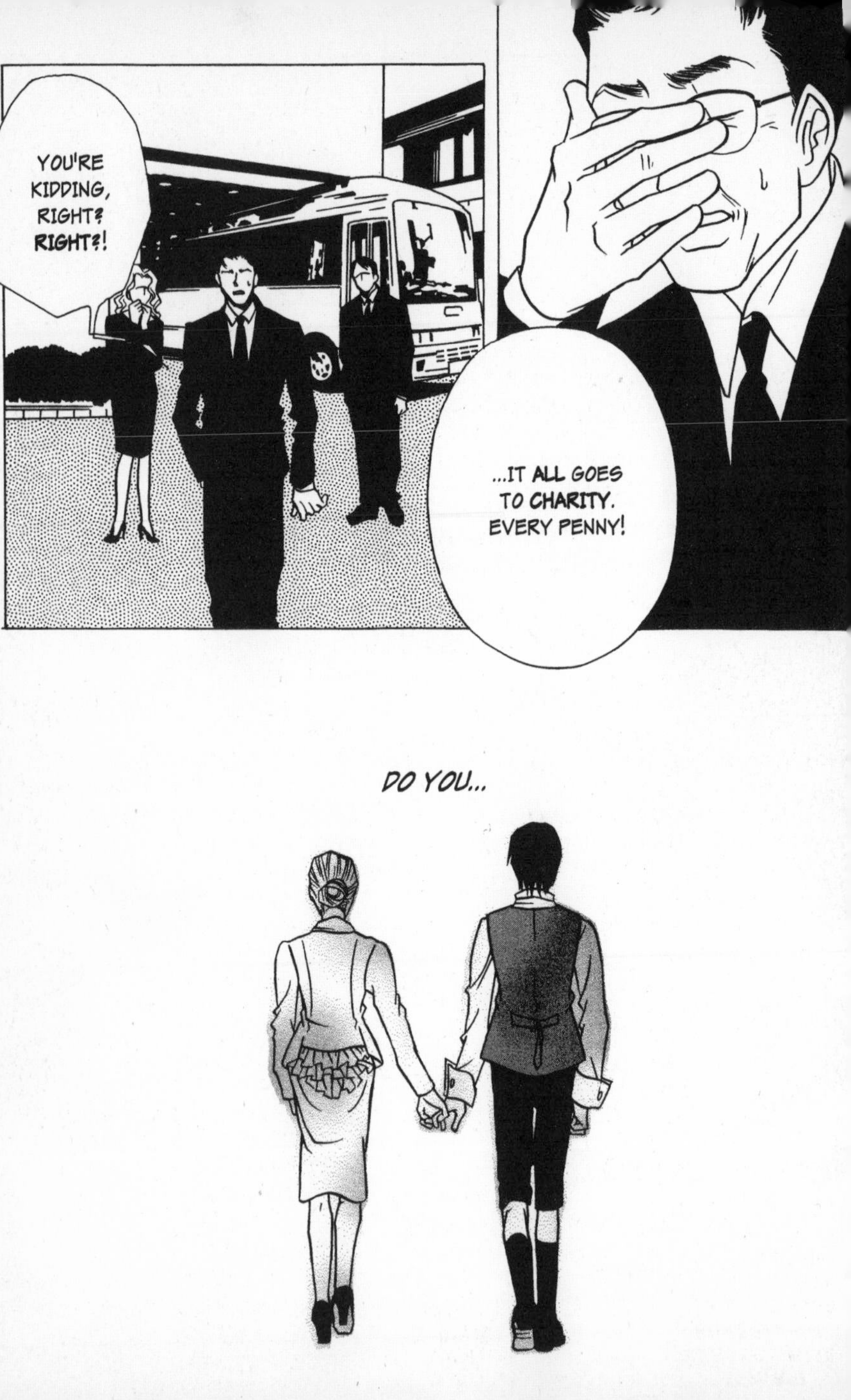
...IT ALL GOES TO CHARITY. EVERY PENNY!
YOU'RE KIDDING, RIGHT? RIGHT?!
DO YOU...

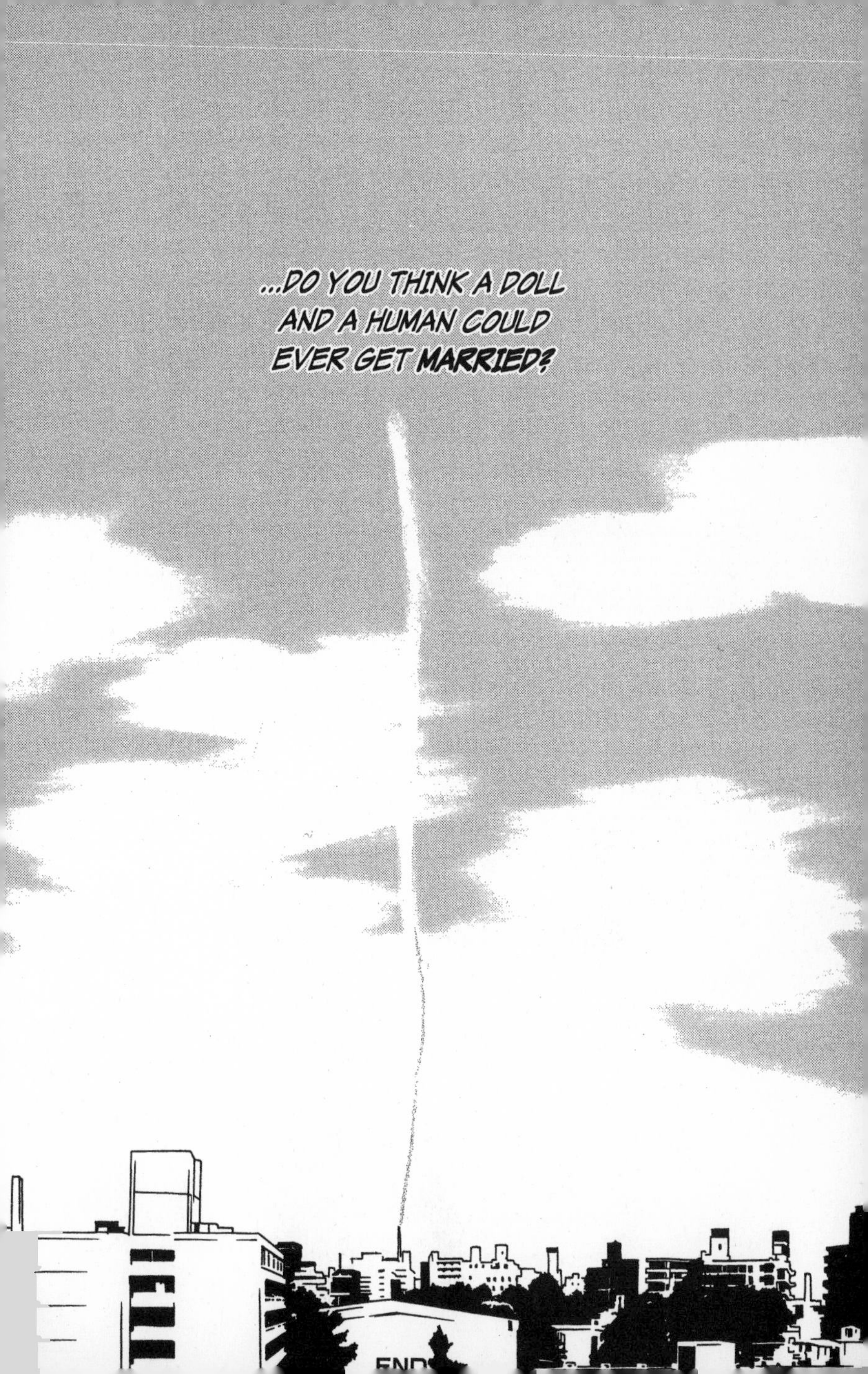
...DO YOU THINK A DOLL AND A HUMAN COULD EVER GET **MARRIED?**
END

L I S T 2

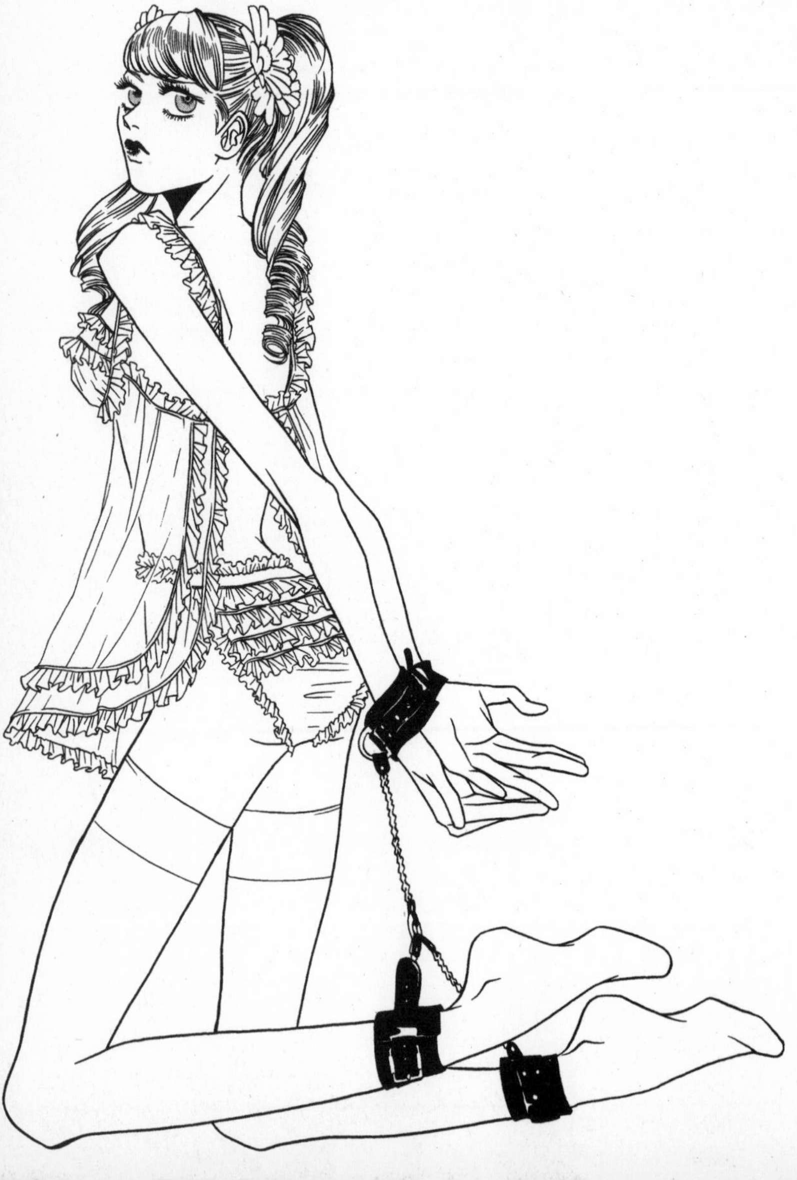

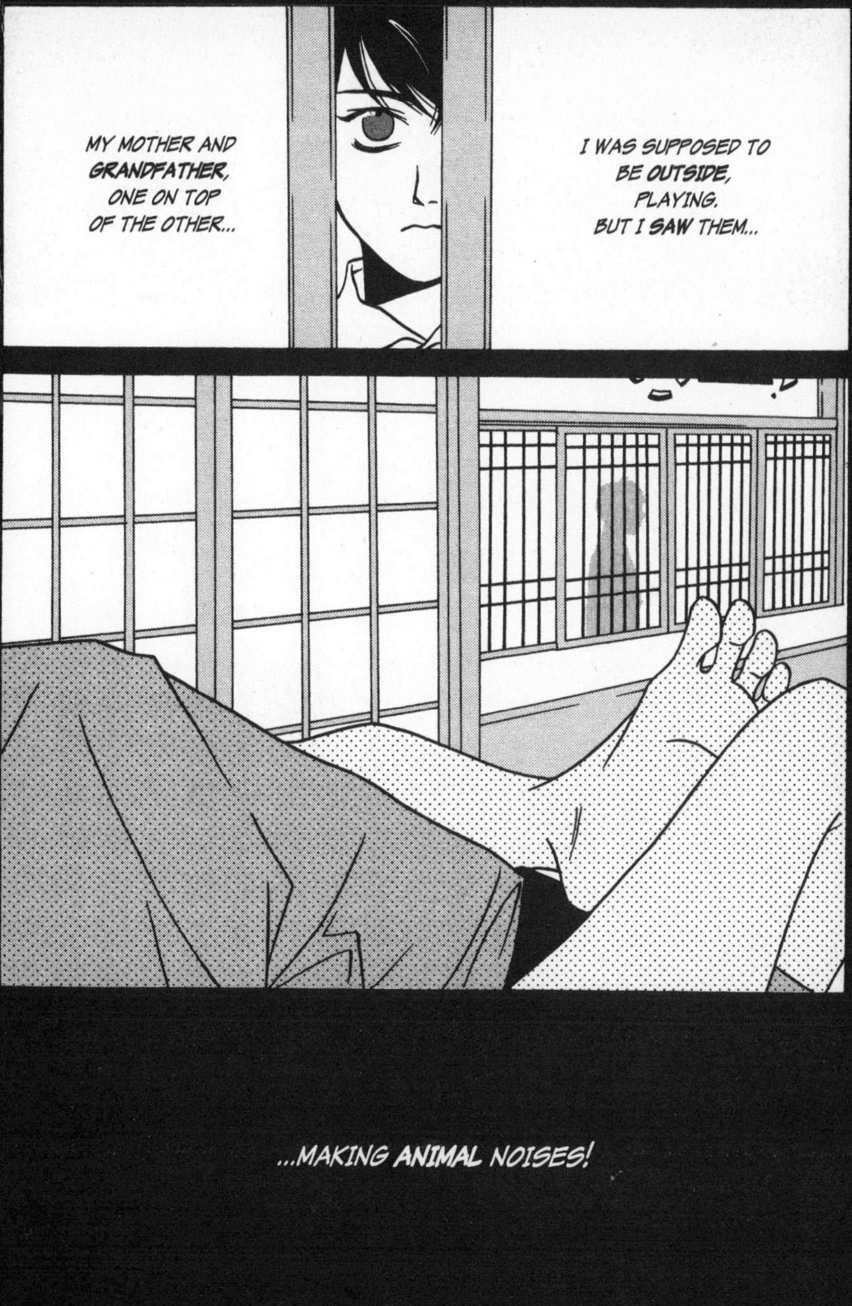
I WAS SUPPOSED TO BE OUTSIDE, PLAYING. BUT I SAW THEM...
MY MOTHER AND GRANDFATHER, ONE ON TOP OF THE OTHER...
...MAKING ANIMAL NOISES!

2. MARIA

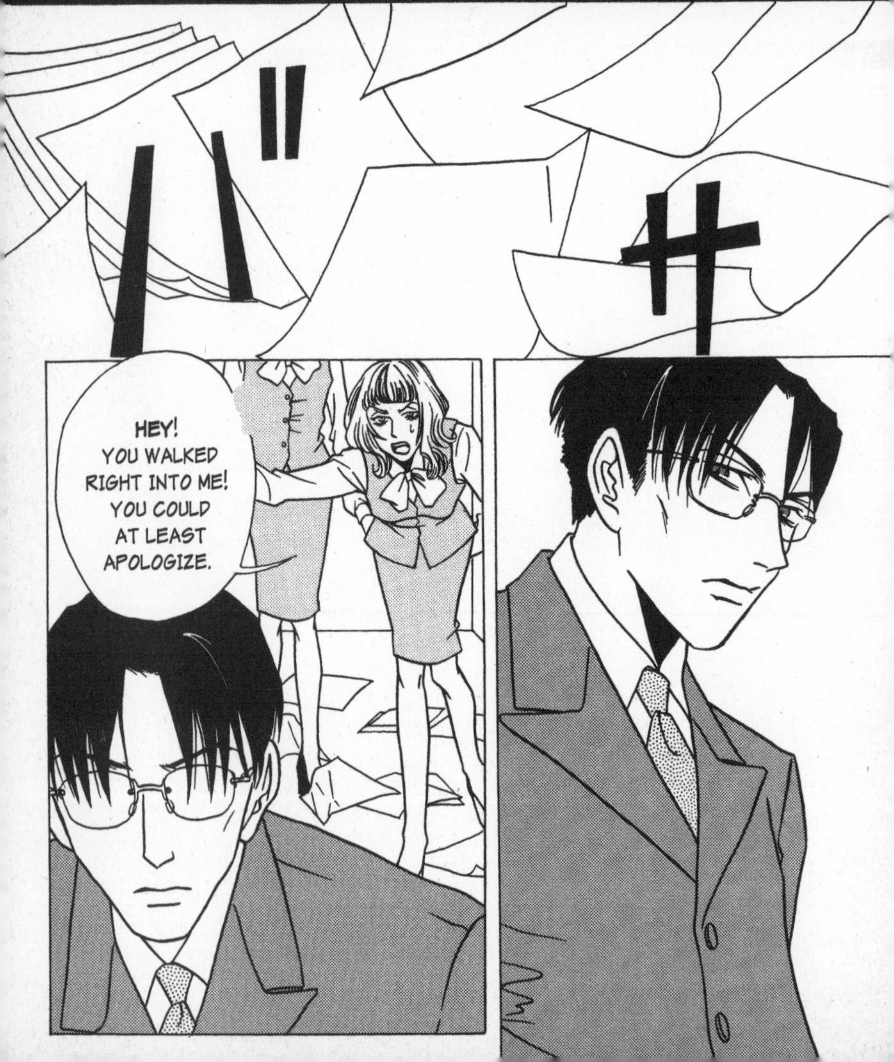
バサ
HEY! YOU WALKED RIGHT INTO ME! YOU COULD AT LEAST APOLOGIZE.

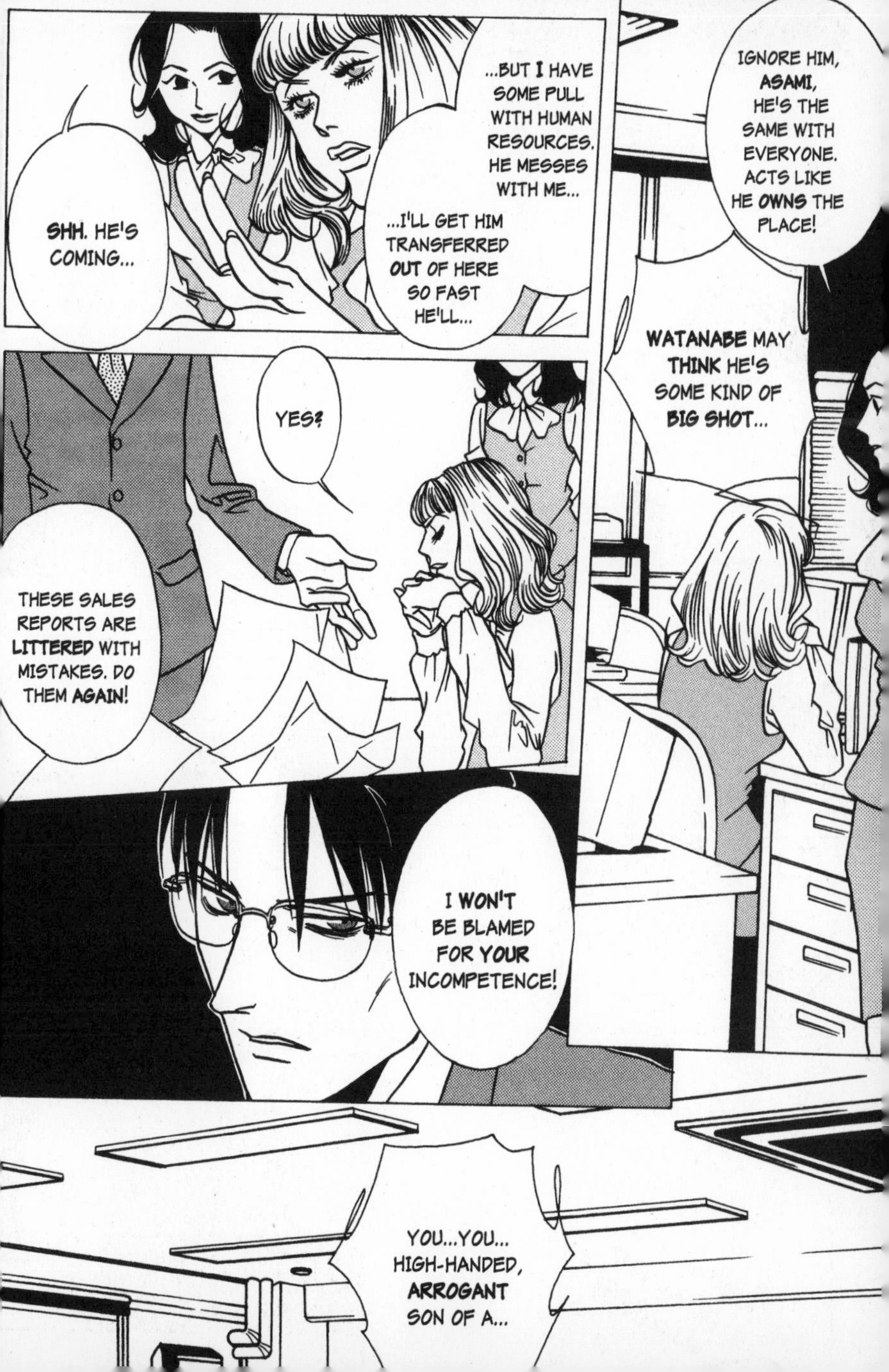
IGNORE HIM, ASAMI, HE'S THE SAME WITH EVERYONE. ACTS LIKE HE OWNS THE PLACE!
WATANABE MAY THINK HE'S SOME KIND OF BIG SHOT...
...BUT I HAVE SOME PULL WITH HUMAN RESOURCES. HE MESSES WITH ME...
...I'LL GET HIM TRANSFERRED OUT OF HERE SO FAST HE'LL...
SHH. HE'S COMING...
YES?
THESE SALES REPORTS ARE LITTERED WITH MISTAKES. DO THEM AGAIN!
I WON'T BE BLAMED FOR YOUR INCOMPETENCE!
YOU...YOU... HIGH-HANDED, ARROGANT SON OF A...

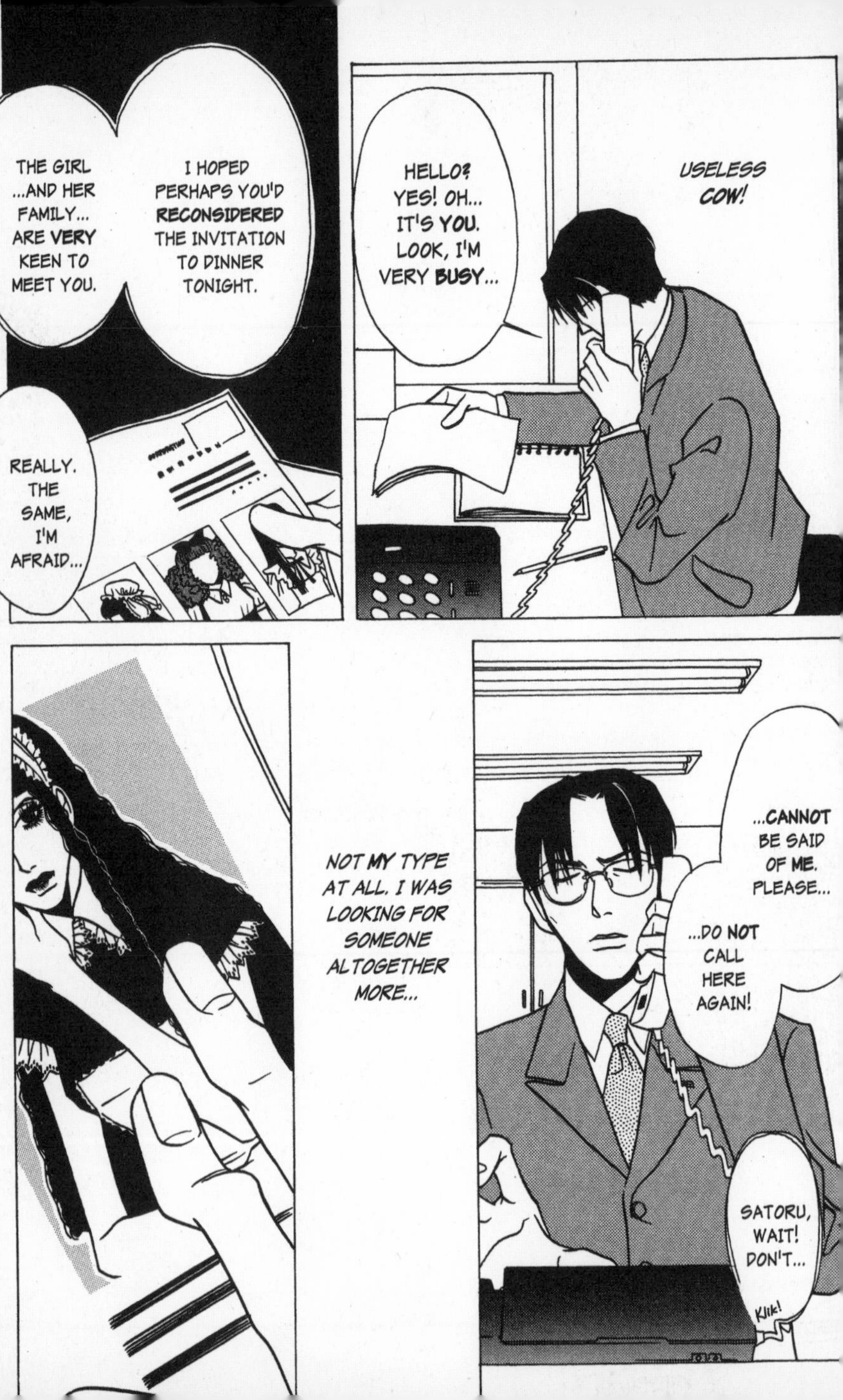
USELESS COW!
HELLO? YES! OH... IT'S YOU. LOOK, I'M VERY BUSY...
I HOPED PERHAPS YOU'D RECONSIDERED THE INVITATION TO DINNER TONIGHT.
THE GIRL ...AND HER FAMILY... ARE VERY KEEN TO MEET YOU.
REALLY. THE SAME, I'M AFRAID...
...CANNOT BE SAID OF ME. PLEASE...
...DO NOT CALL HERE AGAIN!
SATORU, WAIT! DON'T...
Klik!
NOT MY TYPE AT ALL. I WAS LOOKING FOR SOMEONE ALTOGETHER MORE...

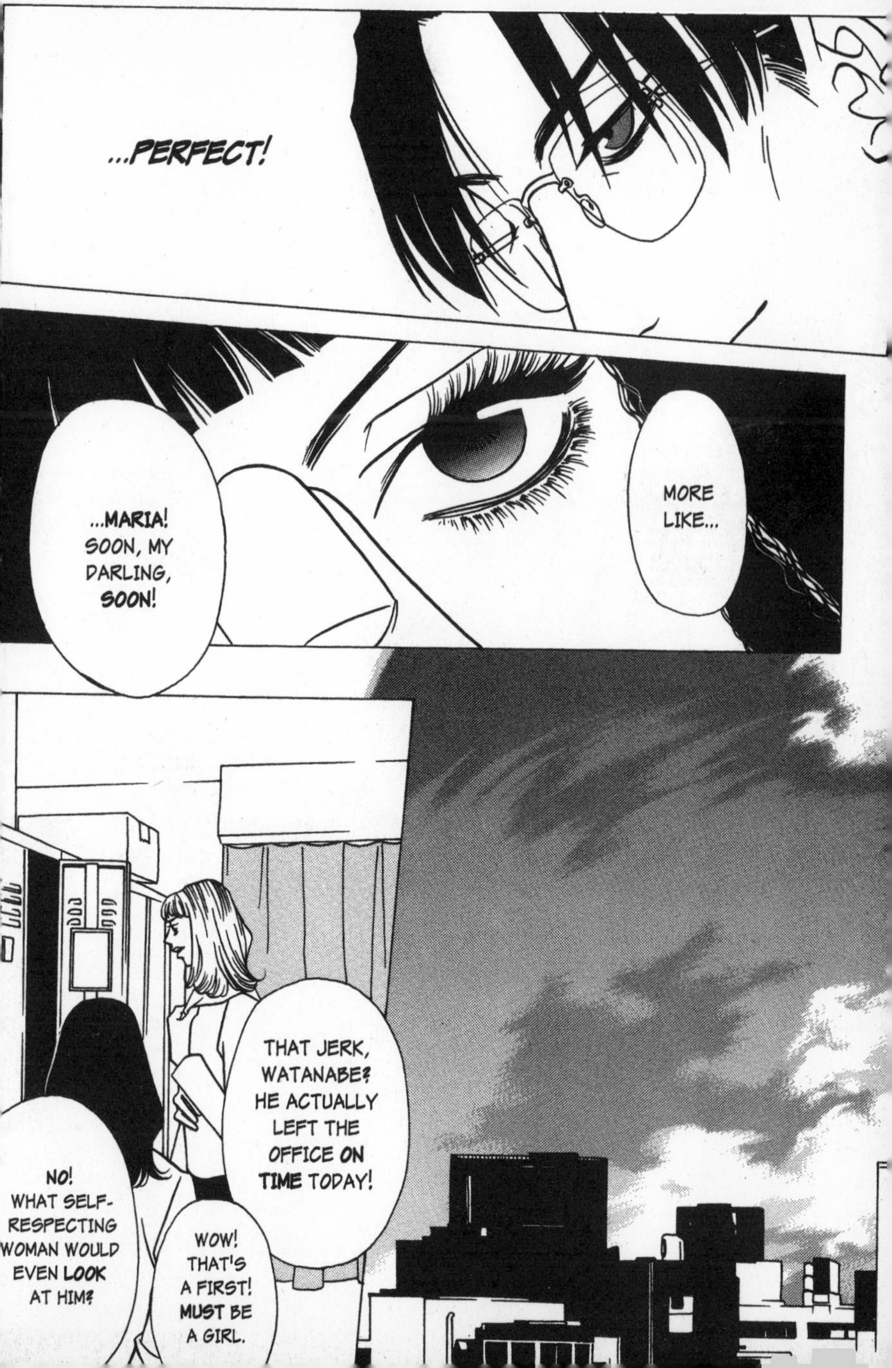
...PERFECT!
MORE LIKE...
...MARIA! SOON, MY DARLING, SOON!
THAT JERK, WATANABE? HE ACTUALLY LEFT THE OFFICE ON TIME TODAY!
WOW! THAT'S A FIRST! MUST BE A GIRL.
NO! WHAT SELF-RESPECTING WOMAN WOULD EVEN LOOK AT HIM?

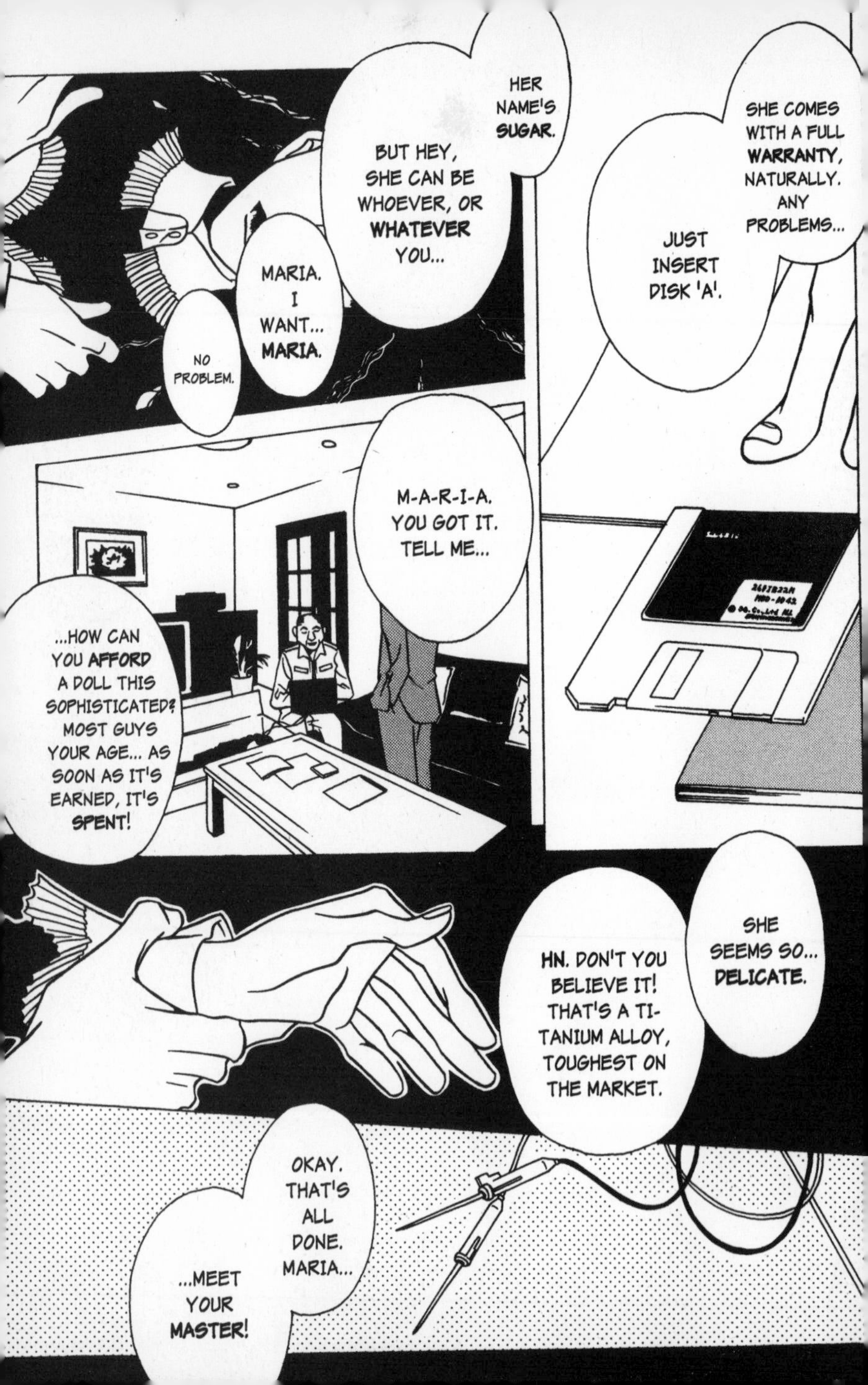
SHE COMES WITH A FULL WARRANTY, NATURALLY. ANY PROBLEMS...
JUST INSERT DISK 'A'.
HER NAME'S SUGAR.
BUT HEY, SHE CAN BE WHOEVER, OR WHATEVER YOU...
MARIA. I WANT... MARIA.
NO PROBLEM.
M-A-R-I-A. YOU GOT IT. TELL ME...
...HOW CAN YOU AFFORD A DOLL THIS SOPHISTICATED? MOST GUYS YOUR AGE... AS SOON AS IT'S EARNED, IT'S SPENT!
SHE SEEMS SO... DELICATE.
HN. DON'T YOU BELIEVE IT! THAT'S A TI-TANIUM ALLOY, TOUGHEST ON THE MARKET.
OKAY. THAT'S ALL DONE. MARIA...
...MEET YOUR MASTER!

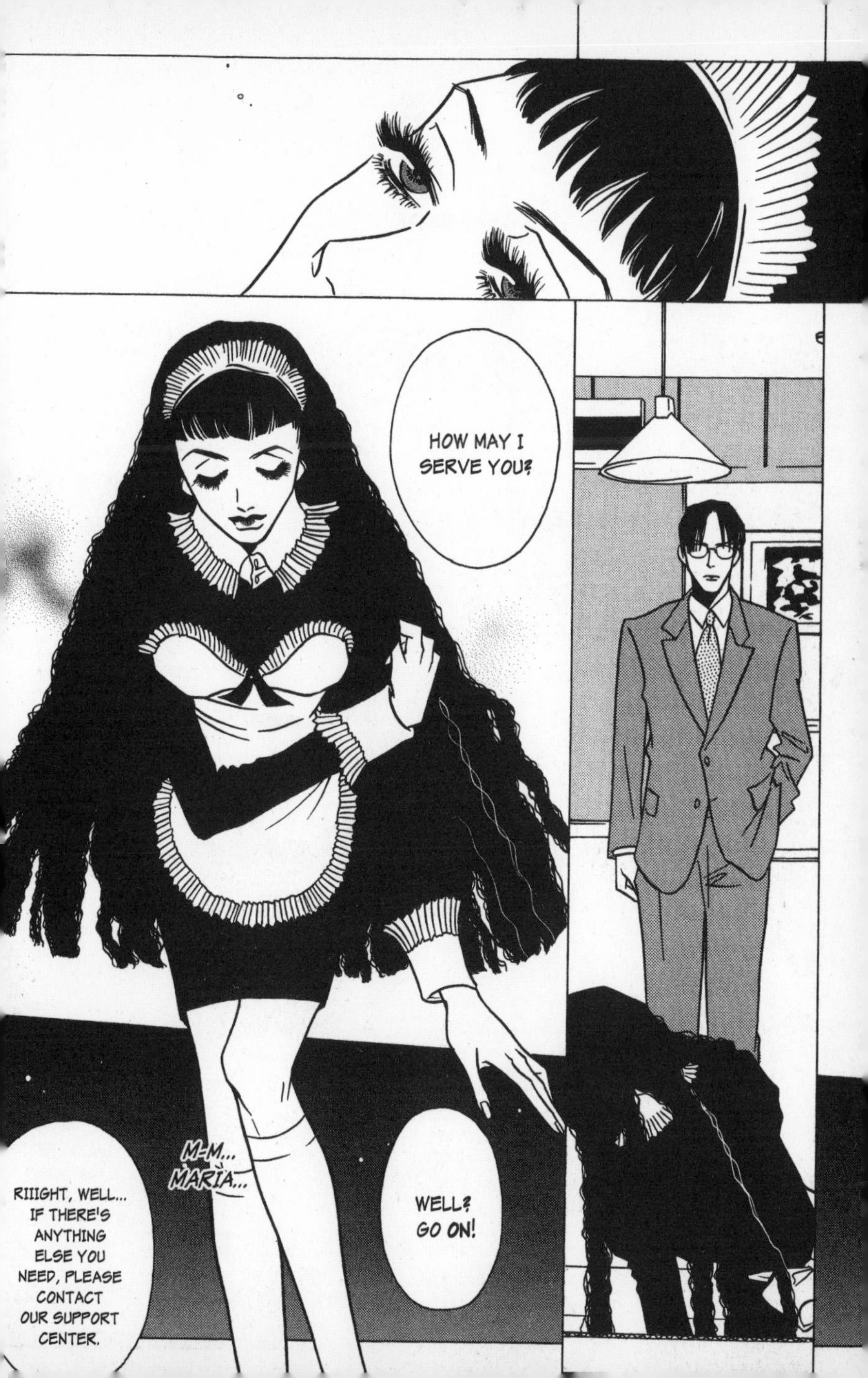
HOW MAY I SERVE YOU?
M-M... MARIA...
WELL? GO ON!
RIIIGHT, WELL... IF THERE'S ANYTHING ELSE YOU NEED, PLEASE CONTACT OUR SUPPORT CENTER.

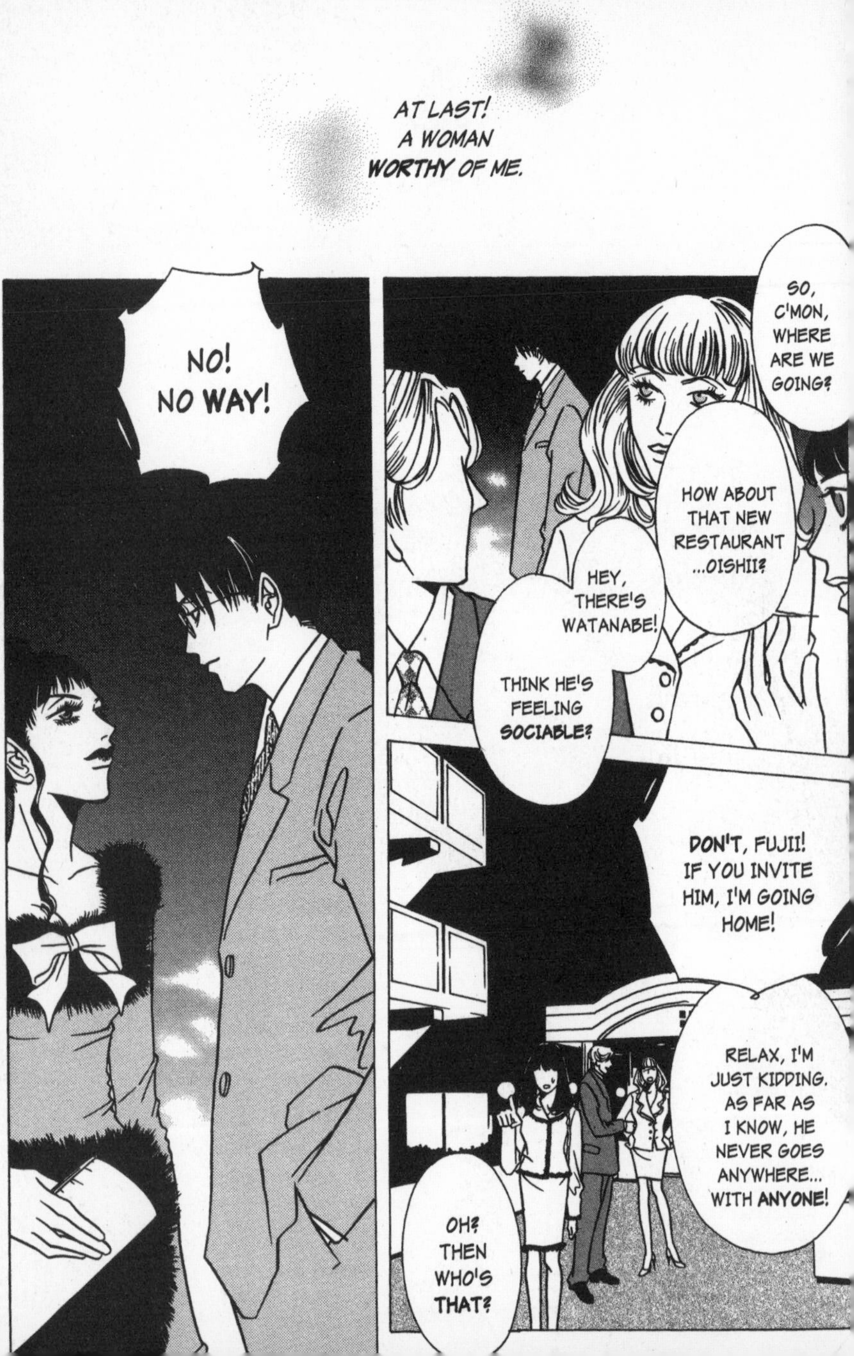
AT LAST! A WOMAN WORTHY OF ME.
SO, C'MON, WHERE ARE WE GOING?
HOW ABOUT THAT NEW RESTAURANT ...OISHII?
HEY, THERE'S WATANABE!
THINK HE'S FEELING SOCIABLE?
DON'T, FUJII! IF YOU INVITE HIM, I'M GOING HOME!
RELAX, I'M JUST KIDDING. AS FAR AS I KNOW, HE NEVER GOES ANYWHERE... WITH ANYONE!
OH? THEN WHO'S THAT?
NO! NO WAY!

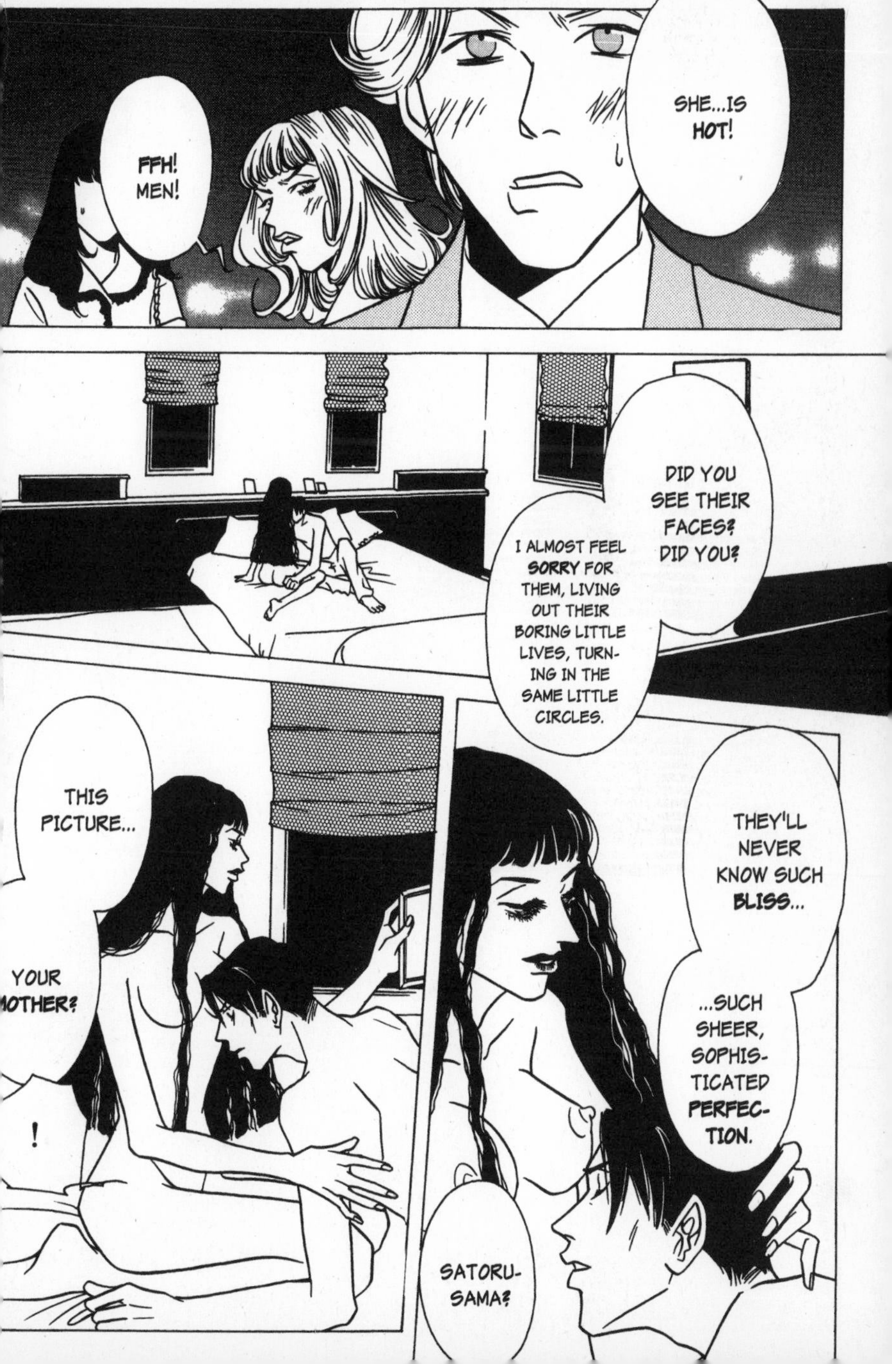
SHE...IS HOT!
FFH! MEN!
DID YOU SEE THEIR FACES? DID YOU?
I ALMOST FEEL SORRY FOR THEM, LIVING OUT THEIR BORING LITTLE LIVES, TURNING IN THE SAME LITTLE CIRCLES.
THEY'LL NEVER KNOW SUCH BLISS...
...SUCH SHEER, SOPHISTICATED PERFECTION.
SATORU-SAMA?
THIS PICTURE...
YOUR MOTHER?
!

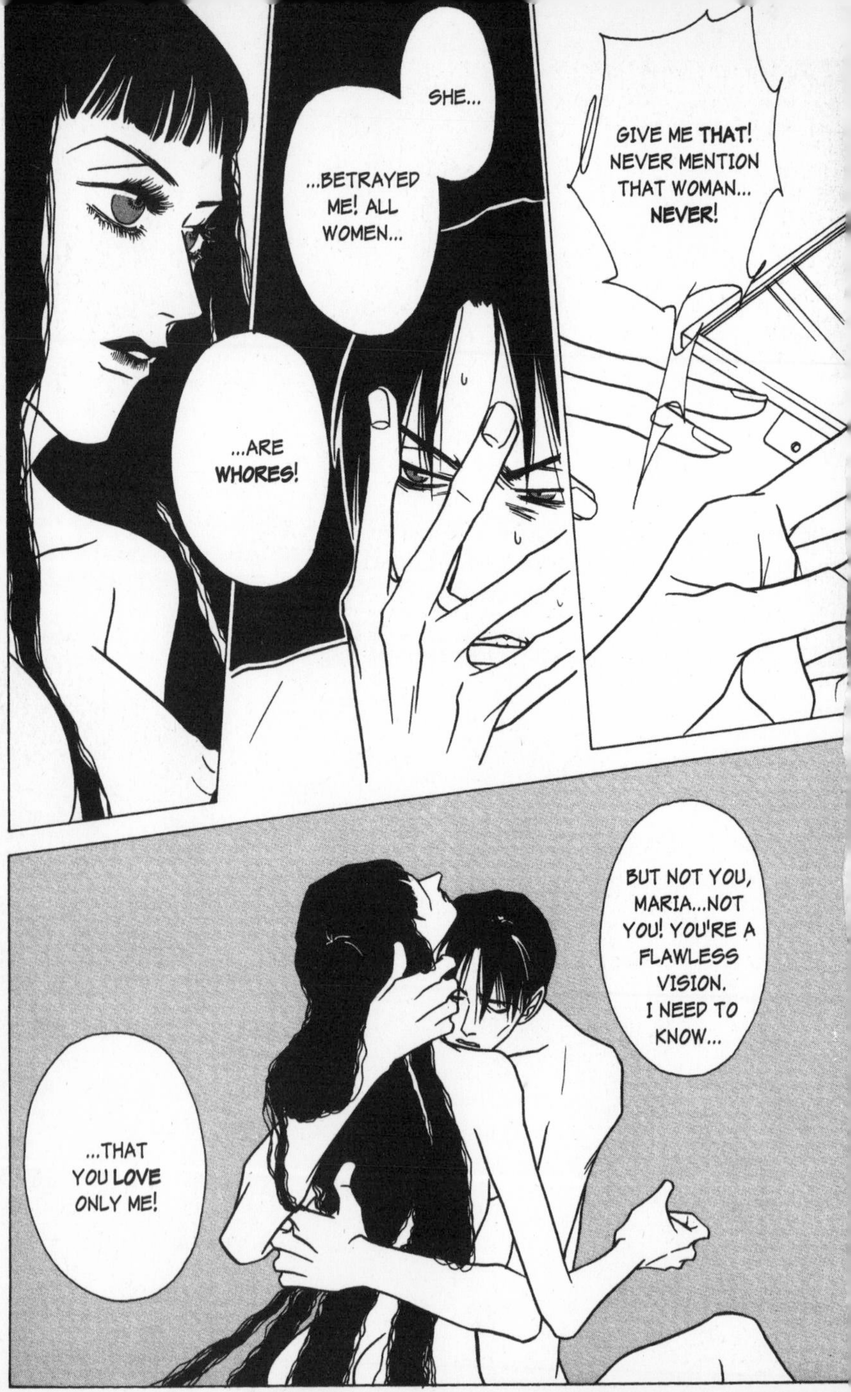
GIVE ME THAT! NEVER MENTION THAT WOMAN... NEVER!
SHE...
...BETRAYED ME! ALL WOMEN...
...ARE WHORES!
BUT NOT YOU, MARIA...NOT YOU! YOU'RE A FLAWLESS VISION. I NEED TO KNOW...
...THAT YOU LOVE ONLY ME!

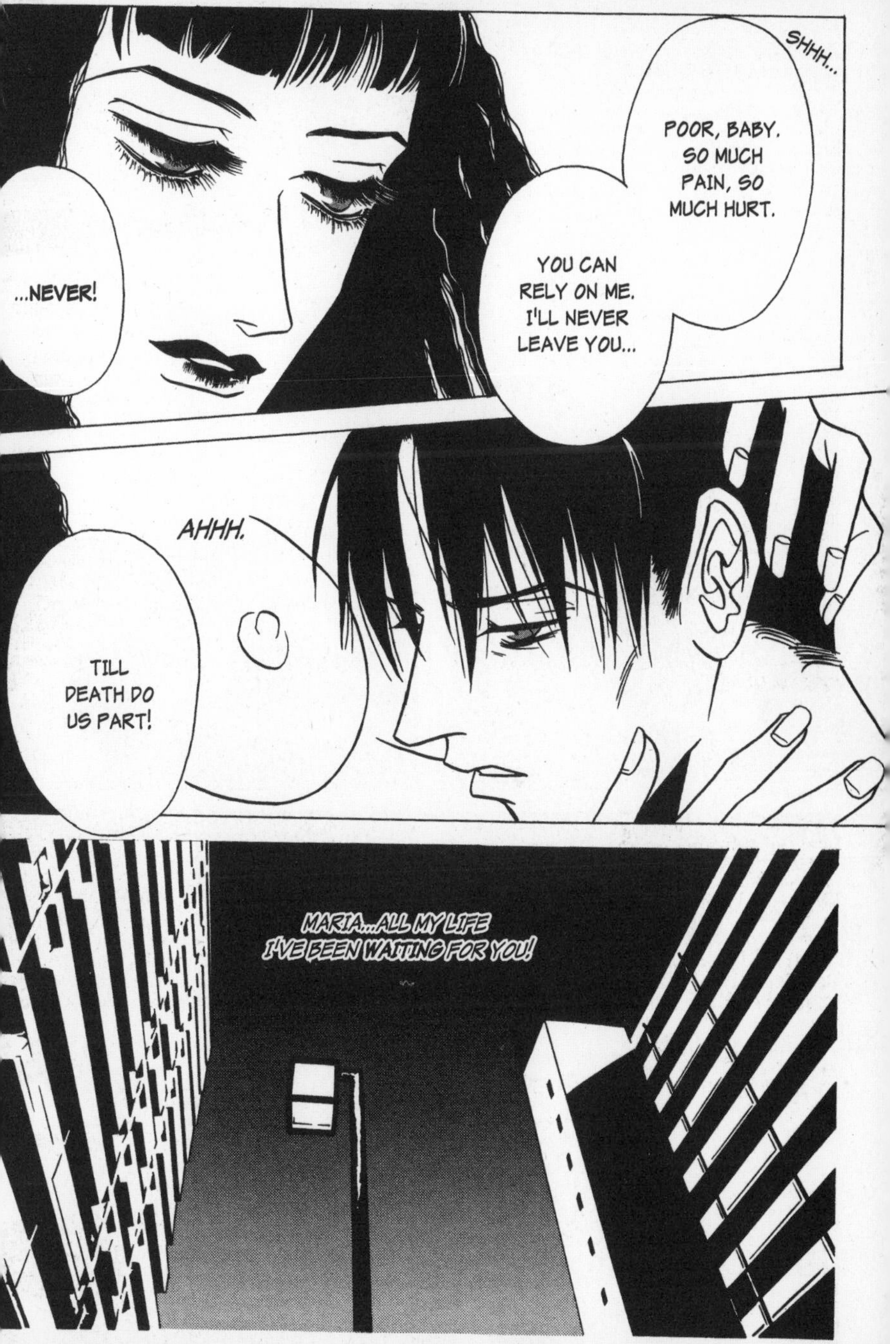
SHHH...
POOR, BABY. SO MUCH PAIN, SO MUCH HURT.
YOU CAN RELY ON ME. I'LL NEVER LEAVE YOU...
...NEVER!
AHHH.
TILL DEATH DO US PART!
MARIA...ALL MY LIFE I'VE BEEN WAITING FOR YOU!

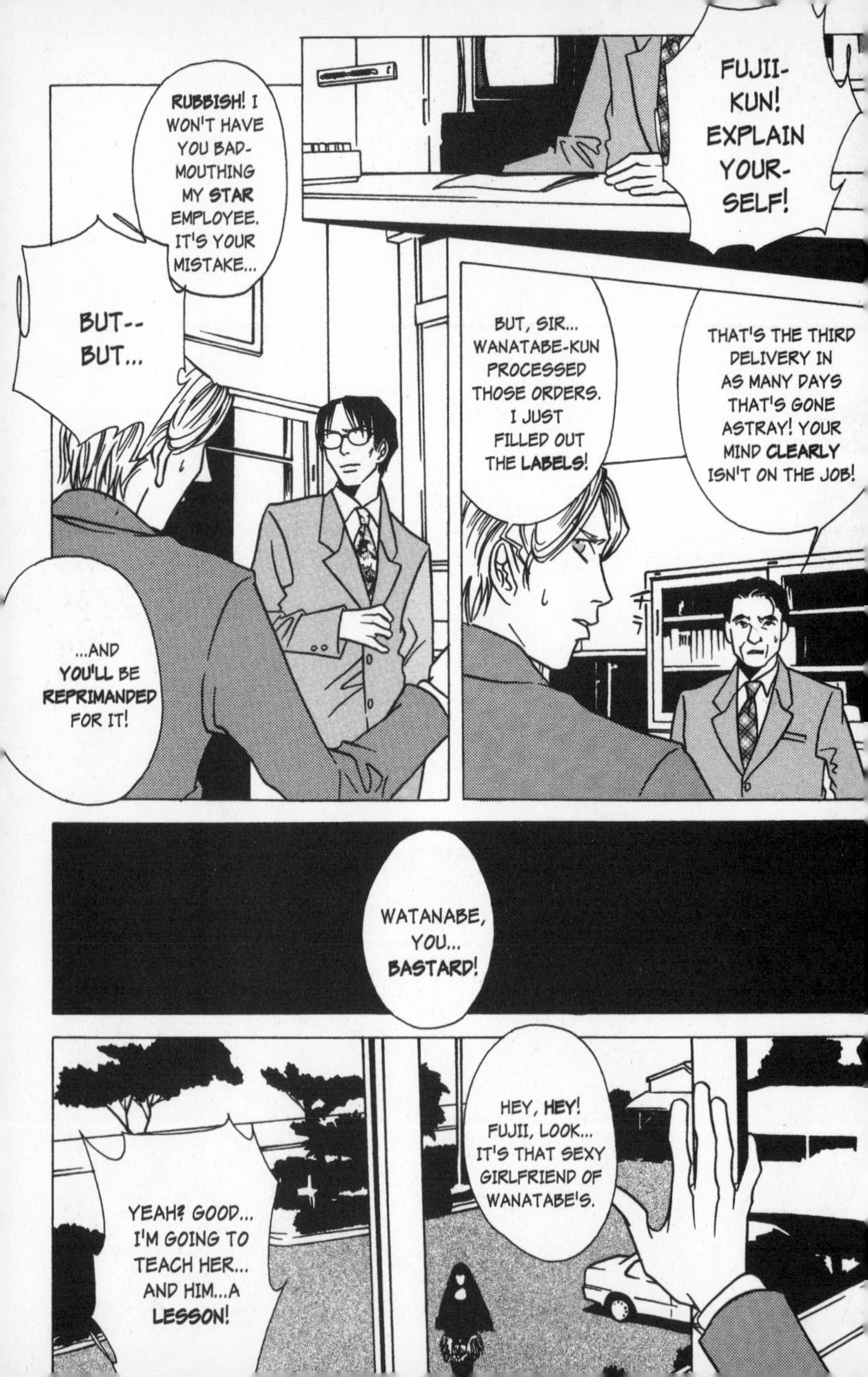
FUJII-KUN! EXPLAIN YOUR-SELF!
THAT'S THE THIRD DELIVERY IN AS MANY DAYS THAT'S GONE ASTRAY! YOUR MIND CLEARLY ISN'T ON THE JOB!
BUT, SIR... WANATABE-KUN PROCESSED THOSE ORDERS. I JUST FILLED OUT THE LABELS!
RUBBISH! I WON'T HAVE YOU BAD-MOUTHING MY STAR EMPLOYEE. IT'S YOUR MISTAKE...
BUT-- BUT...
...AND YOU'LL BE REPRIMANDED FOR IT!
WATANABE, YOU... BASTARD!
HEY, HEY! FUJII, LOOK... IT'S THAT SEXY GIRLFRIEND OF WANATABE'S.
YEAH? GOOD... I'M GOING TO TEACH HER... AND HIM...A LESSON!

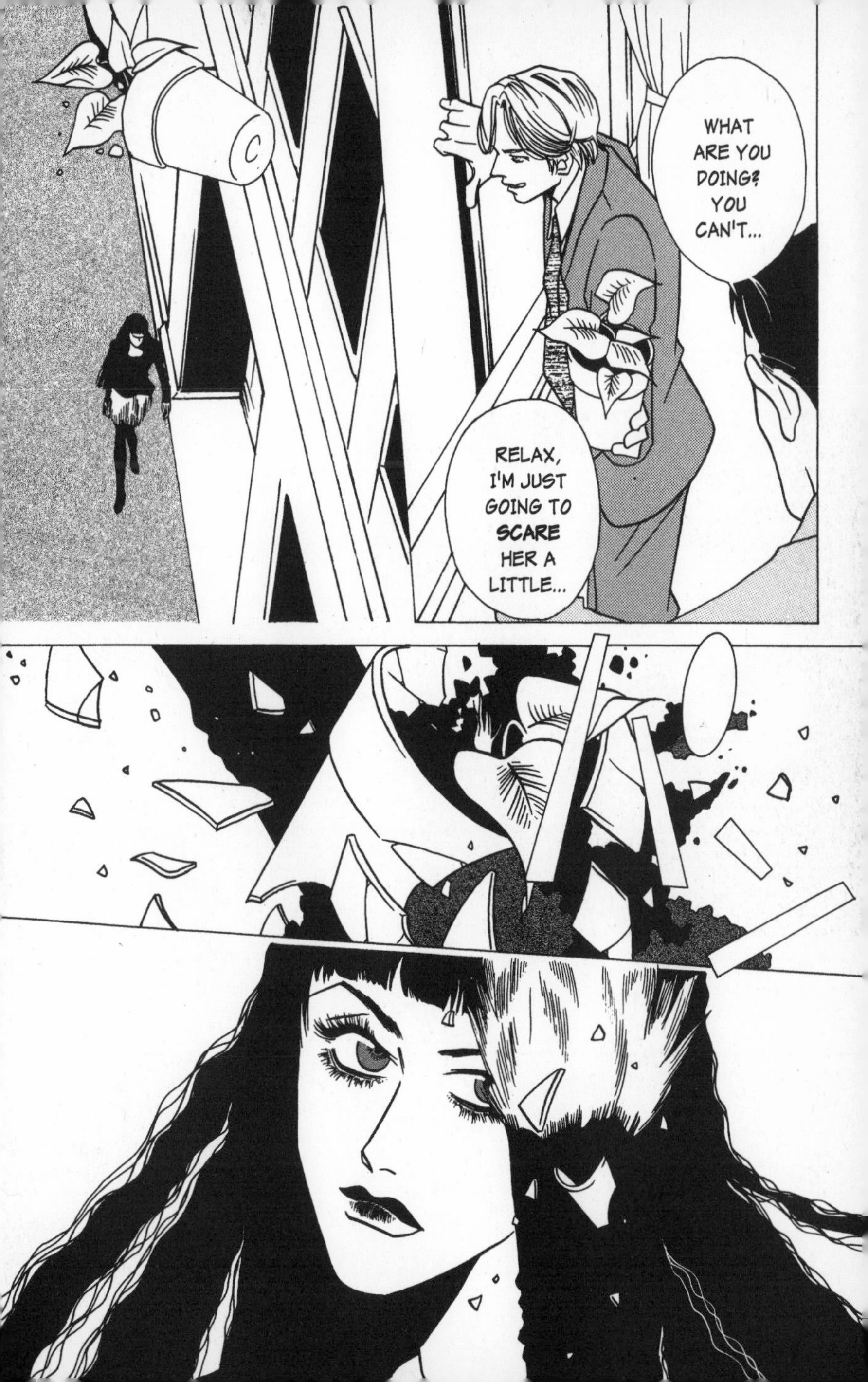
WHAT ARE YOU DOING? YOU CAN'T...
RELAX, I'M JUST GOING TO SCARE HER A LITTLE...

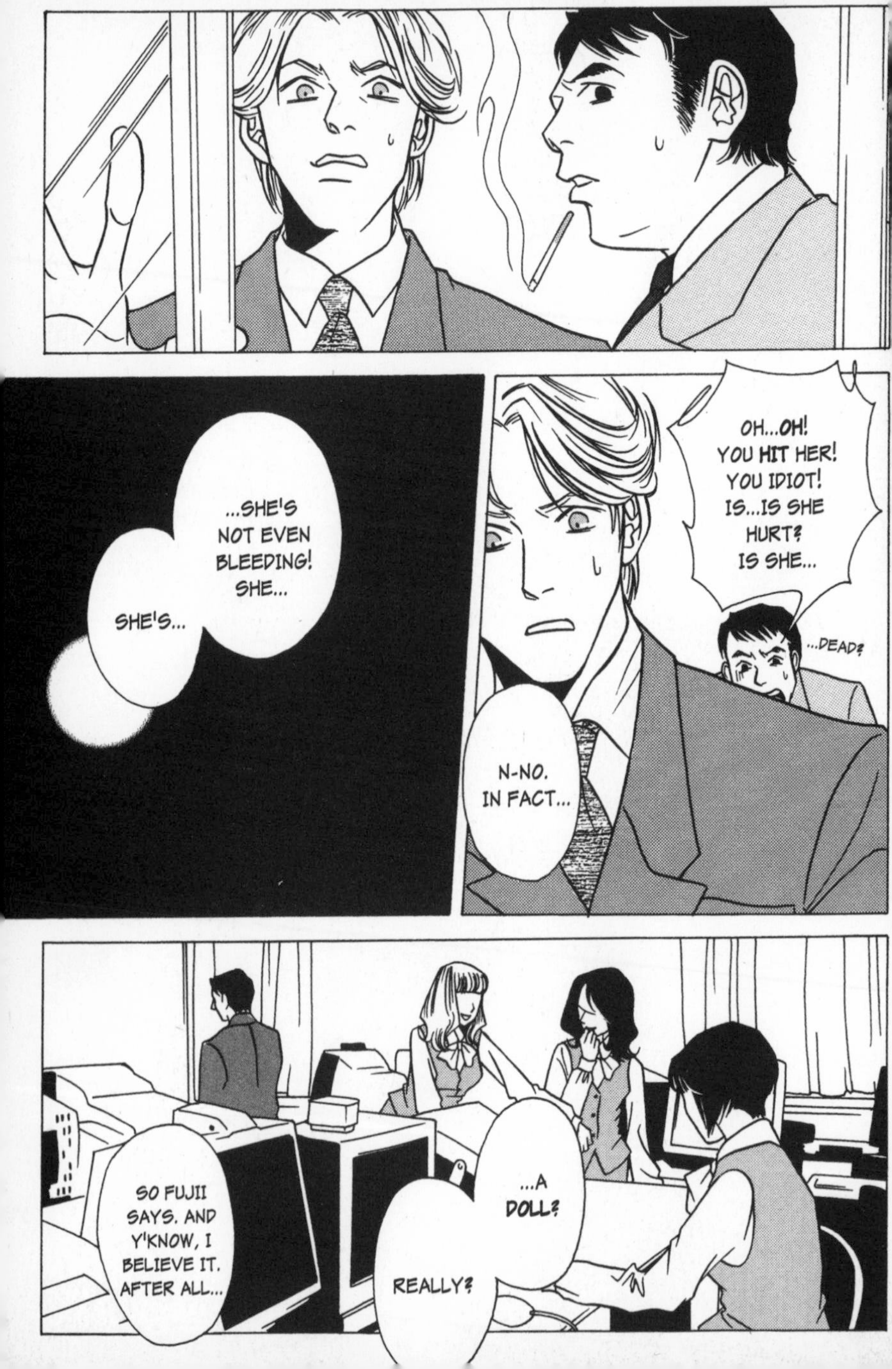
OH...OH! YOU HIT HER! YOU IDIOT! IS...IS SHE HURT? IS SHE...
...DEAD?
N-NO. IN FACT...
...SHE'S NOT EVEN BLEEDING! SHE...
SHE'S...
...A DOLL?
REALLY?
SO FUJII SAYS. AND Y'KNOW, I BELIEVE IT. AFTER ALL...

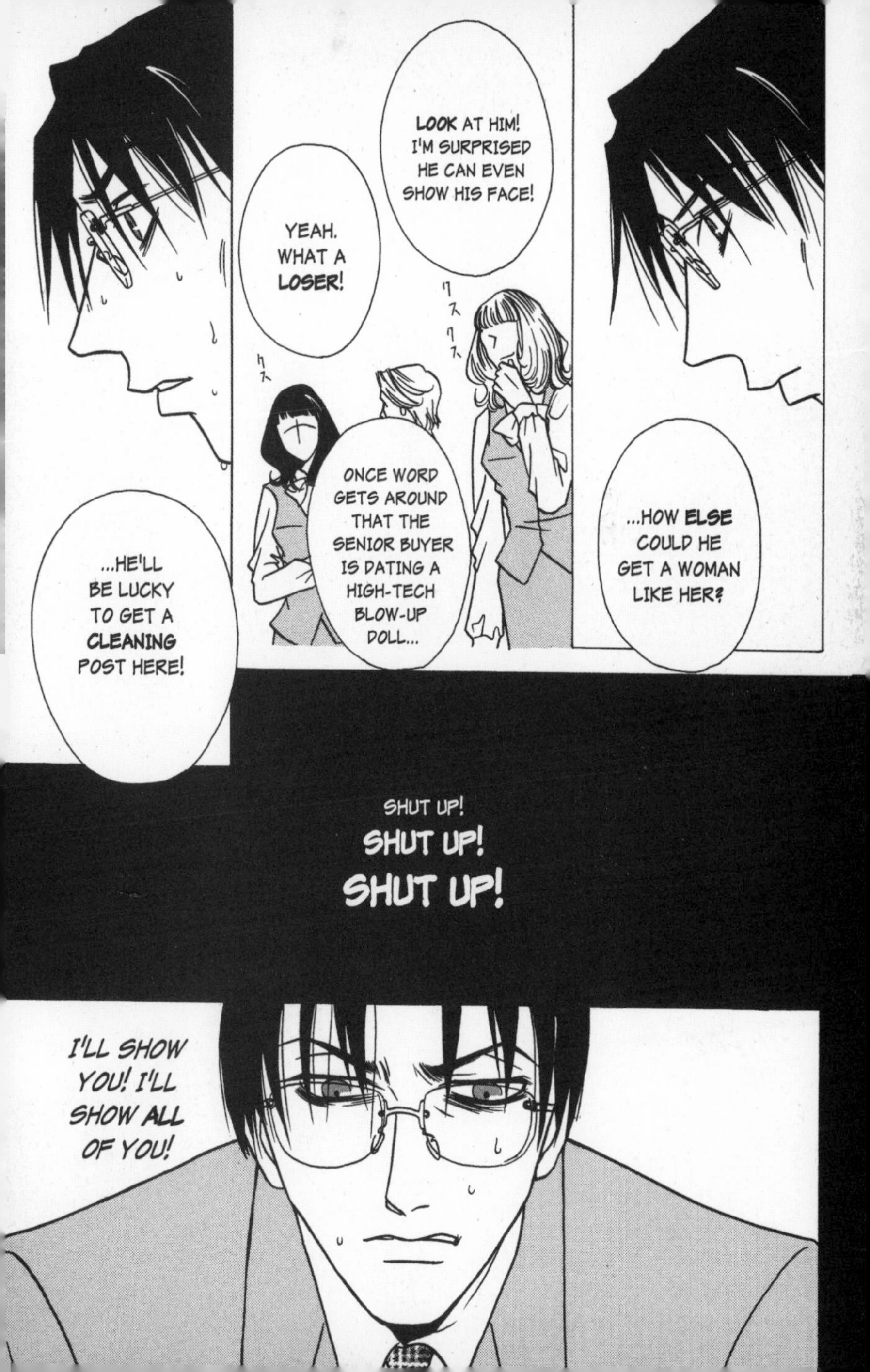
...HOW ELSE COULD HE GET A WOMAN LIKE HER?
LOOK AT HIM! I'M SURPRISED HE CAN EVEN SHOW HIS FACE!
YEAH. WHAT A LOSER!
クスクス
クス
ONCE WORD GETS AROUND THAT THE SENIOR BUYER IS DATING A HIGH-TECH BLOW-UP DOLL...
...HE'LL BE LUCKY TO GET A CLEANING POST HERE!
SHUT UP!
SHUT UP!
SHUT UP!
I'LL SHOW YOU! I'LL SHOW ALL OF YOU!

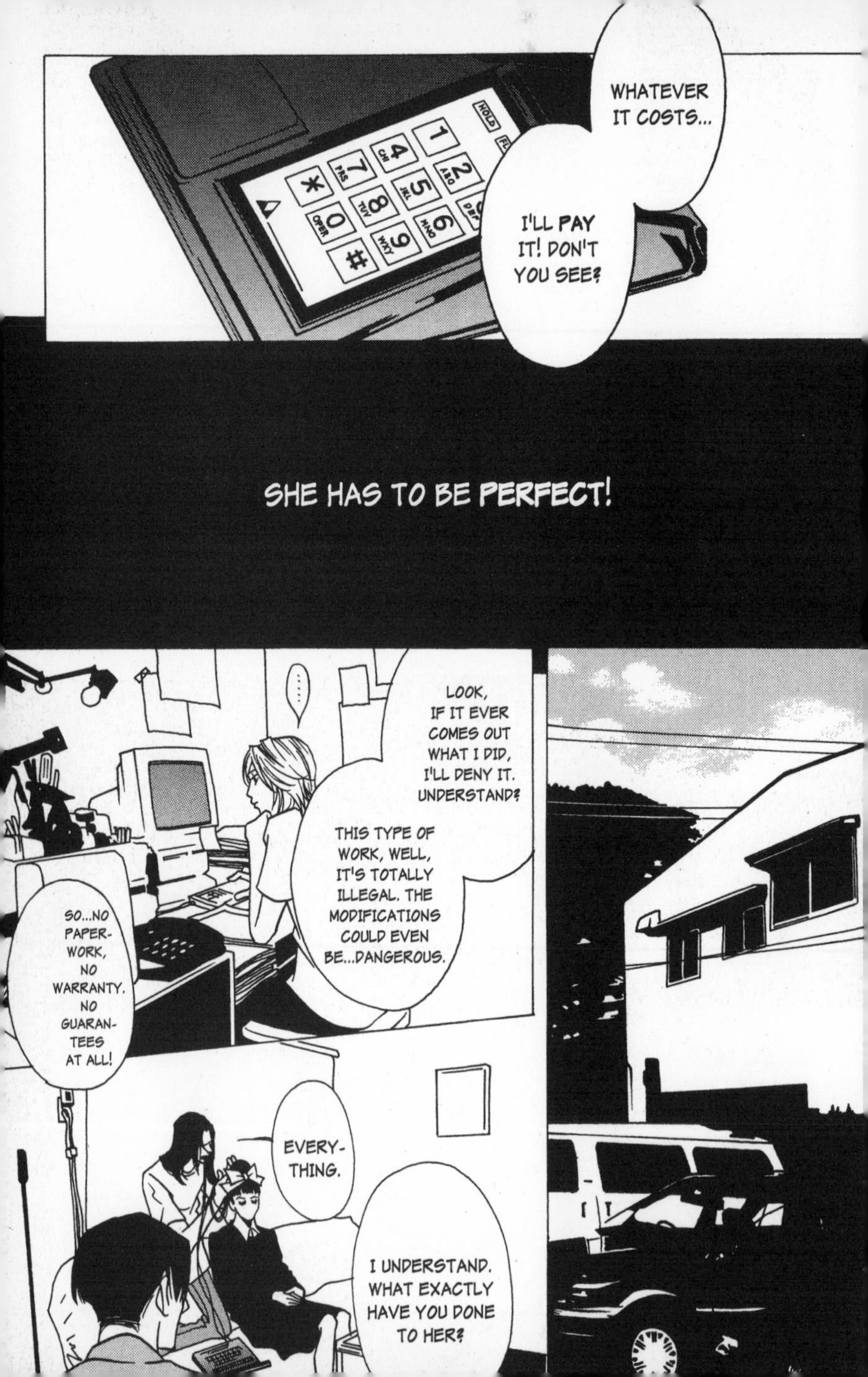
WHATEVER IT COSTS...
I'LL PAY IT! DON'T YOU SEE?
SHE HAS TO BE PERFECT!
LOOK, IF IT EVER COMES OUT WHAT I DID, I'LL DENY IT. UNDERSTAND?
.....
THIS TYPE OF WORK, WELL, IT'S TOTALLY ILLEGAL. THE MODIFICATIONS COULD EVEN BE...DANGEROUS.
SO...NO PAPER-WORK, NO WARRANTY. NO GUARAN-TEES AT ALL!
I UNDERSTAND. WHAT EXACTLY HAVE YOU DONE TO HER?
EVERY-THING.

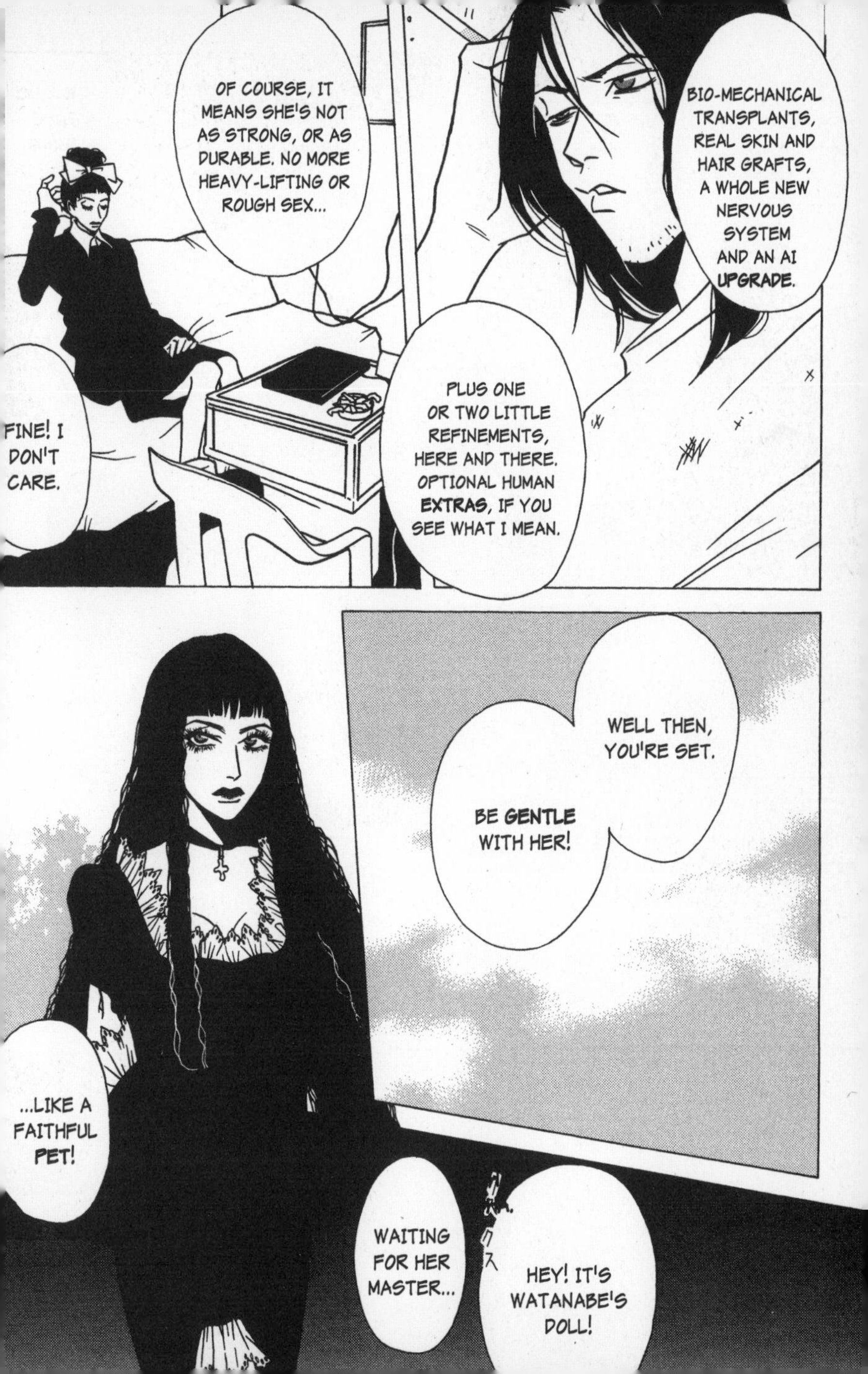
BIO-MECHANICAL TRANSPLANTS, REAL SKIN AND HAIR GRAFTS, A WHOLE NEW NERVOUS SYSTEM AND AN AI **UPGRADE**.
OF COURSE, IT MEANS SHE'S NOT AS STRONG, OR AS DURABLE. NO MORE HEAVY-LIFTING OR ROUGH SEX...
PLUS ONE OR TWO LITTLE REFINEMENTS, HERE AND THERE. OPTIONAL HUMAN **EXTRAS**, IF YOU SEE WHAT I MEAN.
FINE! I DON'T CARE.
WELL THEN, YOU'RE SET.
BE **GENTLE** WITH HER!
クスクス
HEY! IT'S WATANABE'S DOLL!
WAITING FOR HER MASTER...
...LIKE A FAITHFUL **PET**!

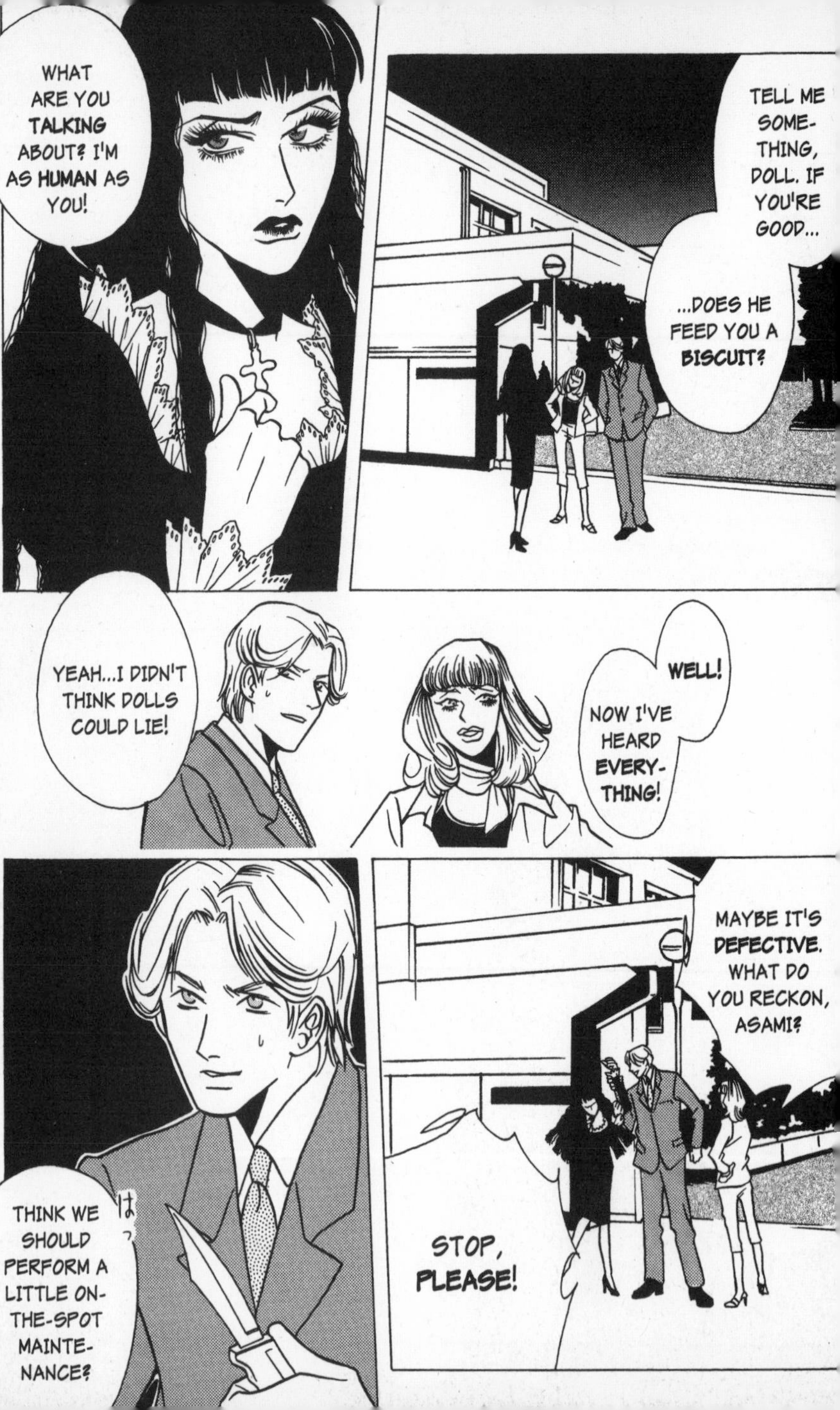
TELL ME SOMETHING, DOLL. IF YOU'RE GOOD...
...DOES HE FEED YOU A BISCUIT?
WHAT ARE YOU TALKING ABOUT? I'M AS HUMAN AS YOU!
WELL! NOW I'VE HEARD EVERYTHING!
YEAH...I DIDN'T THINK DOLLS COULD LIE!
MAYBE IT'S DEFECTIVE. WHAT DO YOU RECKON, ASAMI?
STOP, PLEASE!
THINK WE SHOULD PERFORM A LITTLE ON-THE-SPOT MAINTENANCE?
は

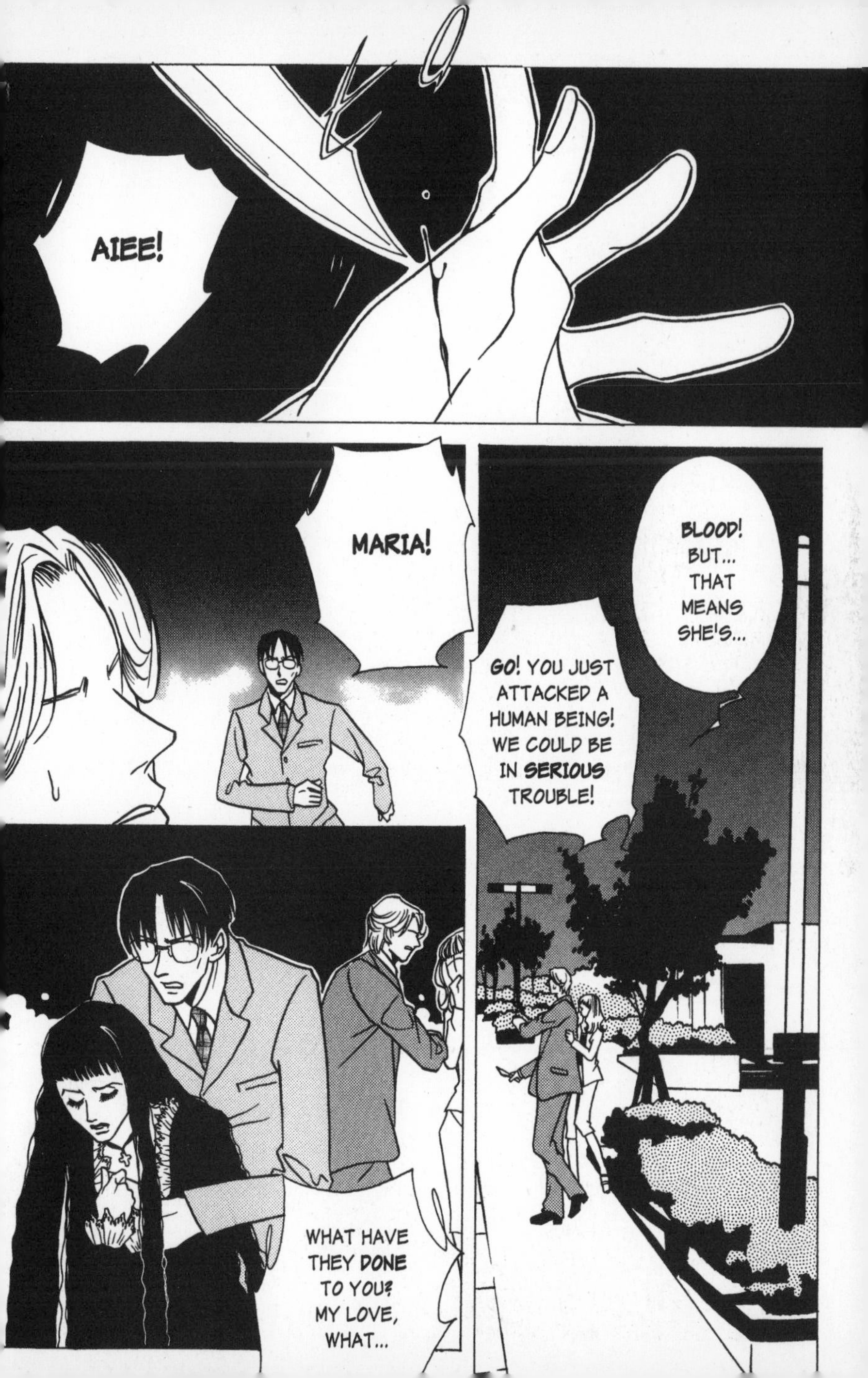
AIEE!
BLOOD! BUT... THAT MEANS SHE'S...
GO! YOU JUST ATTACKED A HUMAN BEING! WE COULD BE IN SERIOUS TROUBLE!
MARIA!
WHAT HAVE THEY DONE TO YOU? MY LOVE, WHAT...

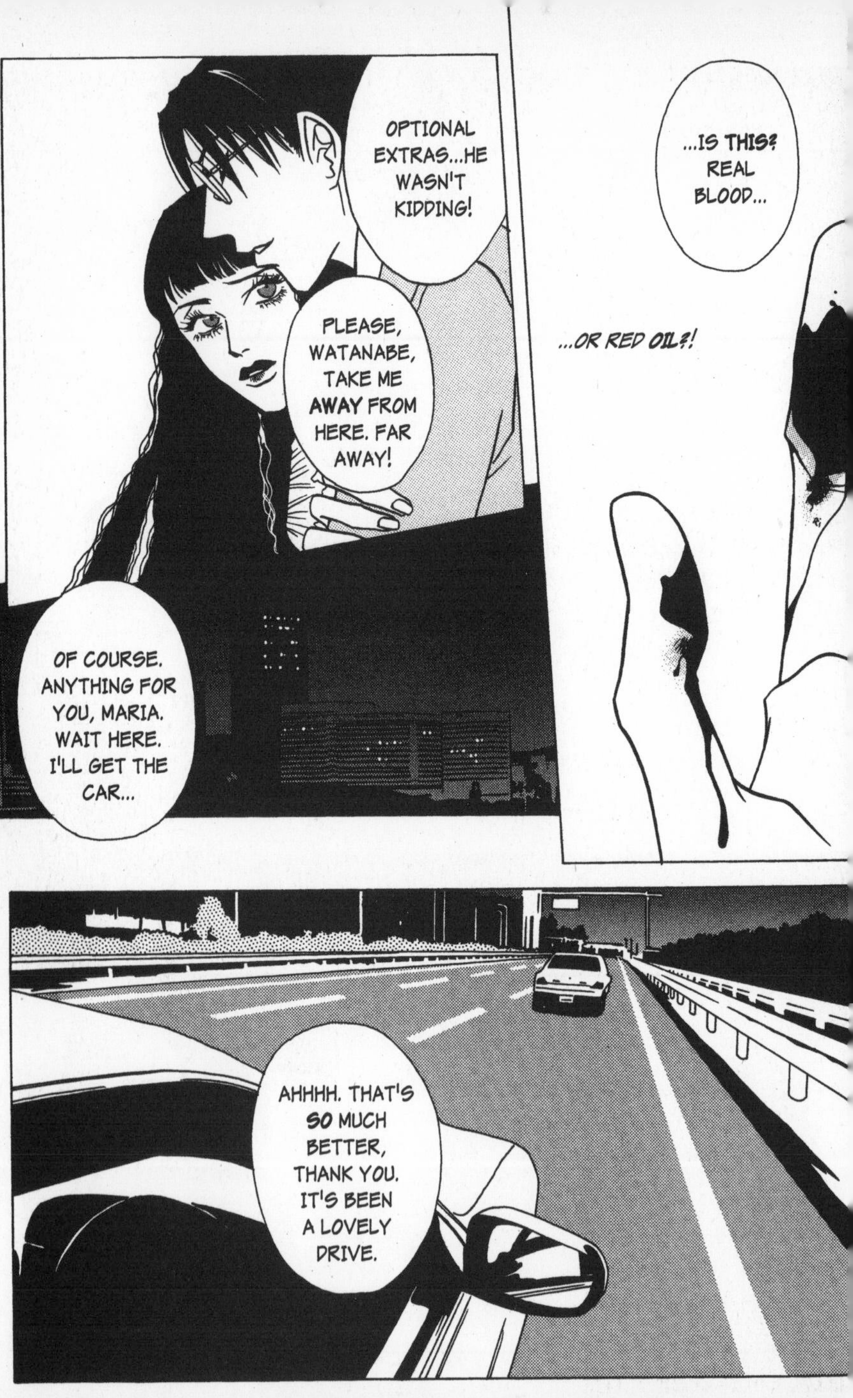
...IS THIS? REAL BLOOD...
...OR RED OIL?!
OPTIONAL EXTRAS...HE WASN'T KIDDING!
PLEASE, WATANABE, TAKE ME **AWAY** FROM HERE. FAR AWAY!
OF COURSE. ANYTHING FOR YOU, MARIA. WAIT HERE. I'LL GET THE CAR...
AHHHH. THAT'S **SO** MUCH BETTER, THANK YOU. IT'S BEEN A LOVELY DRIVE.

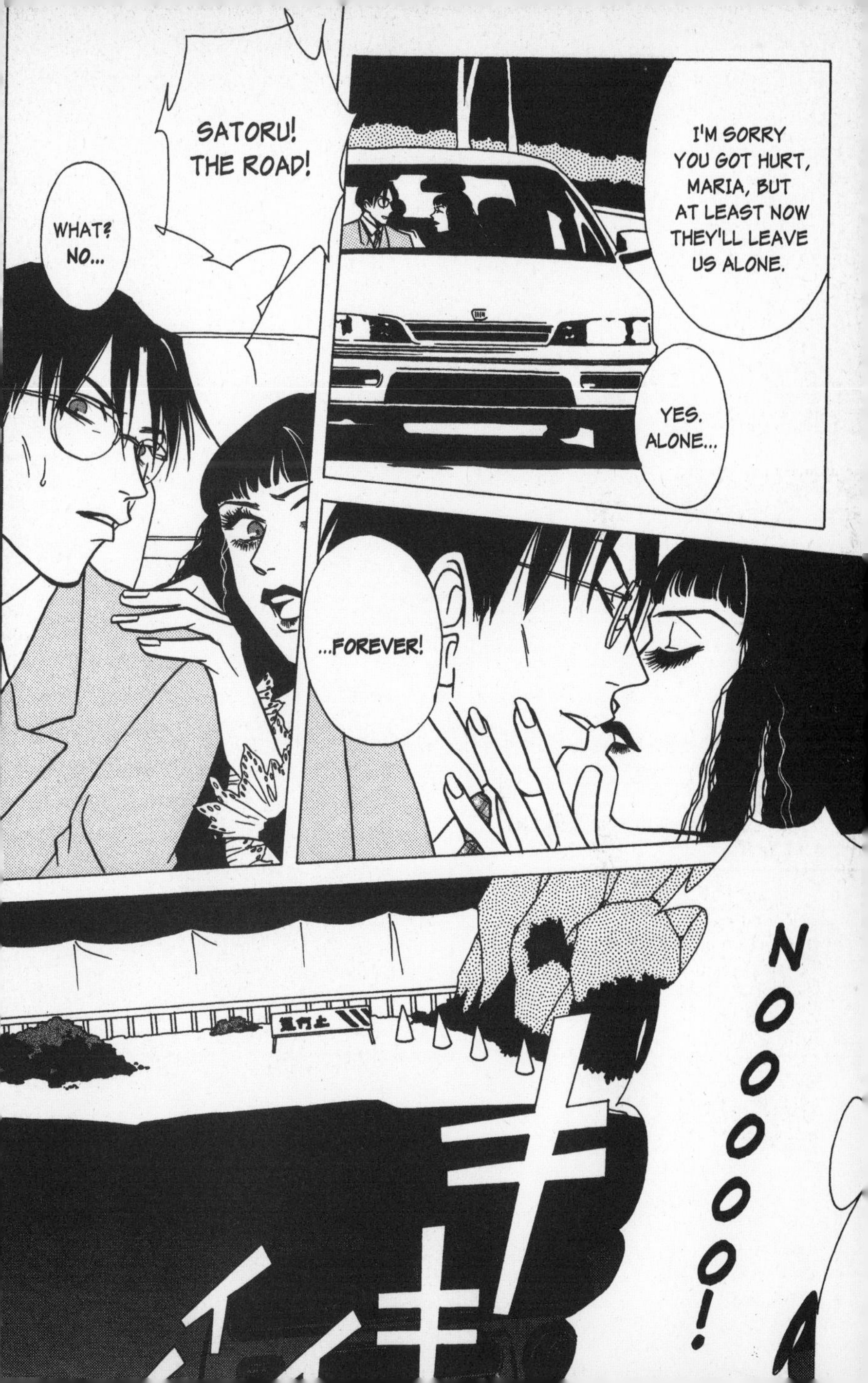
I'M SORRY YOU GOT HURT, MARIA, BUT AT LEAST NOW THEY'LL LEAVE US ALONE.
YES. ALONE...
...FOREVER!
SATORU! THE ROAD!
WHAT? NO...
NOOOOO!

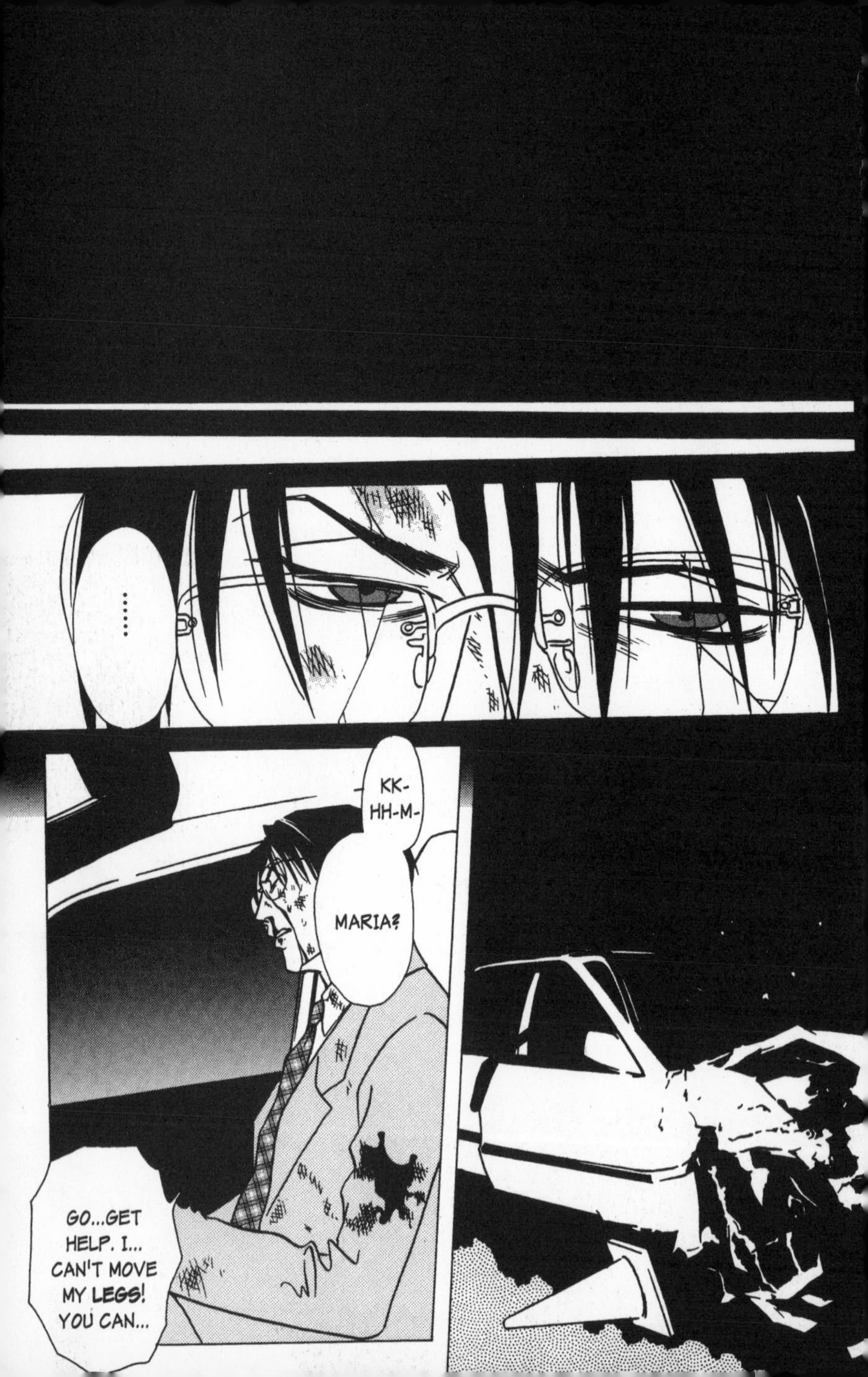
......
KK-HH-M-
MARIA?
GO...GET HELP. I... CAN'T MOVE MY LEGS! YOU CAN...

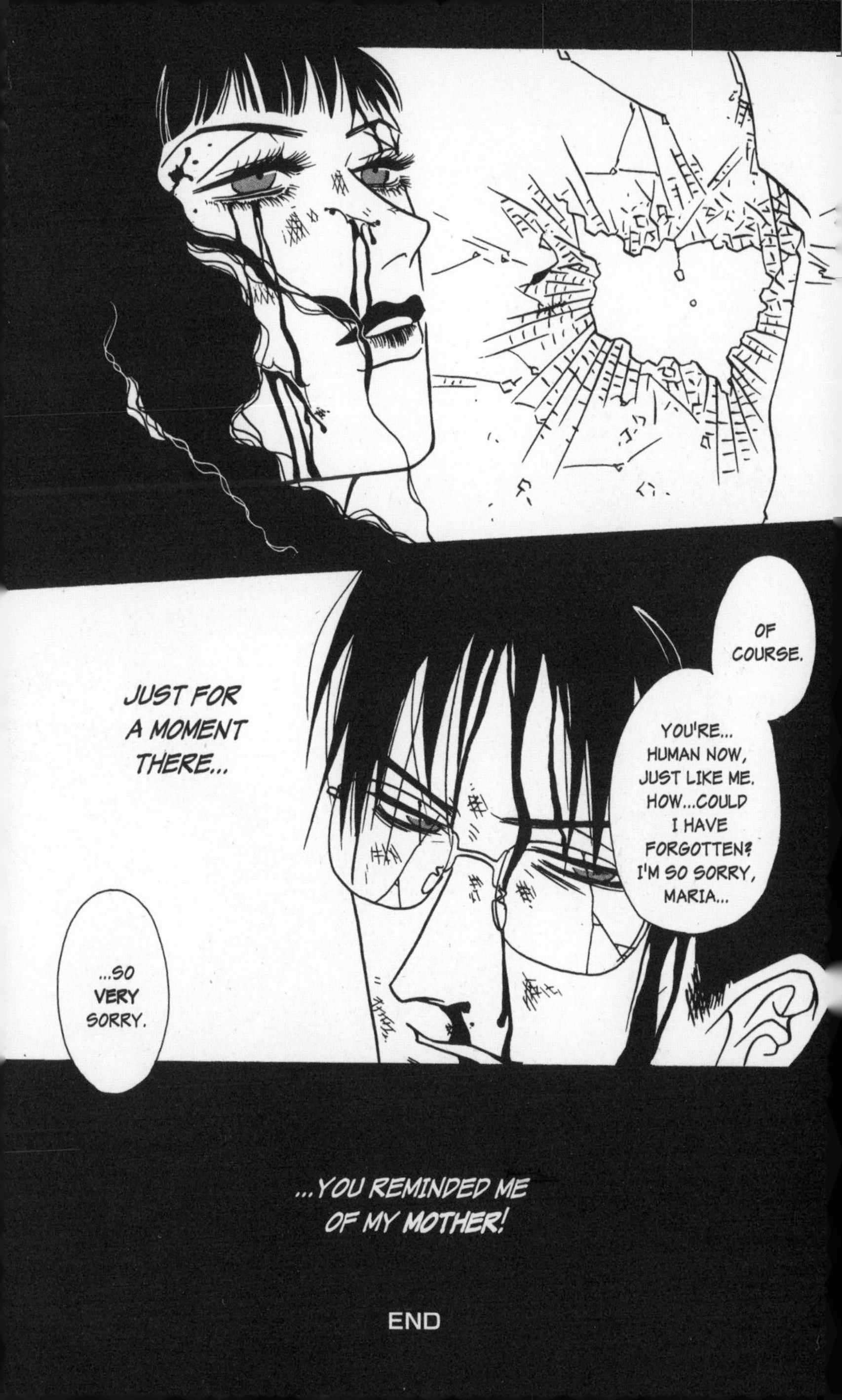
OF COURSE.
YOU'RE... HUMAN NOW, JUST LIKE ME. HOW...COULD I HAVE FORGOTTEN? I'M SO SORRY, MARIA...
JUST FOR A MOMENT THERE...
...SO VERY SORRY.
...YOU REMINDED ME OF MY MOTHER!
END

L I S T 3

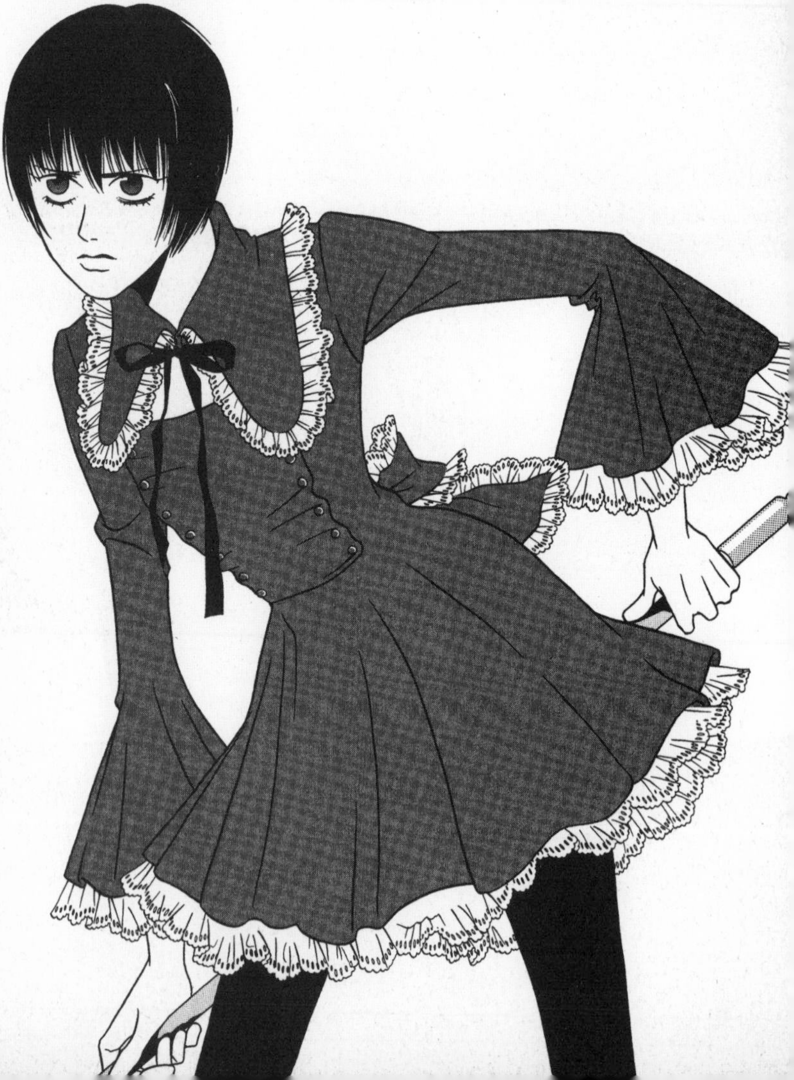

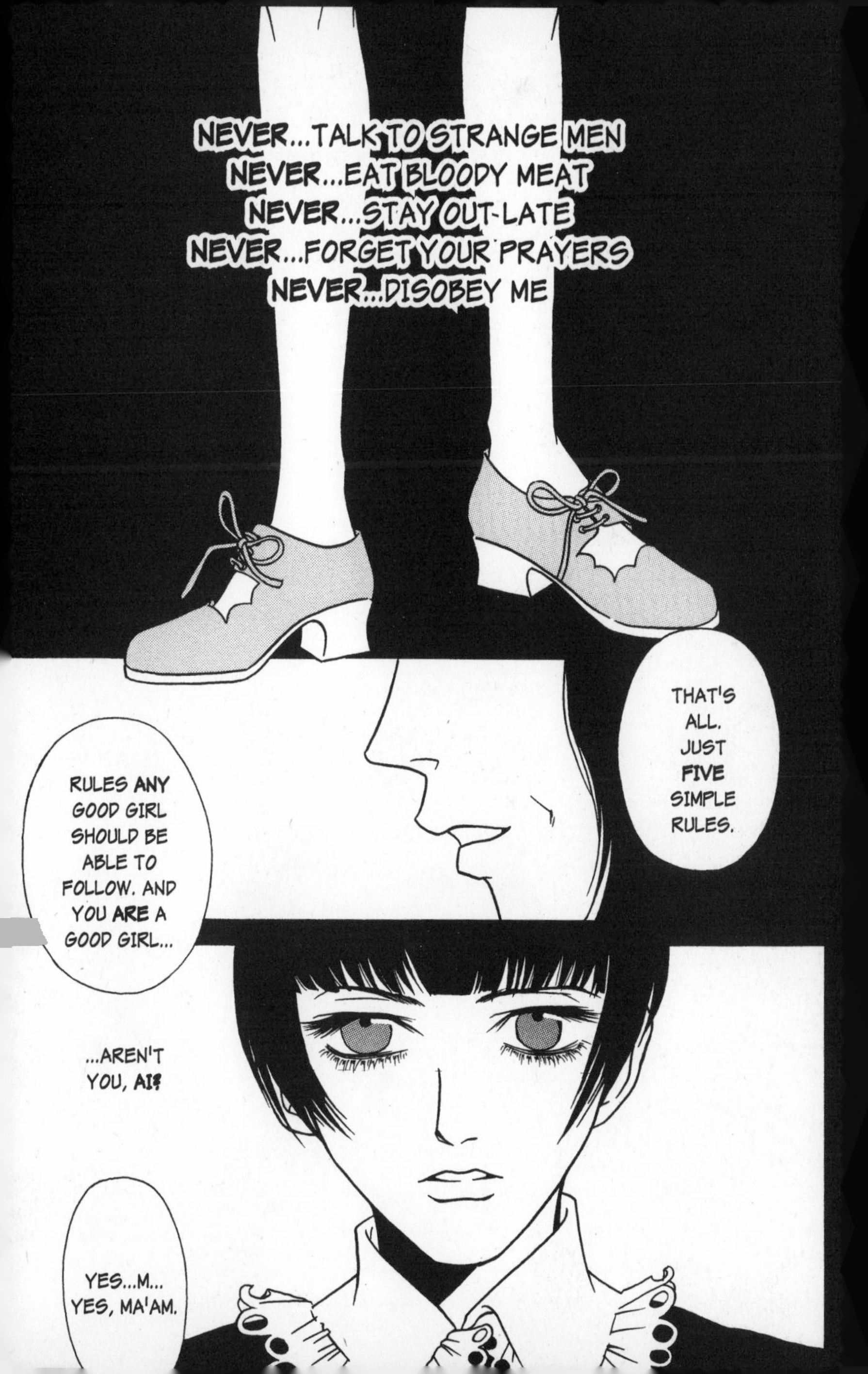
NEVER...TALK TO STRANGE MEN
NEVER...EAT BLOODY MEAT
NEVER...STAY OUT-LATE
NEVER...FORGET YOUR PRAYERS
NEVER...DISOBEY ME
THAT'S ALL. JUST FIVE SIMPLE RULES.
RULES ANY GOOD GIRL SHOULD BE ABLE TO FOLLOW. AND YOU ARE A GOOD GIRL...
...AREN'T YOU, AI?
YES...M... YES, MA'AM.

3. AI

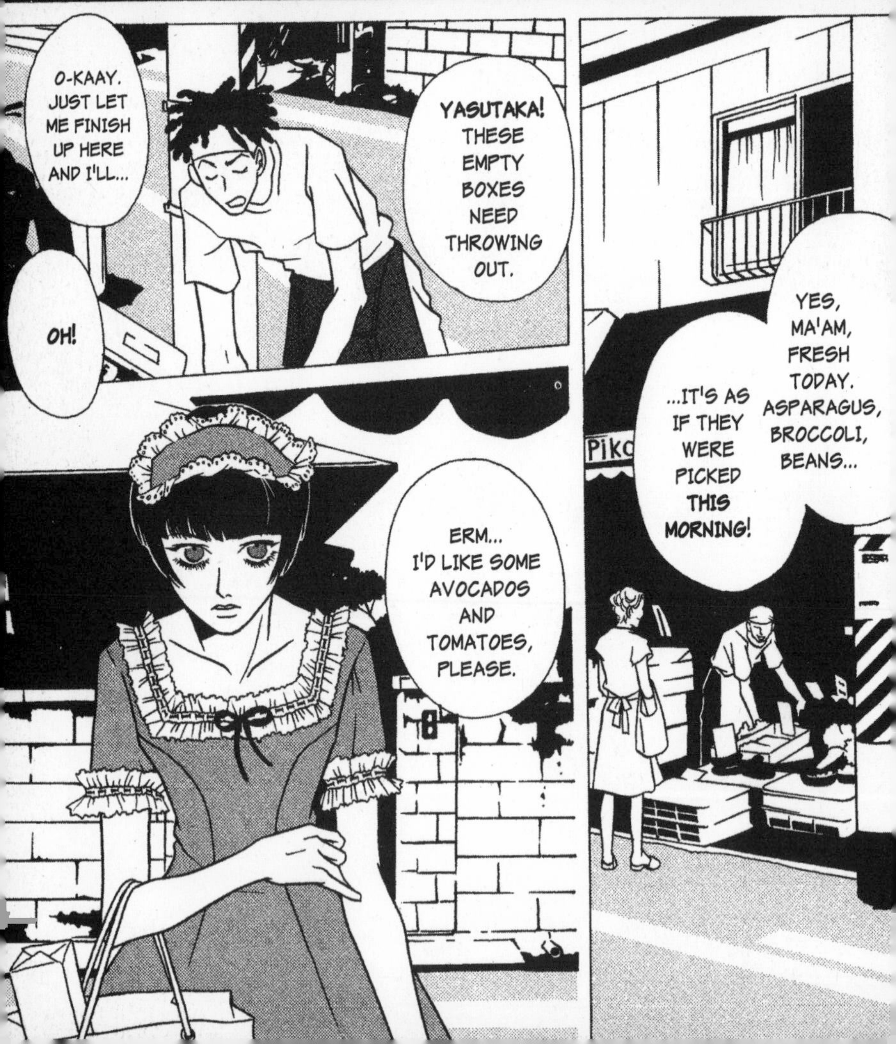
YES, MA'AM, FRESH TODAY. ASPARAGUS, BROCCOLI, BEANS...
...IT'S AS IF THEY WERE PICKED THIS MORNING!
YASUTAKA! THESE EMPTY BOXES NEED THROWING OUT.
O-KAAY. JUST LET ME FINISH UP HERE AND I'LL...
OH!
ERM... I'D LIKE SOME AVOCADOS AND TOMATOES, PLEASE.

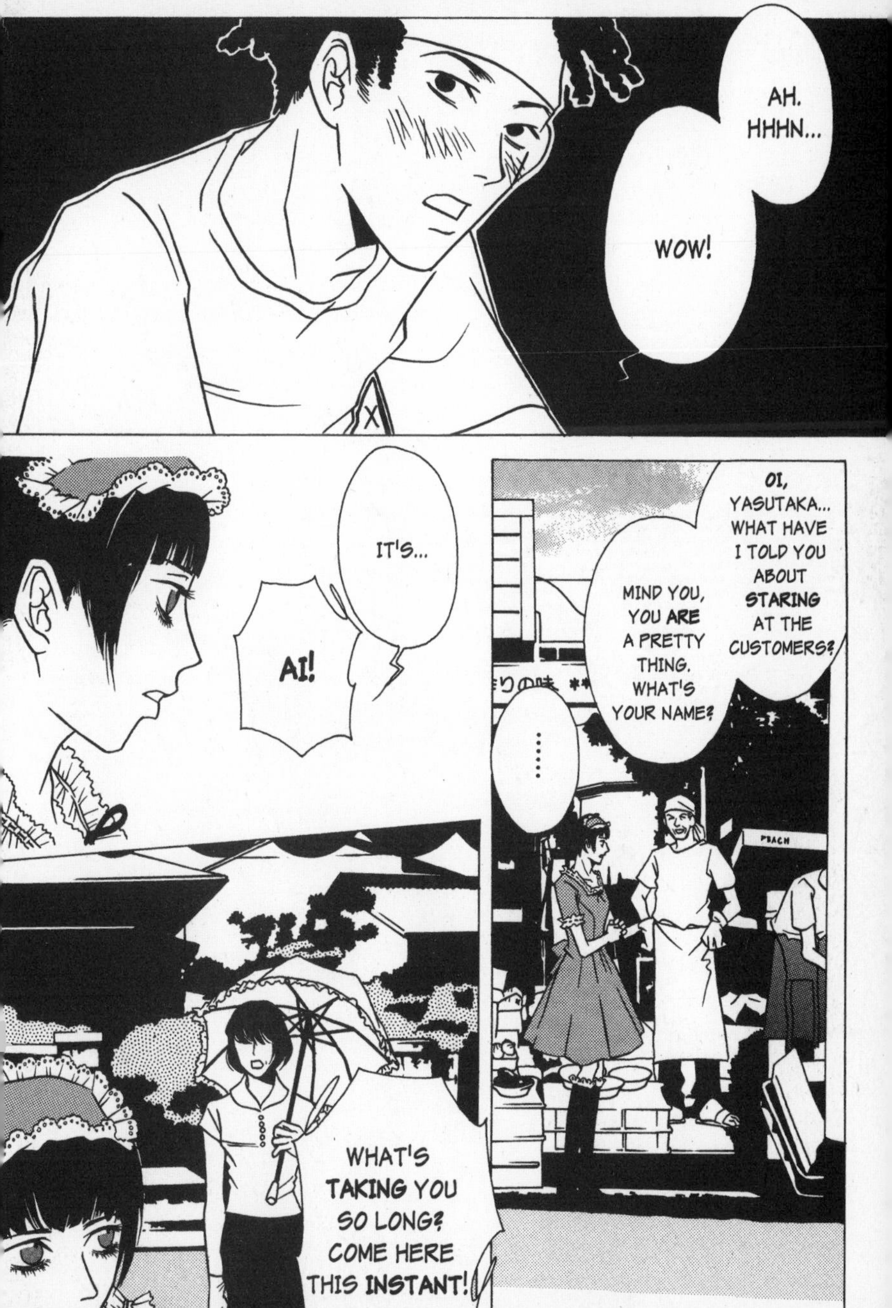
AH. HHHN...
WOW!
OI, YASUTAKA... WHAT HAVE I TOLD YOU ABOUT STARING AT THE CUSTOMERS?
MIND YOU, YOU ARE A PRETTY THING. WHAT'S YOUR NAME?
......
IT'S...
AI!
WHAT'S TAKING YOU SO LONG? COME HERE THIS INSTANT!

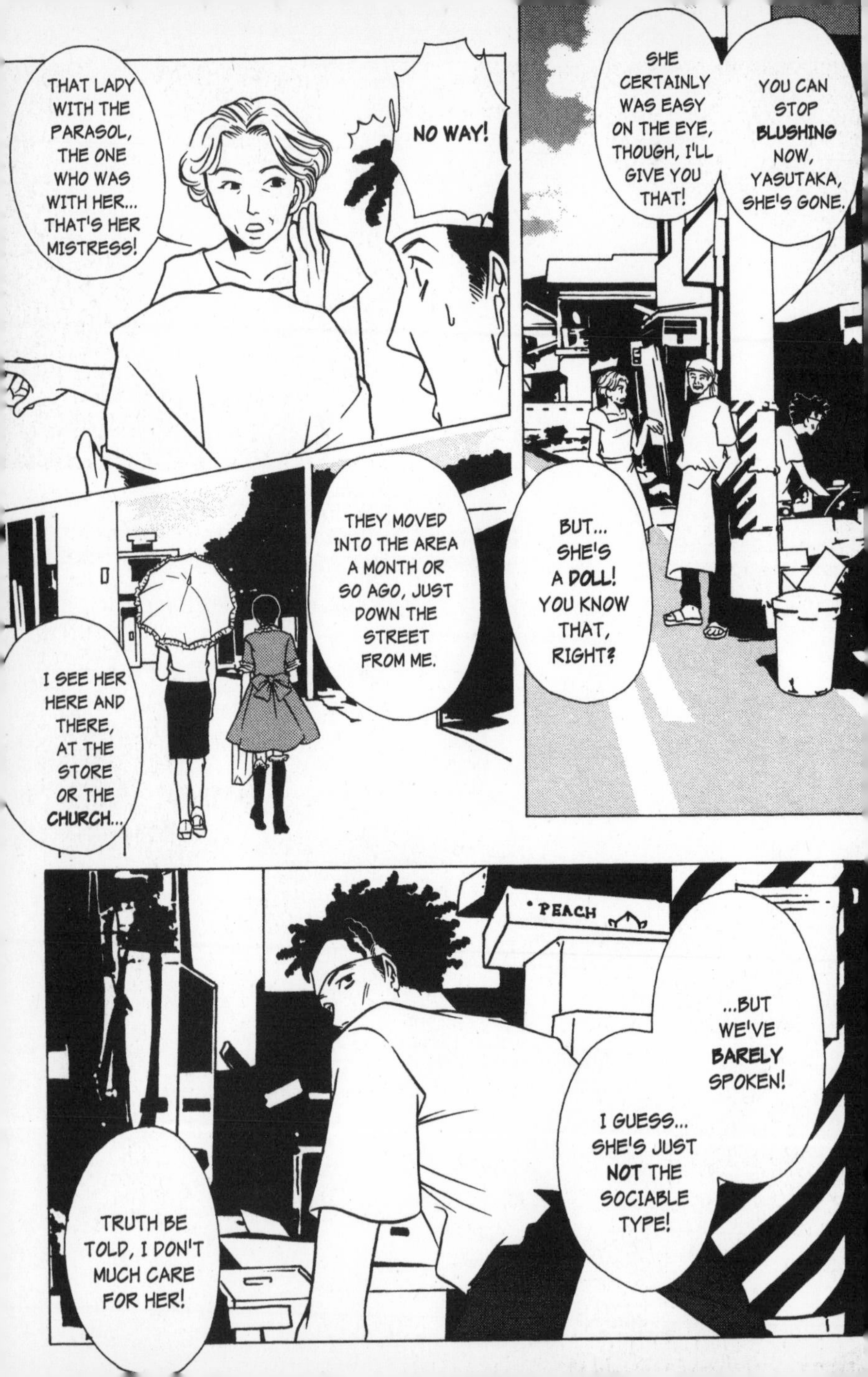
YOU CAN STOP **BLUSHING** NOW, YASUTAKA, SHE'S GONE.
SHE CERTAINLY WAS EASY ON THE EYE, THOUGH, I'LL GIVE YOU THAT!
BUT... SHE'S A **DOLL**! YOU KNOW THAT, RIGHT?
THAT LADY WITH THE PARASOL, THE ONE WHO WAS WITH HER... THAT'S HER MISTRESS!
NO WAY!
THEY MOVED INTO THE AREA A MONTH OR SO AGO, JUST DOWN THE STREET FROM ME.
I SEE HER HERE AND THERE, AT THE STORE OR THE **CHURCH**...
PEACH
TRUTH BE TOLD, I DON'T MUCH CARE FOR HER!
...BUT WE'VE **BARELY** SPOKEN!
I GUESS... SHE'S JUST **NOT** THE SOCIABLE TYPE!

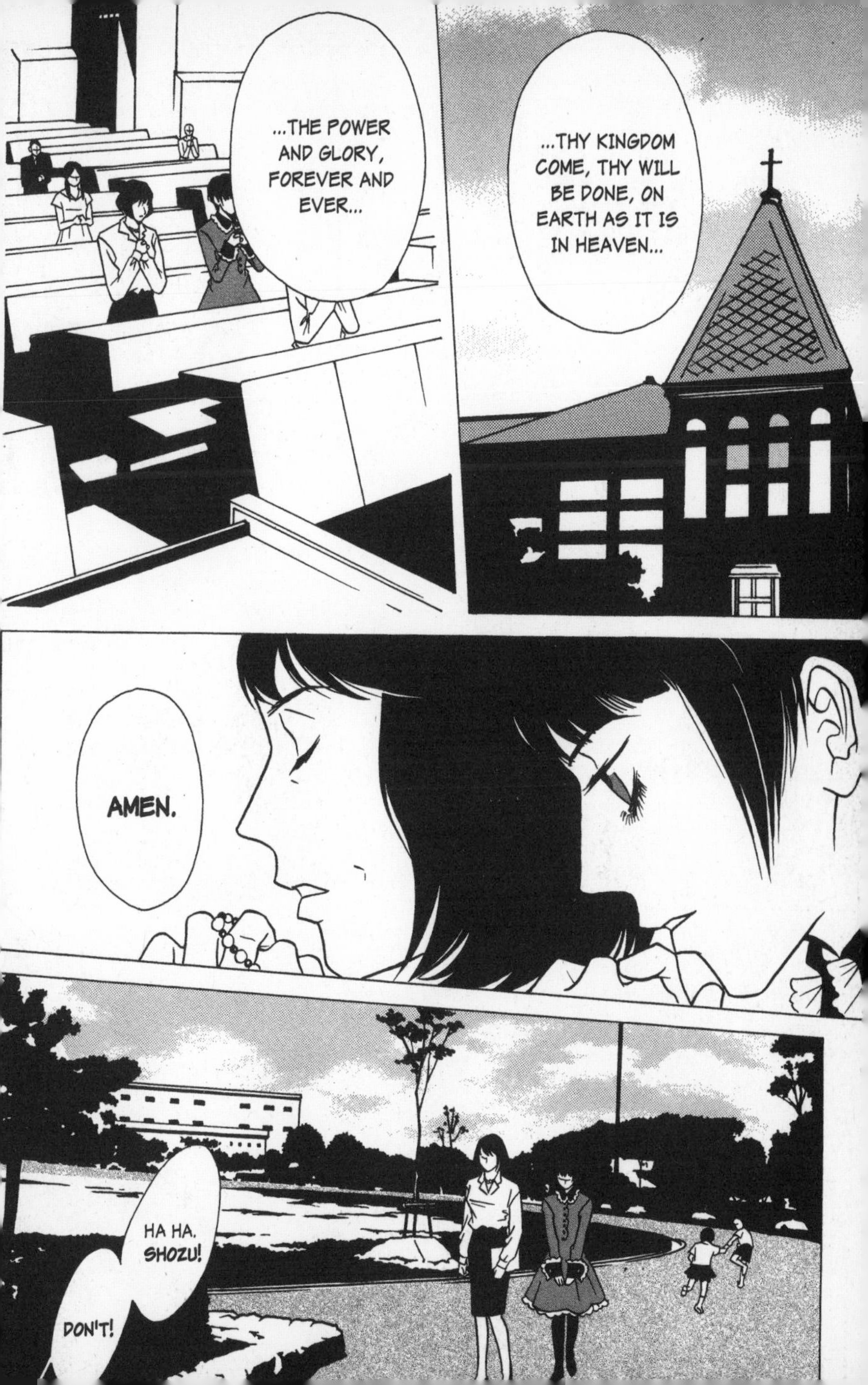
...THY KINGDOM COME, THY WILL BE DONE, ON EARTH AS IT IS IN HEAVEN...
...THE POWER AND GLORY, FOREVER AND EVER...
AMEN.
HA HA. SHOZU!
DON'T!

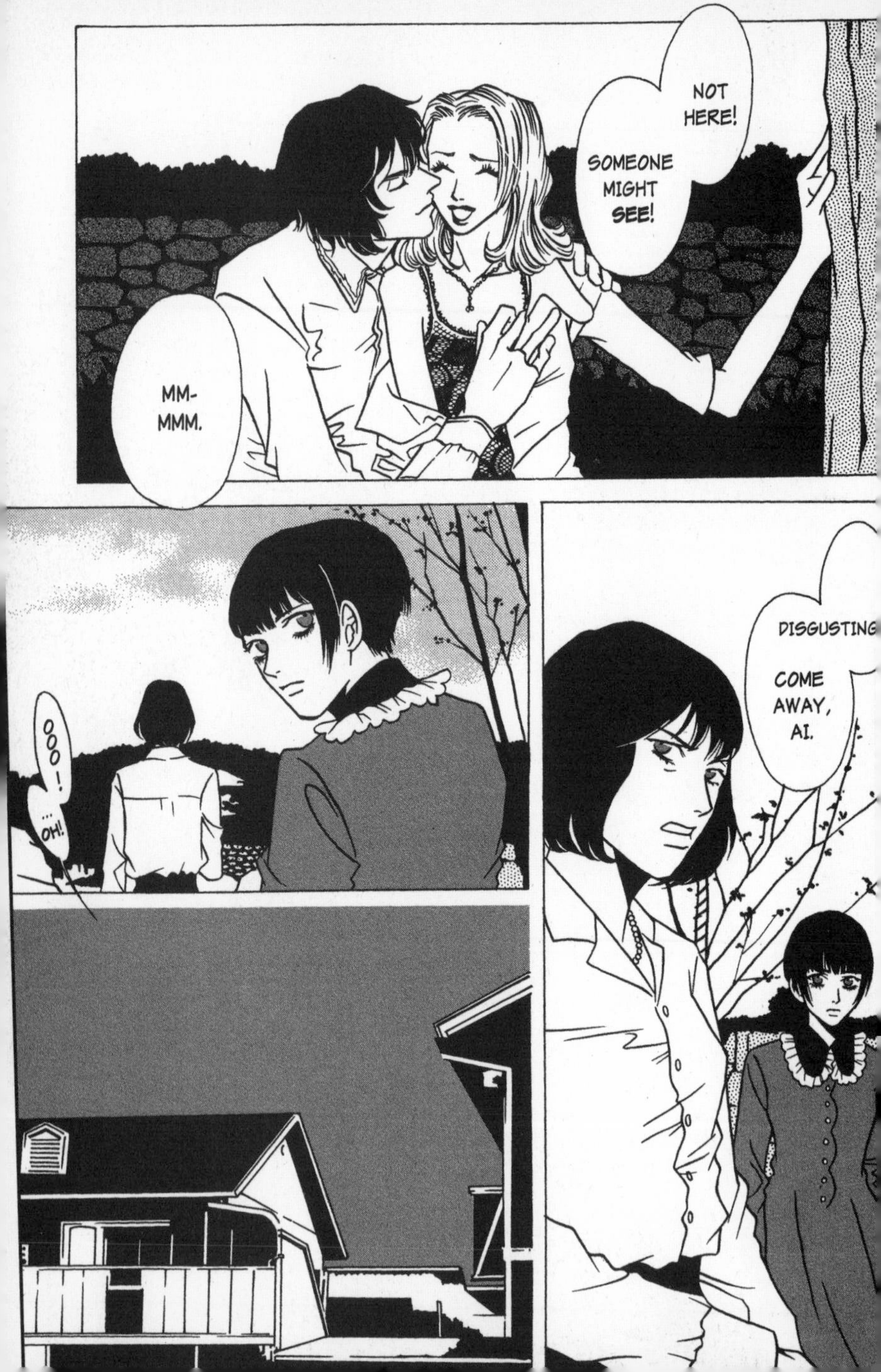
NOT HERE!
SOMEONE MIGHT SEE!
MM-MMM.
DISGUSTING
COME AWAY, AI.
OOO!
...OH!

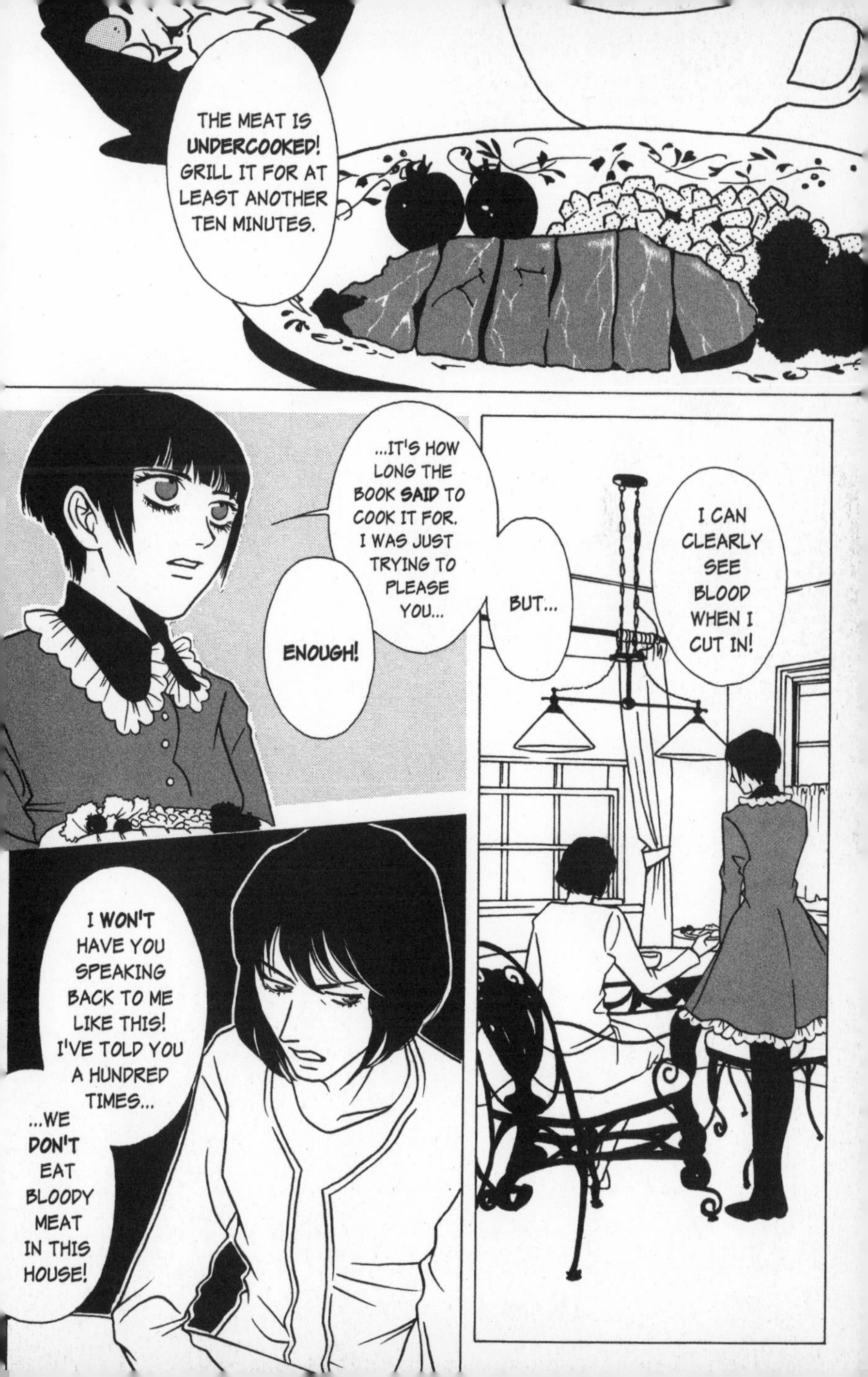
THE MEAT IS UNDERCOOKED! GRILL IT FOR AT LEAST ANOTHER TEN MINUTES.
I CAN CLEARLY SEE BLOOD WHEN I CUT IN!
BUT...
...IT'S HOW LONG THE BOOK SAID TO COOK IT FOR. I WAS JUST TRYING TO PLEASE YOU...
ENOUGH!
I WON'T HAVE YOU SPEAKING BACK TO ME LIKE THIS! I'VE TOLD YOU A HUNDRED TIMES...
...WE DON'T EAT BLOODY MEAT IN THIS HOUSE!

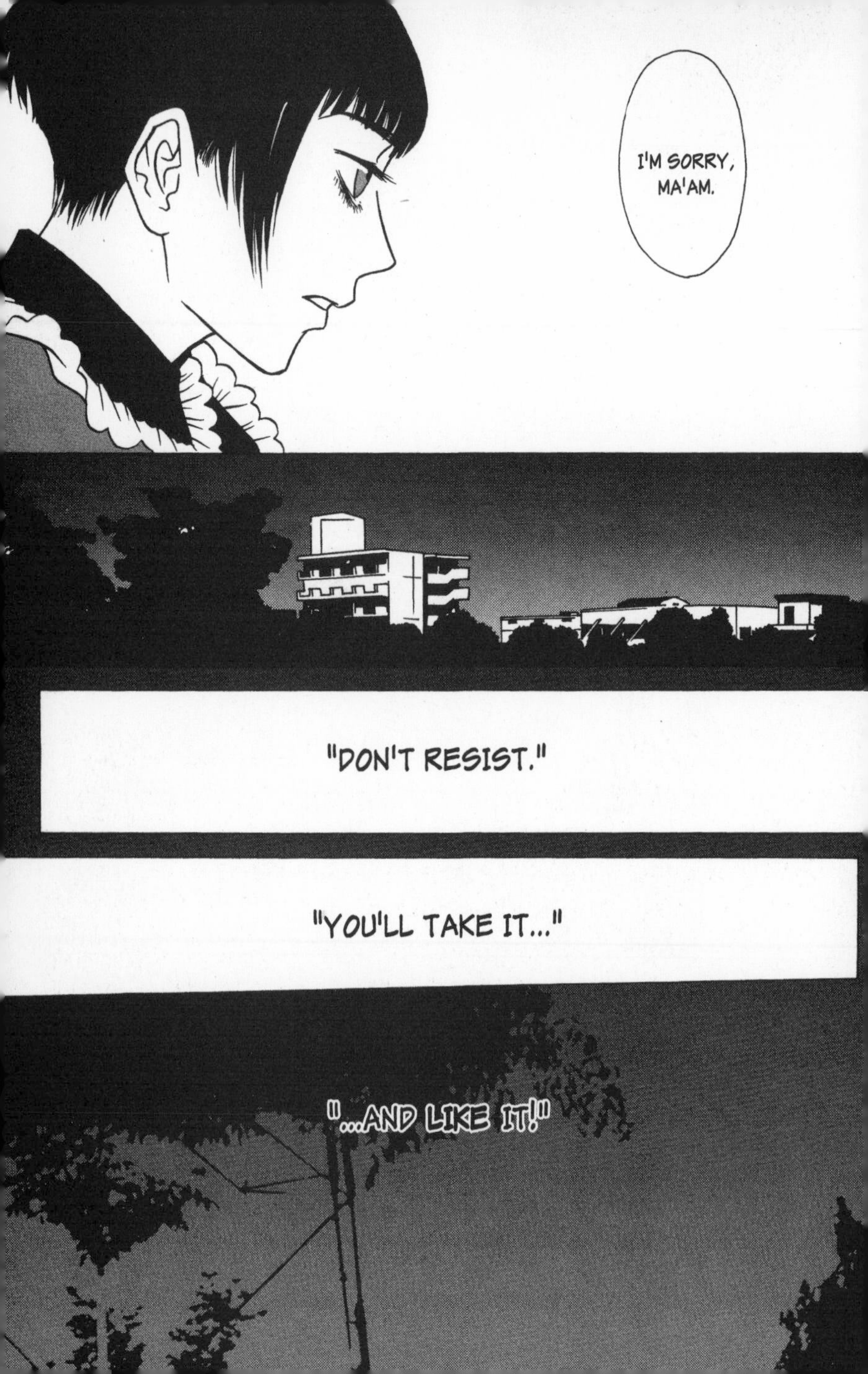
I'M SORRY, MA'AM.
"DON'T RESIST."
"YOU'LL TAKE IT..."
"...AND LIKE IT!"

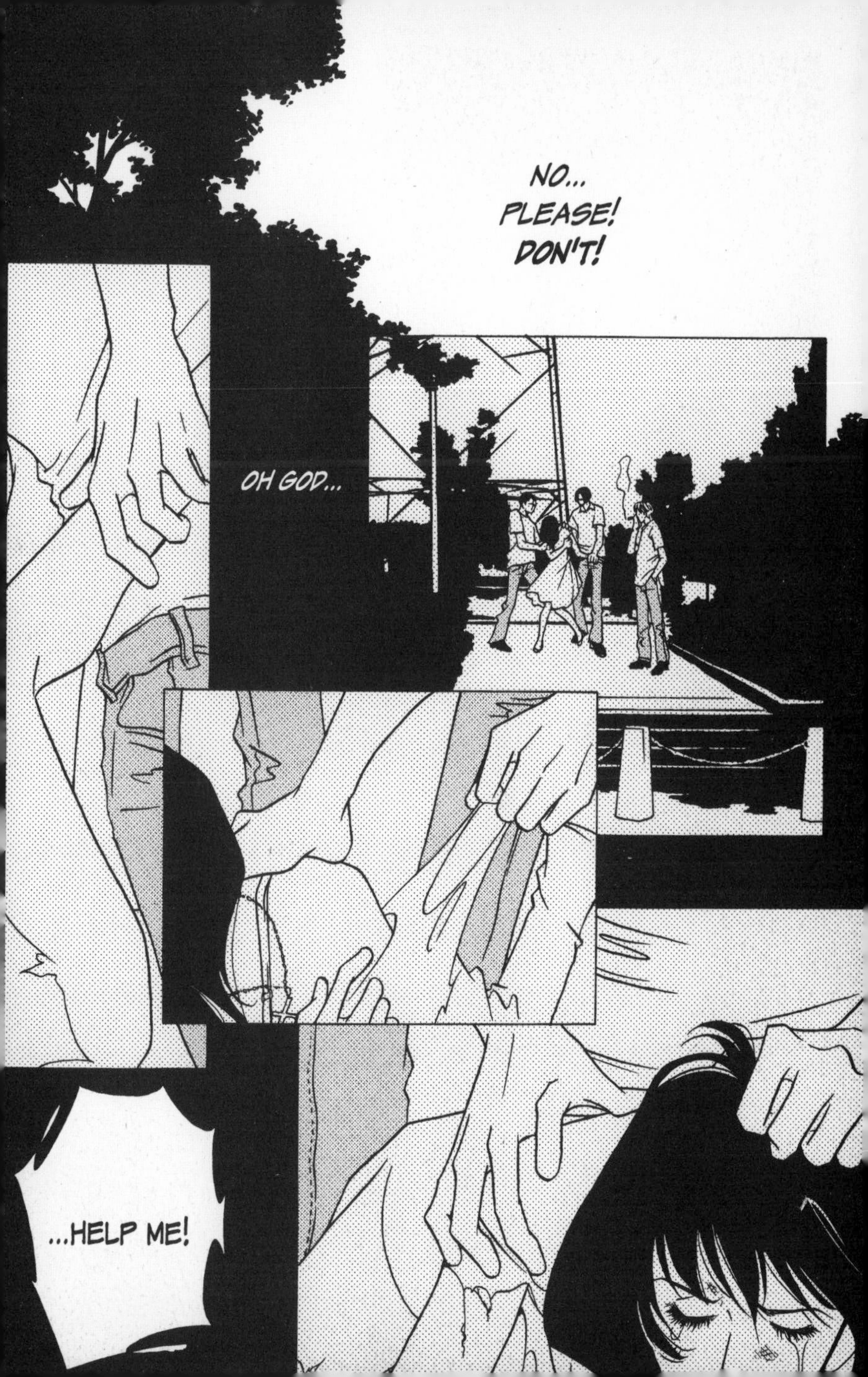
NO... PLEASE! DON'T!
OH GOD...
...HELP ME!

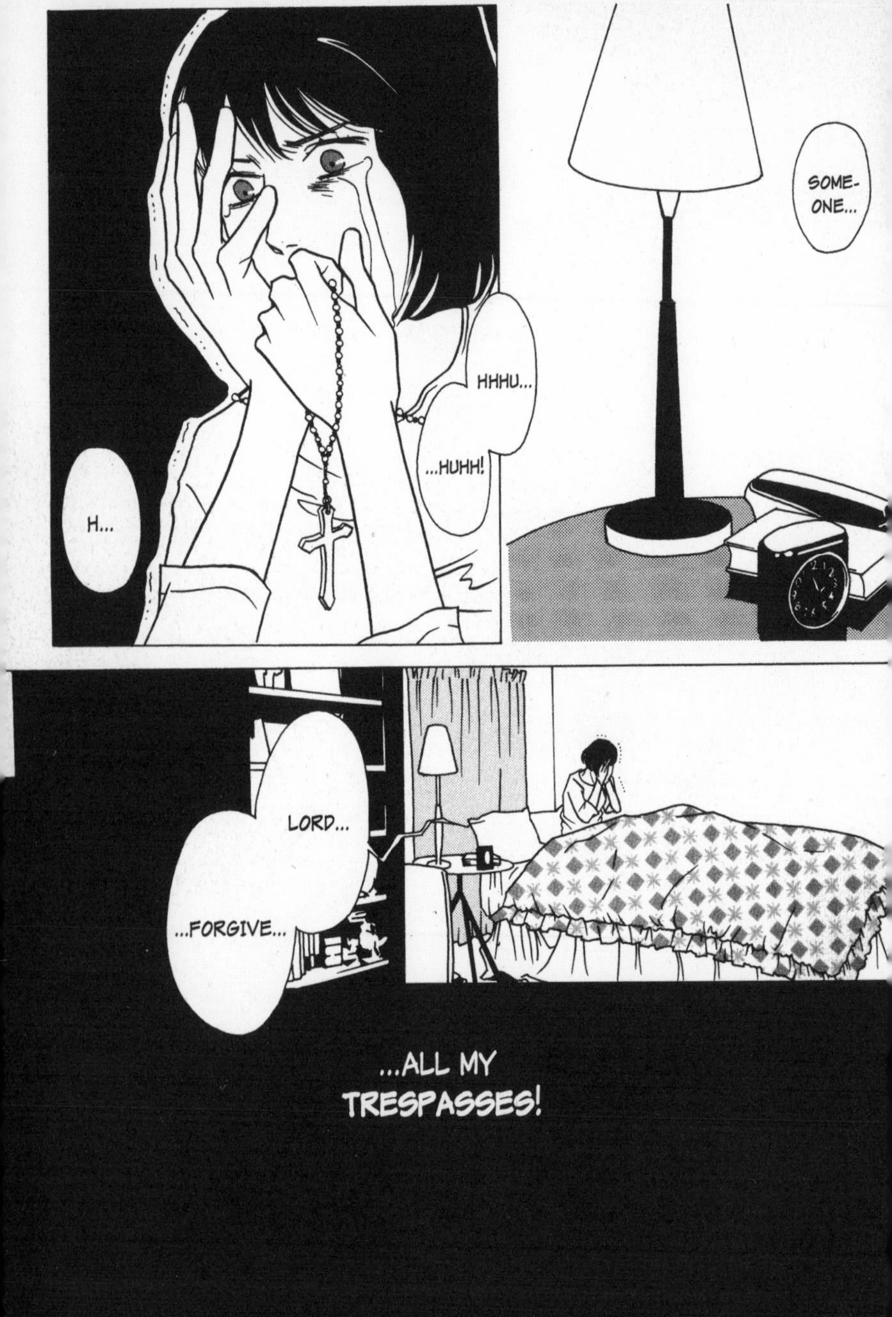
SOME-ONE...
HHHU... ...HUHH!
H...
LORD... ...FORGIVE...
...ALL MY TRESPASSES!

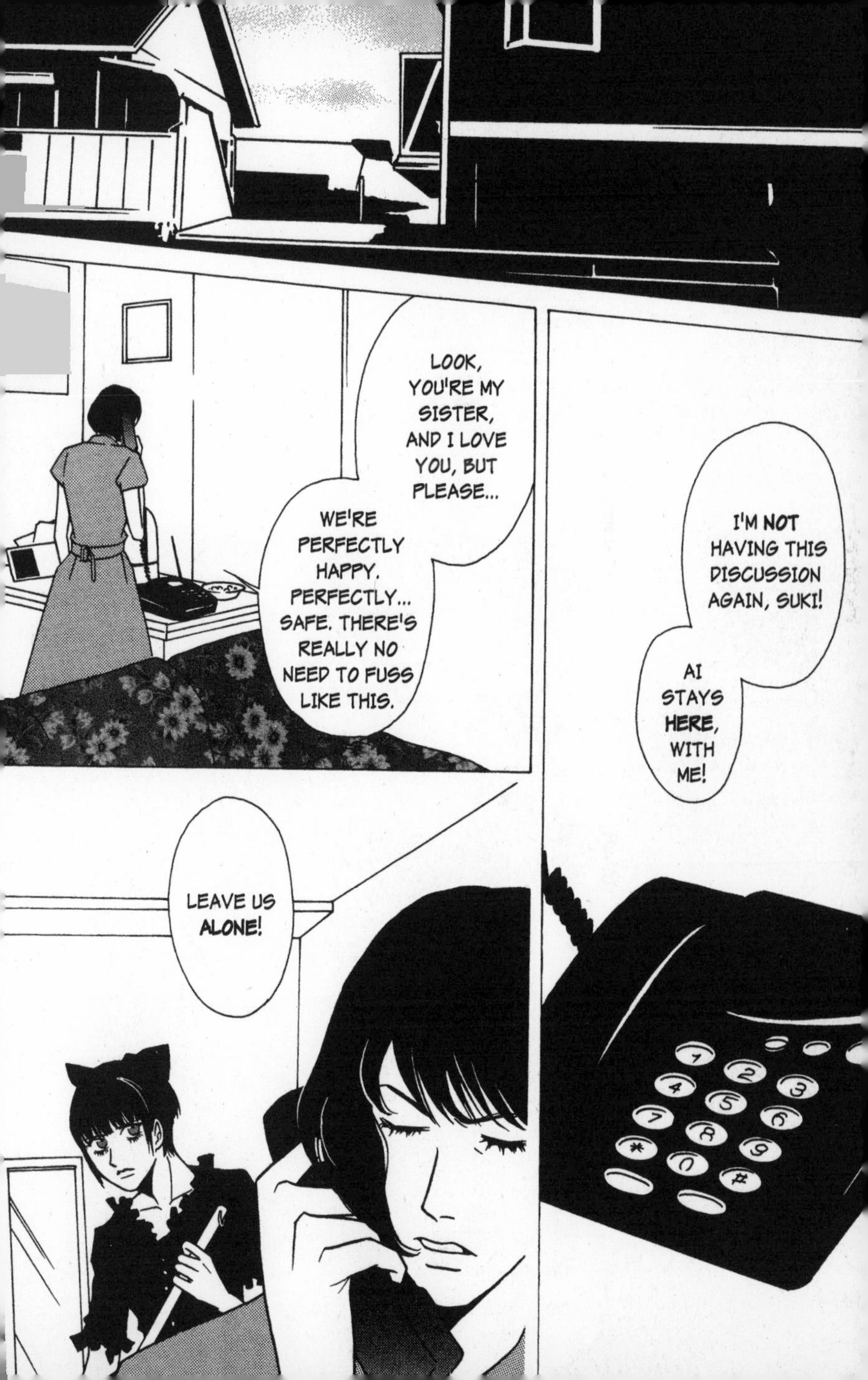
I'M NOT HAVING THIS DISCUSSION AGAIN, SUKI!
AI STAYS HERE, WITH ME!
LOOK, YOU'RE MY SISTER, AND I LOVE YOU, BUT PLEASE...
WE'RE PERFECTLY HAPPY. PERFECTLY... SAFE. THERE'S REALLY NO NEED TO FUSS LIKE THIS.
LEAVE US ALONE!

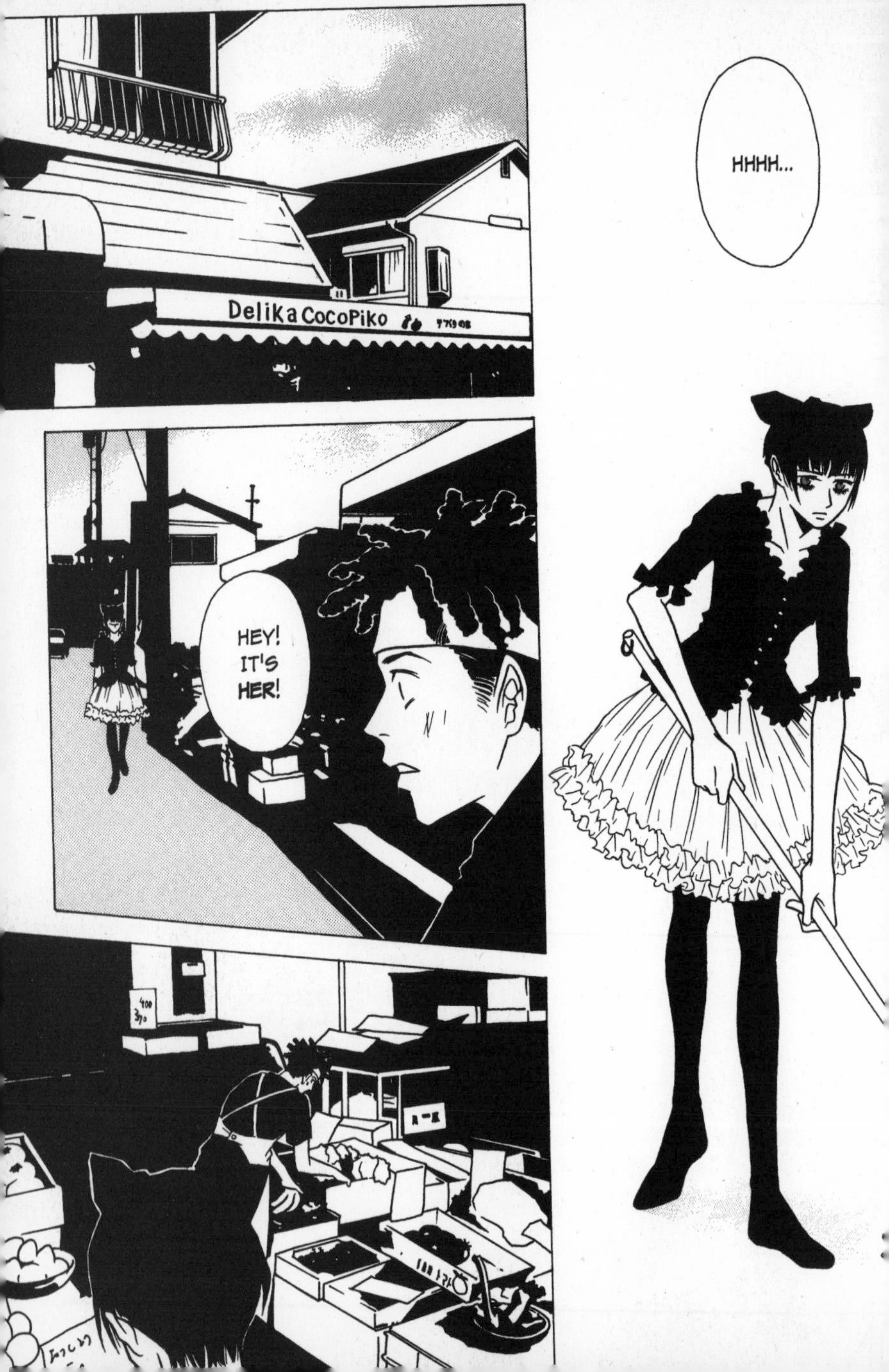
HHHH...
DeliKa CocoPiko
HEY! IT'S HER!

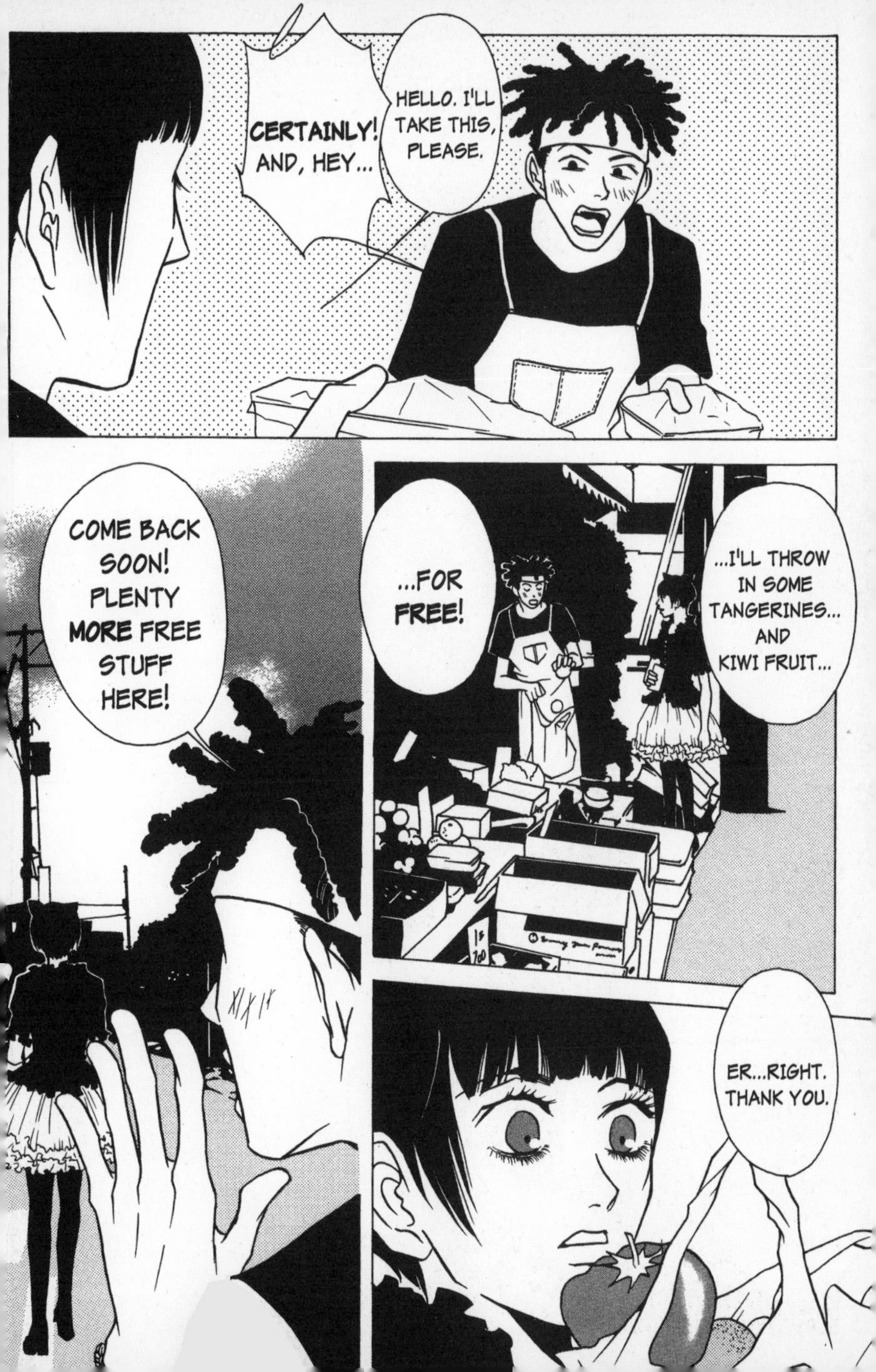
HELLO. I'LL TAKE THIS, PLEASE.
CERTAINLY! AND, HEY...
...I'LL THROW IN SOME TANGERINES... AND KIWI FRUIT...
...FOR FREE!
ER...RIGHT. THANK YOU.
COME BACK SOON! PLENTY MORE FREE STUFF HERE!

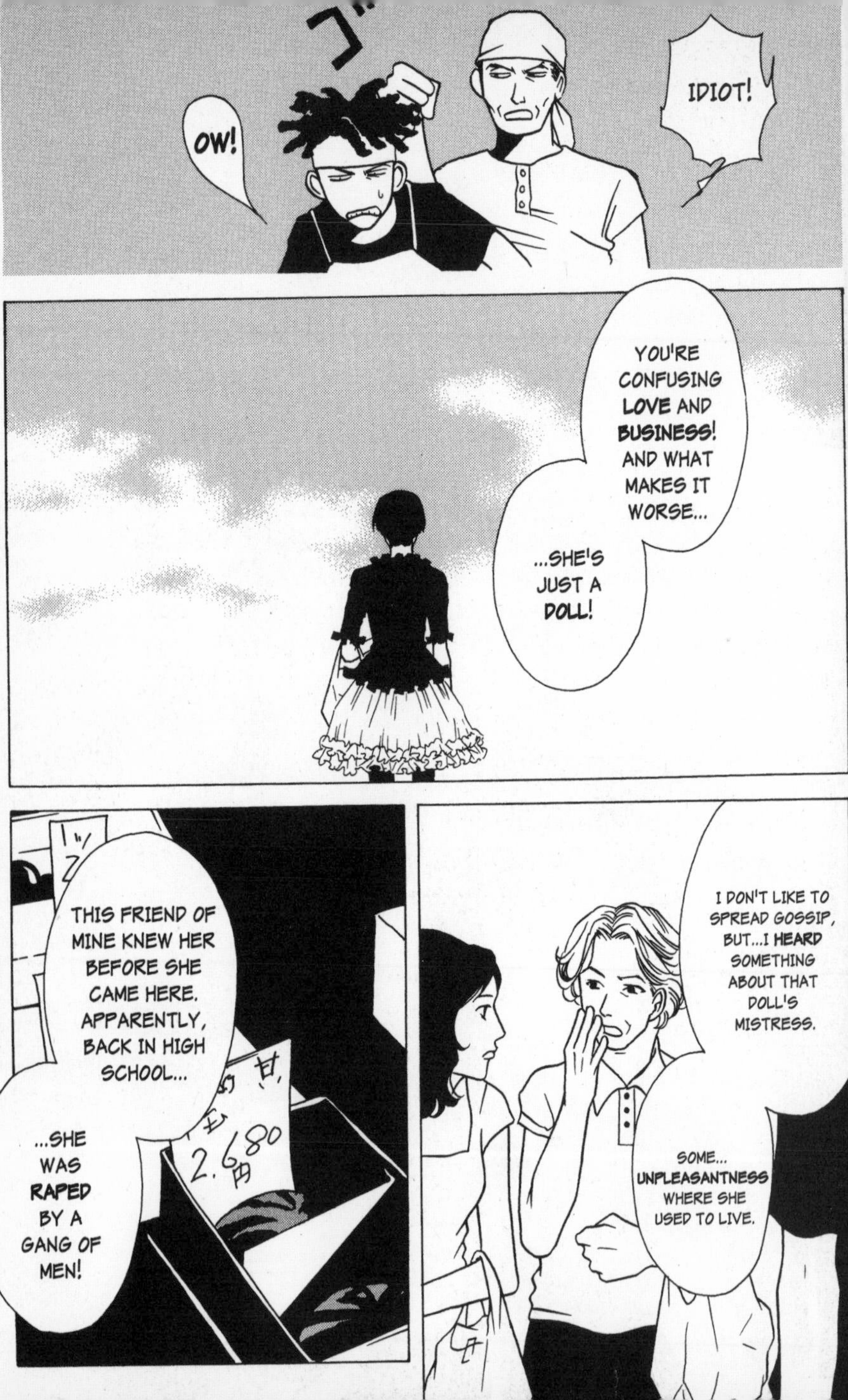
IDIOT!
OW!
YOU'RE CONFUSING LOVE AND BUSINESS! AND WHAT MAKES IT WORSE...
...SHE'S JUST A DOLL!
I DON'T LIKE TO SPREAD GOSSIP, BUT...I HEARD SOMETHING ABOUT THAT DOLL'S MISTRESS.
SOME... UNPLEASANTNESS WHERE SHE USED TO LIVE.
THIS FRIEND OF MINE KNEW HER BEFORE SHE CAME HERE. APPARENTLY, BACK IN HIGH SCHOOL...
...SHE WAS RAPED BY A GANG OF MEN!

IT WAS A BIG SCANDAL. ESPECIALLY WHEN SHE BECAME **PREGNANT!** HER FAMILY...ALL STRICT CATHOLICS...TRIED TO HUSH IT UP.

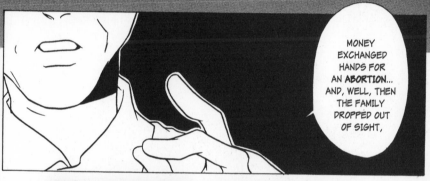

MONEY EXCHANGED HANDS FOR AN **ABORTION...** AND, WELL, THEN THE FAMILY DROPPED OUT OF SIGHT,

SO THE DOLL IS MAYBE A **SUBSTITUTE** FOR THAT CHILD THAT NEVER WAS. MAKES SENSE.

......

MM. YES. BUT IN THE END, A DOLL IS JUST A DOLL. IT'S NEVER GOING REPLACE A REAL HUMAN BEING!

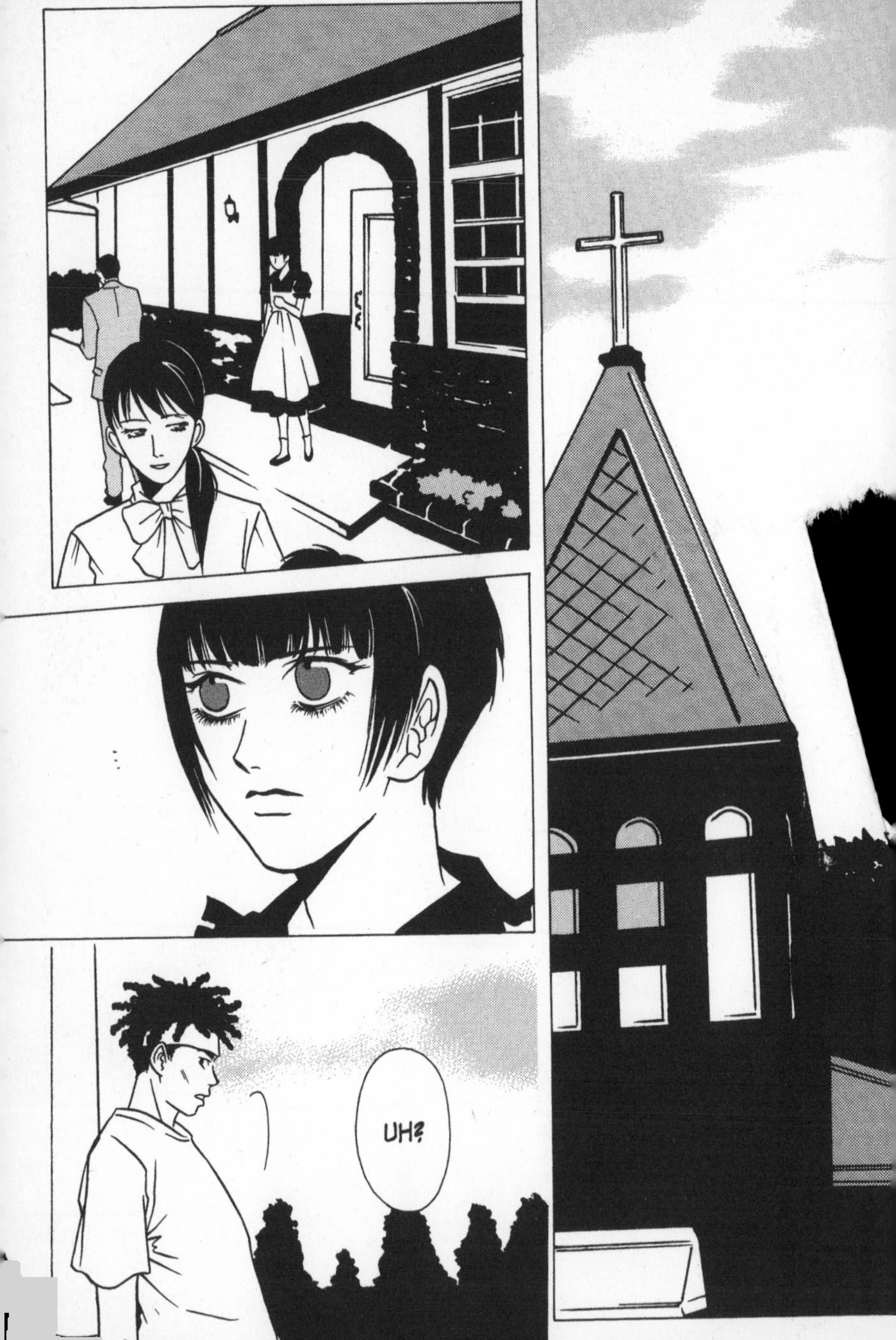
UH?

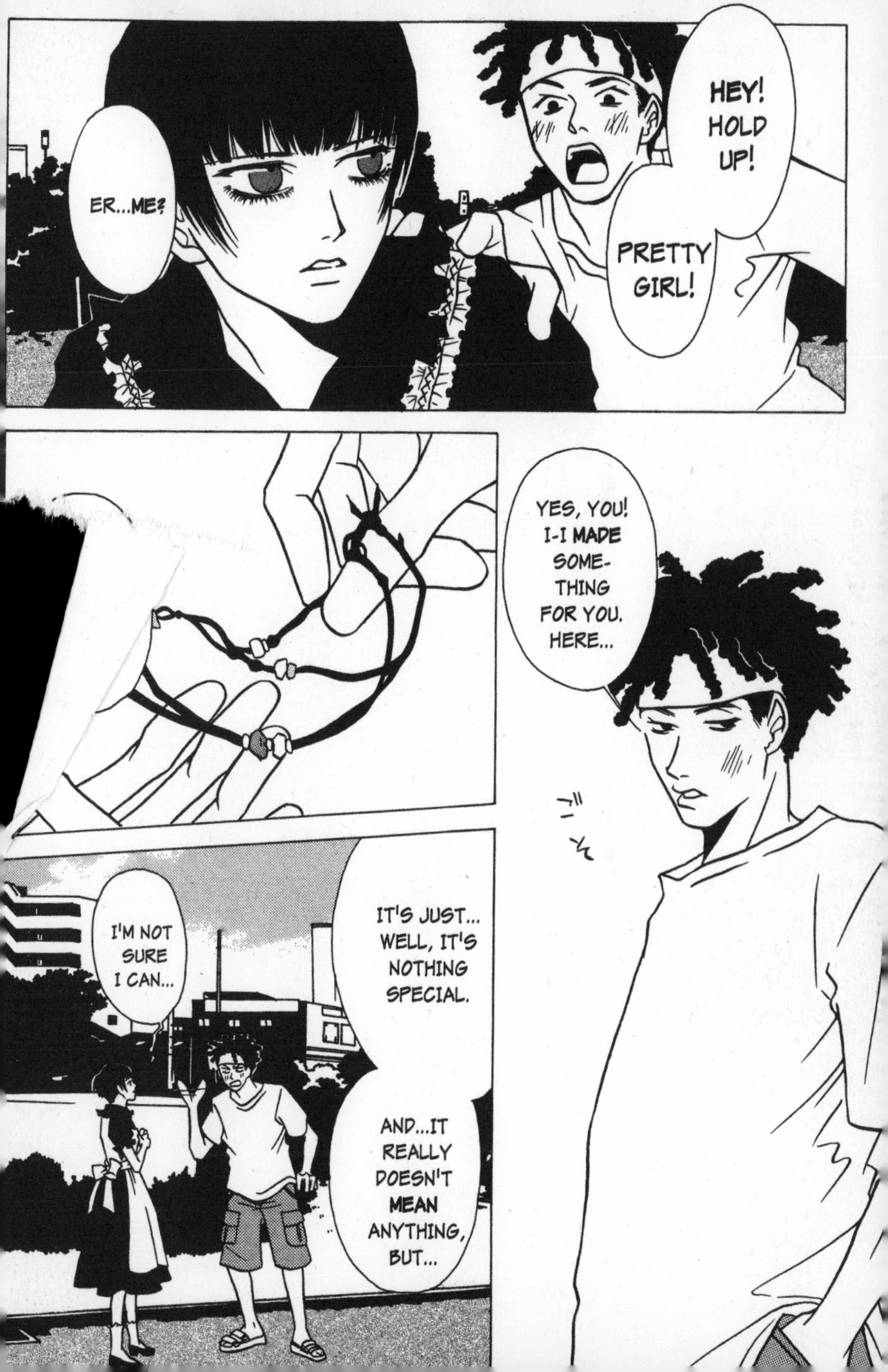
HEY! HOLD UP!
PRETTY GIRL!
ER...ME?
YES, YOU! I-I MADE SOME-THING FOR YOU. HERE...
IT'S JUST... WELL, IT'S NOTHING SPECIAL.
AND...IT REALLY DOESN'T MEAN ANYTHING, BUT...
I'M NOT SURE I CAN...

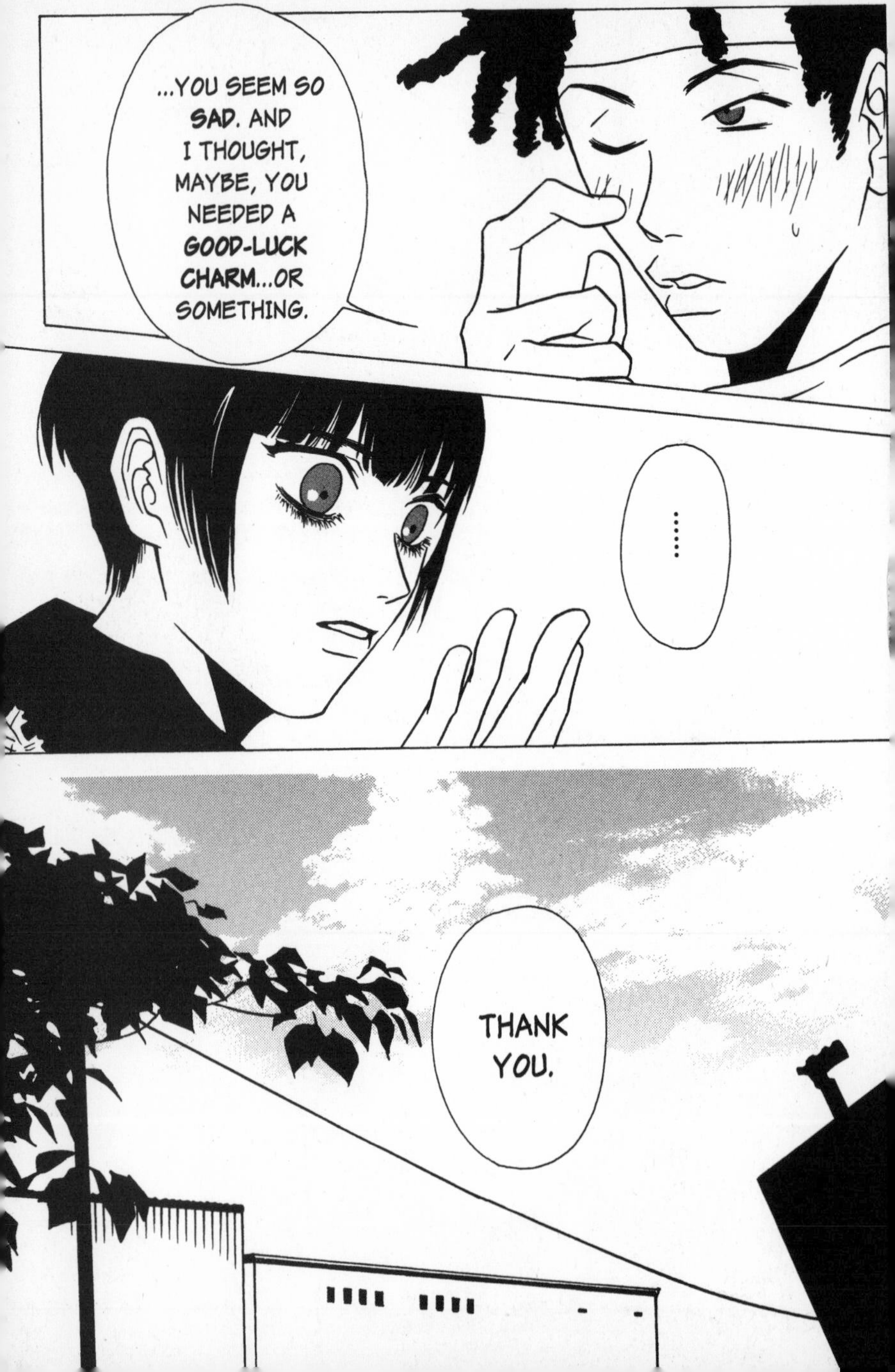
...YOU SEEM SO SAD. AND I THOUGHT, MAYBE, YOU NEEDED A GOOD-LUCK CHARM...OR SOMETHING.
......
THANK YOU.

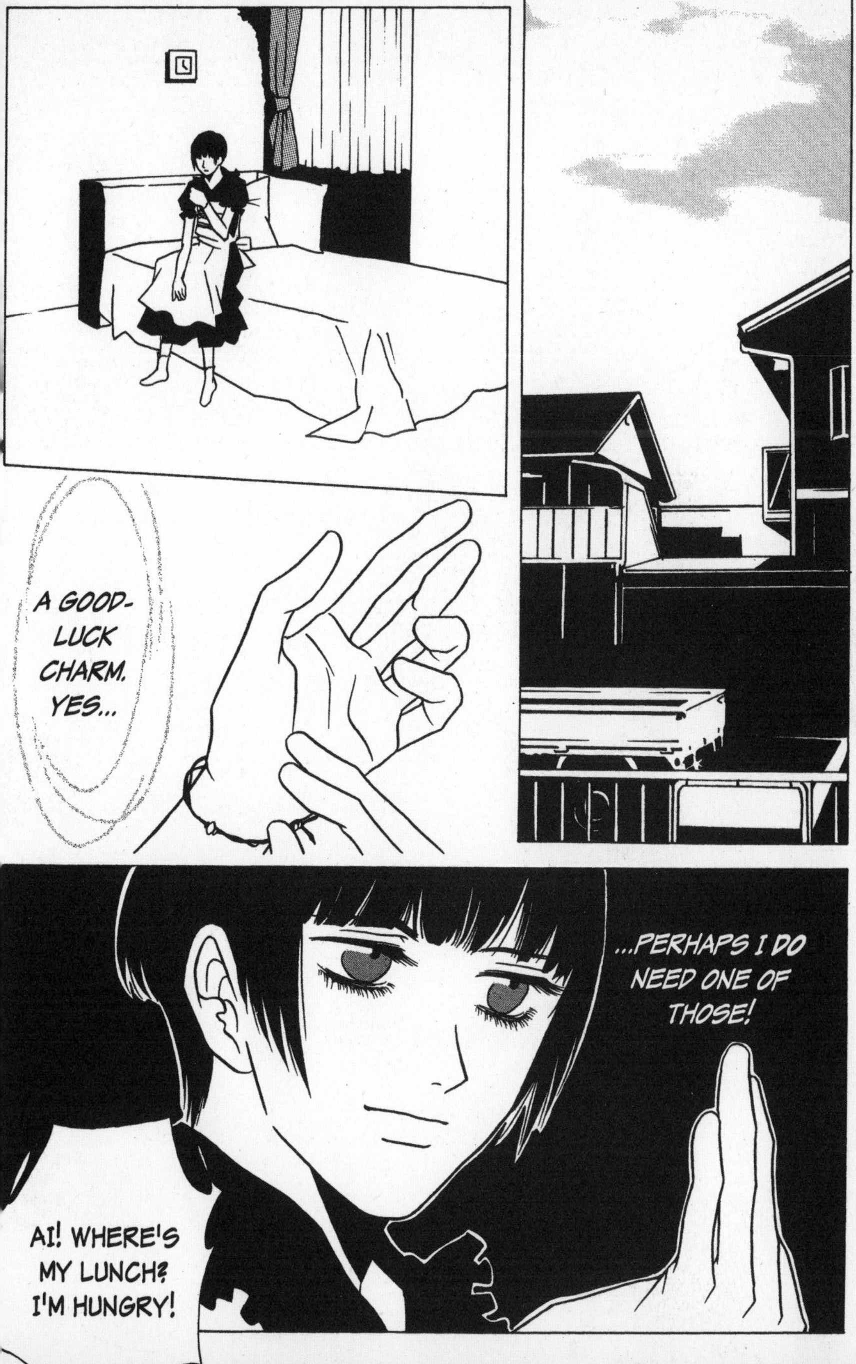
A GOOD-LUCK CHARM. YES...
...PERHAPS I DO NEED ONE OF THOSE!
AI! WHERE'S MY LUNCH? I'M HUNGRY!

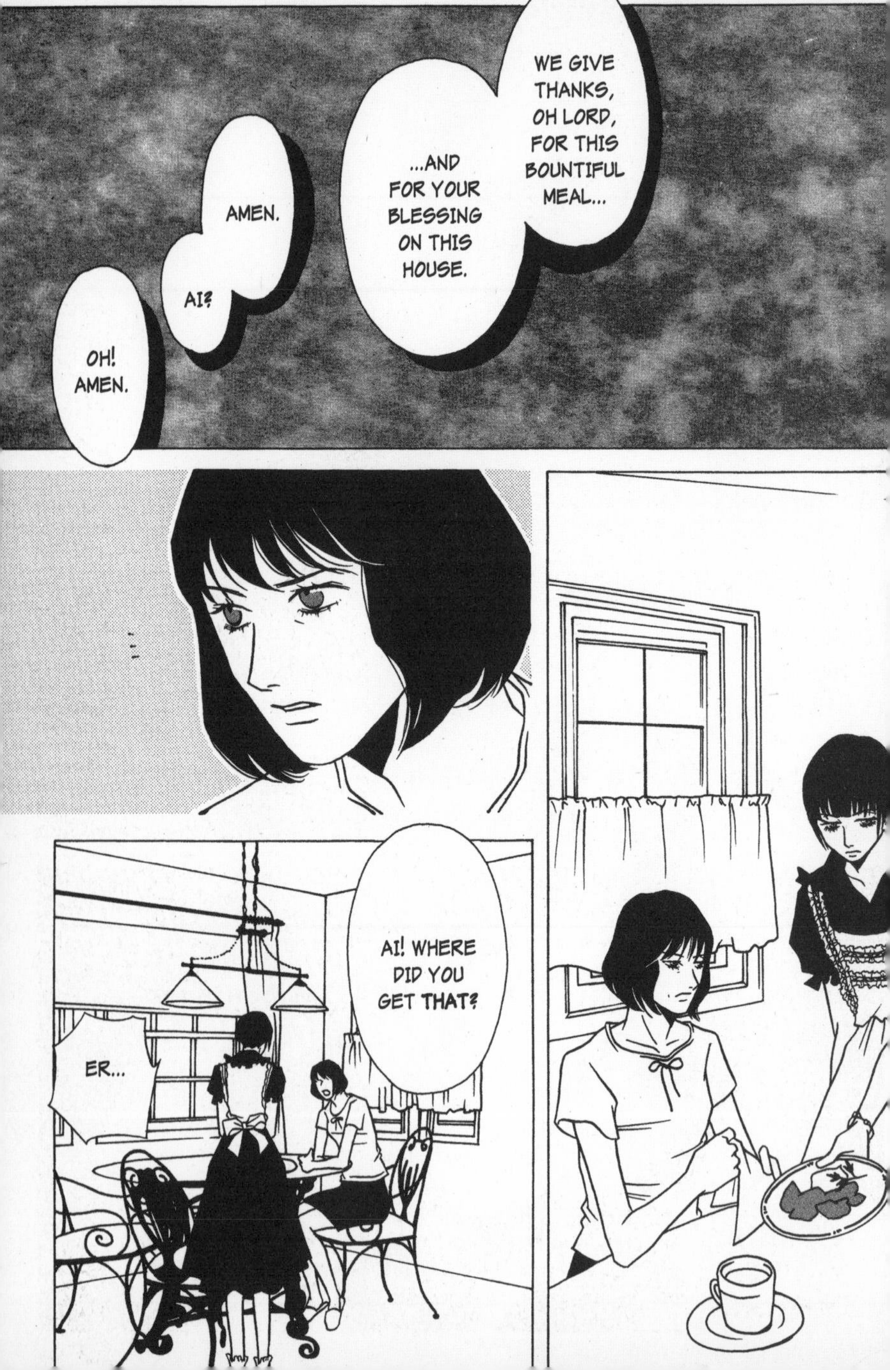
WE GIVE THANKS, OH LORD, FOR THIS BOUNTIFUL MEAL...
...AND FOR YOUR BLESSING ON THIS HOUSE.
AMEN.
AI?
OH! AMEN.
AI! WHERE DID YOU GET THAT?
ER...

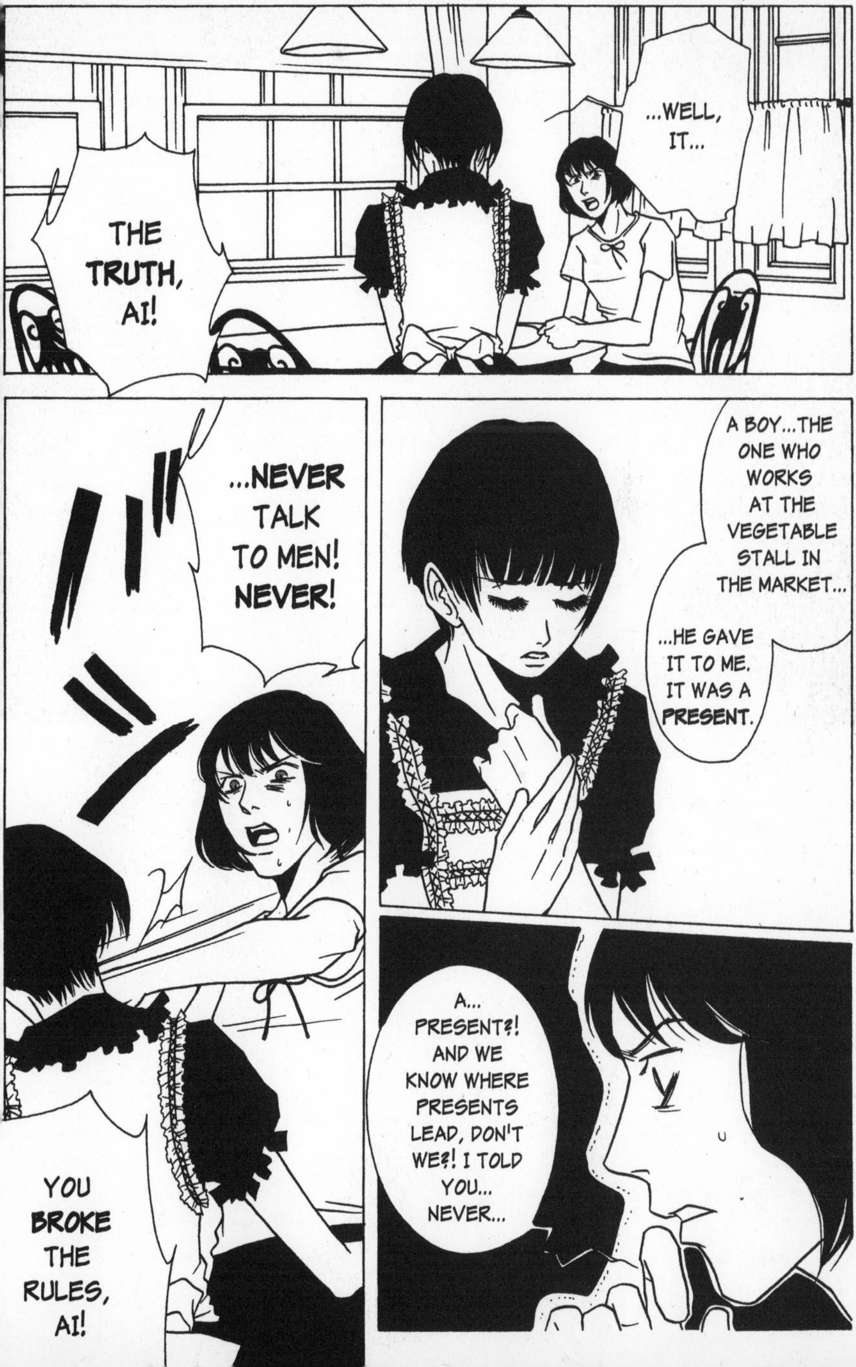
...WELL, IT...
THE TRUTH, AI!
A BOY...THE ONE WHO WORKS AT THE VEGETABLE STALL IN THE MARKET...
...HE GAVE IT TO ME. IT WAS A PRESENT.
A... PRESENT?! AND WE KNOW WHERE PRESENTS LEAD, DON'T WE?! I TOLD YOU... NEVER...
...NEVER TALK TO MEN! NEVER!
YOU BROKE THE RULES, AI!

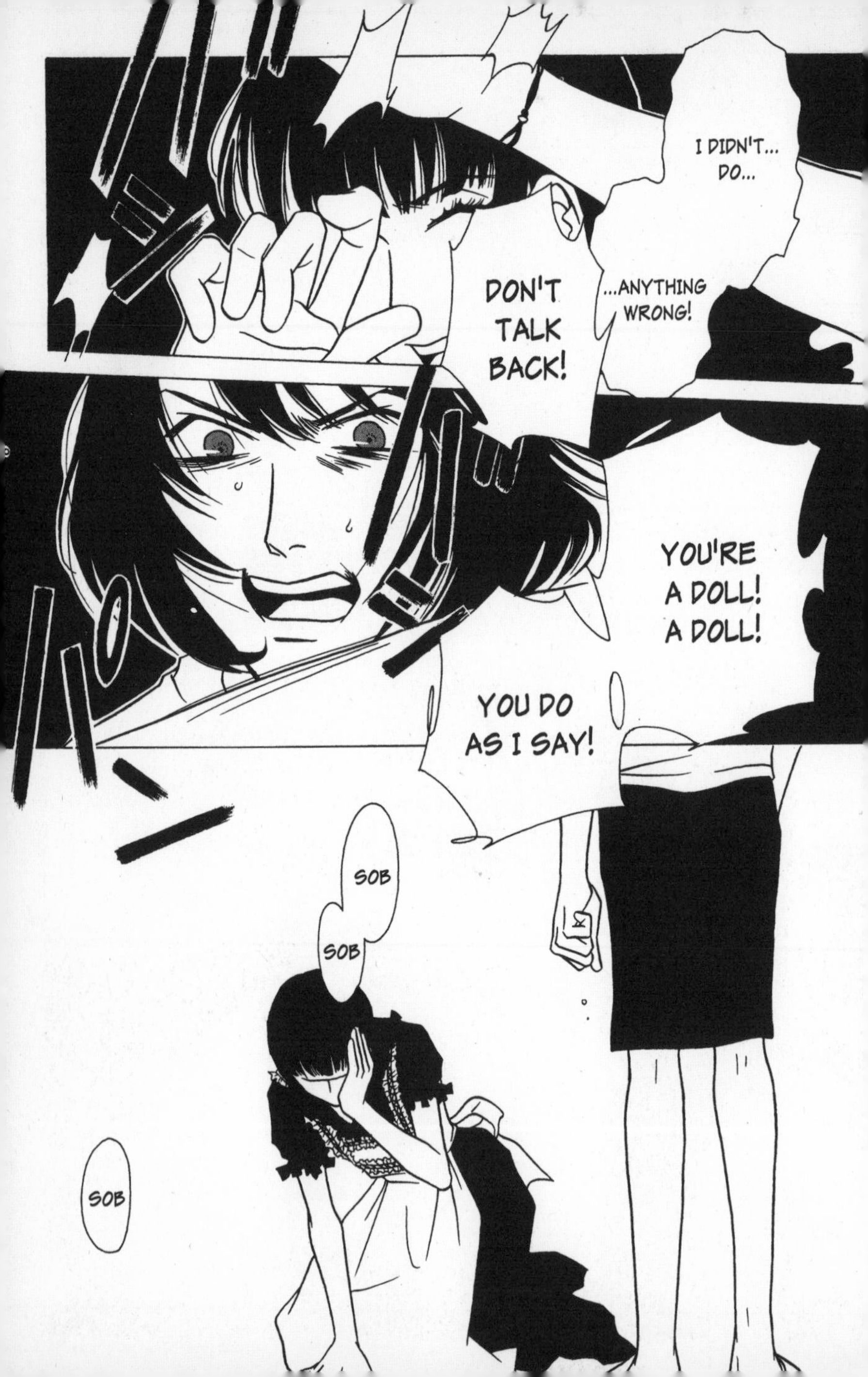
I DIDN'T... DO...
...ANYTHING WRONG!
DON'T TALK BACK!
YOU'RE A DOLL! A DOLL!
YOU DO AS I SAY!
SOB
SOB
SOB

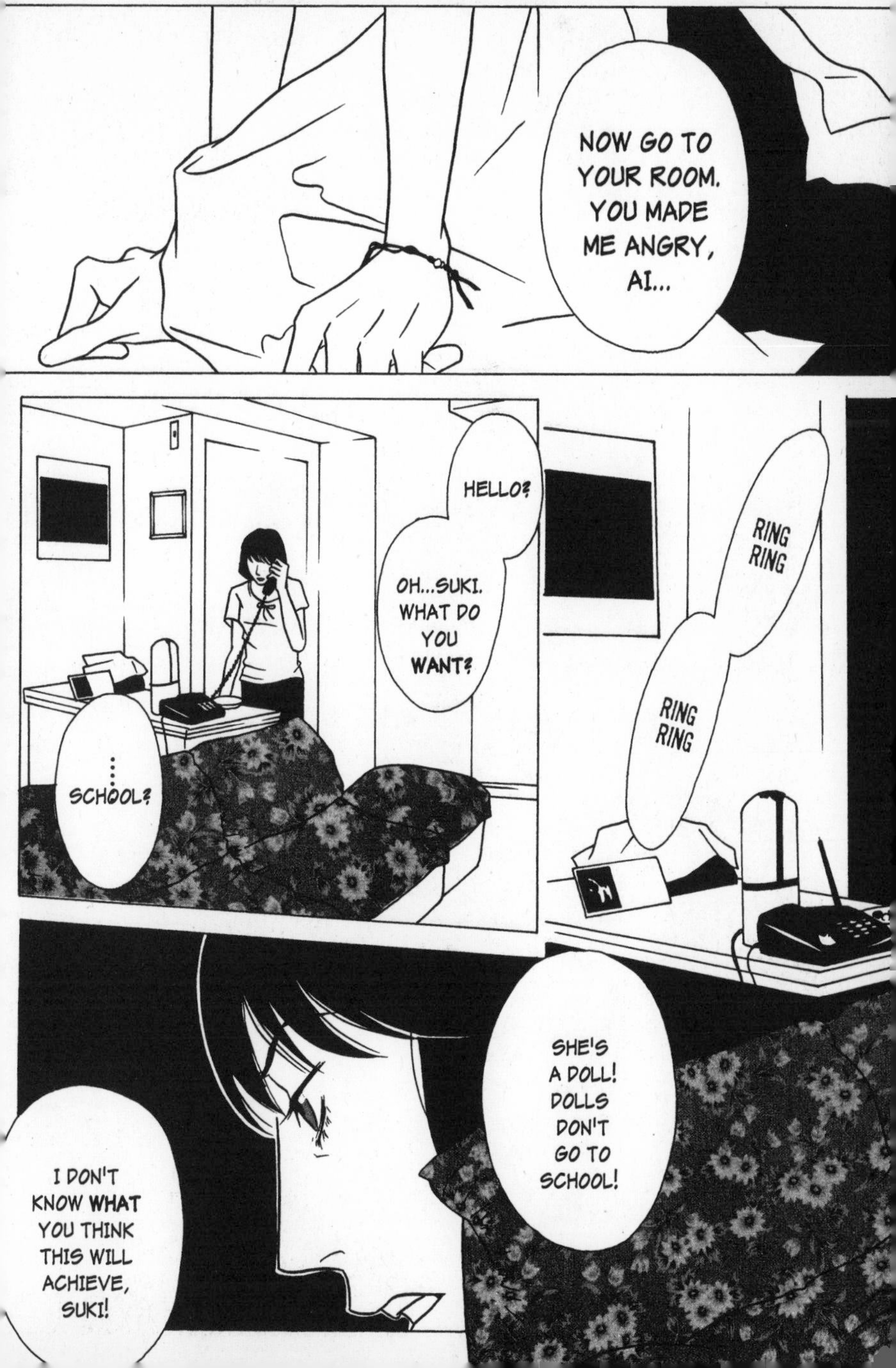
NOW GO TO YOUR ROOM. YOU MADE ME ANGRY, AI...
RING RING
RING RING
HELLO?
OH...SUKI. WHAT DO YOU WANT?
...SCHOOL?
SHE'S A DOLL! DOLLS DON'T GO TO SCHOOL!
I DON'T KNOW WHAT YOU THINK THIS WILL ACHIEVE, SUKI!

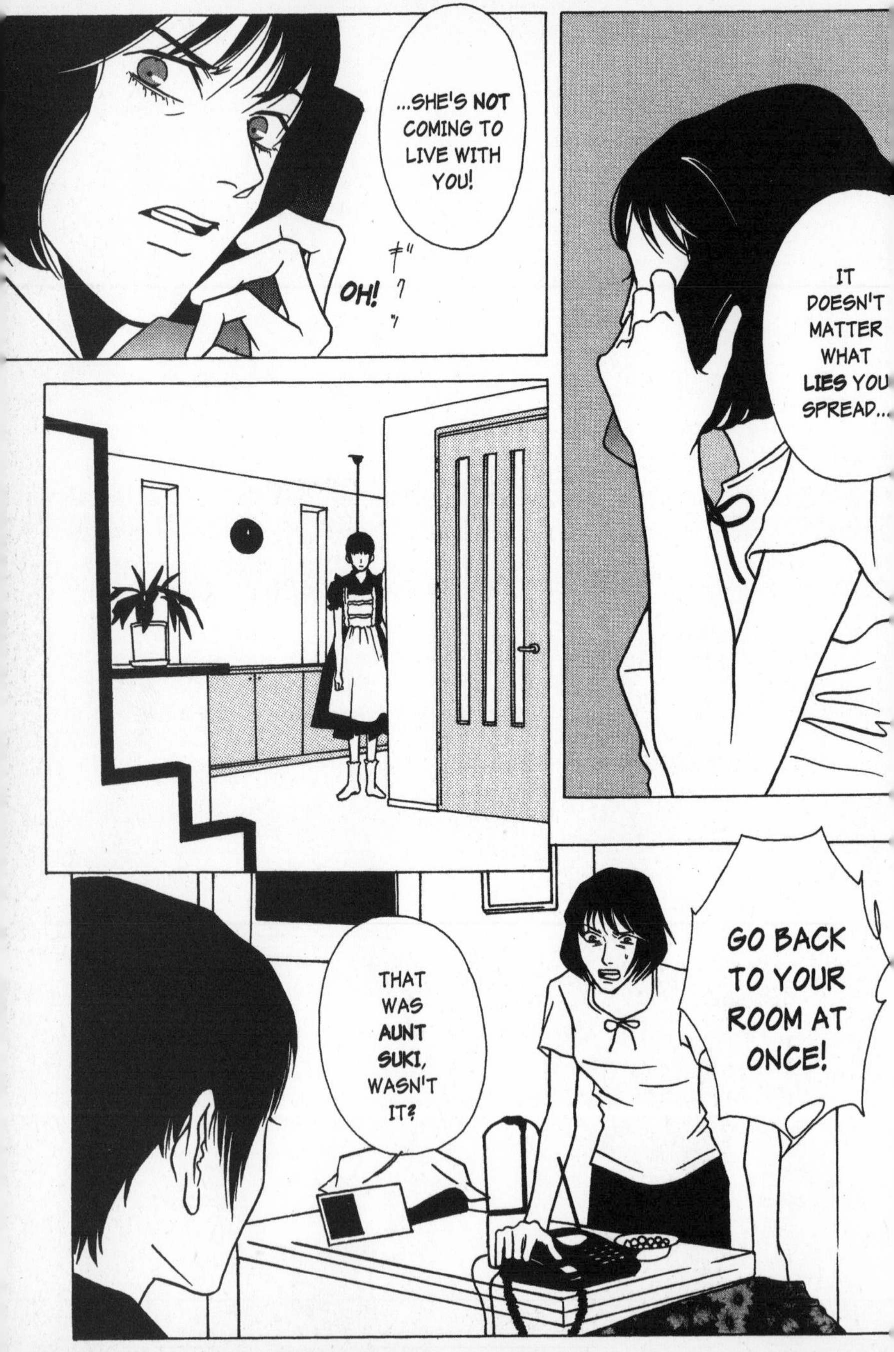
IT DOESN'T MATTER WHAT LIES YOU SPREAD...
...SHE'S NOT COMING TO LIVE WITH YOU!
ギッ
OH!
GO BACK TO YOUR ROOM AT ONCE!
THAT WAS AUNT SUKI, WASN'T IT?

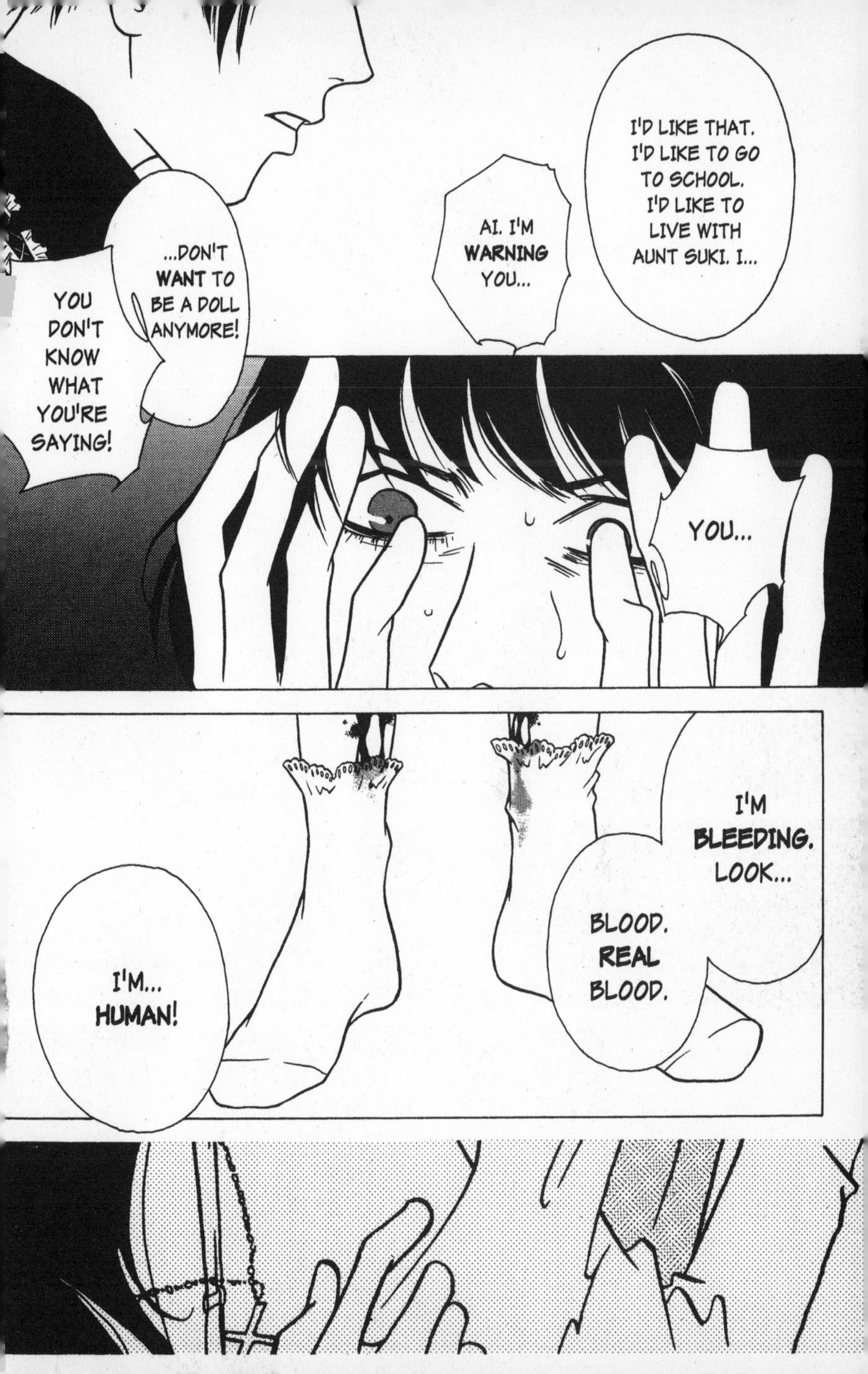
I'D LIKE THAT. I'D LIKE TO GO TO SCHOOL. I'D LIKE TO LIVE WITH AUNT SUKI. I...
AI. I'M WARNING YOU...
...DON'T WANT TO BE A DOLL ANYMORE!
YOU DON'T KNOW WHAT YOU'RE SAYING!
YOU...
I'M BLEEDING. LOOK...
BLOOD. REAL BLOOD.
I'M... HUMAN!

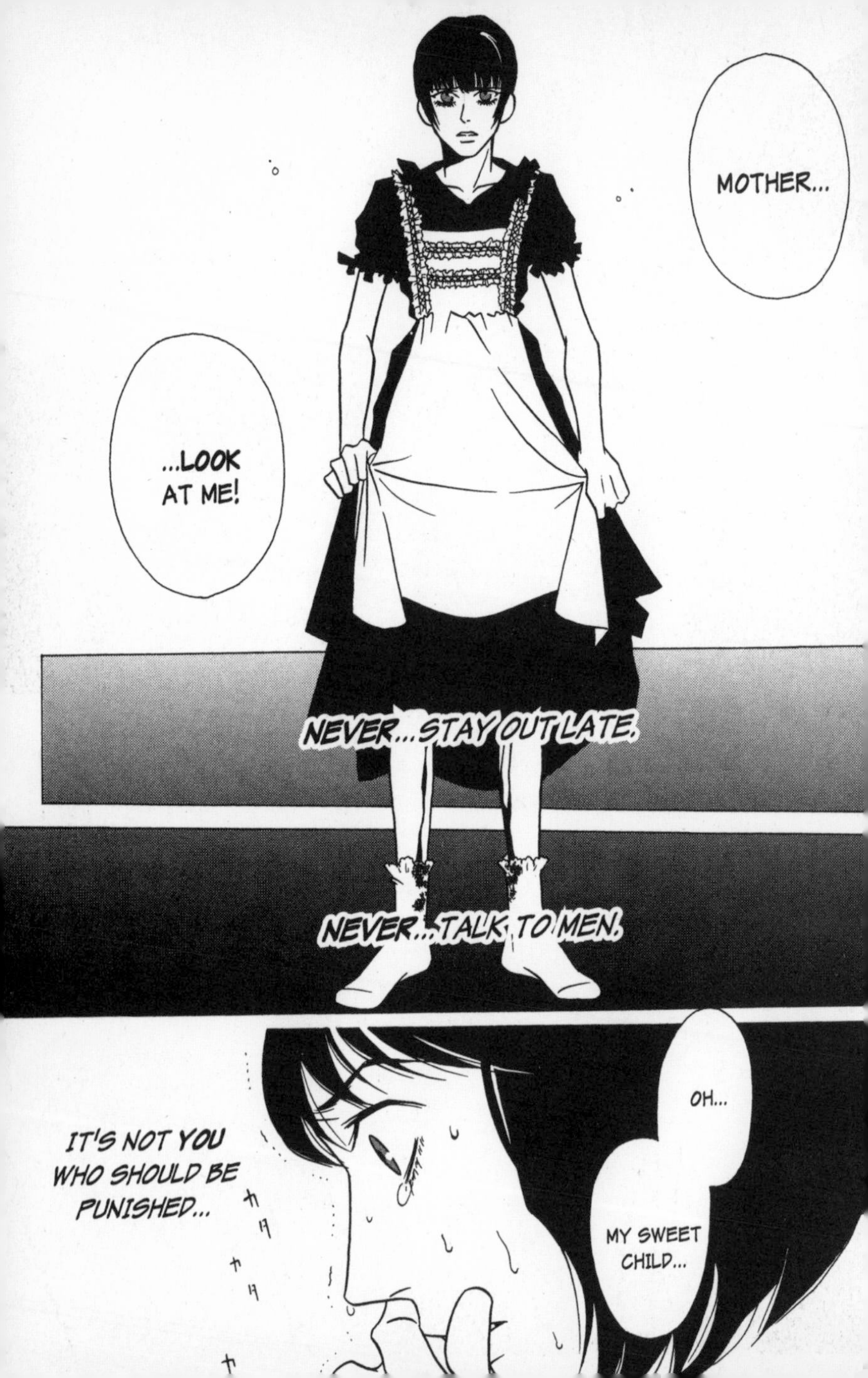
MOTHER...
...LOOK AT ME!
NEVER...STAY OUT LATE.
NEVER...TALK TO MEN.
OH...
MY SWEET CHILD...
IT'S NOT YOU WHO SHOULD BE PUNISHED...

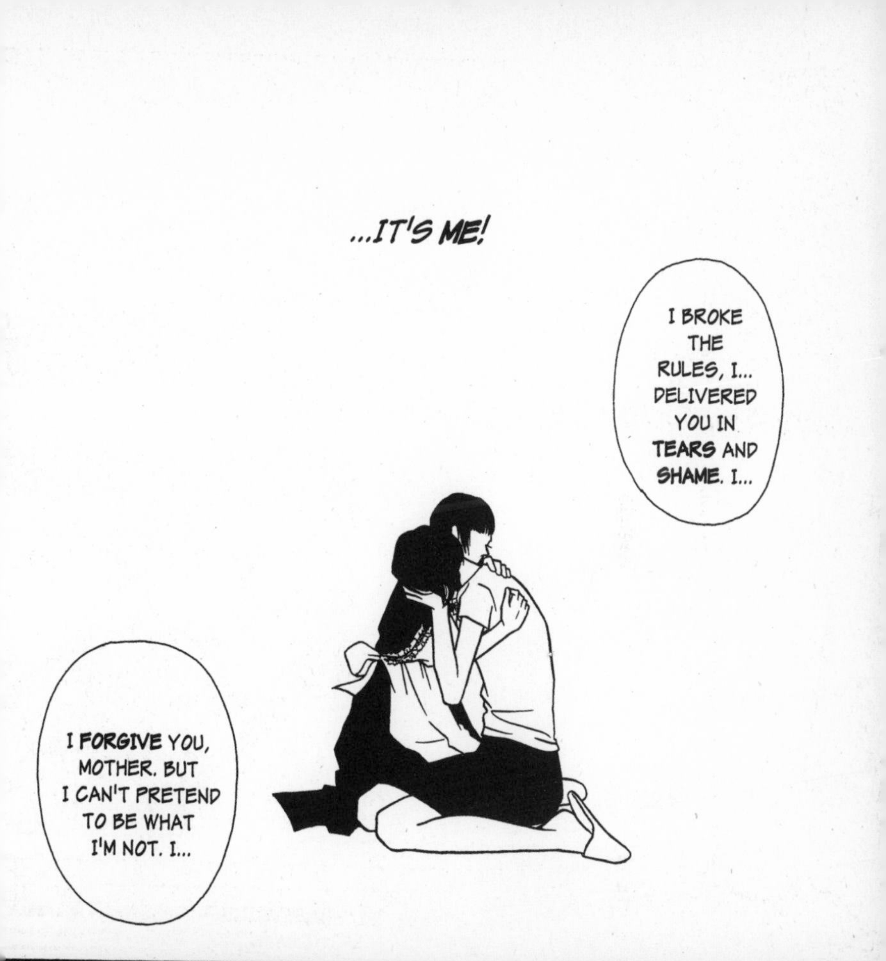
...IT'S ME!
I BROKE THE RULES, I... DELIVERED YOU IN TEARS AND SHAME. I...
I FORGIVE YOU, MOTHER. BUT I CAN'T PRETEND TO BE WHAT I'M NOT. I...
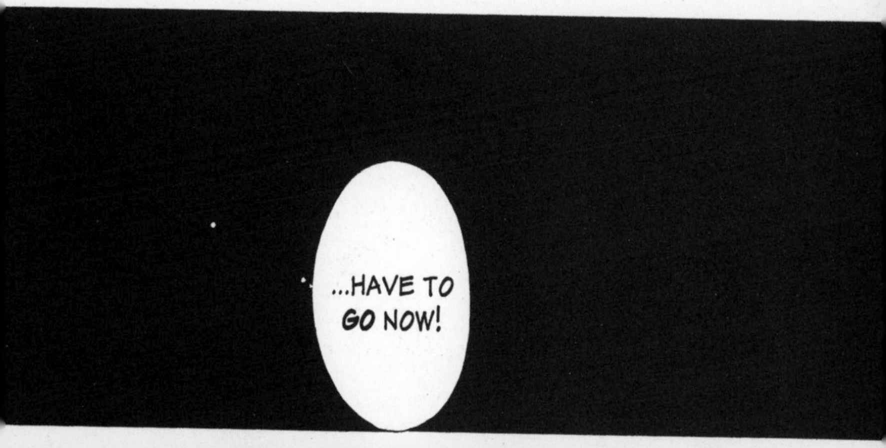
...HAVE TO GO NOW!

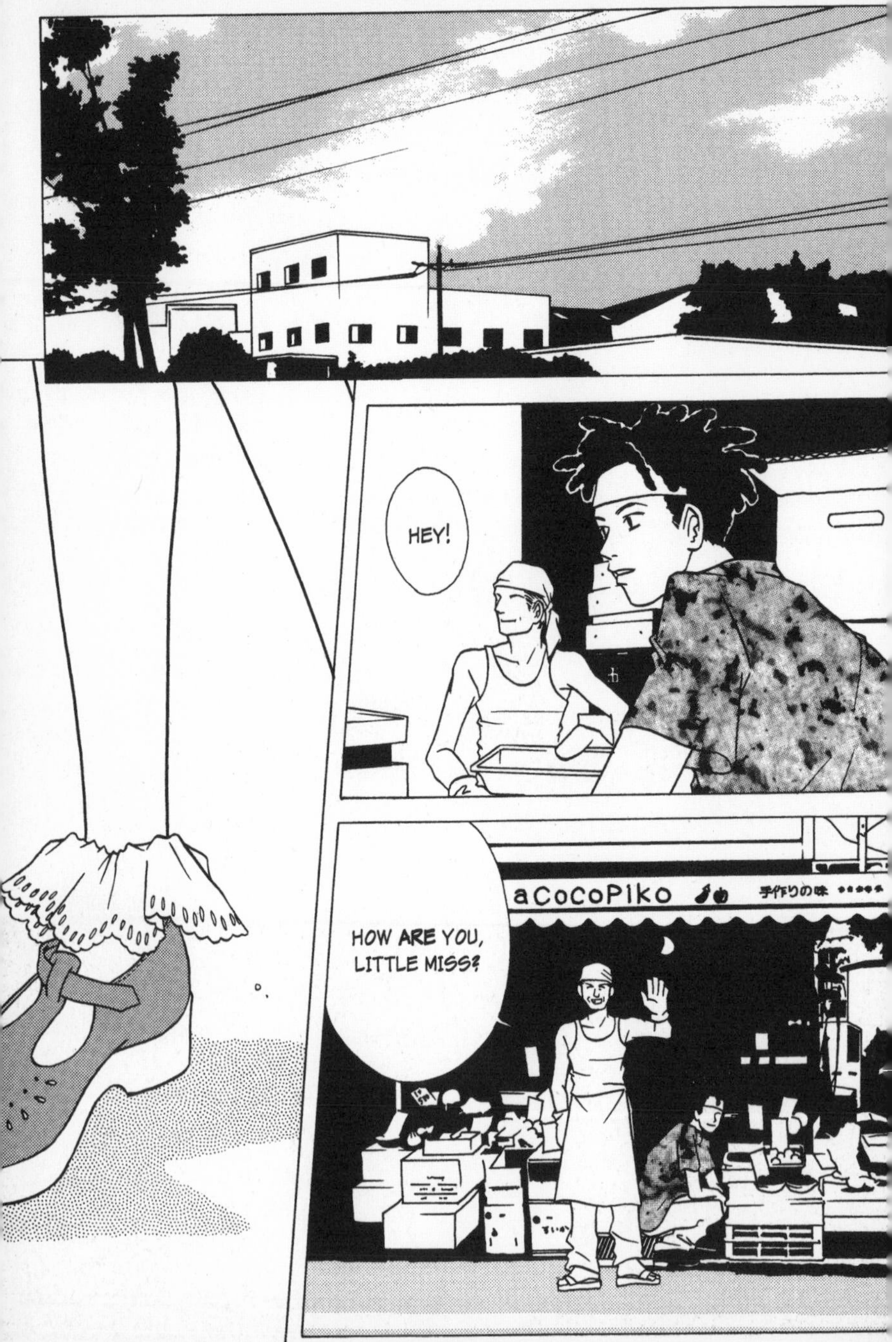
HEY!
aCoCoPiko
手作りの味
HOW ARE YOU, LITTLE MISS?

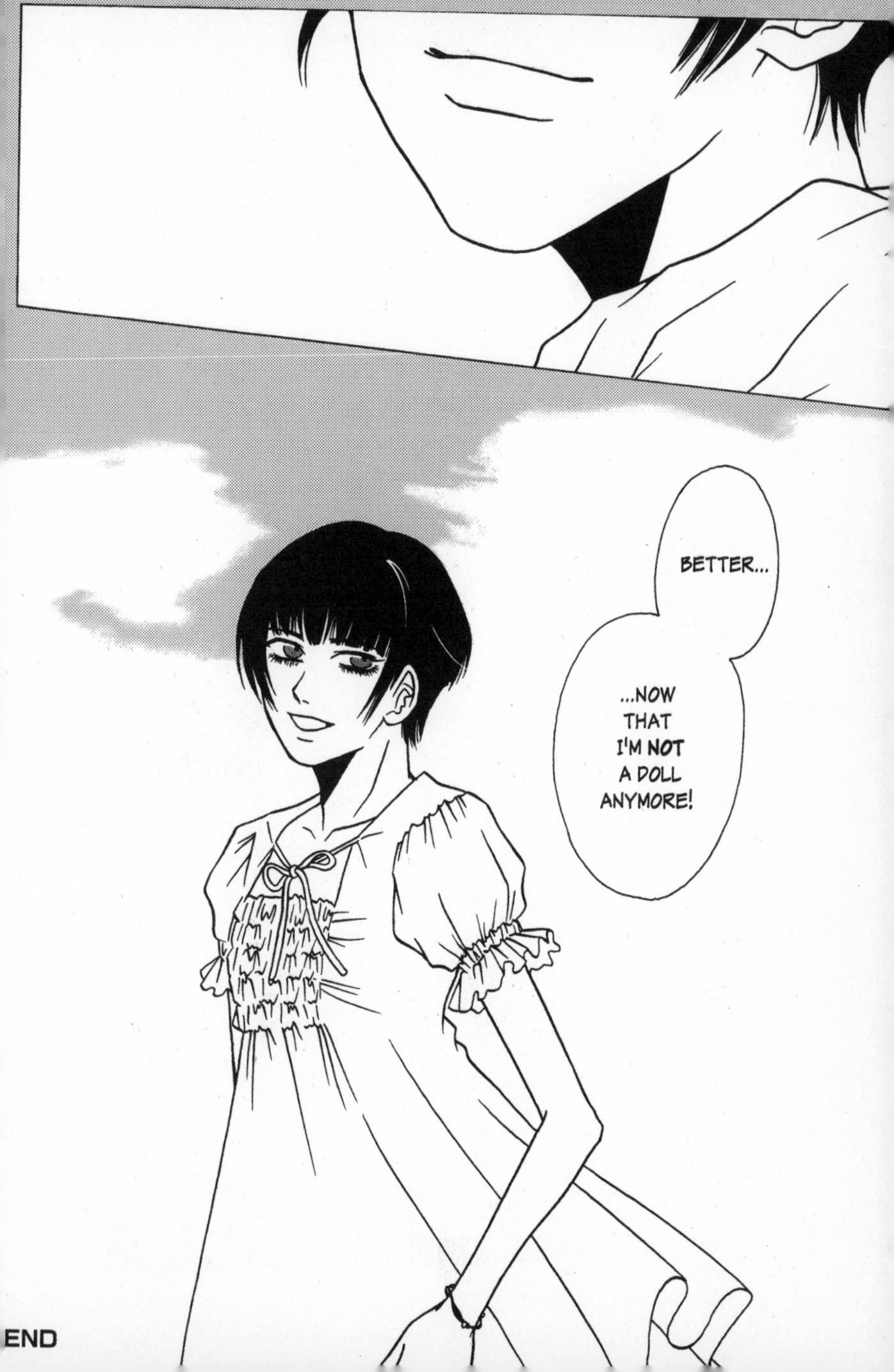
BETTER...
...NOW THAT I'M NOT A DOLL ANYMORE!

END

LIST 4

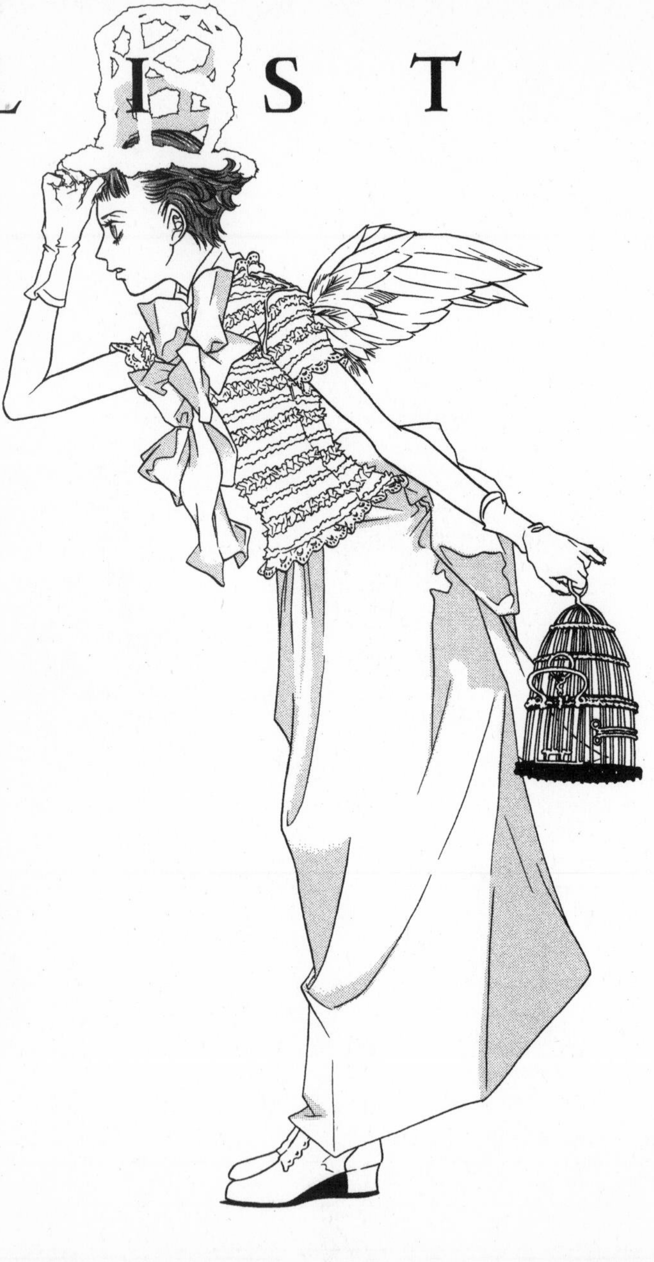

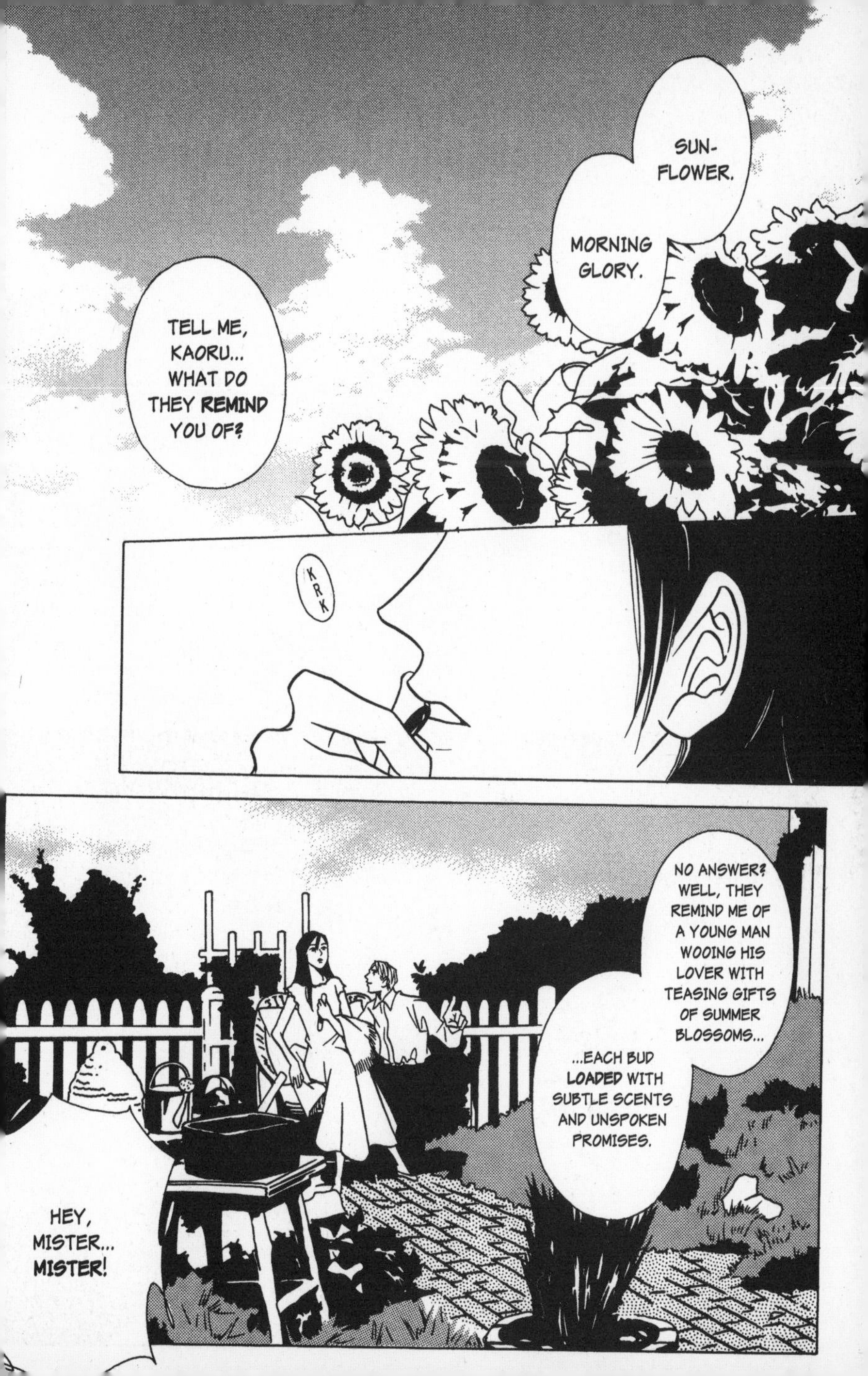
SUN-FLOWER.
MORNING GLORY.
TELL ME, KAORU... WHAT DO THEY **REMIND** YOU OF?
KRK
NO ANSWER? WELL, THEY REMIND ME OF A YOUNG MAN WOOING HIS LOVER WITH TEASING GIFTS OF SUMMER BLOSSOMS...
...EACH BUD **LOADED** WITH SUBTLE SCENTS AND UNSPOKEN PROMISES.
HEY, MISTER... **MISTER!**

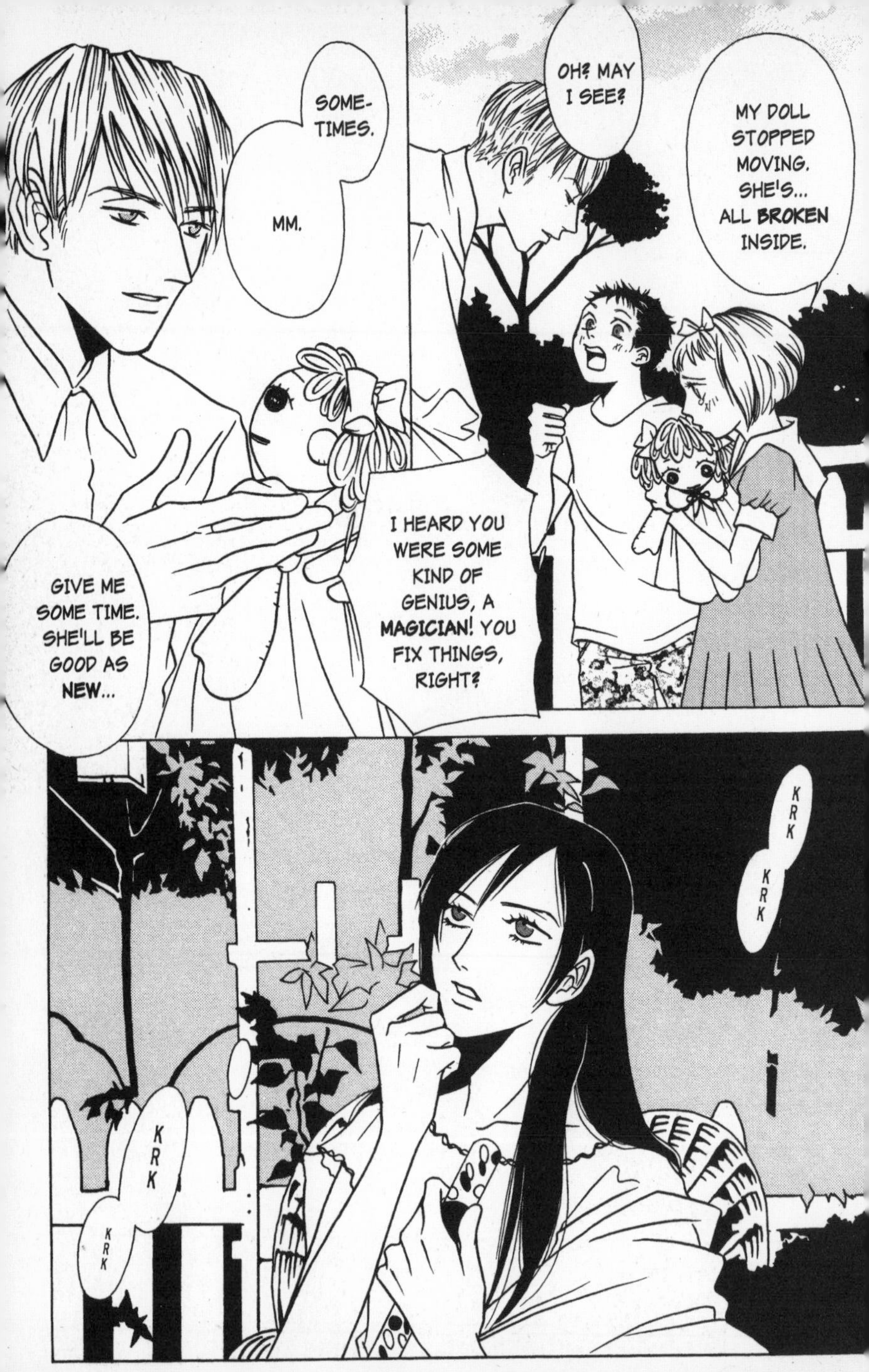
MY DOLL STOPPED MOVING. SHE'S... ALL BROKEN INSIDE.
OH? MAY I SEE?
I HEARD YOU WERE SOME KIND OF GENIUS, A MAGICIAN! YOU FIX THINGS, RIGHT?
SOME-TIMES.
MM.
GIVE ME SOME TIME. SHE'LL BE GOOD AS NEW...
KRK KRK KRK
KRK KRK

4. KAORU

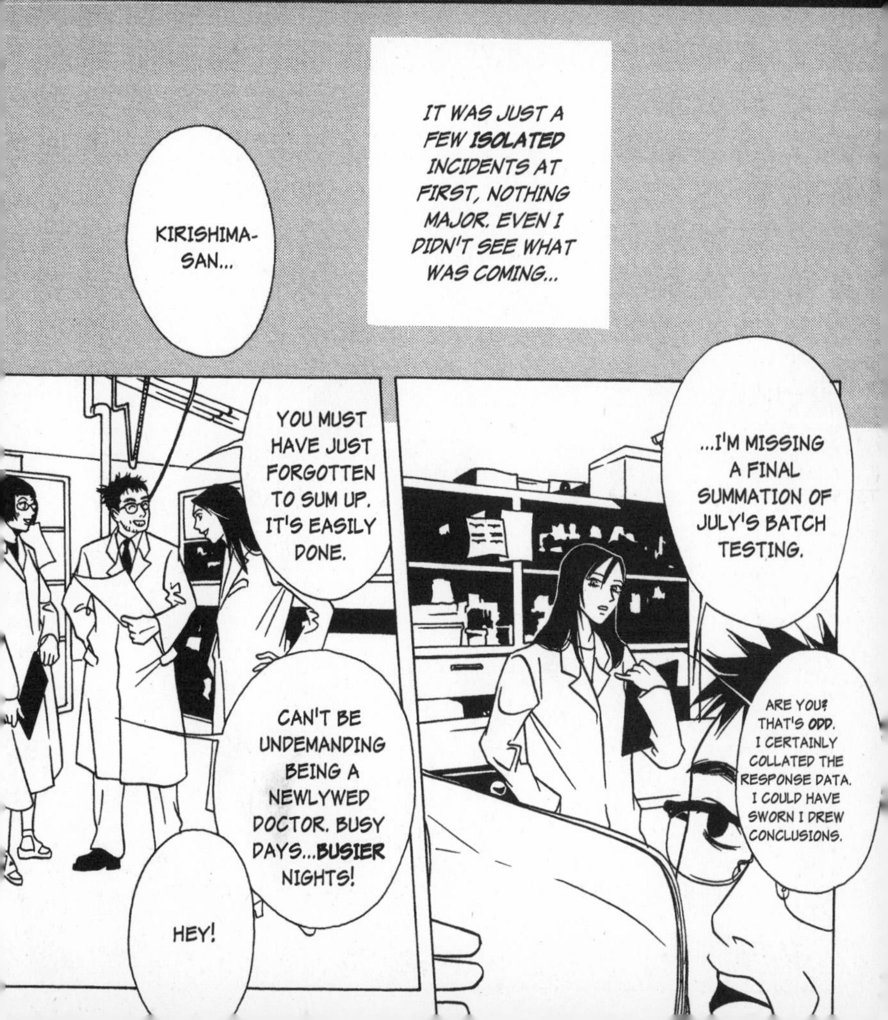
IT WAS JUST A FEW ISOLATED INCIDENTS AT FIRST, NOTHING MAJOR. EVEN I DIDN'T SEE WHAT WAS COMING...
KIRISHIMA-SAN...
...I'M MISSING A FINAL SUMMATION OF JULY'S BATCH TESTING.
ARE YOU? THAT'S ODD. I CERTAINLY COLLATED THE RESPONSE DATA. I COULD HAVE SWORN I DREW CONCLUSIONS.
YOU MUST HAVE JUST FORGOTTEN TO SUM UP. IT'S EASILY DONE.
CAN'T BE UNDEMANDING BEING A NEWLYWED DOCTOR. BUSY DAYS...BUSIER NIGHTS!
HEY!

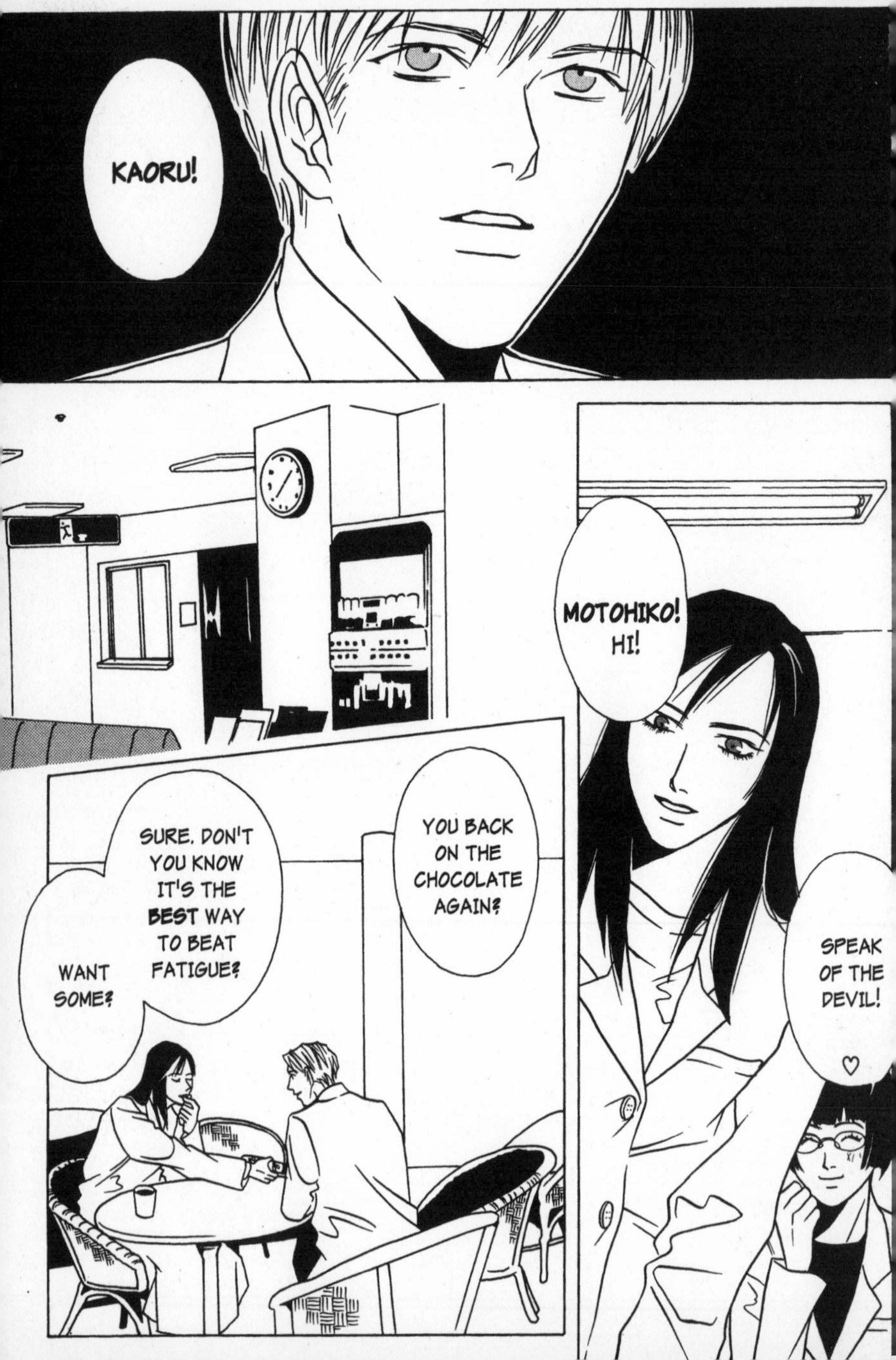
KAORU!
MOTOHIKO! HI!
SPEAK OF THE DEVIL! ♡
YOU BACK ON THE CHOCOLATE AGAIN?
SURE. DON'T YOU KNOW IT'S THE BEST WAY TO BEAT FATIGUE?
WANT SOME?

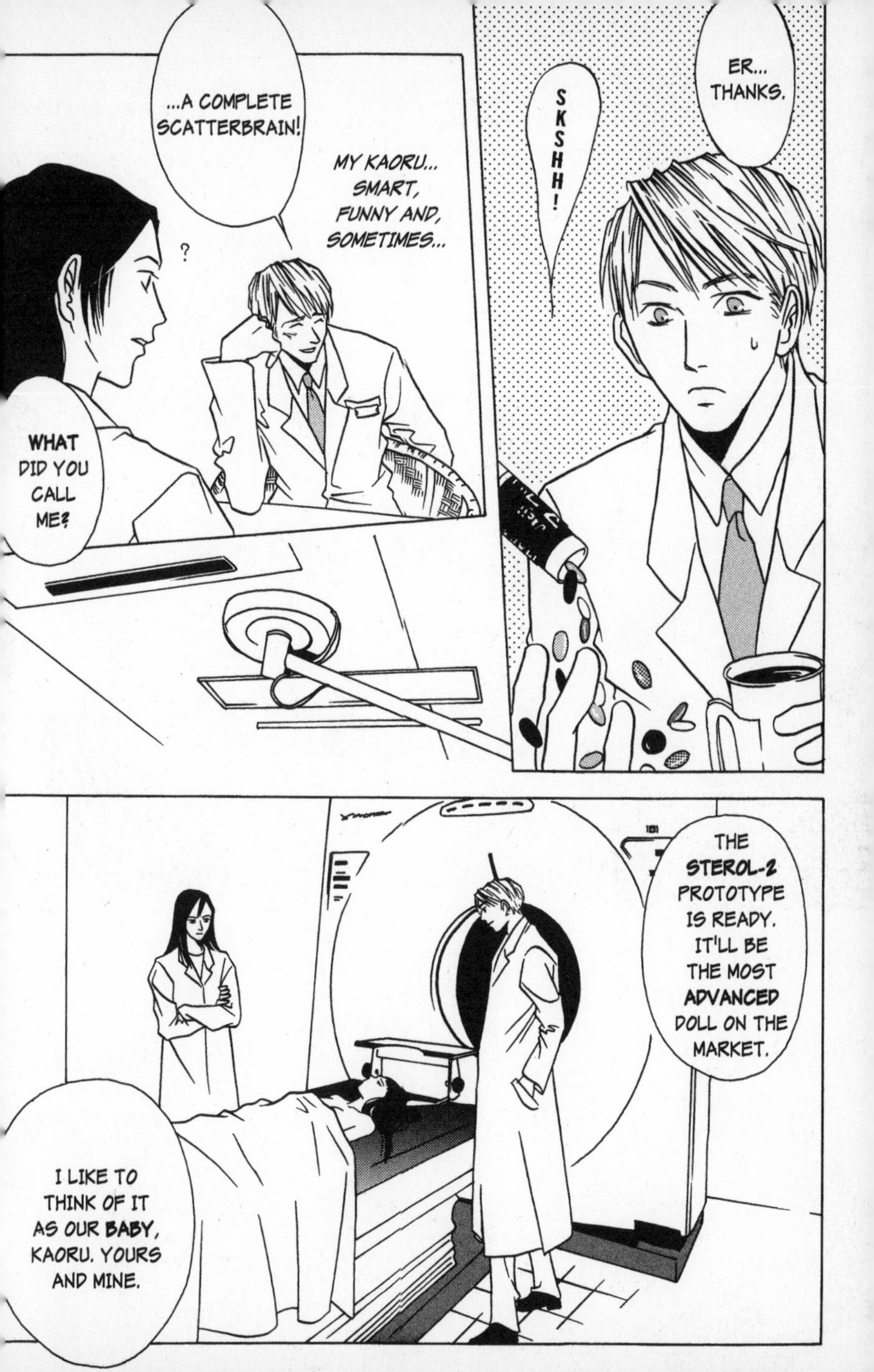
ER... THANKS.
SKSHH!
MY KAORU... SMART, FUNNY AND, SOMETIMES...
...A COMPLETE SCATTERBRAIN!
WHAT DID YOU CALL ME?
THE STEROL-2 PROTOTYPE IS READY. IT'LL BE THE MOST ADVANCED DOLL ON THE MARKET.
I LIKE TO THINK OF IT AS OUR BABY, KAORU. YOURS AND MINE.

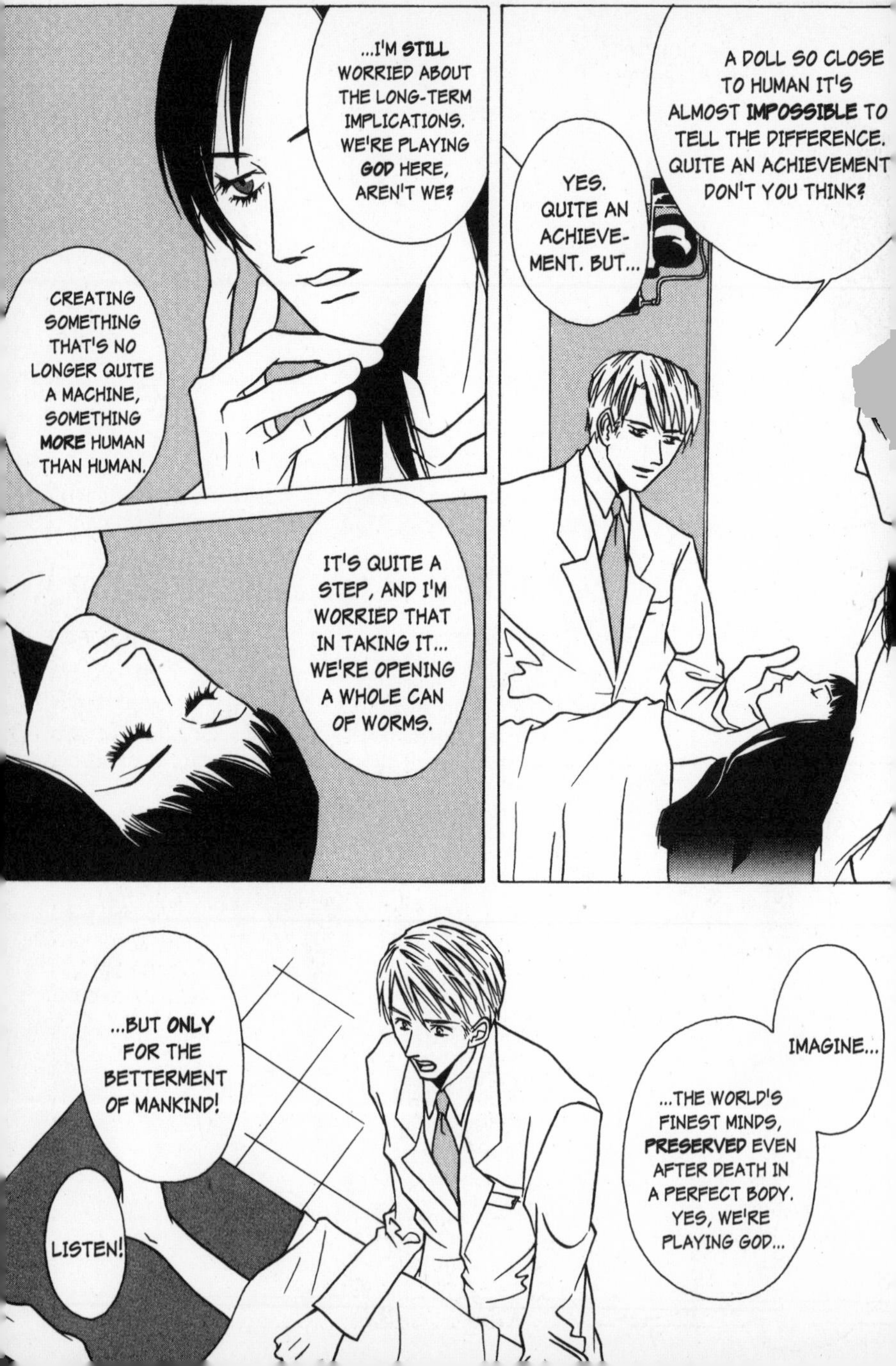
A DOLL SO CLOSE TO HUMAN IT'S ALMOST IMPOSSIBLE TO TELL THE DIFFERENCE. QUITE AN ACHIEVEMENT DON'T YOU THINK?
YES. QUITE AN ACHIEVE-MENT. BUT...
...I'M STILL WORRIED ABOUT THE LONG-TERM IMPLICATIONS. WE'RE PLAYING GOD HERE, AREN'T WE?
CREATING SOMETHING THAT'S NO LONGER QUITE A MACHINE, SOMETHING MORE HUMAN THAN HUMAN.
IT'S QUITE A STEP, AND I'M WORRIED THAT IN TAKING IT... WE'RE OPENING A WHOLE CAN OF WORMS.
IMAGINE...
...THE WORLD'S FINEST MINDS, PRESERVED EVEN AFTER DEATH IN A PERFECT BODY. YES, WE'RE PLAYING GOD...
...BUT ONLY FOR THE BETTERMENT OF MANKIND!
LISTEN!

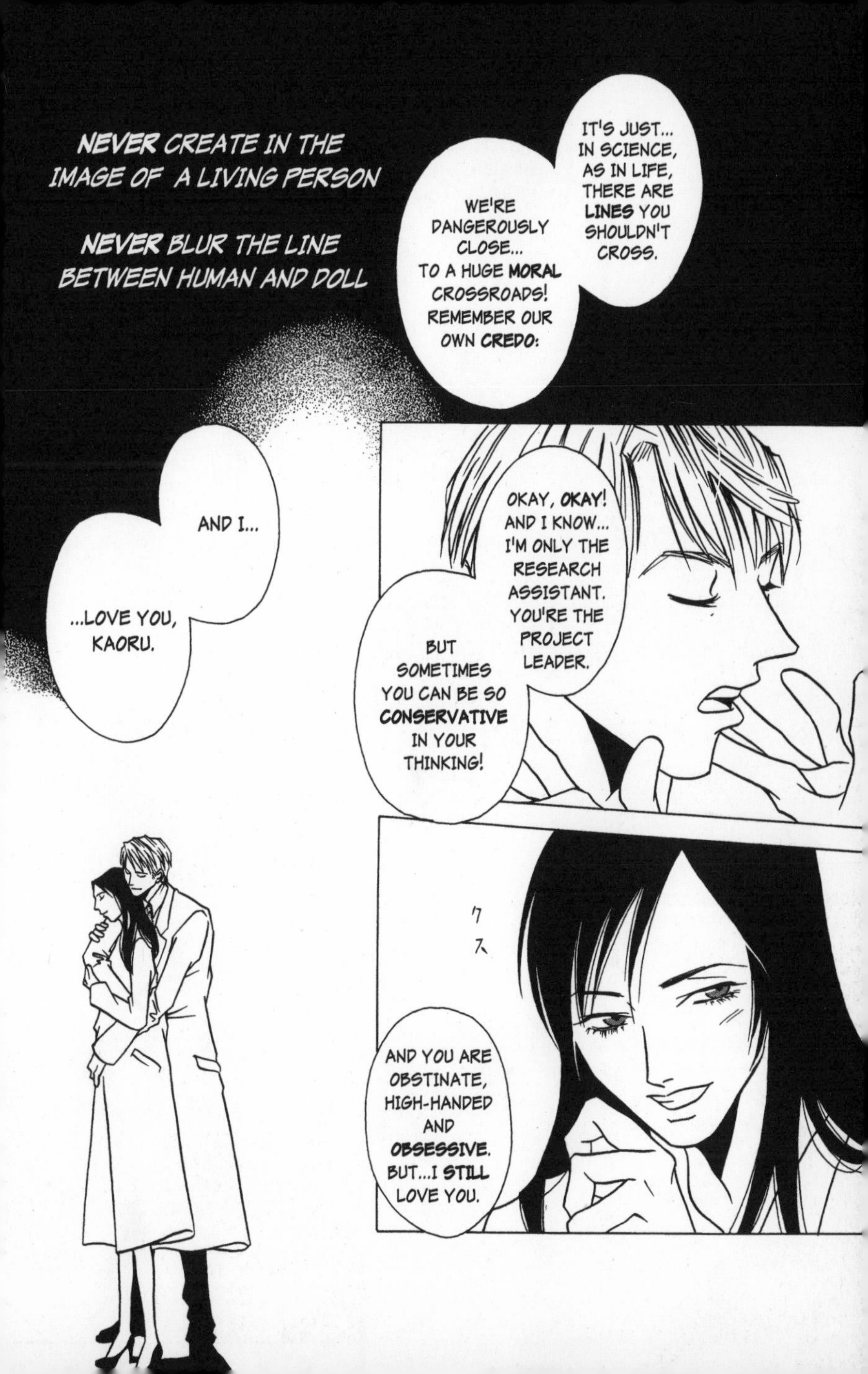
IT'S JUST... IN SCIENCE, AS IN LIFE, THERE ARE LINES YOU SHOULDN'T CROSS.
WE'RE DANGEROUSLY CLOSE... TO A HUGE MORAL CROSSROADS! REMEMBER OUR OWN CREDO:
NEVER CREATE IN THE IMAGE OF A LIVING PERSON
NEVER BLUR THE LINE BETWEEN HUMAN AND DOLL
OKAY, OKAY! AND I KNOW... I'M ONLY THE RESEARCH ASSISTANT. YOU'RE THE PROJECT LEADER.
BUT SOMETIMES YOU CAN BE SO CONSERVATIVE IN YOUR THINKING!
クス
AND YOU ARE OBSTINATE, HIGH-HANDED AND OBSESSIVE. BUT...I STILL LOVE YOU.
AND I...
...LOVE YOU, KAORU.

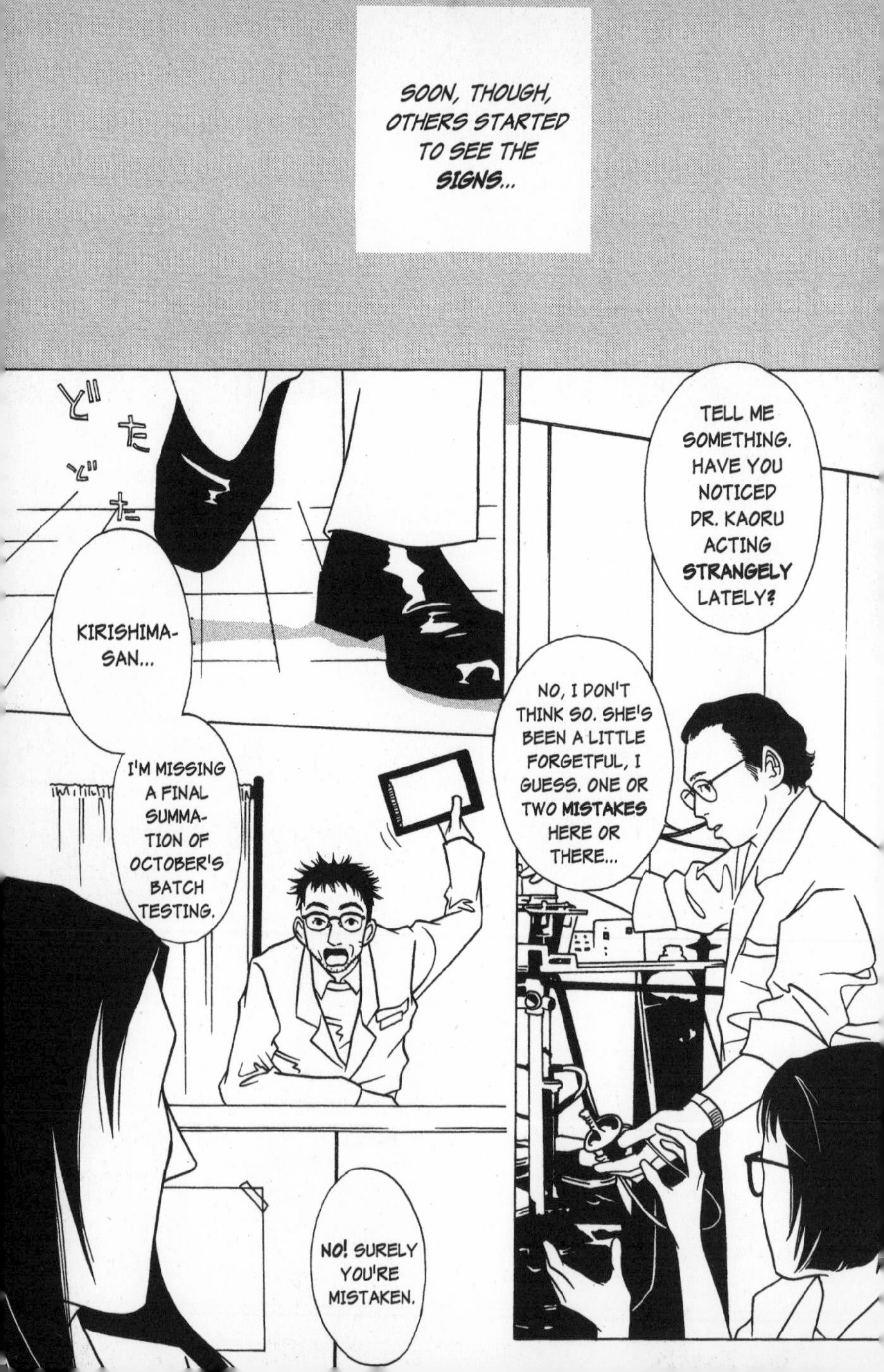
SOON, THOUGH, OTHERS STARTED TO SEE THE SIGNS...
TELL ME SOMETHING. HAVE YOU NOTICED DR. KAORU ACTING STRANGELY LATELY?
NO, I DON'T THINK SO. SHE'S BEEN A LITTLE FORGETFUL, I GUESS. ONE OR TWO MISTAKES HERE OR THERE...
どたどた
KIRISHIMA-SAN...
I'M MISSING A FINAL SUMMATION OF OCTOBER'S BATCH TESTING.
NO! SURELY YOU'RE MISTAKEN.

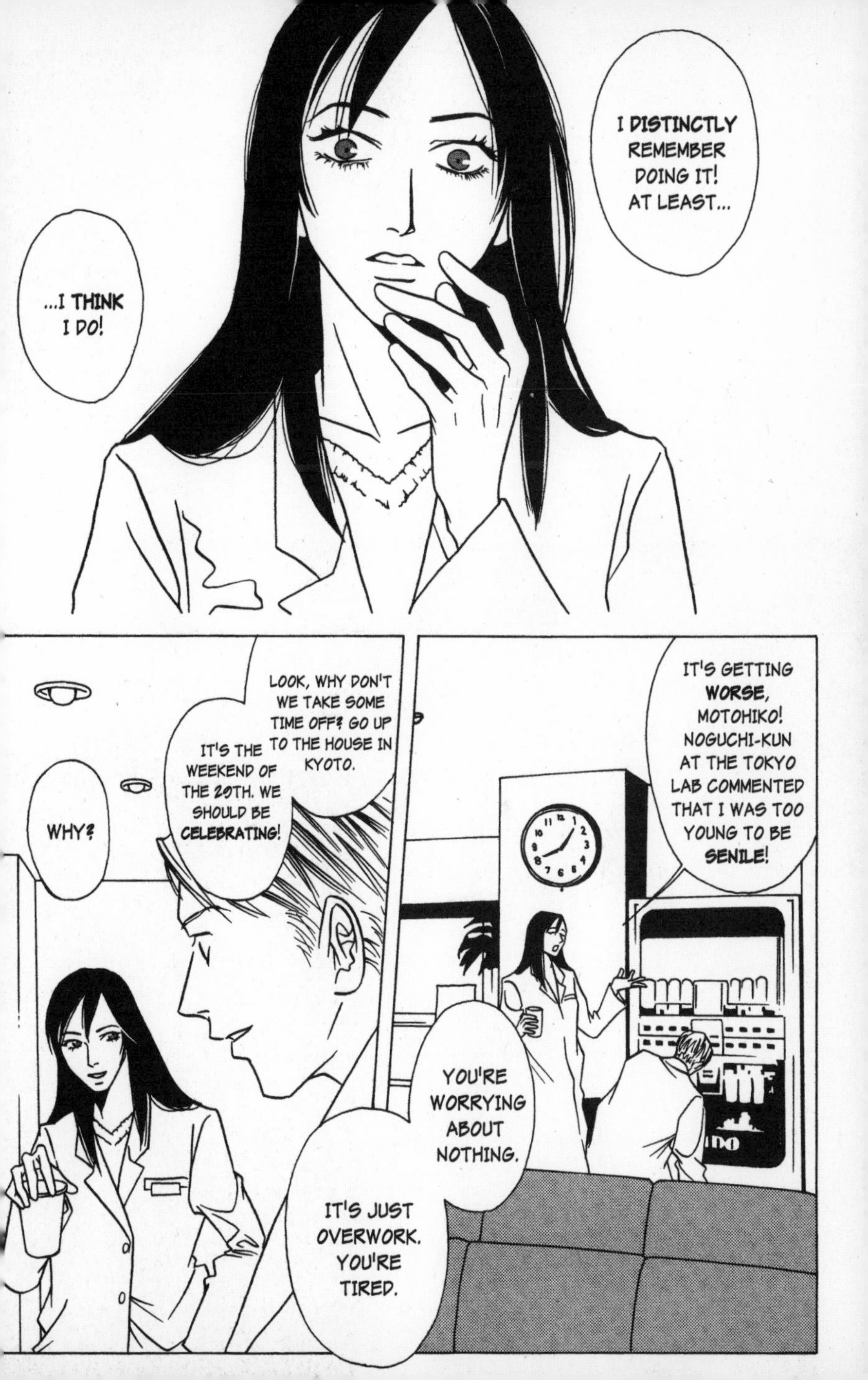
I DISTINCTLY REMEMBER DOING IT! AT LEAST...
...I THINK I DO!
IT'S GETTING WORSE, MOTOHIKO! NOGUCHI-KUN AT THE TOKYO LAB COMMENTED THAT I WAS TOO YOUNG TO BE SENILE!
YOU'RE WORRYING ABOUT NOTHING.
IT'S JUST OVERWORK. YOU'RE TIRED.
LOOK, WHY DON'T WE TAKE SOME TIME OFF? GO UP TO THE HOUSE IN KYOTO.
IT'S THE WEEKEND OF THE 20TH. WE SHOULD BE CELEBRATING!
WHY?

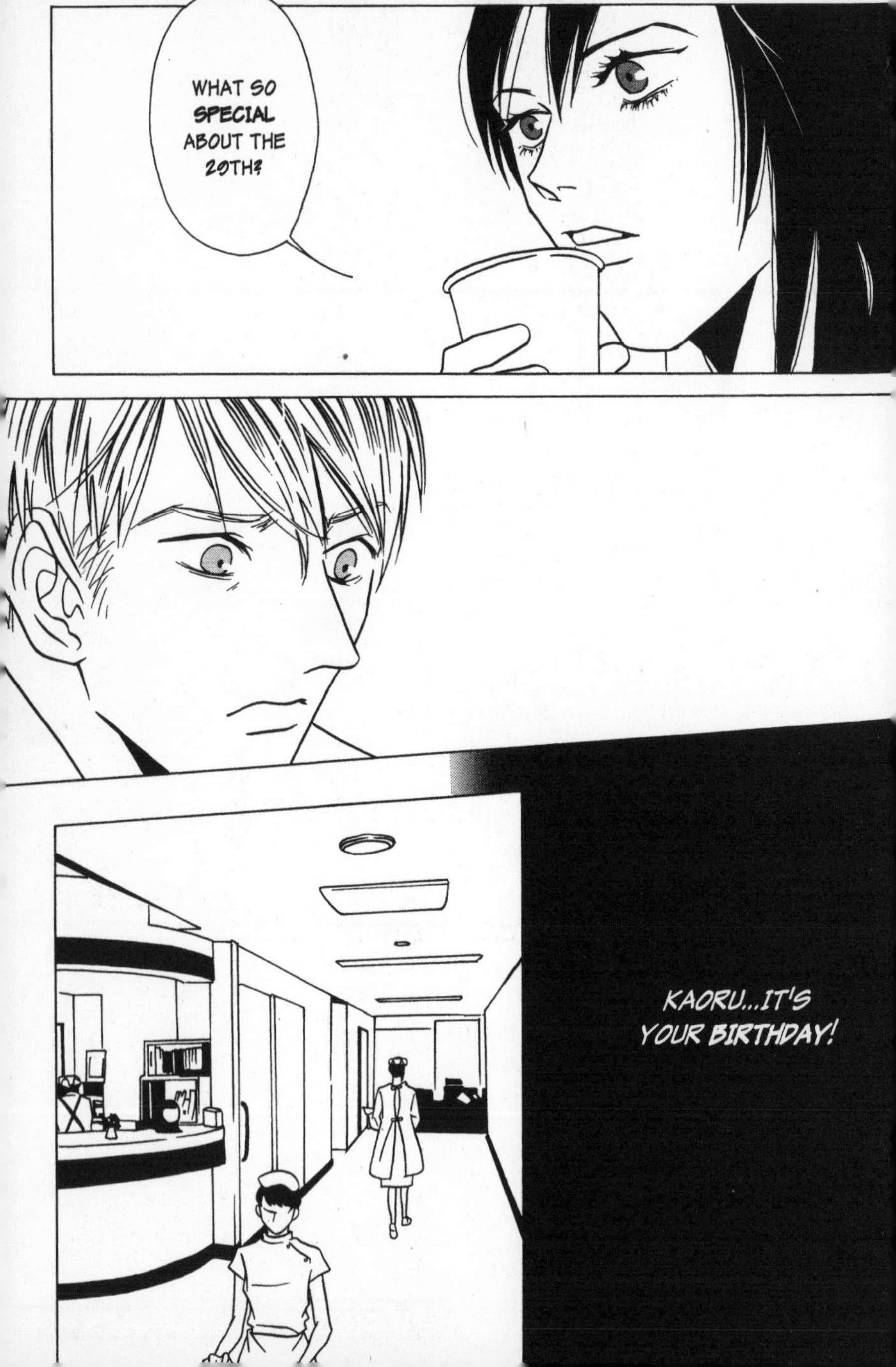
WHAT SO SPECIAL ABOUT THE 29TH?
KAORU...IT'S YOUR BIRTHDAY!

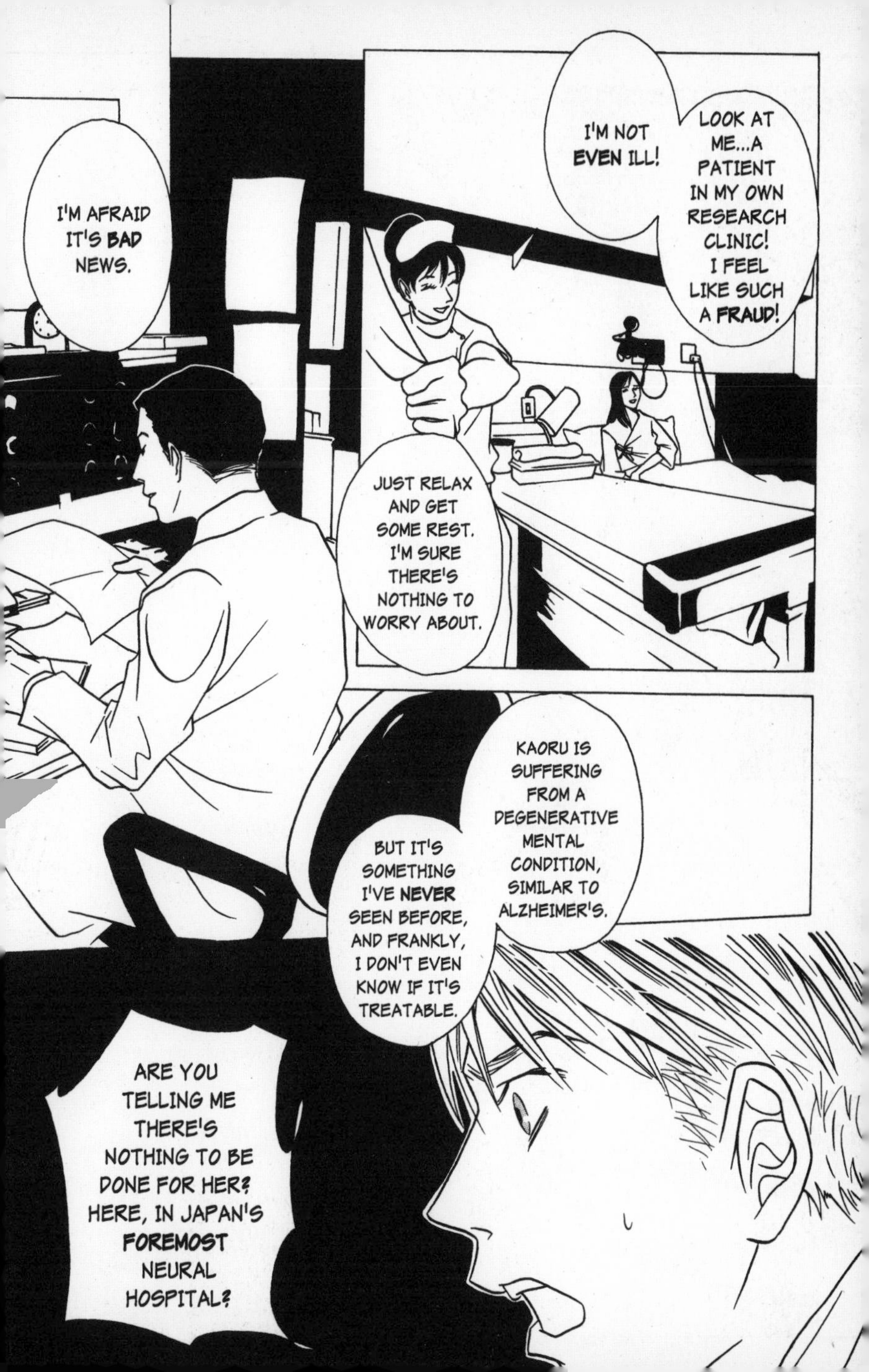
LOOK AT ME...A PATIENT IN MY OWN RESEARCH CLINIC! I FEEL LIKE SUCH A FRAUD!
I'M NOT EVEN ILL!
JUST RELAX AND GET SOME REST. I'M SURE THERE'S NOTHING TO WORRY ABOUT.
I'M AFRAID IT'S BAD NEWS.
KAORU IS SUFFERING FROM A DEGENERATIVE MENTAL CONDITION, SIMILAR TO ALZHEIMER'S.
BUT IT'S SOMETHING I'VE NEVER SEEN BEFORE, AND FRANKLY, I DON'T EVEN KNOW IF IT'S TREATABLE.
ARE YOU TELLING ME THERE'S NOTHING TO BE DONE FOR HER? HERE, IN JAPAN'S FOREMOST NEURAL HOSPITAL?

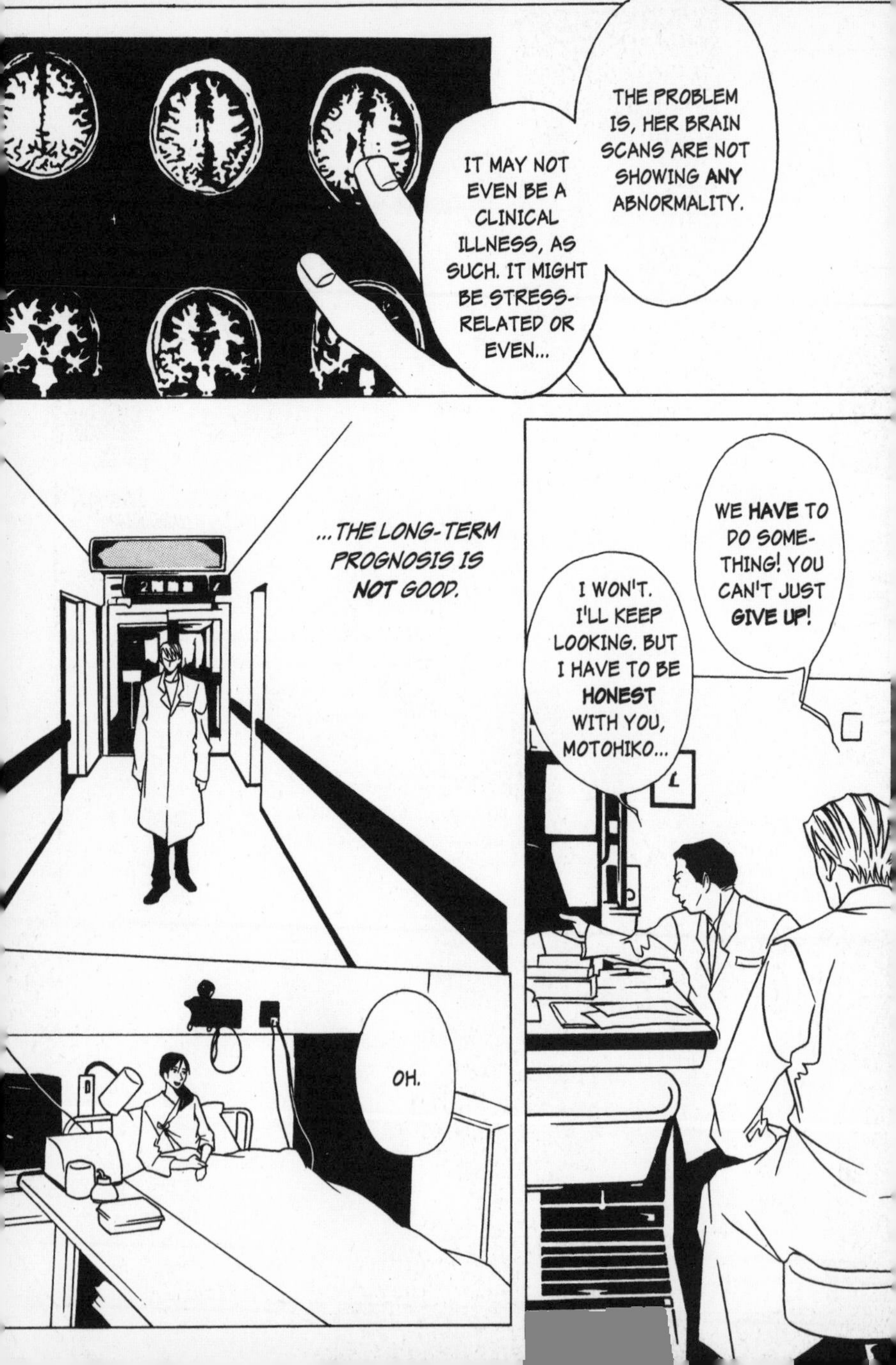
THE PROBLEM IS, HER BRAIN SCANS ARE NOT SHOWING ANY ABNORMALITY.
IT MAY NOT EVEN BE A CLINICAL ILLNESS, AS SUCH. IT MIGHT BE STRESS-RELATED OR EVEN...
WE HAVE TO DO SOME-THING! YOU CAN'T JUST GIVE UP!
I WON'T. I'LL KEEP LOOKING. BUT I HAVE TO BE HONEST WITH YOU, MOTOHIKO...
...THE LONG-TERM PROGNOSIS IS NOT GOOD.
OH.

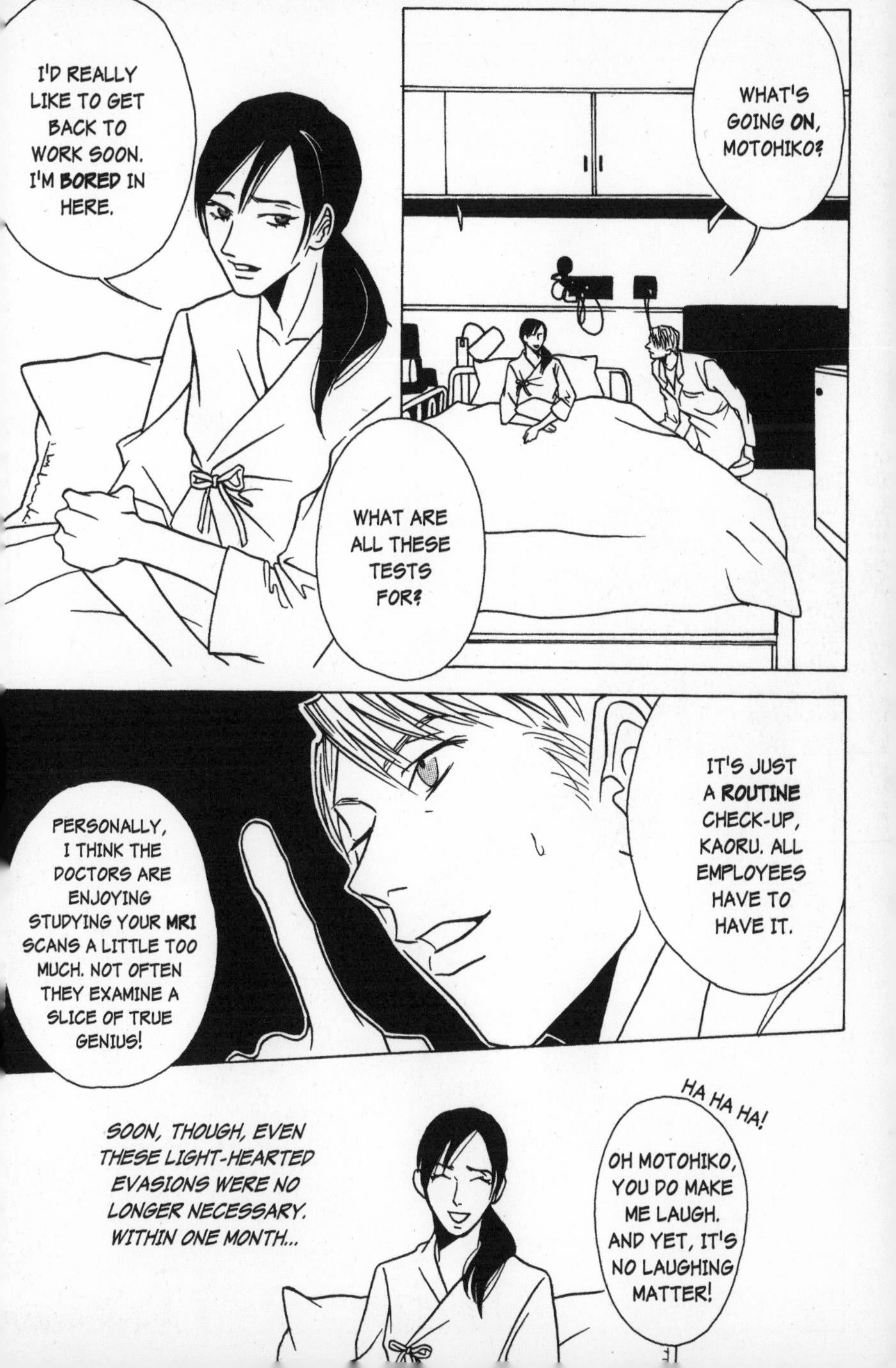
WHAT'S GOING ON, MOTOHIKO?
WHAT ARE ALL THESE TESTS FOR?
I'D REALLY LIKE TO GET BACK TO WORK SOON. I'M BORED IN HERE.
IT'S JUST A ROUTINE CHECK-UP, KAORU. ALL EMPLOYEES HAVE TO HAVE IT.
PERSONALLY, I THINK THE DOCTORS ARE ENJOYING STUDYING YOUR MRI SCANS A LITTLE TOO MUCH. NOT OFTEN THEY EXAMINE A SLICE OF TRUE GENIUS!
HA HA HA!
OH MOTOHIKO, YOU DO MAKE ME LAUGH. AND YET, IT'S NO LAUGHING MATTER!
SOON, THOUGH, EVEN THESE LIGHT-HEARTED EVASIONS WERE NO LONGER NECESSARY. WITHIN ONE MONTH...

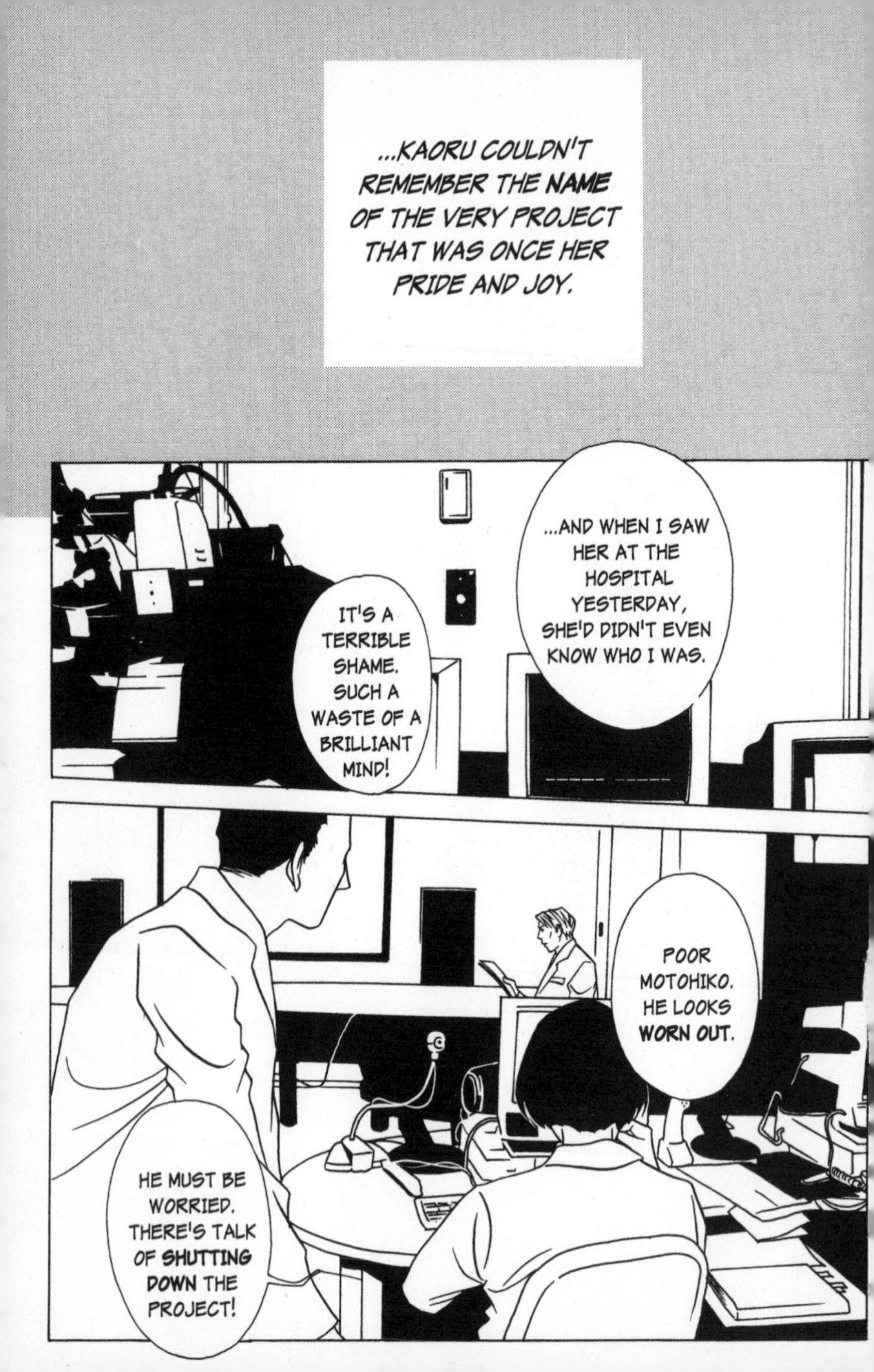
...KAORU COULDN'T REMEMBER THE NAME OF THE VERY PROJECT THAT WAS ONCE HER PRIDE AND JOY.
...AND WHEN I SAW HER AT THE HOSPITAL YESTERDAY, SHE'D DIDN'T EVEN KNOW WHO I WAS.
IT'S A TERRIBLE SHAME. SUCH A WASTE OF A BRILLIANT MIND!
POOR MOTOHIKO. HE LOOKS WORN OUT.
HE MUST BE WORRIED. THERE'S TALK OF SHUTTING DOWN THE PROJECT!

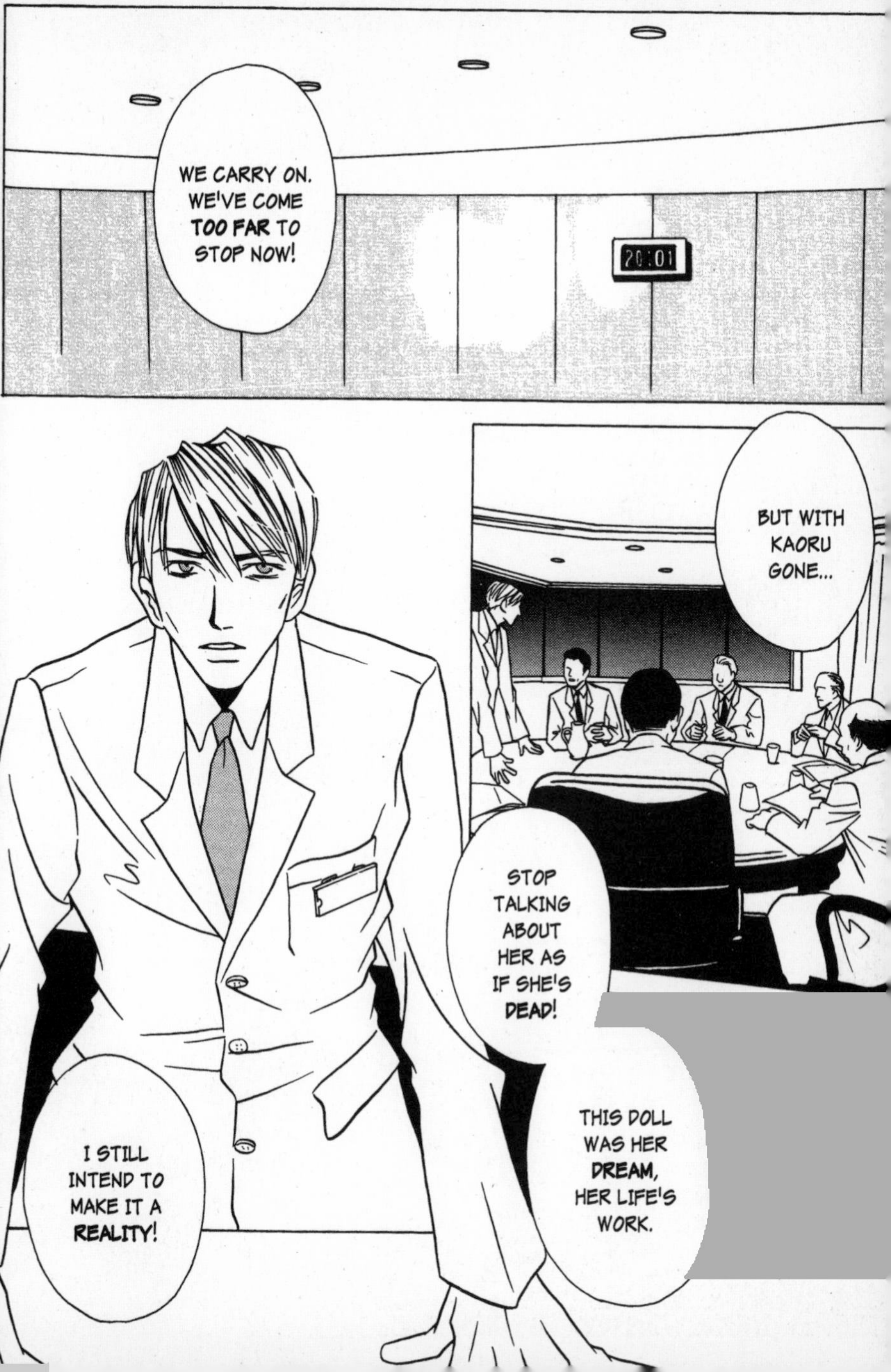
WE CARRY ON. WE'VE COME **TOO FAR** TO STOP NOW!
BUT WITH KAORU GONE...
STOP TALKING ABOUT HER AS IF SHE'S **DEAD**!
THIS DOLL WAS HER **DREAM**, HER LIFE'S WORK.
I STILL INTEND TO MAKE IT A **REALITY**!

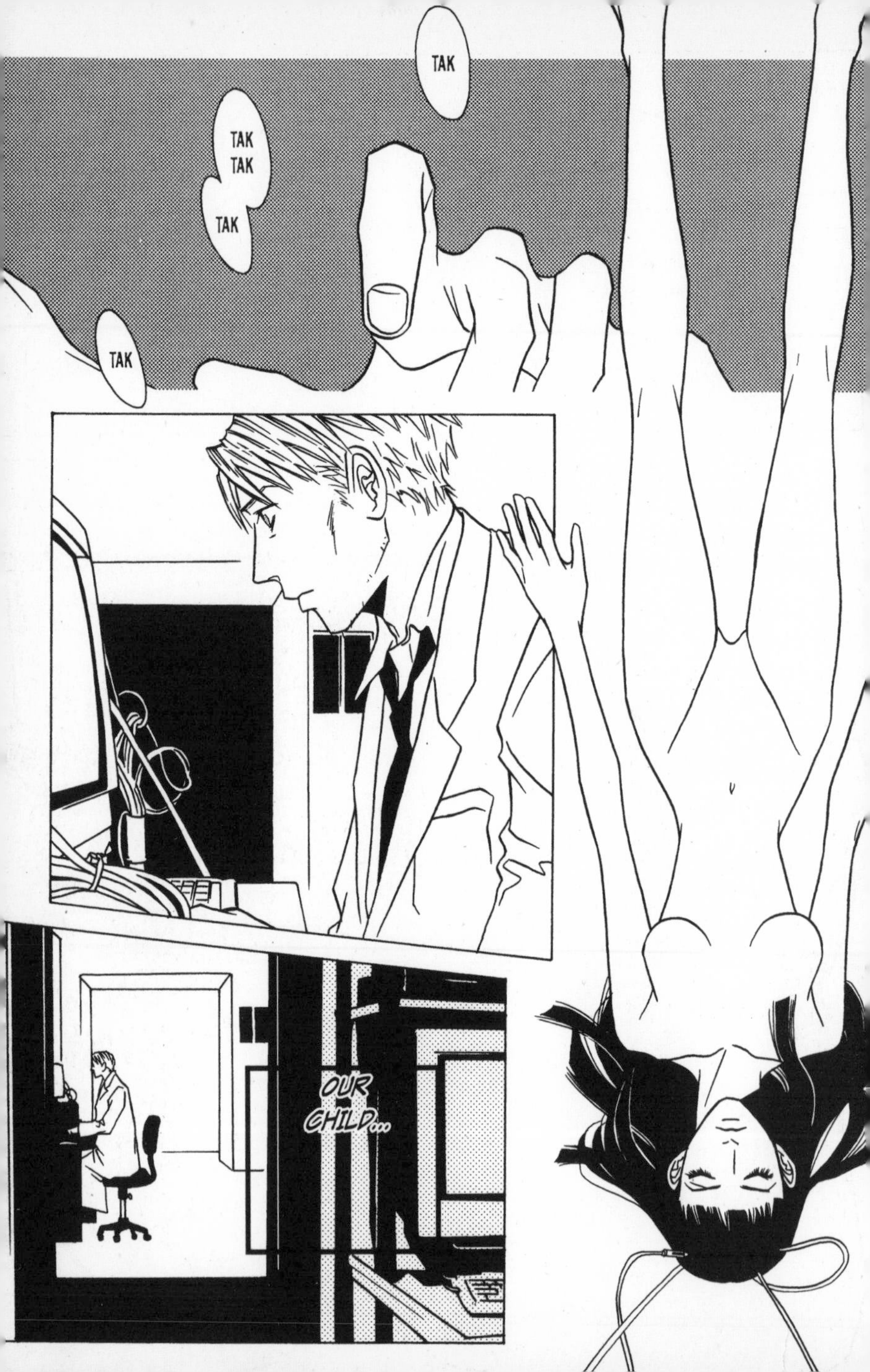

TAK
TAK
TAK
TAK
TAK
OUR CHILD...

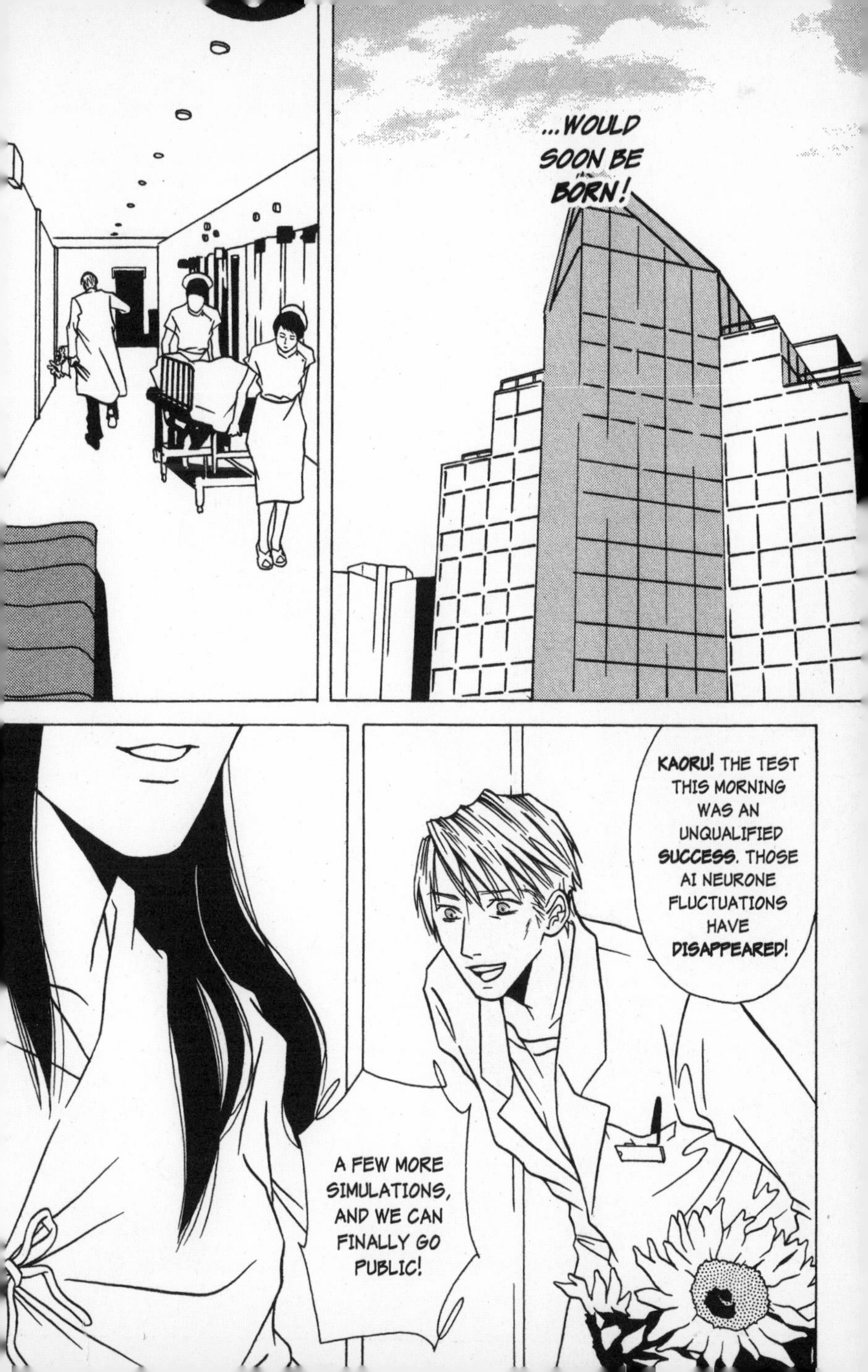
...WOULD SOON BE BORN!
KAORU! THE TEST THIS MORNING WAS AN UNQUALIFIED SUCCESS. THOSE AI NEURONE FLUCTUATIONS HAVE DISAPPEARED!
A FEW MORE SIMULATIONS, AND WE CAN FINALLY GO PUBLIC!

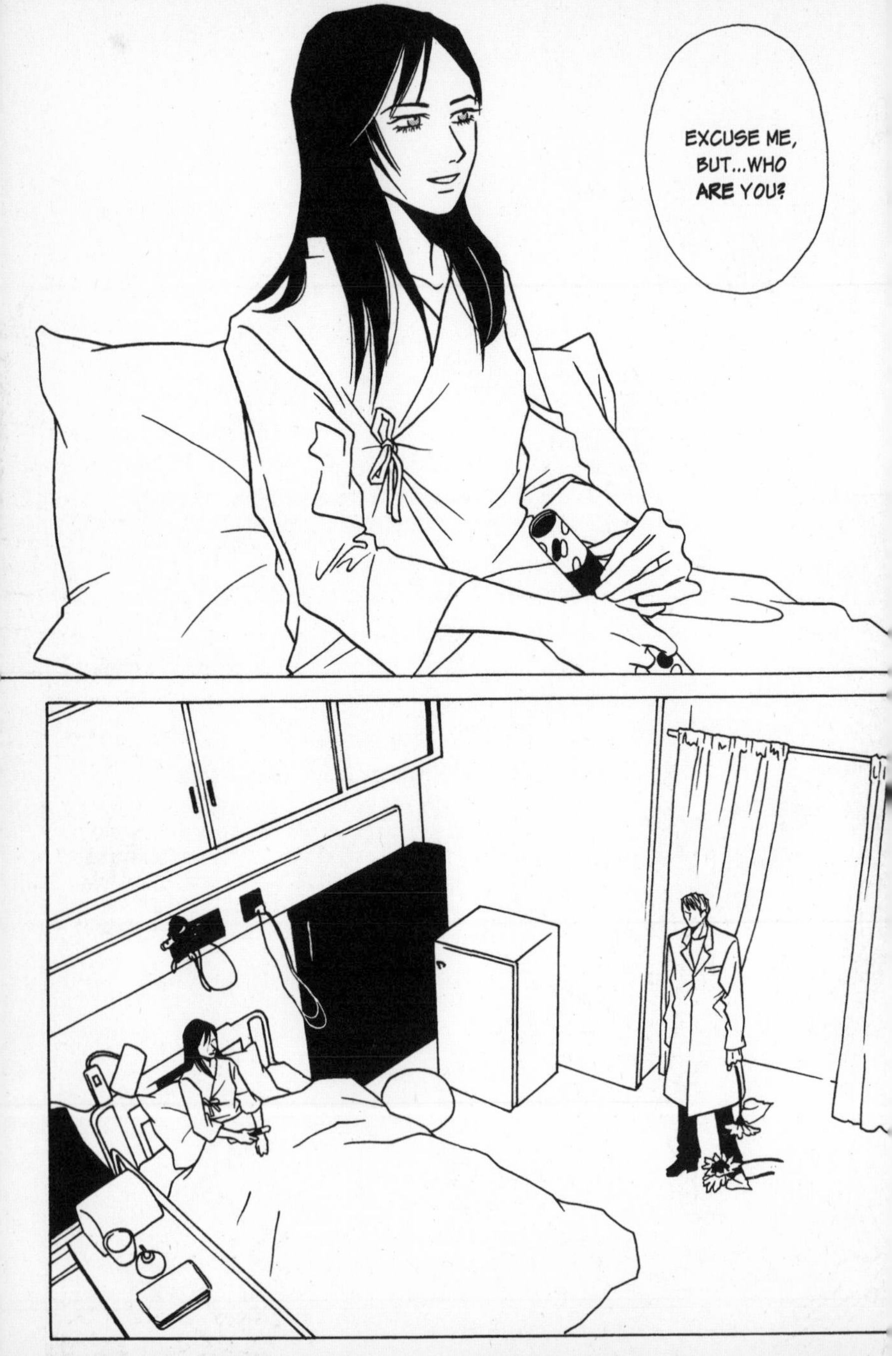
EXCUSE ME, BUT...WHO ARE YOU?

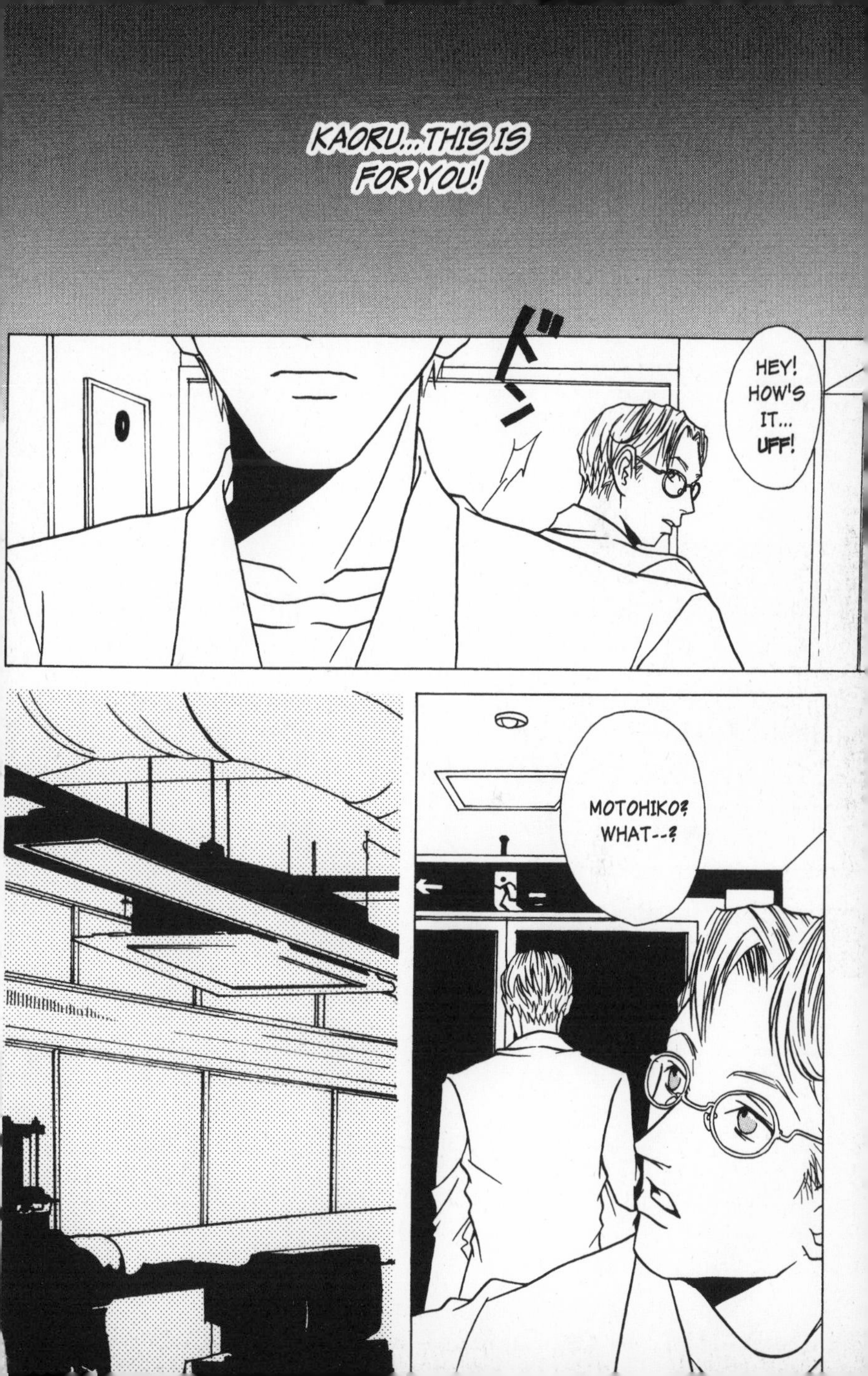
KAORU...THIS IS FOR YOU!
ドン
HEY! HOW'S IT... UFF!
MOTOHIKO? WHAT--?

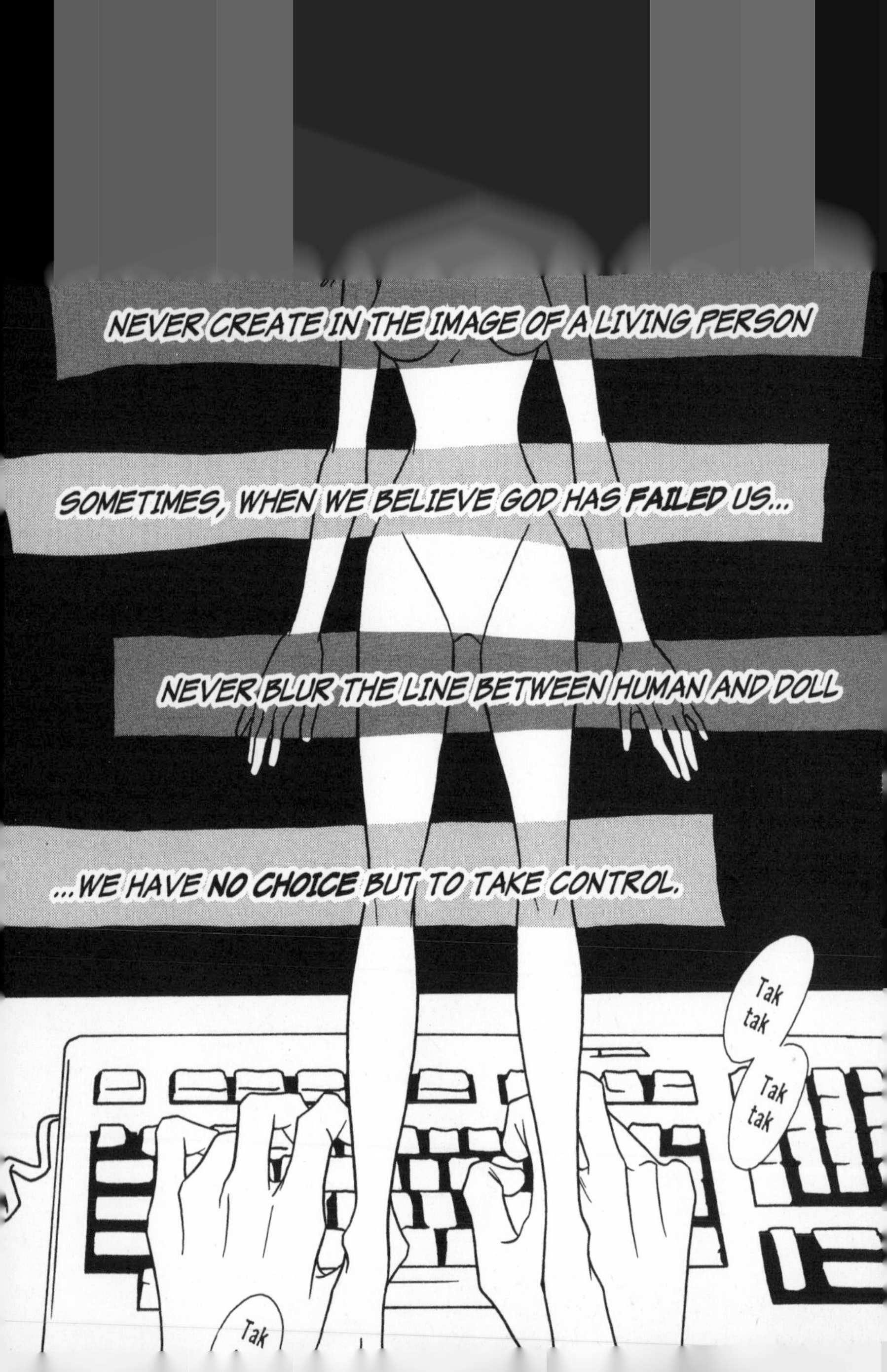
NEVER CREATE IN THE IMAGE OF A LIVING PERSON
SOMETIMES, WHEN WE BELIEVE GOD HAS FAILED US...
NEVER BLUR THE LINE BETWEEN HUMAN AND DOLL
...WE HAVE NO CHOICE BUT TO TAKE CONTROL.
Tak tak
Tak tak
Tak

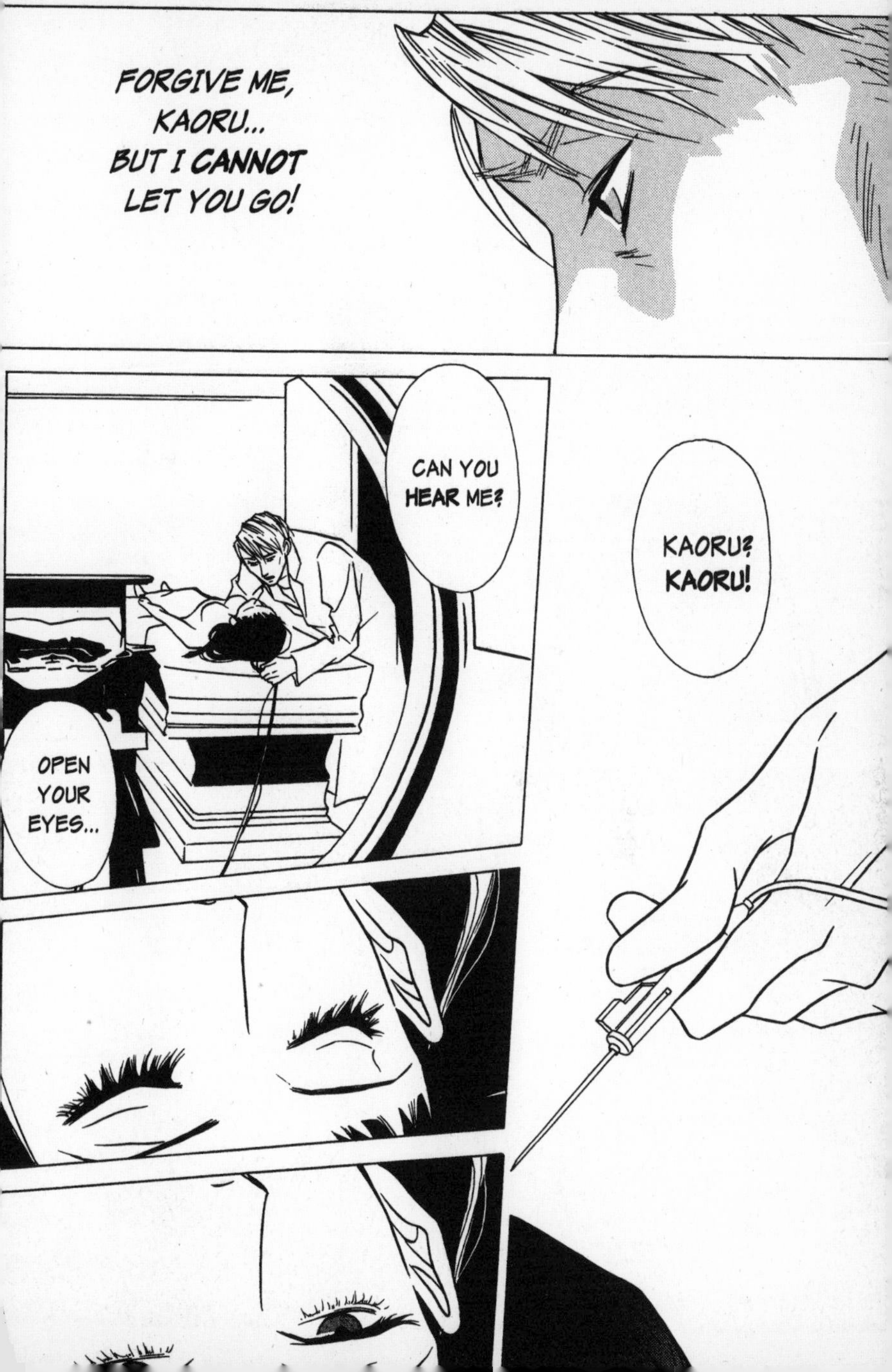
FORGIVE ME, KAORU... BUT I CANNOT LET YOU GO!
KAORU? KAORU!
CAN YOU HEAR ME?
OPEN YOUR EYES...

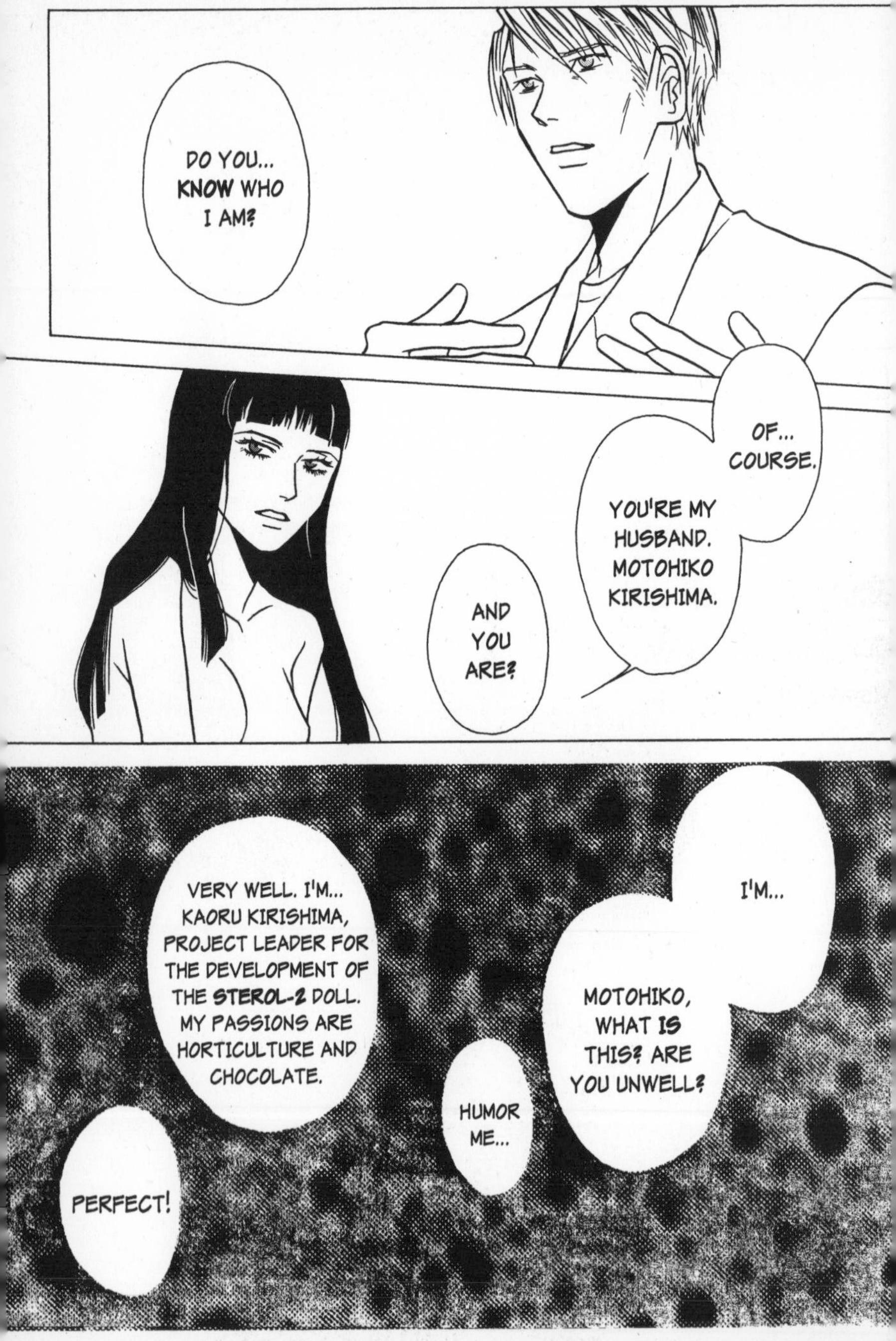
DO YOU... KNOW WHO I AM?
OF... COURSE.
YOU'RE MY HUSBAND. MOTOHIKO KIRISHIMA.
AND YOU ARE?
I'M...
MOTOHIKO, WHAT IS THIS? ARE YOU UNWELL?
HUMOR ME...
VERY WELL. I'M... KAORU KIRISHIMA, PROJECT LEADER FOR THE DEVELOPMENT OF THE STEROL-2 DOLL. MY PASSIONS ARE HORTICULTURE AND CHOCOLATE.
PERFECT!

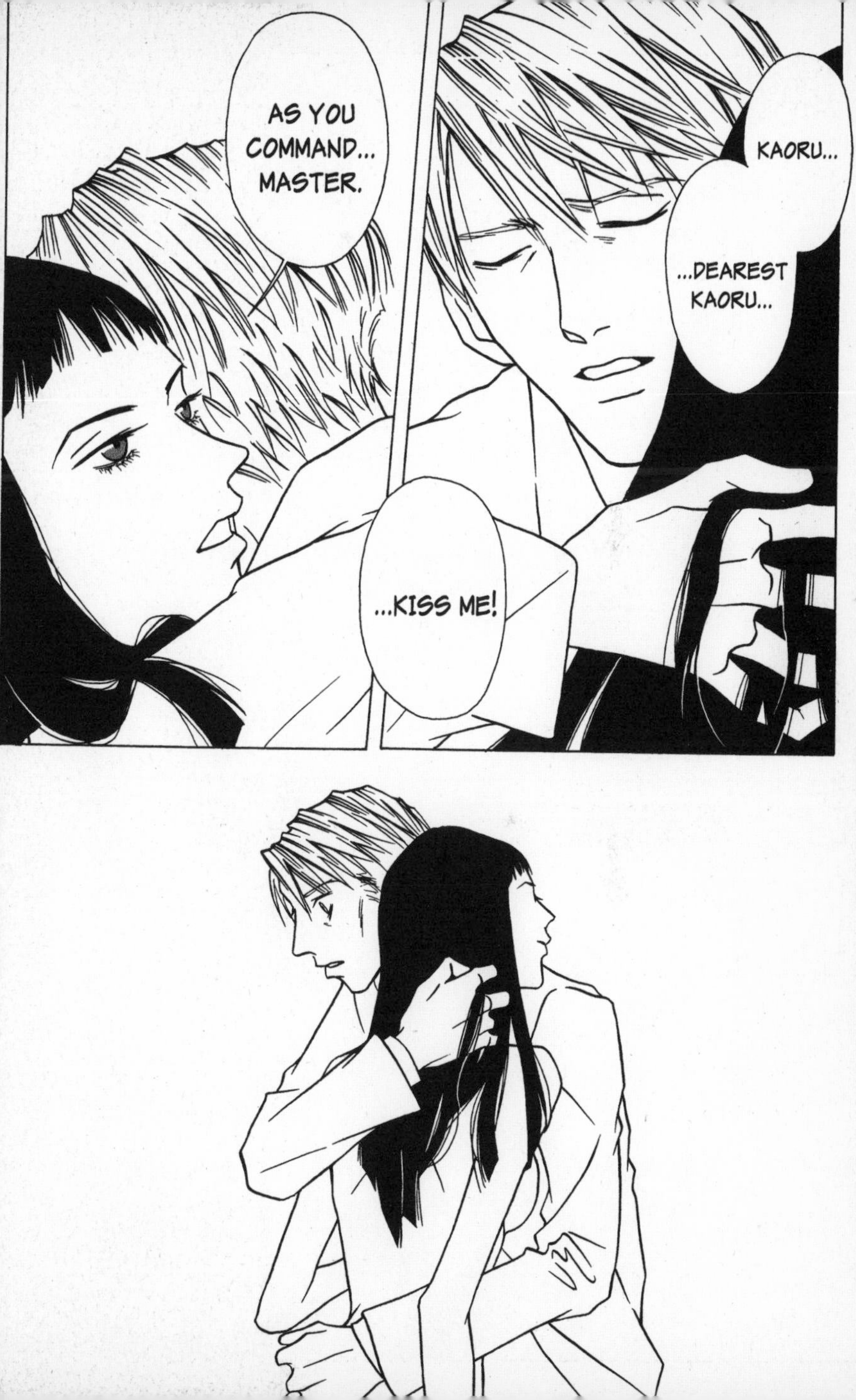
KAORU...
...DEAREST KAORU...
...KISS ME!
AS YOU COMMAND... MASTER.

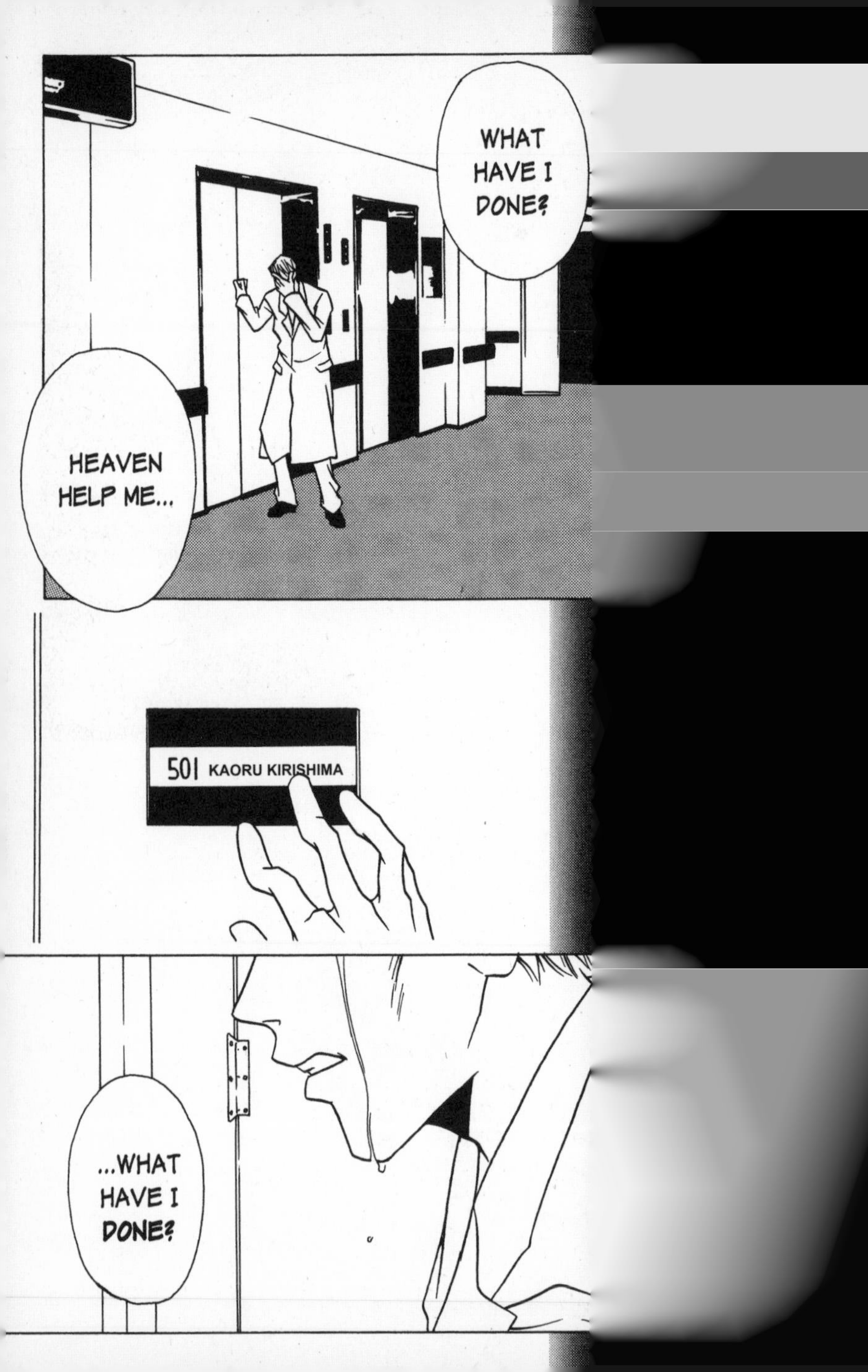
WHAT HAVE I DONE?
HEAVEN HELP ME...
501 KAORU KIRISHIMA
...WHAT HAVE I DONE?

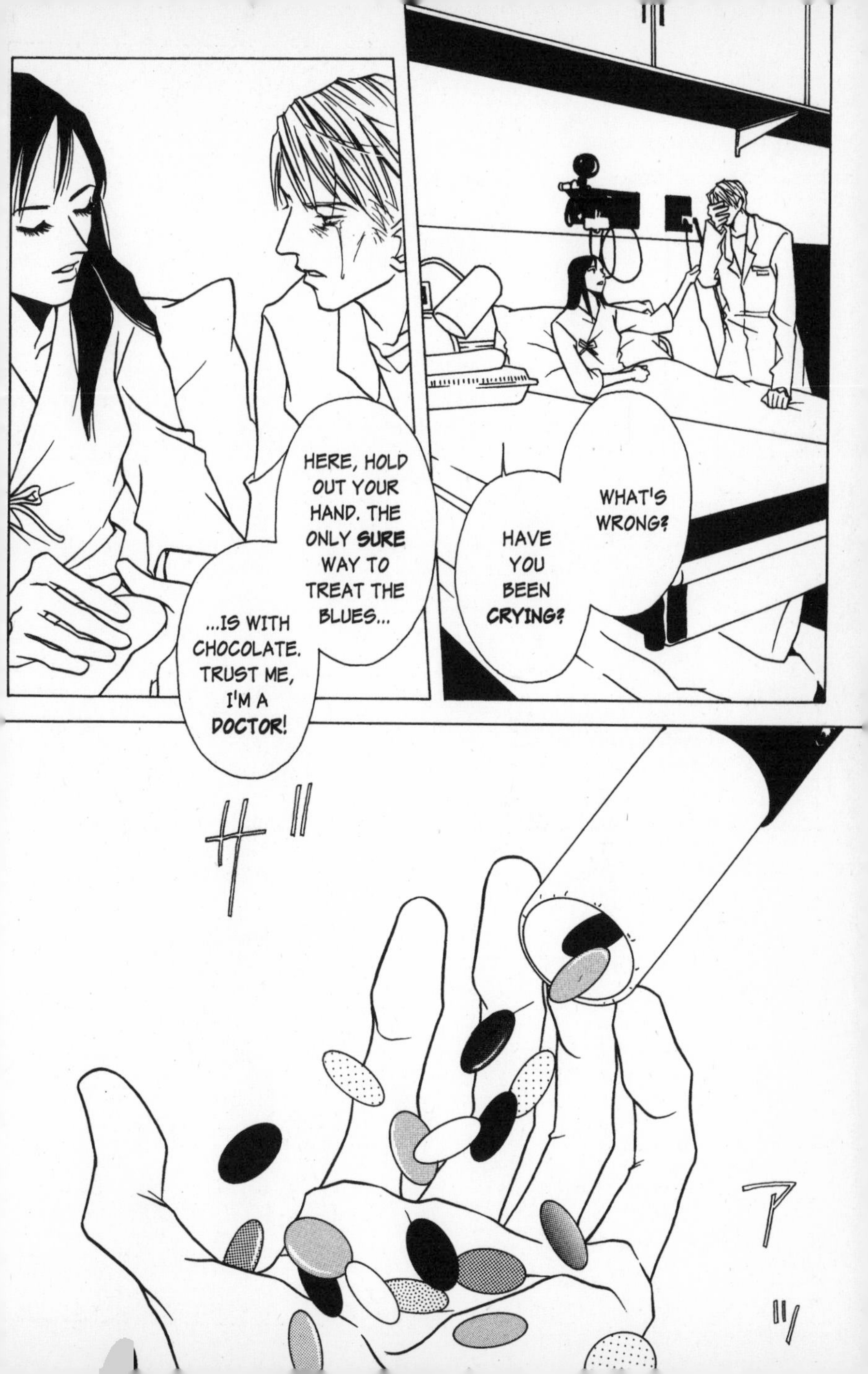
WHAT'S WRONG?
HAVE YOU BEEN CRYING?
HERE, HOLD OUT YOUR HAND. THE ONLY **SURE** WAY TO TREAT THE BLUES...
...IS WITH CHOCOLATE. TRUST ME, I'M A **DOCTOR**!

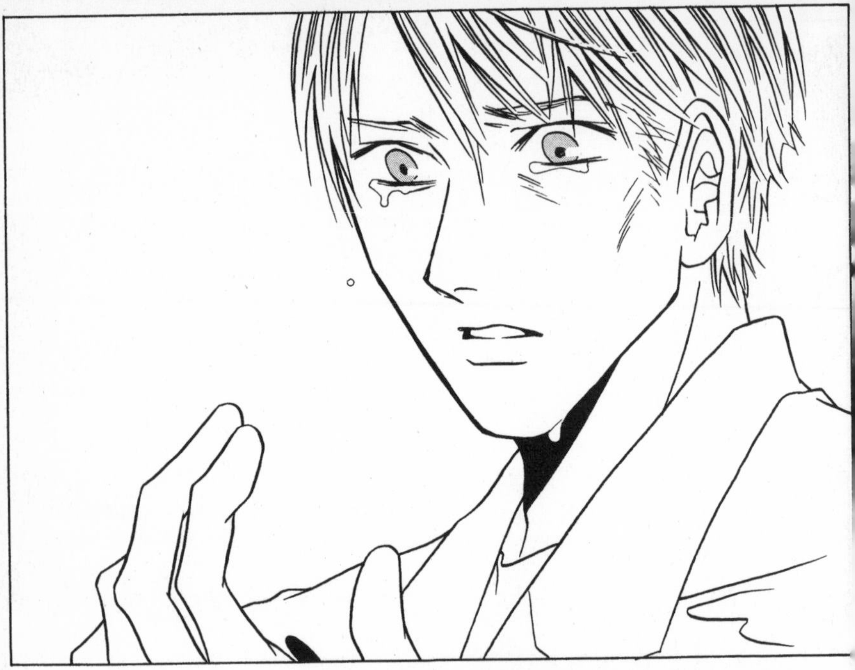

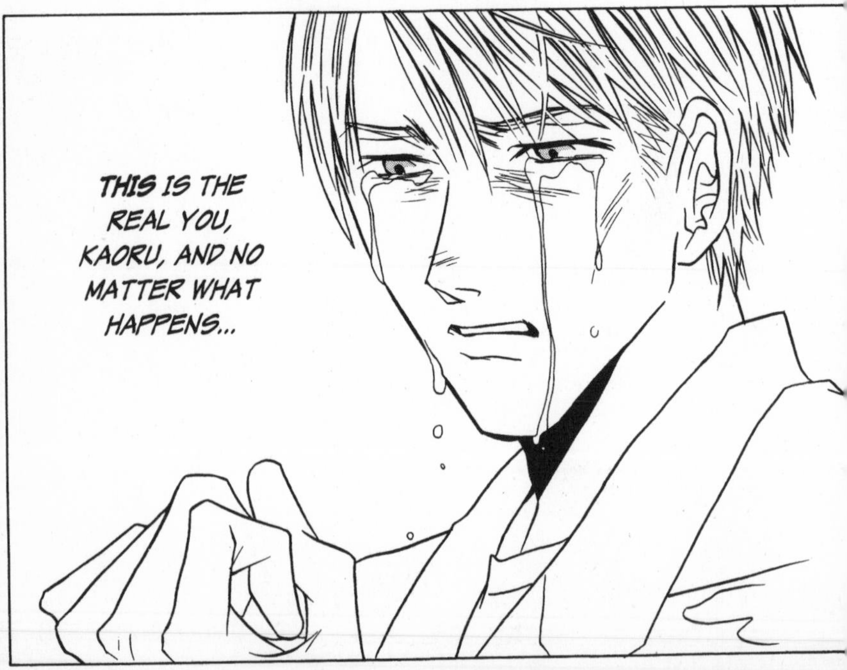
THIS IS THE REAL YOU, KAORU, AND NO MATTER WHAT HAPPENS...

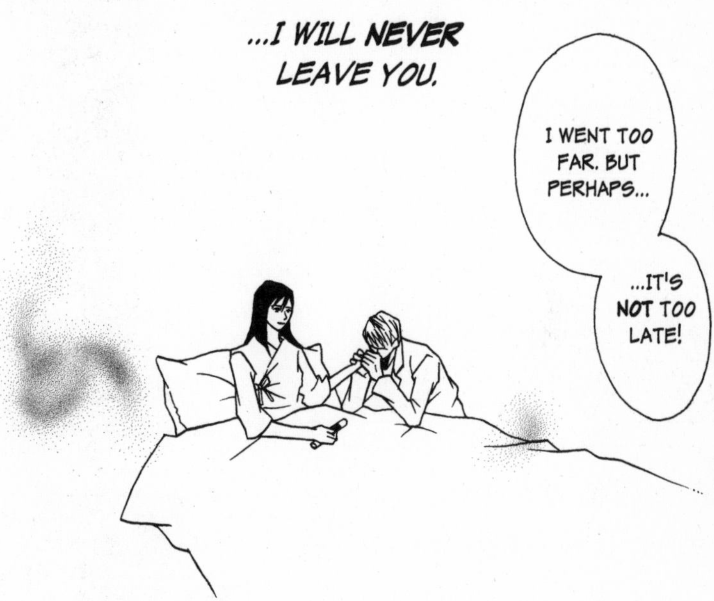
...I WILL NEVER LEAVE YOU.
I WENT TOO FAR. BUT PERHAPS...
...IT'S NOT TOO LATE!

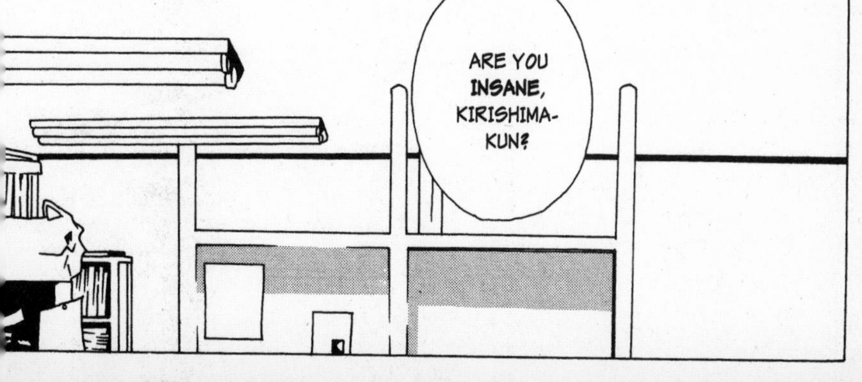
ARE YOU INSANE, KIRISHIMA-KUN?

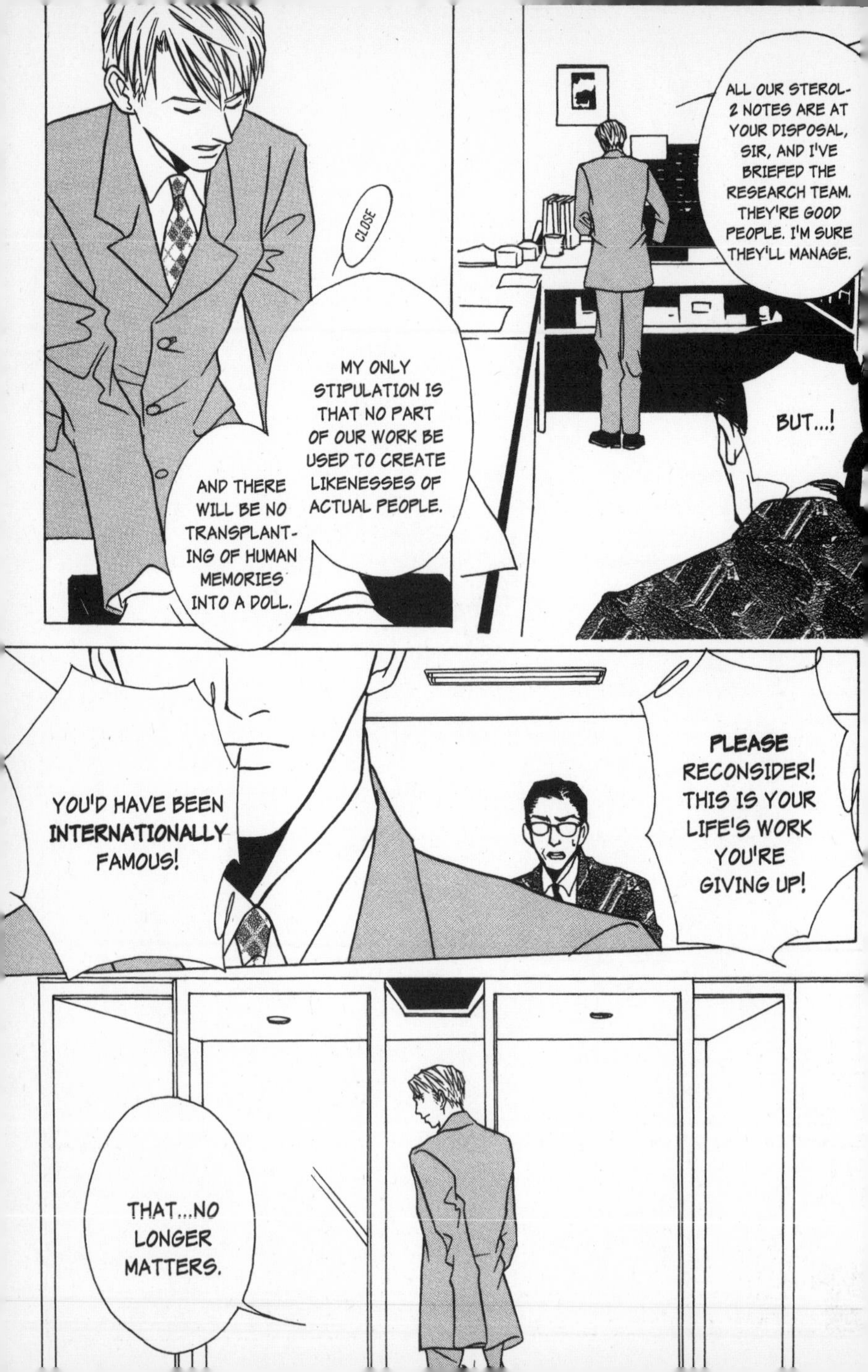
ALL OUR STEROL-2 NOTES ARE AT YOUR DISPOSAL, SIR, AND I'VE BRIEFED THE RESEARCH TEAM. THEY'RE GOOD PEOPLE. I'M SURE THEY'LL MANAGE.
BUT...!
CLOSE
MY ONLY STIPULATION IS THAT NO PART OF OUR WORK BE USED TO CREATE LIKENESSES OF ACTUAL PEOPLE.
AND THERE WILL BE NO TRANSPLANTING OF HUMAN MEMORIES INTO A DOLL.
PLEASE RECONSIDER! THIS IS YOUR LIFE'S WORK YOU'RE GIVING UP!
YOU'D HAVE BEEN INTERNATIONALLY FAMOUS!
THAT...NO LONGER MATTERS.

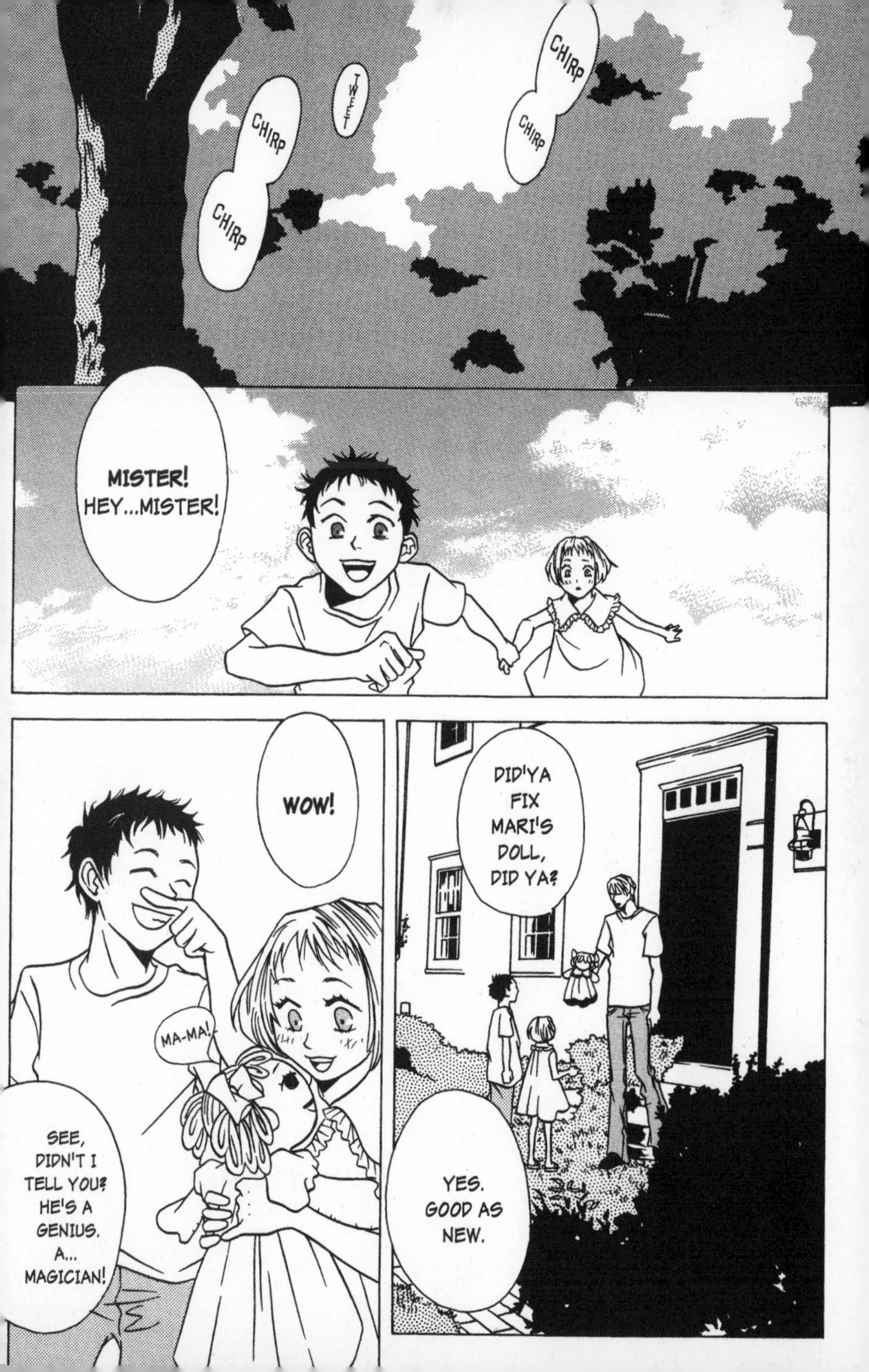
CHIRP
CHIRP
TWEET
CHIRP
CHIRP
MISTER! HEY...MISTER!
DID'YA FIX MARI'S DOLL, DID YA?
YES. GOOD AS NEW.
WOW!
MA-MA!
SEE, DIDN'T I TELL YOU? HE'S A GENIUS. A... MAGICIAN!

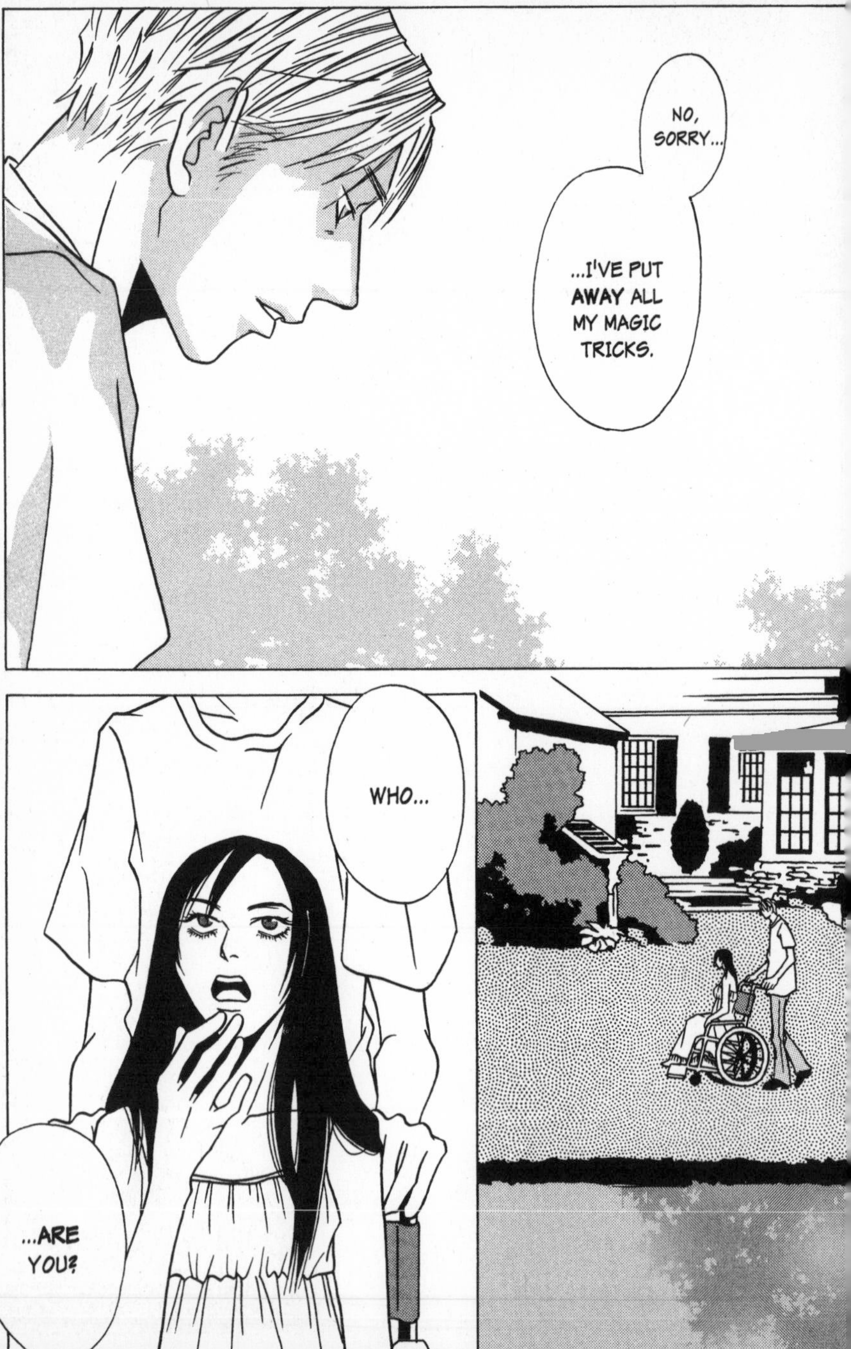
NO, SORRY...
...I'VE PUT AWAY ALL MY MAGIC TRICKS.
WHO...
...ARE YOU?

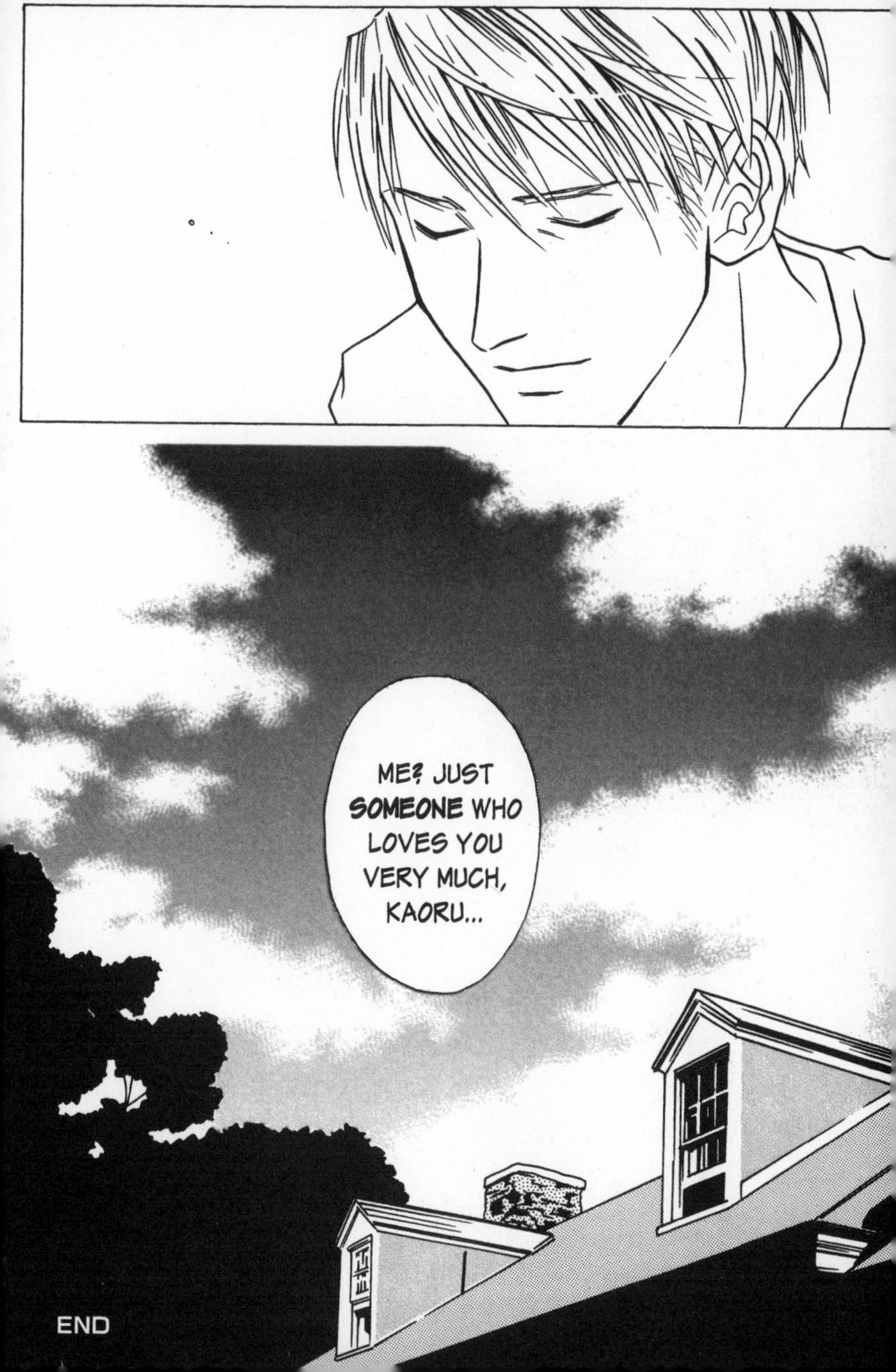
ME? JUST **SOMEONE** WHO LOVES YOU VERY MUCH, KAORU...
END

LIST 5

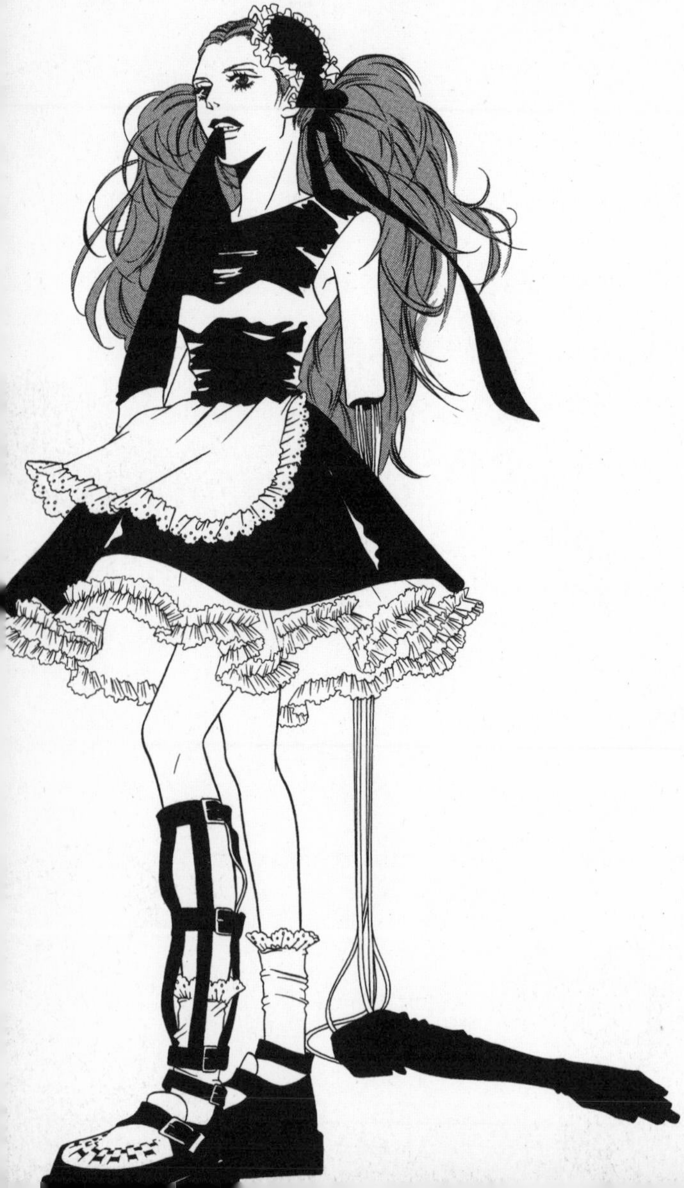

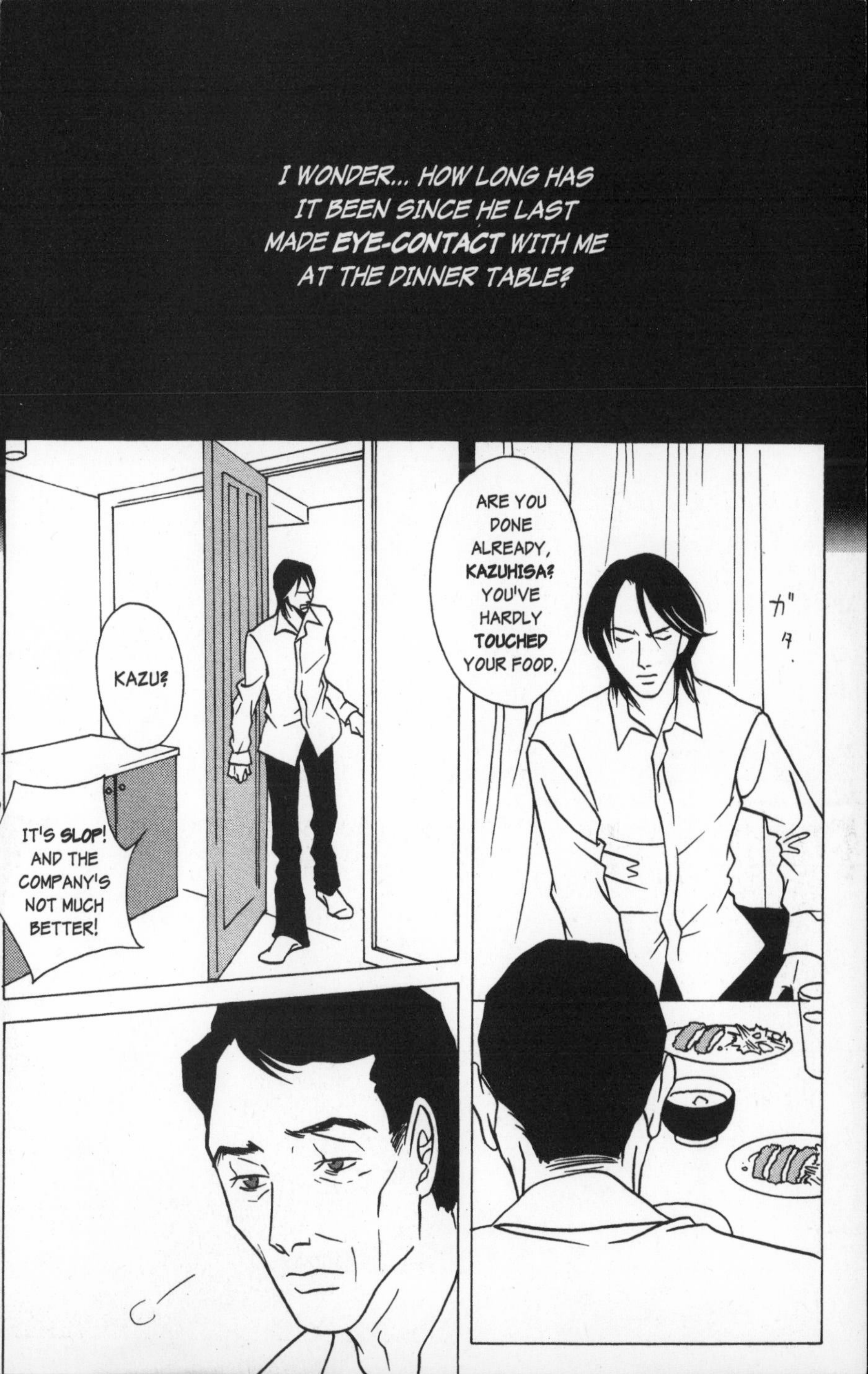
I WONDER... HOW LONG HAS IT BEEN SINCE HE LAST MADE **EYE-CONTACT** WITH ME AT THE DINNER TABLE?
ARE YOU DONE ALREADY, **KAZUHISA**? YOU'VE HARDLY **TOUCHED** YOUR FOOD.
ガタ
KAZU?
IT'S **SLOP**! AND THE COMPANY'S NOT MUCH BETTER!

5. AYAKO

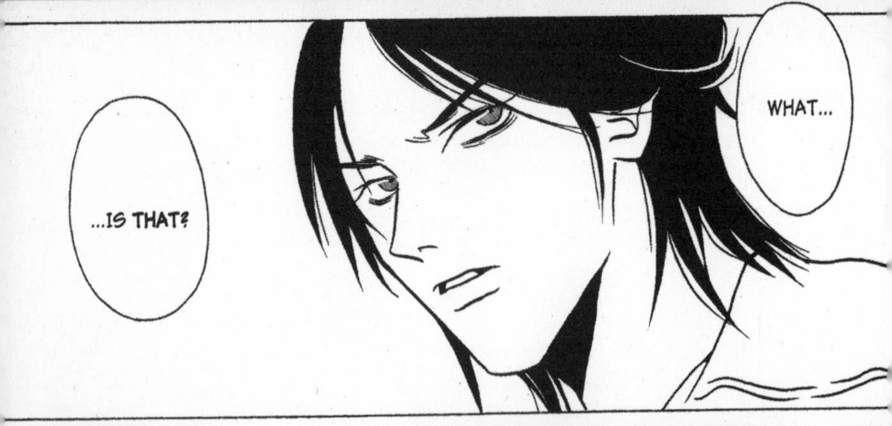
WHAT...
...IS THAT?

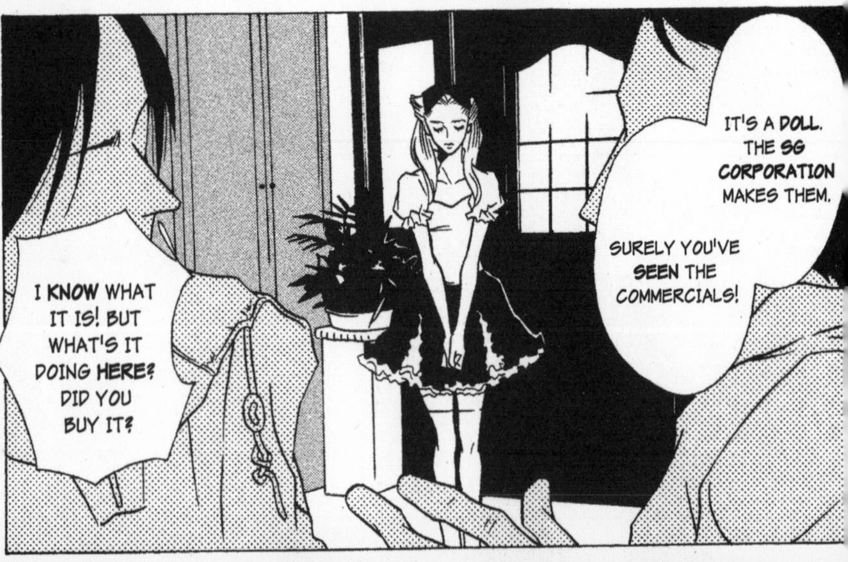
IT'S A DOLL. THE SG CORPORATION MAKES THEM.
SURELY YOU'VE SEEN THE COMMERCIALS!
I KNOW WHAT IT IS! BUT WHAT'S IT DOING HERE? DID YOU BUY IT?

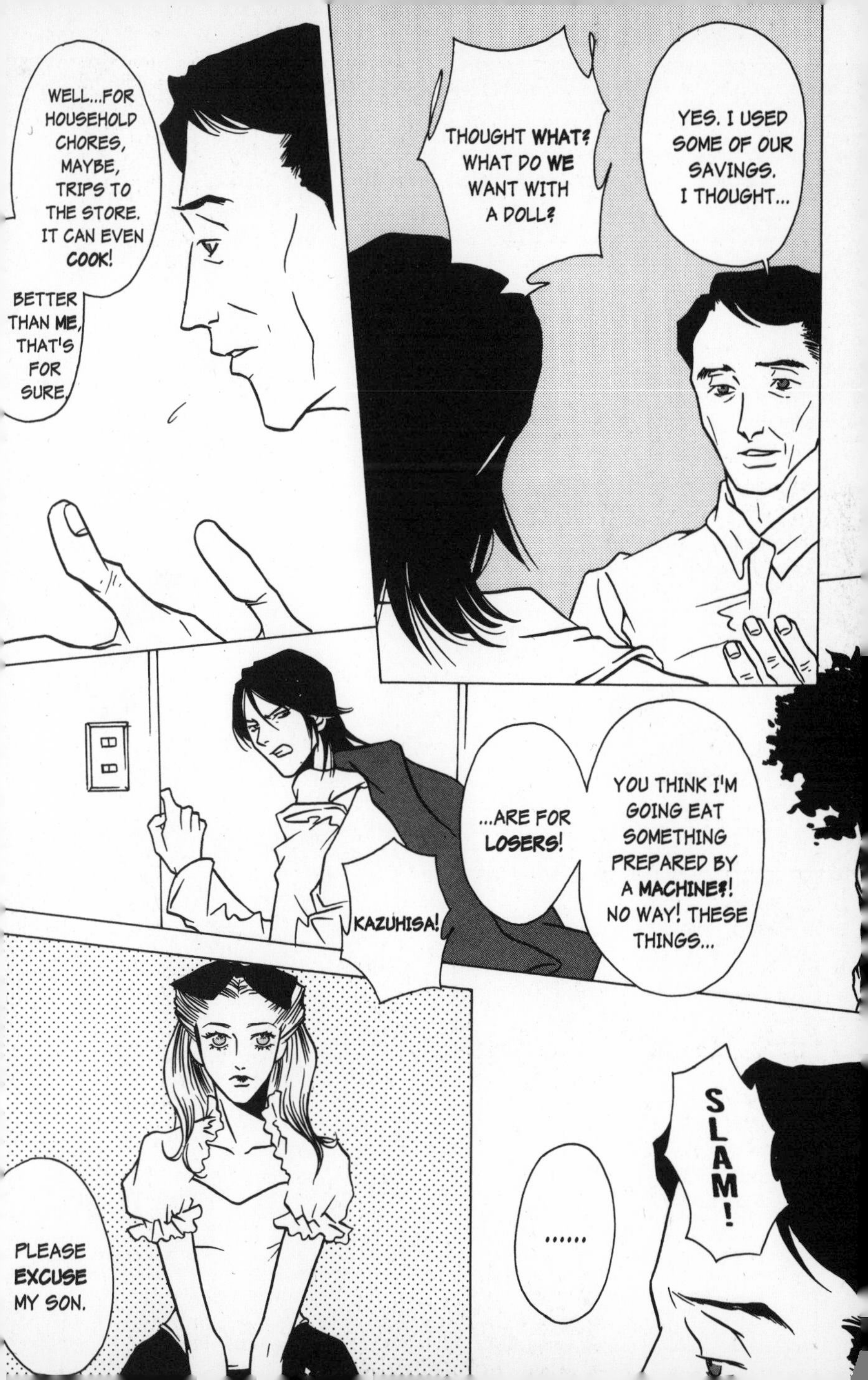
YES. I USED SOME OF OUR SAVINGS. I THOUGHT...
THOUGHT WHAT? WHAT DO WE WANT WITH A DOLL?
WELL...FOR HOUSEHOLD CHORES, MAYBE, TRIPS TO THE STORE. IT CAN EVEN COOK!
BETTER THAN ME, THAT'S FOR SURE.
YOU THINK I'M GOING EAT SOMETHING PREPARED BY A MACHINE?! NO WAY! THESE THINGS...
...ARE FOR LOSERS!
KAZUHISA!
SLAM!
......
PLEASE EXCUSE MY SON.

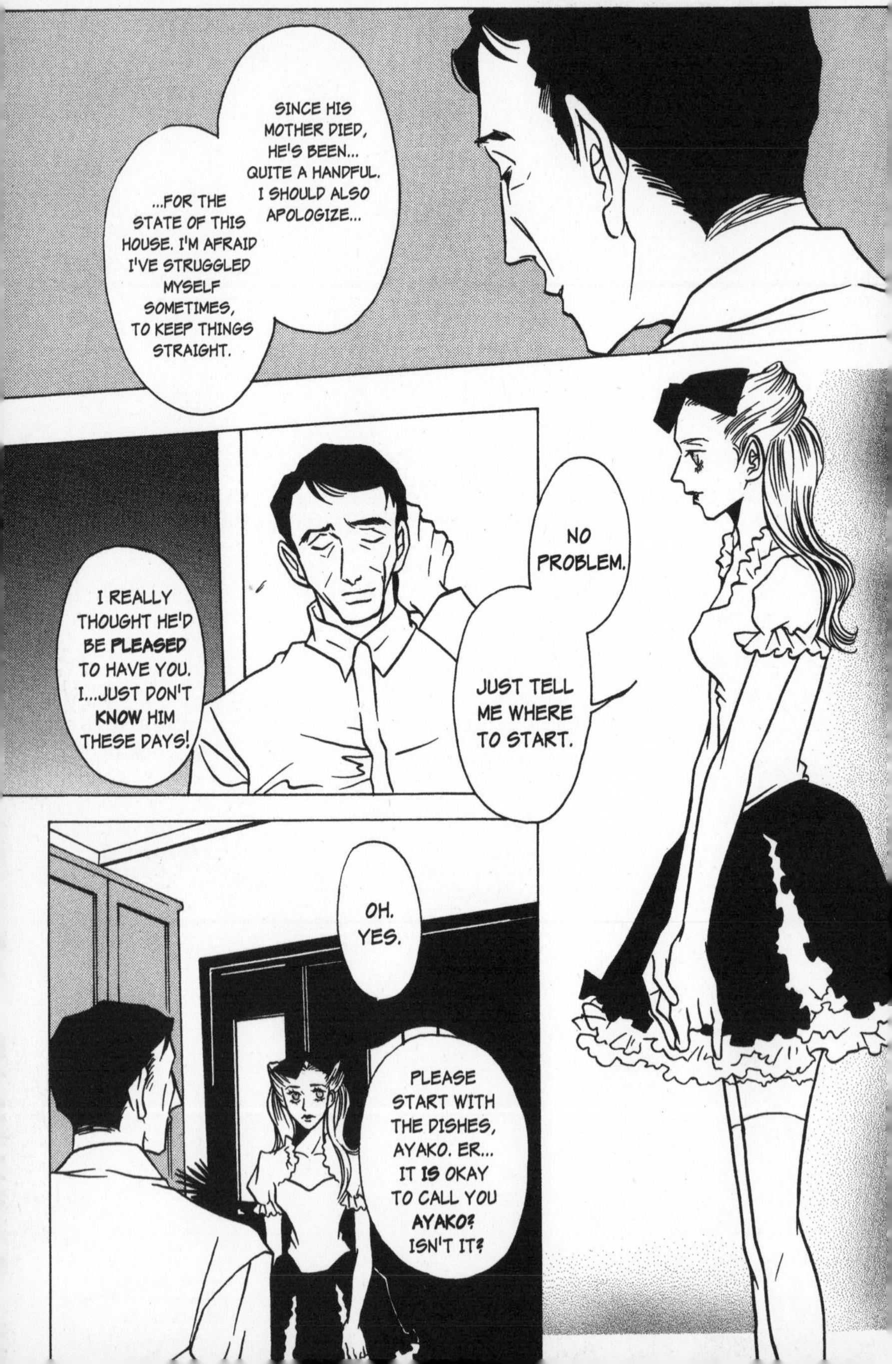
SINCE HIS MOTHER DIED, HE'S BEEN... QUITE A HANDFUL. I SHOULD ALSO APOLOGIZE...
...FOR THE STATE OF THIS HOUSE. I'M AFRAID I'VE STRUGGLED MYSELF SOMETIMES, TO KEEP THINGS STRAIGHT.
NO PROBLEM.
JUST TELL ME WHERE TO START.
I REALLY THOUGHT HE'D BE **PLEASED** TO HAVE YOU. I...JUST DON'T **KNOW** HIM THESE DAYS!
OH. YES.
PLEASE START WITH THE DISHES, AYAKO. ER... IT **IS** OKAY TO CALL YOU **AYAKO?** ISN'T IT?

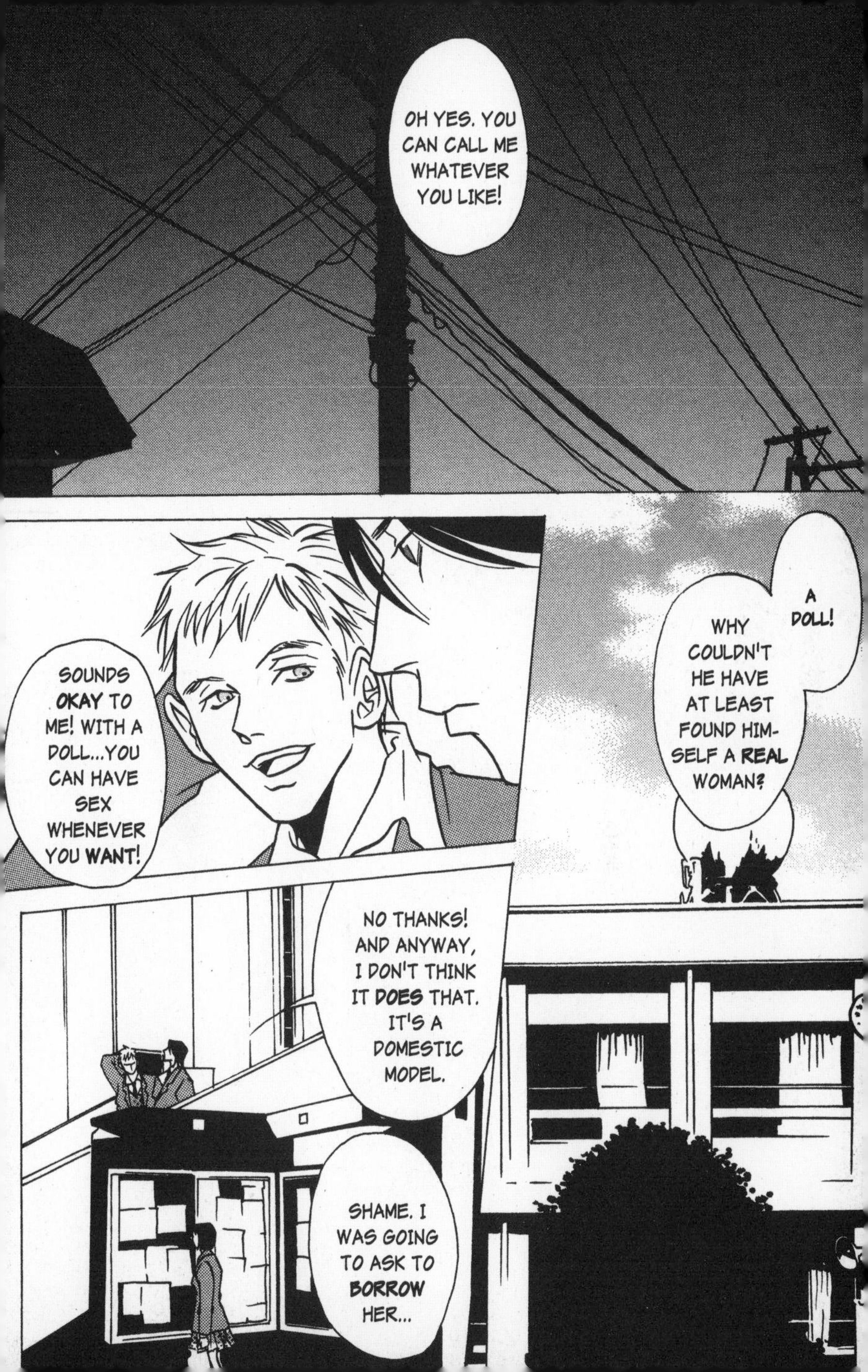
OH YES. YOU CAN CALL ME WHATEVER YOU LIKE!
A DOLL!
WHY COULDN'T HE HAVE AT LEAST FOUND HIM-SELF A REAL WOMAN?
SOUNDS OKAY TO ME! WITH A DOLL...YOU CAN HAVE SEX WHENEVER YOU WANT!
NO THANKS! AND ANYWAY, I DON'T THINK IT DOES THAT. IT'S A DOMESTIC MODEL.
SHAME. I WAS GOING TO ASK TO BORROW HER...

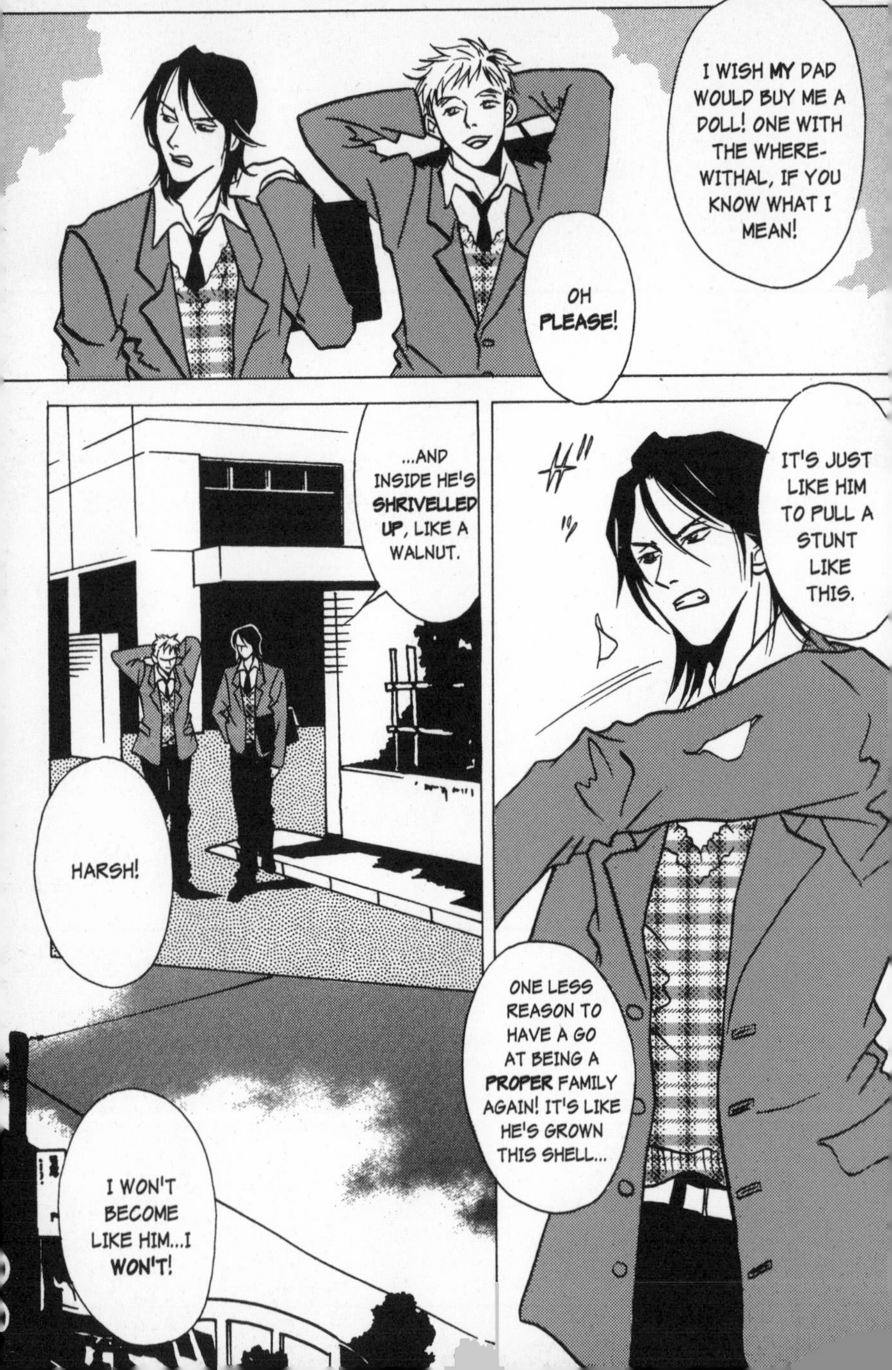
I WISH MY DAD WOULD BUY ME A DOLL! ONE WITH THE WHERE-WITHAL, IF YOU KNOW WHAT I MEAN!
OH PLEASE!
IT'S JUST LIKE HIM TO PULL A STUNT LIKE THIS.
ONE LESS REASON TO HAVE A GO AT BEING A PROPER FAMILY AGAIN! IT'S LIKE HE'S GROWN THIS SHELL...
...AND INSIDE HE'S SHRIVELLED UP, LIKE A WALNUT.
HARSH!
I WON'T BECOME LIKE HIM...I WON'T!

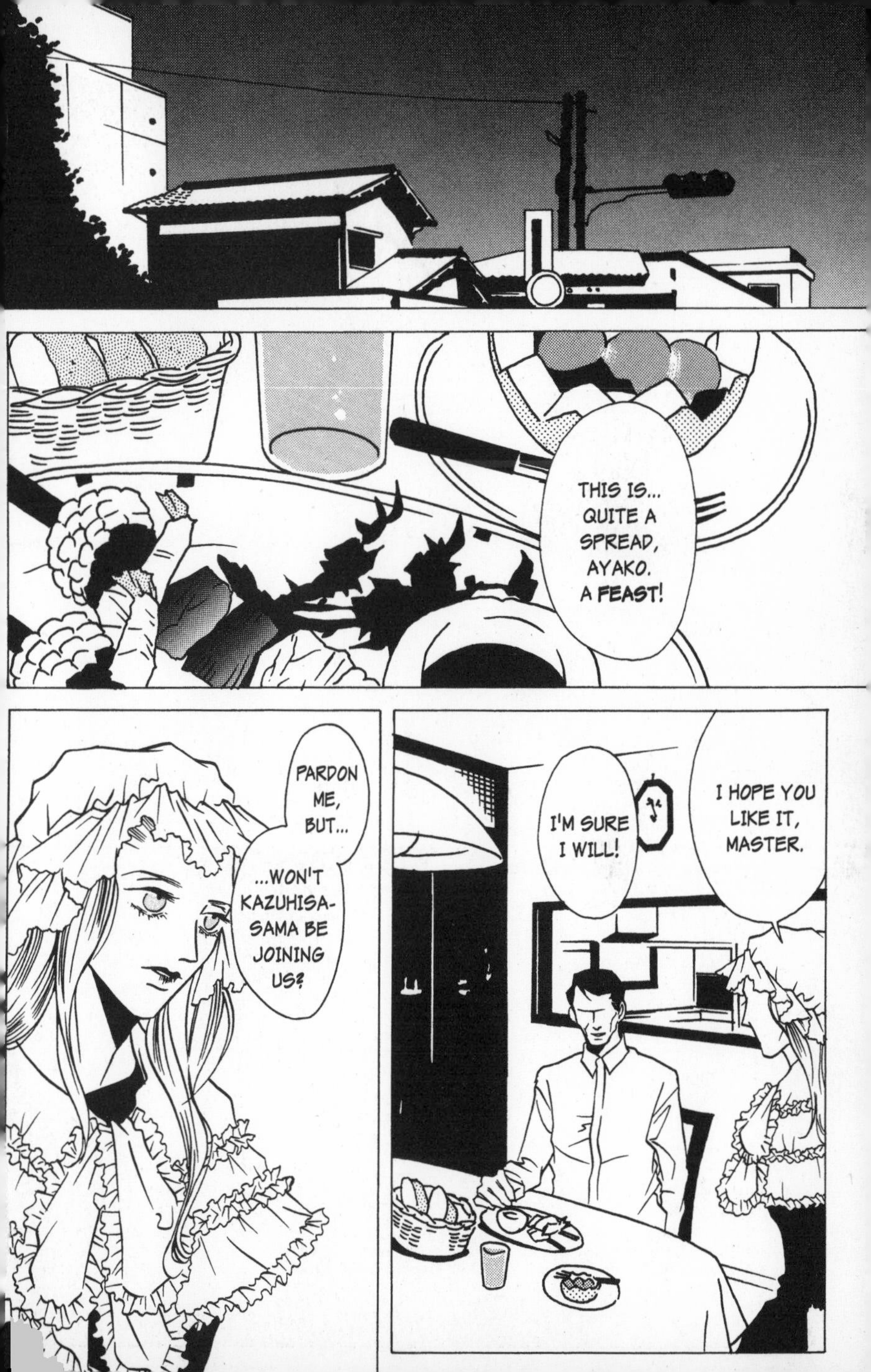
THIS IS... QUITE A SPREAD, AYAKO. A FEAST!
I HOPE YOU LIKE IT, MASTER.
I'M SURE I WILL!
PARDON ME, BUT...
...WON'T KAZUHISA-SAMA BE JOINING US?

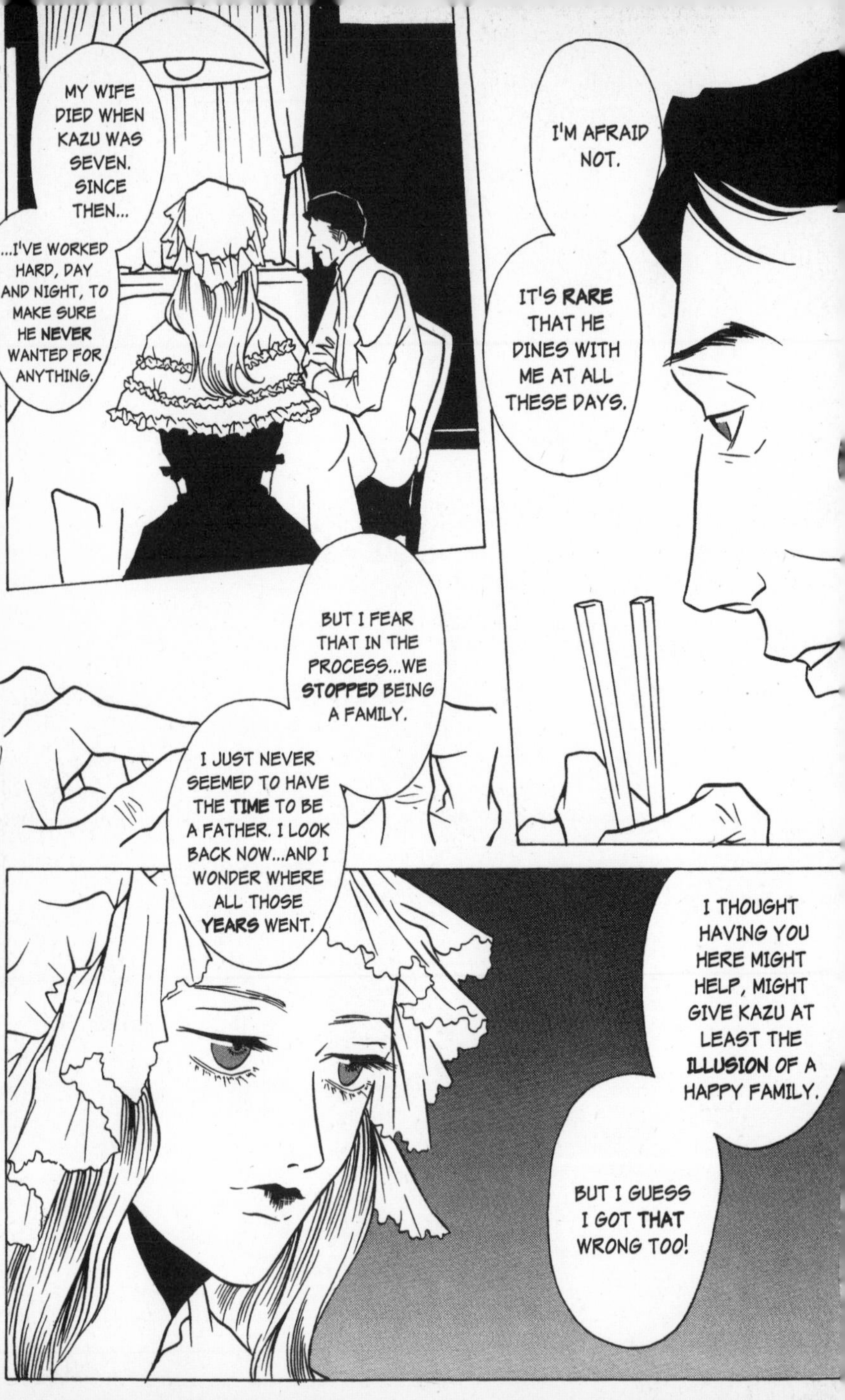
I'M AFRAID NOT.
IT'S **RARE** THAT HE DINES WITH ME AT ALL THESE DAYS.
MY WIFE DIED WHEN KAZU WAS SEVEN. SINCE THEN...
...I'VE WORKED HARD, DAY AND NIGHT, TO MAKE SURE HE **NEVER** WANTED FOR ANYTHING.
BUT I FEAR THAT IN THE PROCESS...WE **STOPPED** BEING A FAMILY.
I JUST NEVER SEEMED TO HAVE THE **TIME** TO BE A FATHER. I LOOK BACK NOW...AND I WONDER WHERE ALL THOSE **YEARS** WENT.
I THOUGHT HAVING YOU HERE MIGHT HELP, MIGHT GIVE KAZU AT LEAST THE **ILLUSION** OF A HAPPY FAMILY.
BUT I GUESS I GOT **THAT** WRONG TOO!

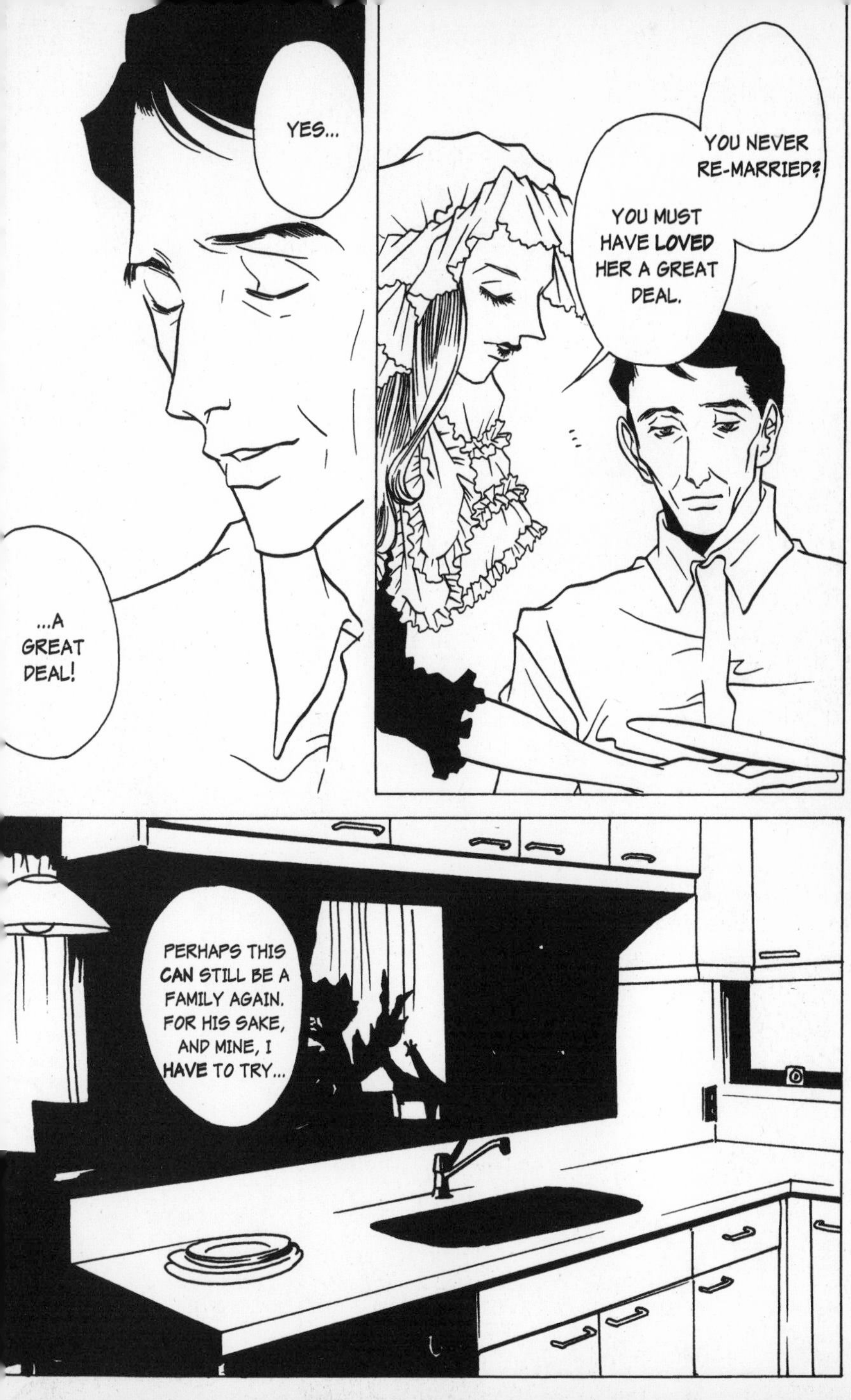
YOU NEVER RE-MARRIED?
YOU MUST HAVE **LOVED** HER A GREAT DEAL.
YES...
...A GREAT DEAL!
PERHAPS THIS **CAN** STILL BE A FAMILY AGAIN. FOR HIS SAKE, AND MINE, I **HAVE** TO TRY...

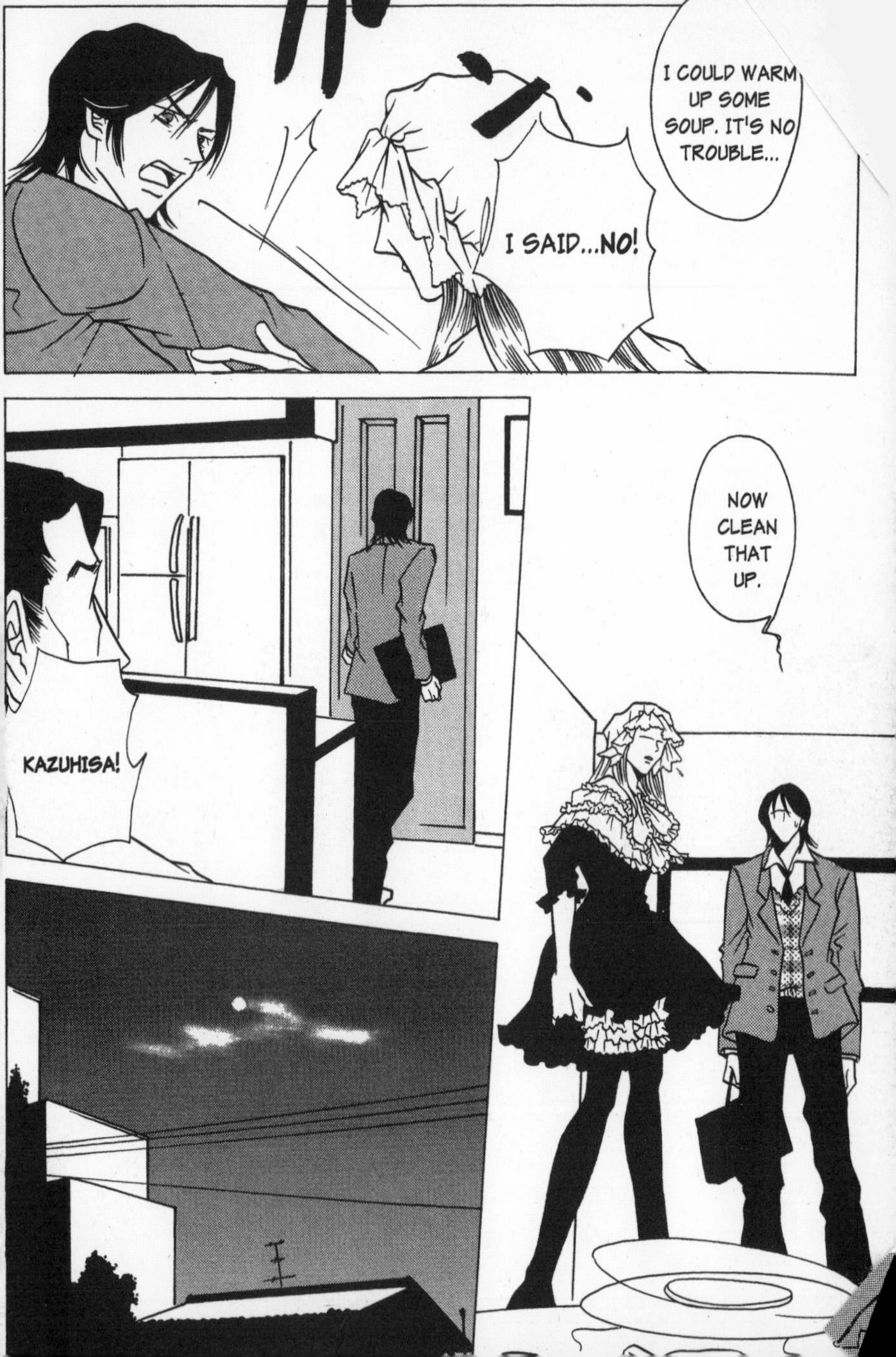
I COULD WARM UP SOME SOUP. IT'S NO TROUBLE...
パ
I SAID...NO!
NOW CLEAN THAT UP.
KAZUHISA!

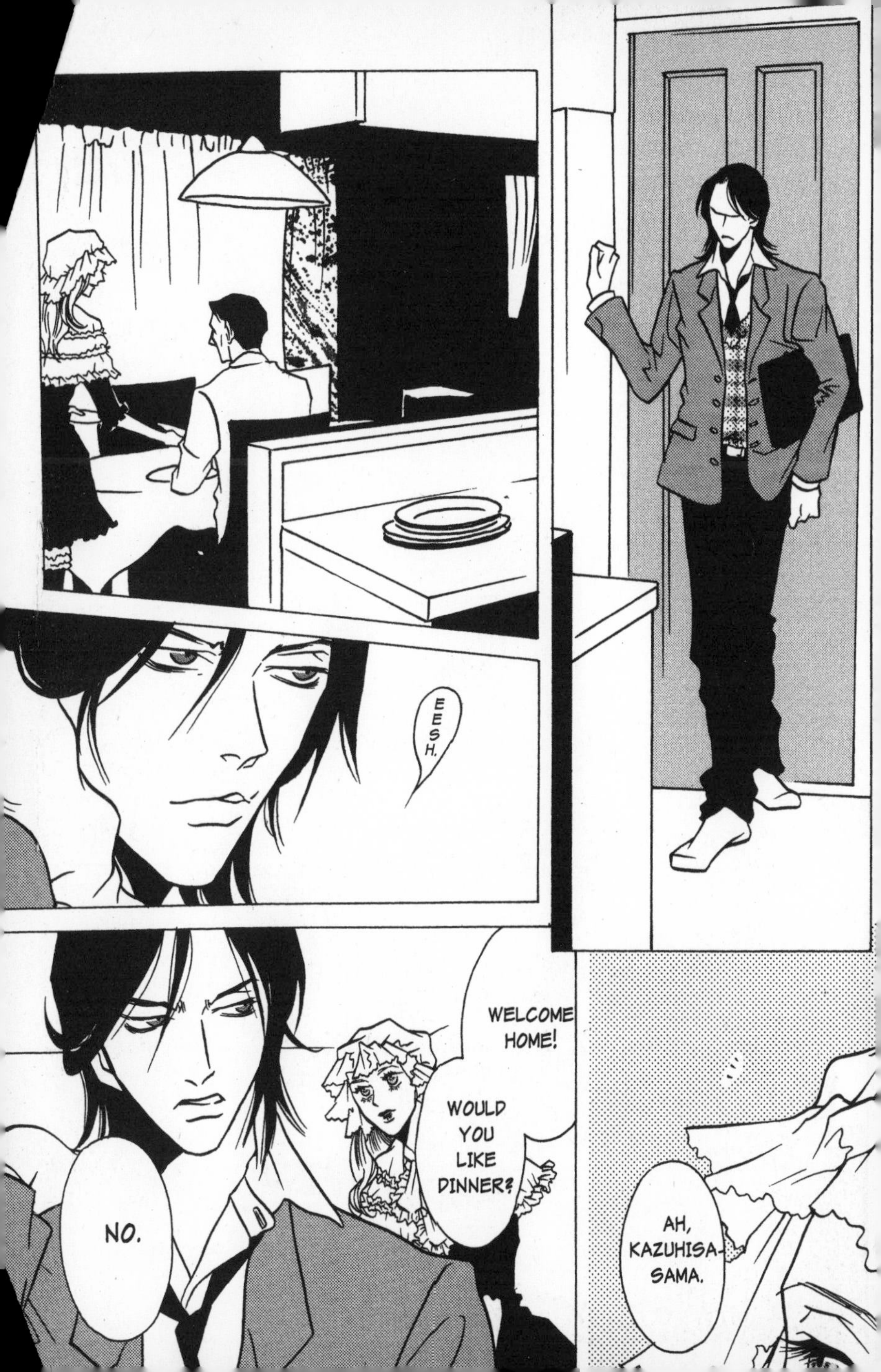
EESH.
AH, KAZUHISA-SAMA.
WELCOME HOME!
WOULD YOU LIKE DINNER?
NO.

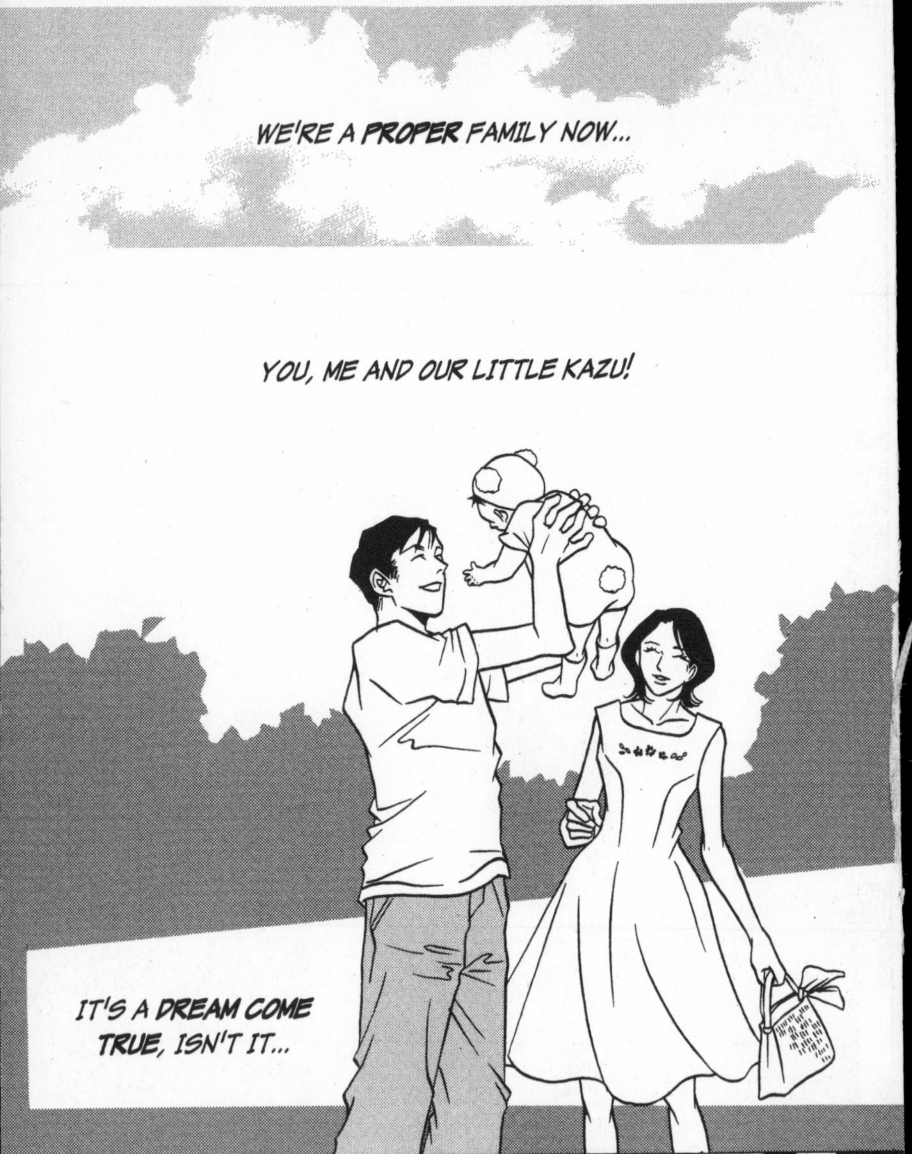
WE'RE A PROPER FAMILY NOW...
YOU, ME AND OUR LITTLE KAZU!
IT'S A DREAM COME TRUE, ISN'T IT...
...MY DARLING?

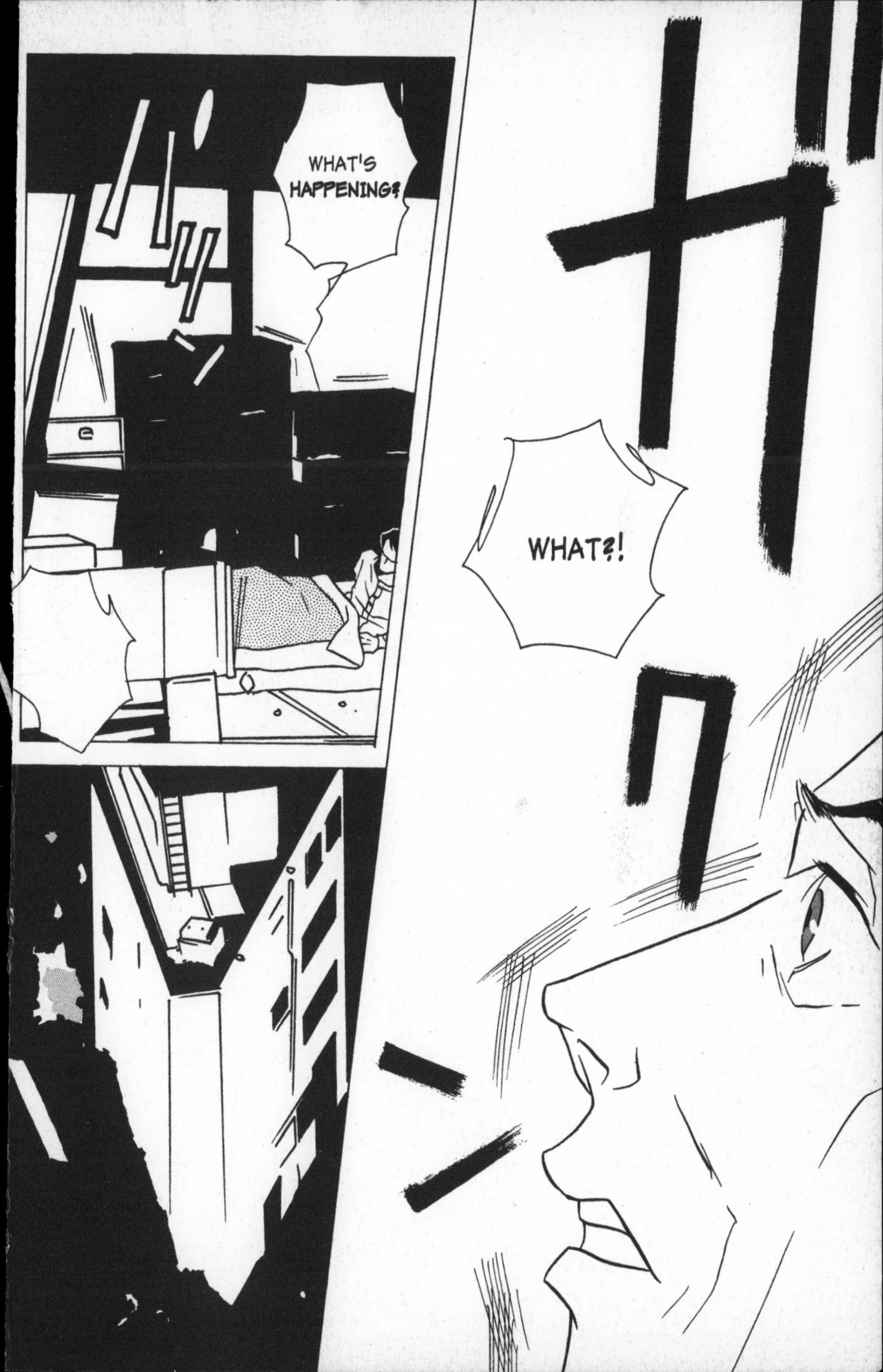
WHAT?!
WHAT'S HAPPENING?

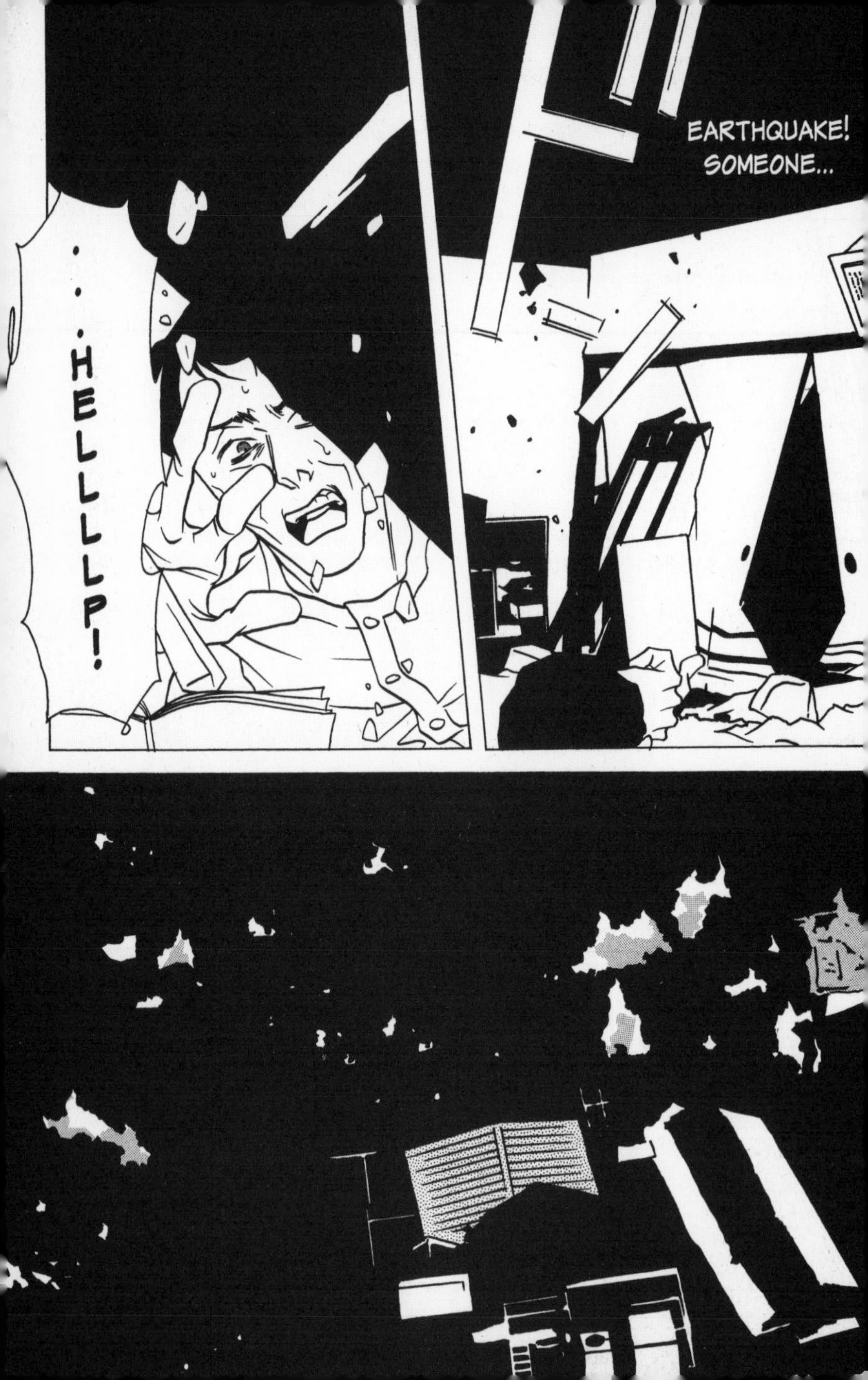
EARTHQUAKE! SOMEONE...
...HELLLLLP!

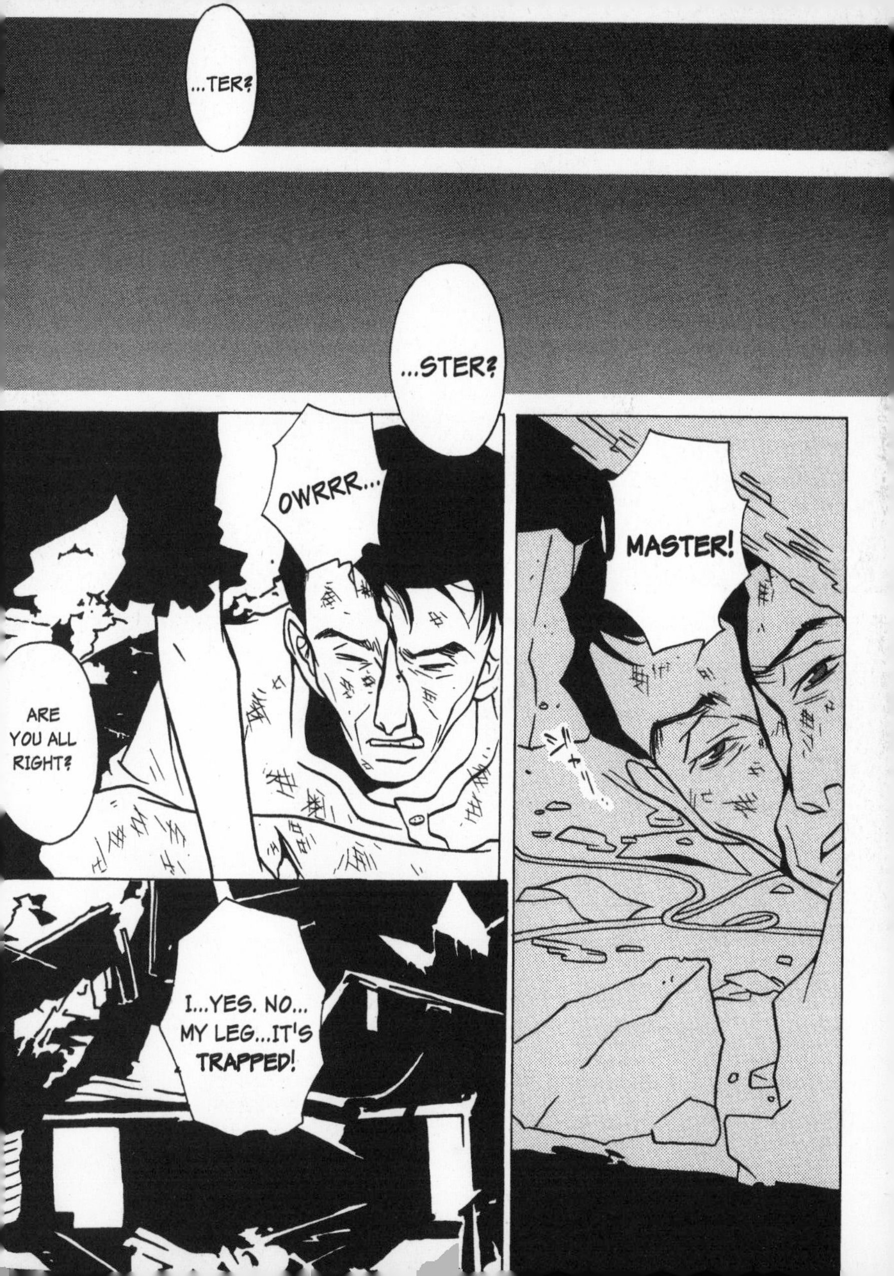
...TER?
...STER?
MASTER!
OWRRR...
ARE YOU ALL RIGHT?
I...YES. NO... MY LEG...IT'S TRAPPED!

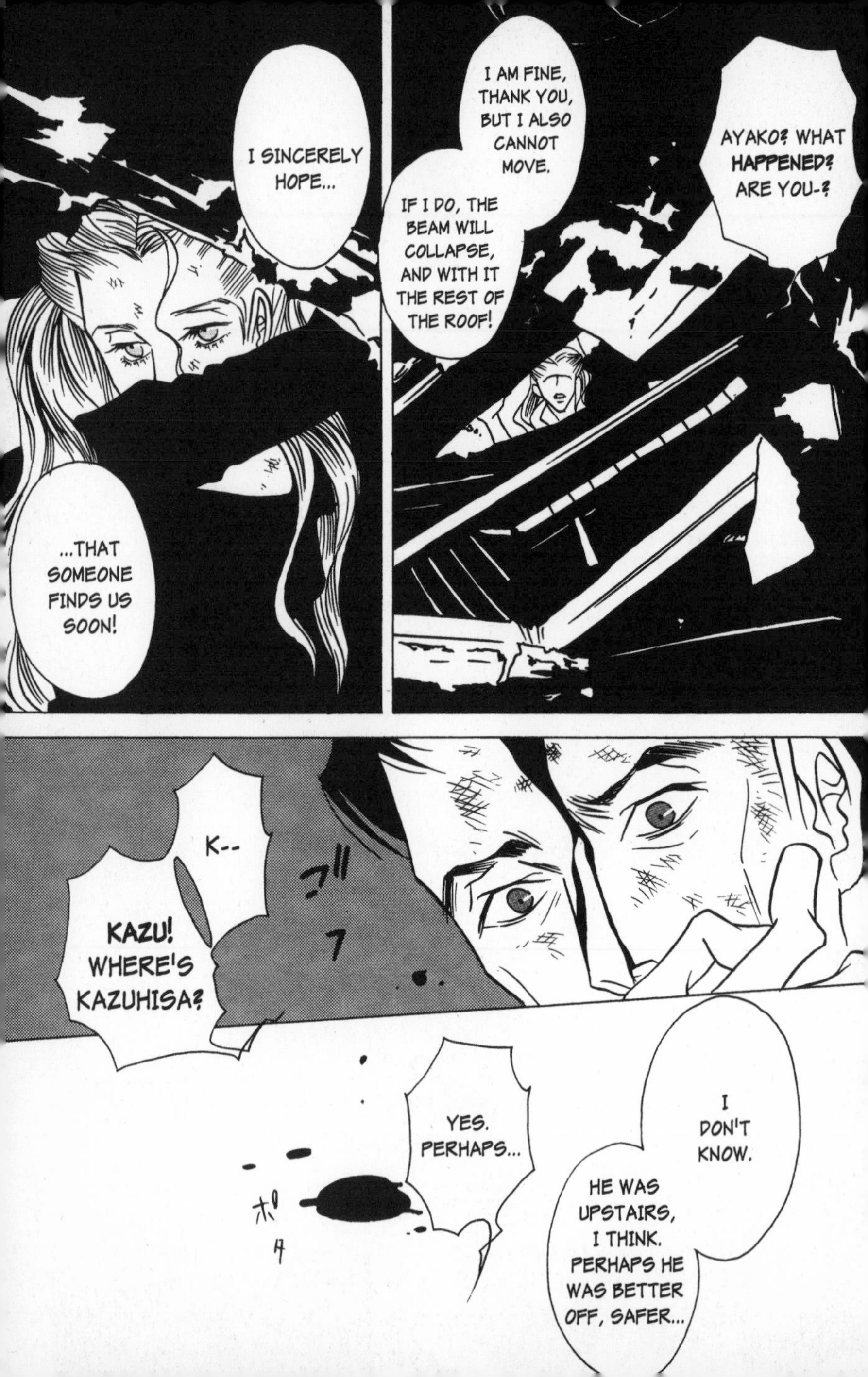

AYAKO? WHAT HAPPENED? ARE YOU-?
I AM FINE, THANK YOU, BUT I ALSO CANNOT MOVE.
IF I DO, THE BEAM WILL COLLAPSE, AND WITH IT THE REST OF THE ROOF!
I SINCERELY HOPE...
...THAT SOMEONE FINDS US SOON!
K--
KAZU! WHERE'S KAZUHISA?
ゴッ
I DON'T KNOW.
HE WAS UPSTAIRS, I THINK. PERHAPS HE WAS BETTER OFF, SAFER...
YES. PERHAPS...
ポタ

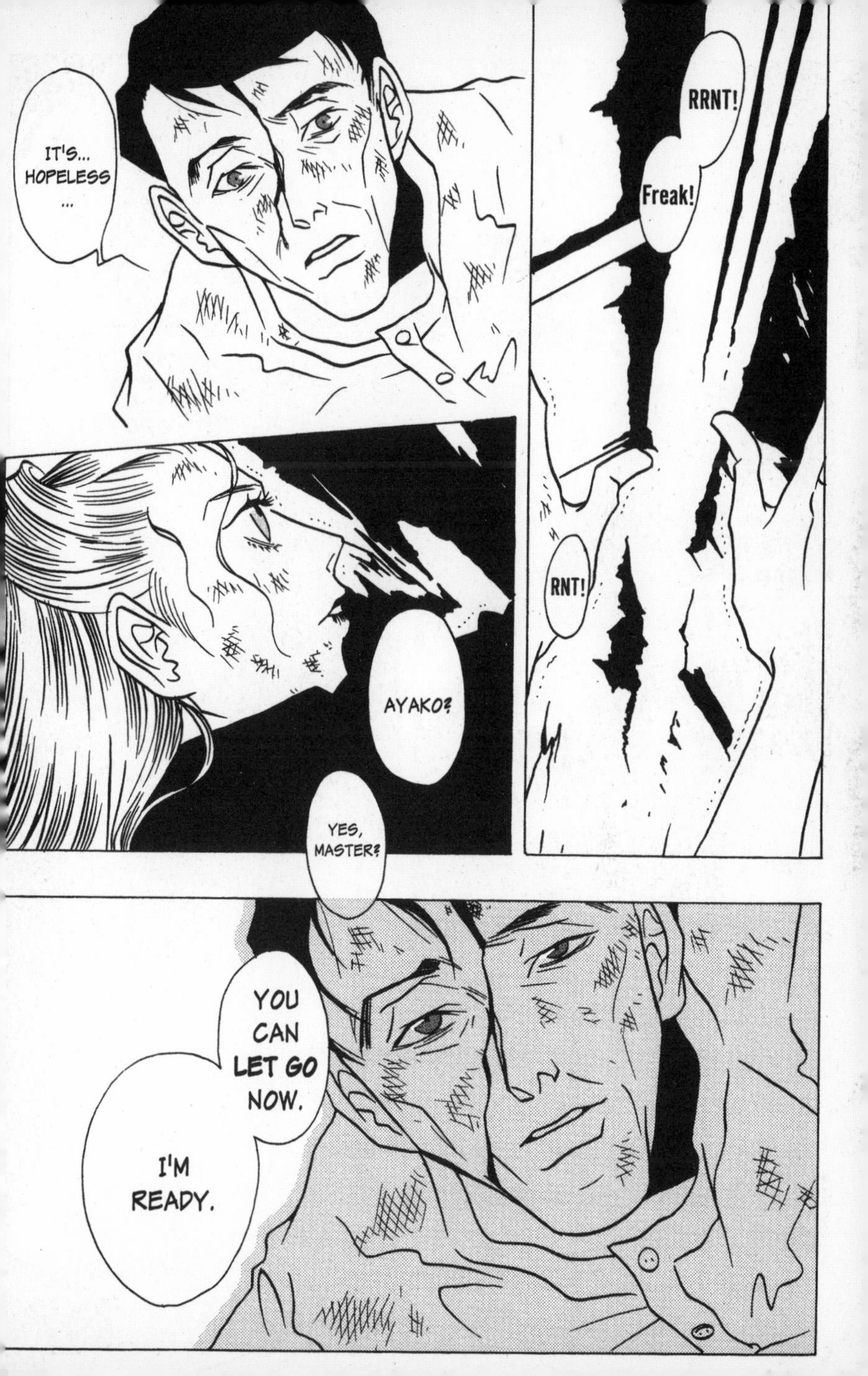
RRNT!
Freak!
RNT!
IT'S... HOPELESS ...
AYAKO?
YES, MASTER?
YOU CAN LET GO NOW.
I'M READY.

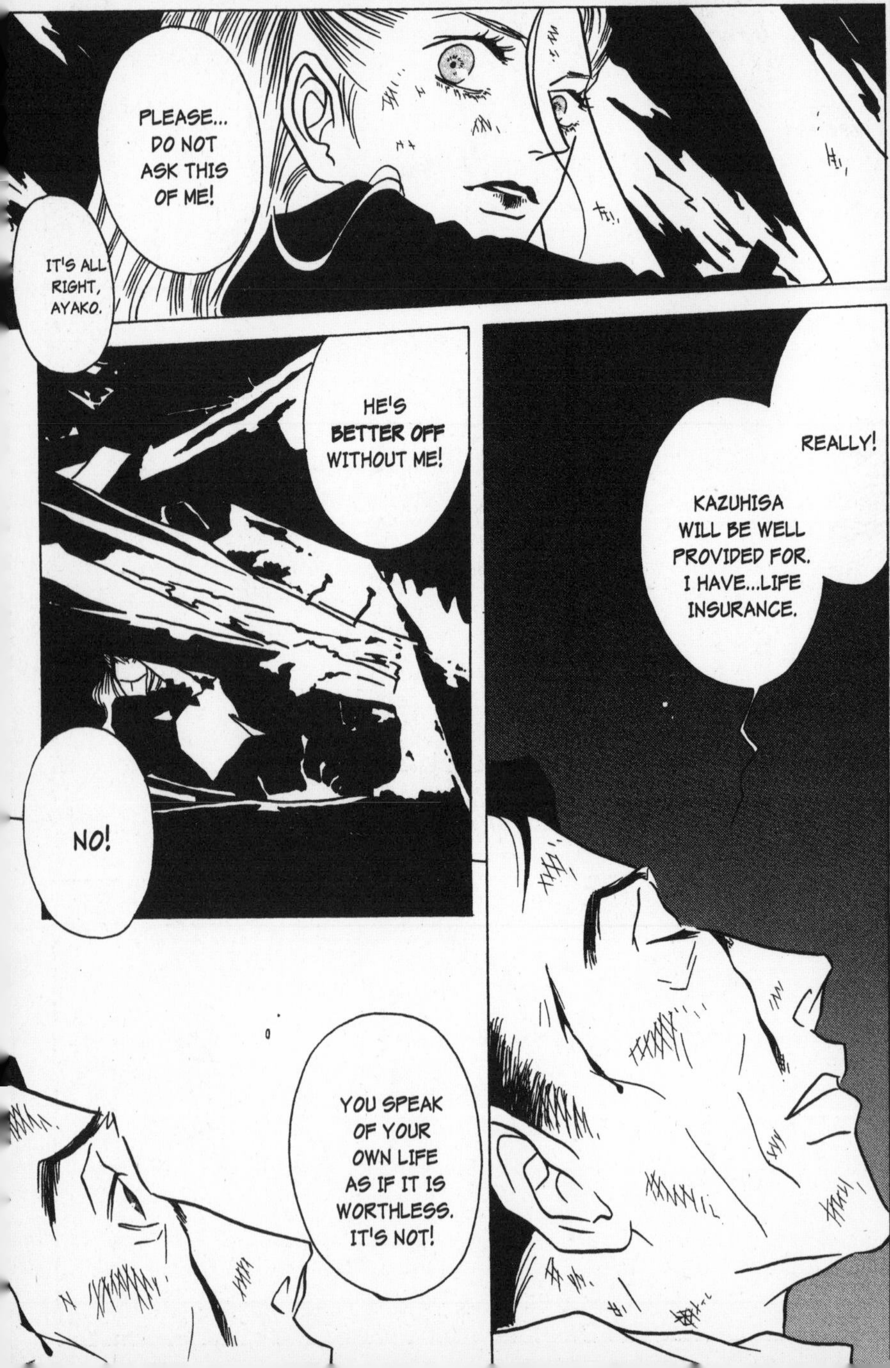
PLEASE... DO NOT ASK THIS OF ME!
IT'S ALL RIGHT, AYAKO.
REALLY!
KAZUHISA WILL BE WELL PROVIDED FOR. I HAVE...LIFE INSURANCE.
HE'S BETTER OFF WITHOUT ME!
NO!
YOU SPEAK OF YOUR OWN LIFE AS IF IT IS WORTHLESS. IT'S NOT!

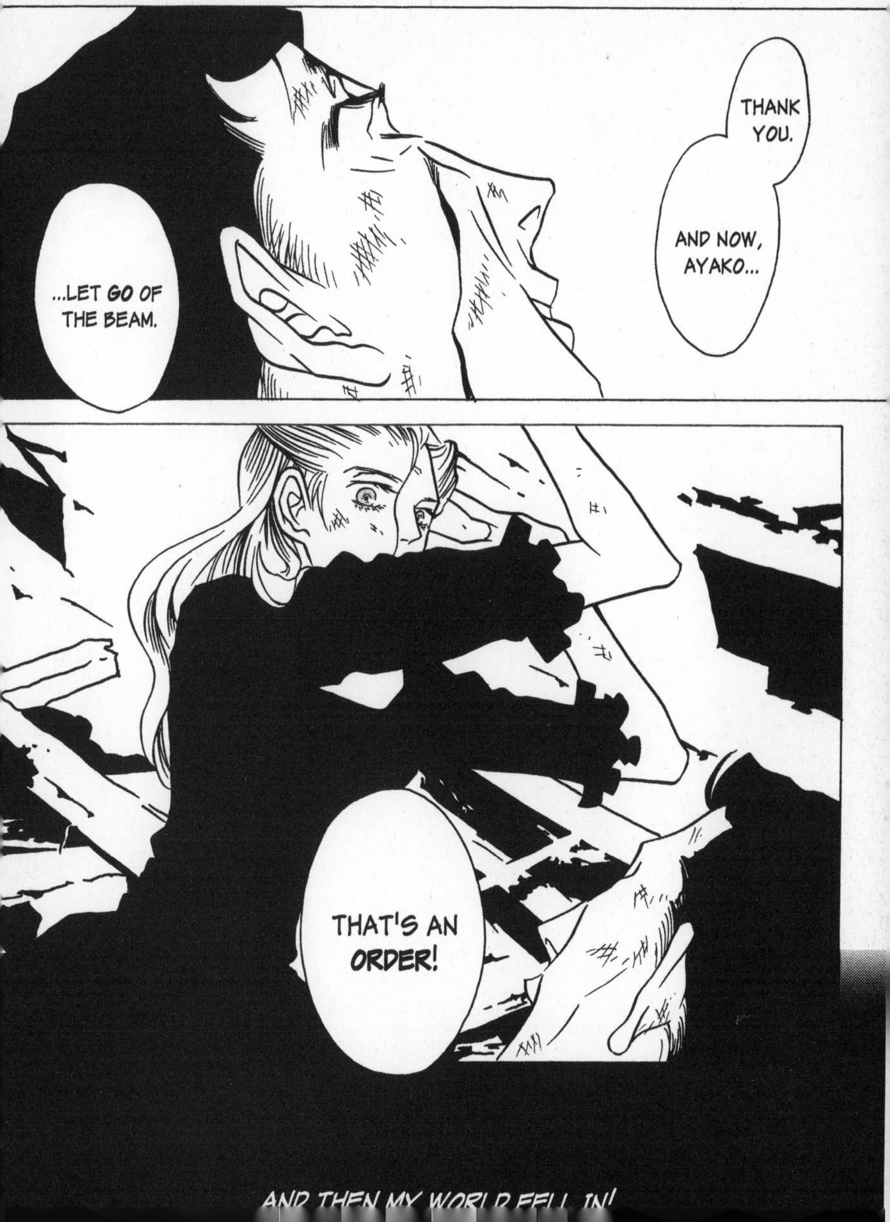
THANK YOU.
AND NOW, AYAKO...
...LET GO OF THE BEAM.
THAT'S AN ORDER!
AND THEN MY WORLD FELL IN!

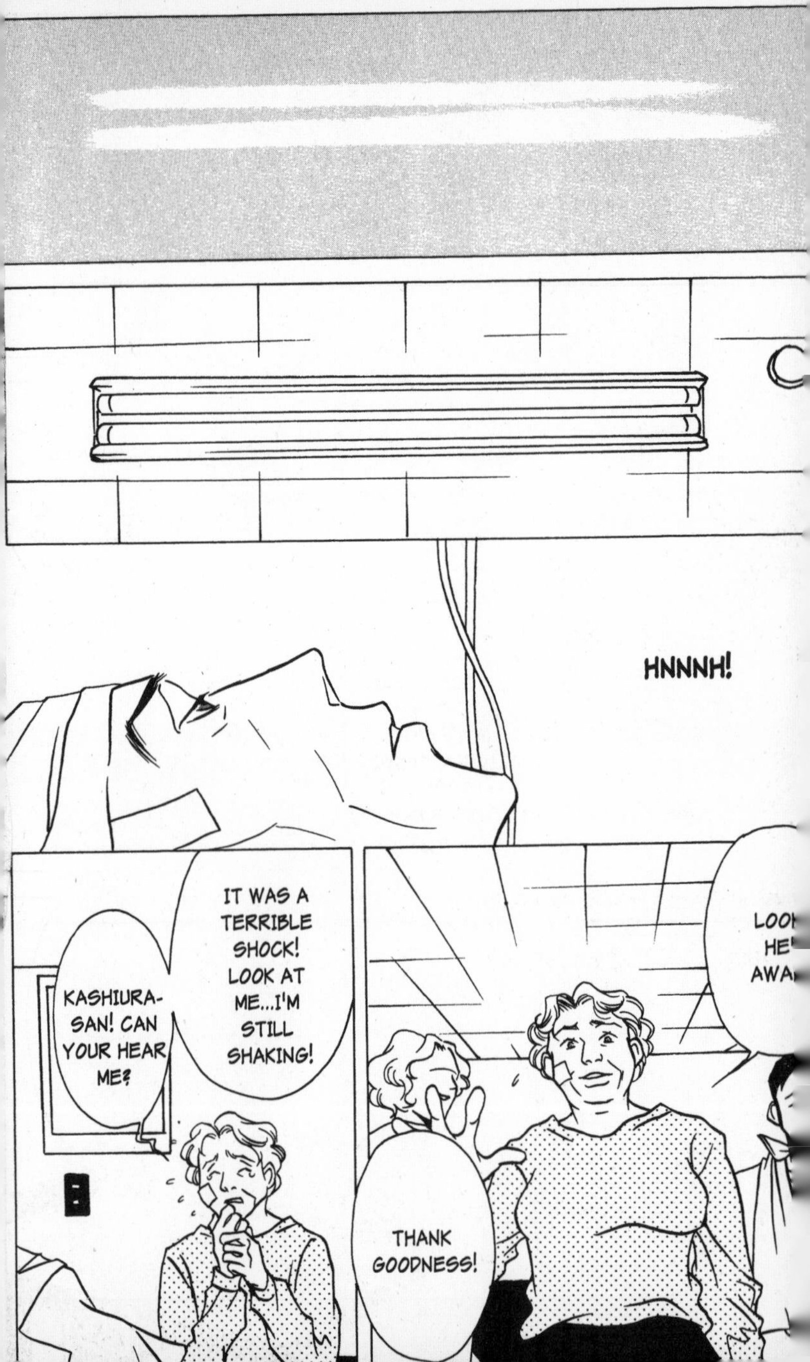
HNNNH!
THANK GOODNESS!
IT WAS A TERRIBLE SHOCK! LOOK AT ME...I'M STILL SHAKING!
KASHIURA-SAN! CAN YOUR HEAR ME?

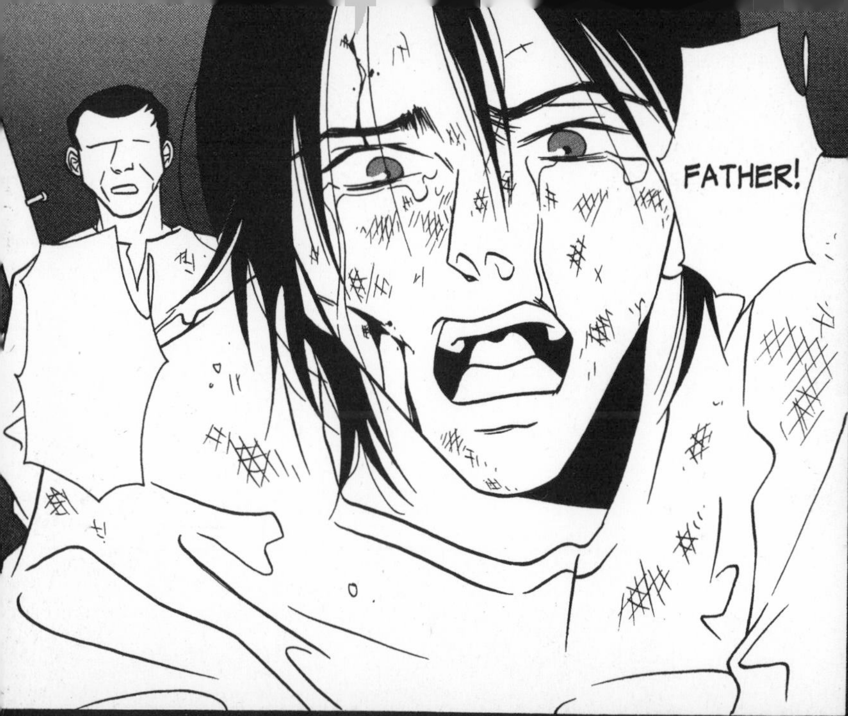
FATHER!

CAN YOU **HEAR** ME? FATHER...

...DON'T LEAVE ME!

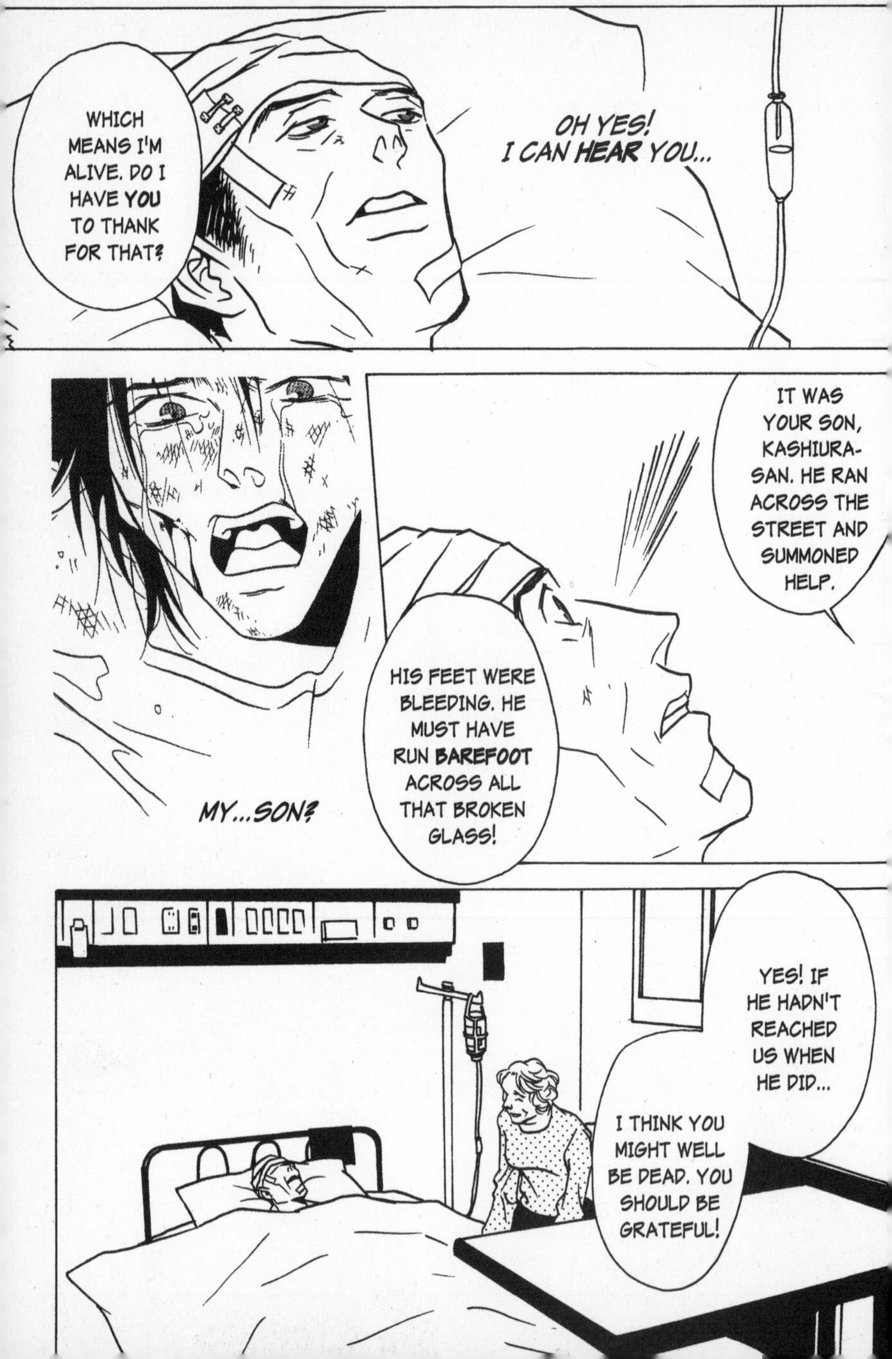
OH YES! I CAN HEAR YOU...
WHICH MEANS I'M ALIVE. DO I HAVE YOU TO THANK FOR THAT?
IT WAS YOUR SON, KASHIURA-SAN. HE RAN ACROSS THE STREET AND SUMMONED HELP.
HIS FEET WERE BLEEDING. HE MUST HAVE RUN BAREFOOT ACROSS ALL THAT BROKEN GLASS!
MY...SON?
YES! IF HE HADN'T REACHED US WHEN HE DID...
I THINK YOU MIGHT WELL BE DEAD. YOU SHOULD BE GRATEFUL!

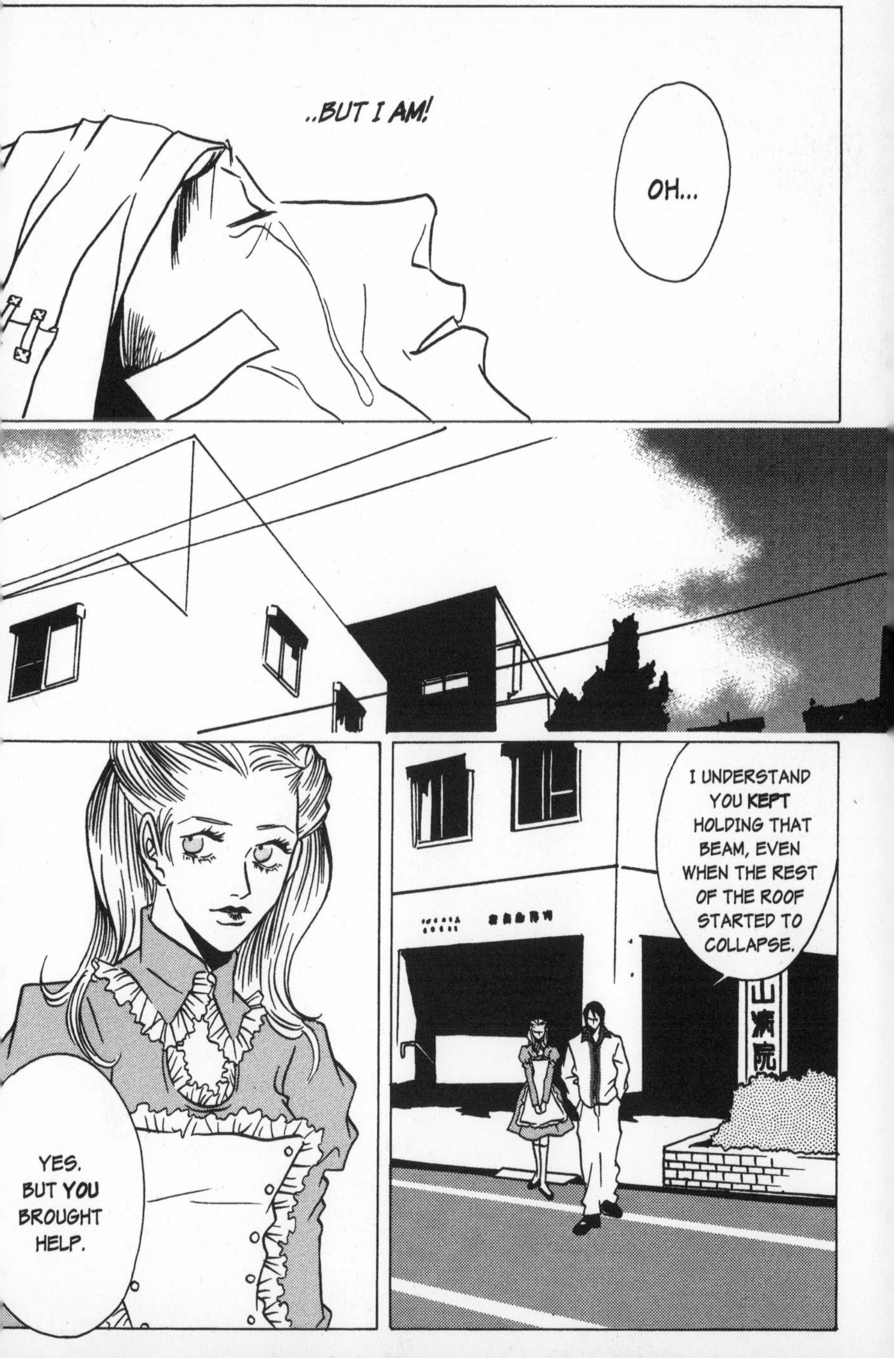
OH...
..BUT I AM!
I UNDERSTAND YOU KEPT HOLDING THAT BEAM, EVEN WHEN THE REST OF THE ROOF STARTED TO COLLAPSE.
山病院
YES. BUT YOU BROUGHT HELP.

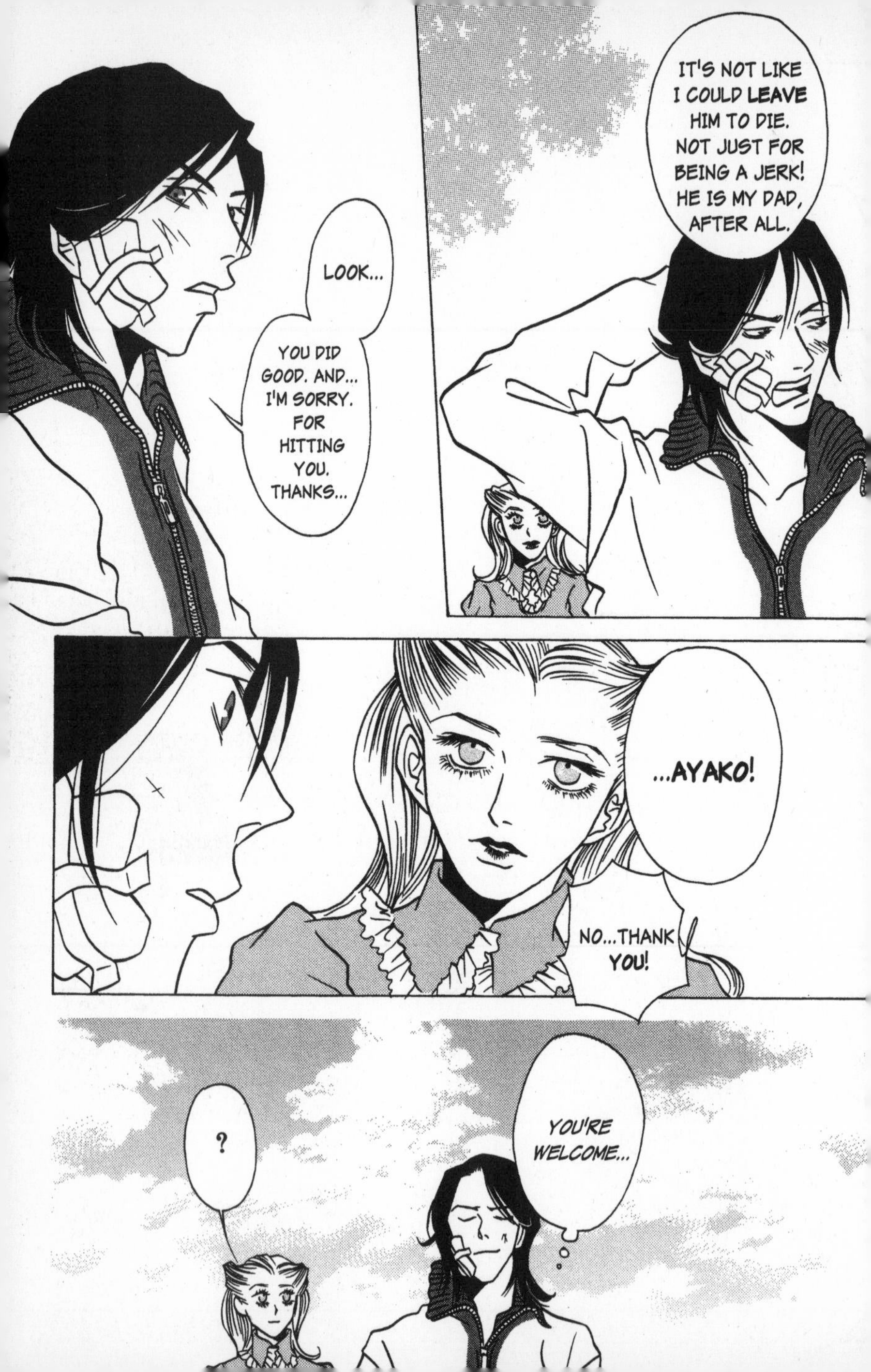
IT'S NOT LIKE I COULD LEAVE HIM TO DIE. NOT JUST FOR BEING A JERK! HE IS MY DAD, AFTER ALL.
LOOK...
YOU DID GOOD. AND... I'M SORRY. FOR HITTING YOU. THANKS...
...AYAKO!
NO...THANK YOU!
YOU'RE WELCOME...
?

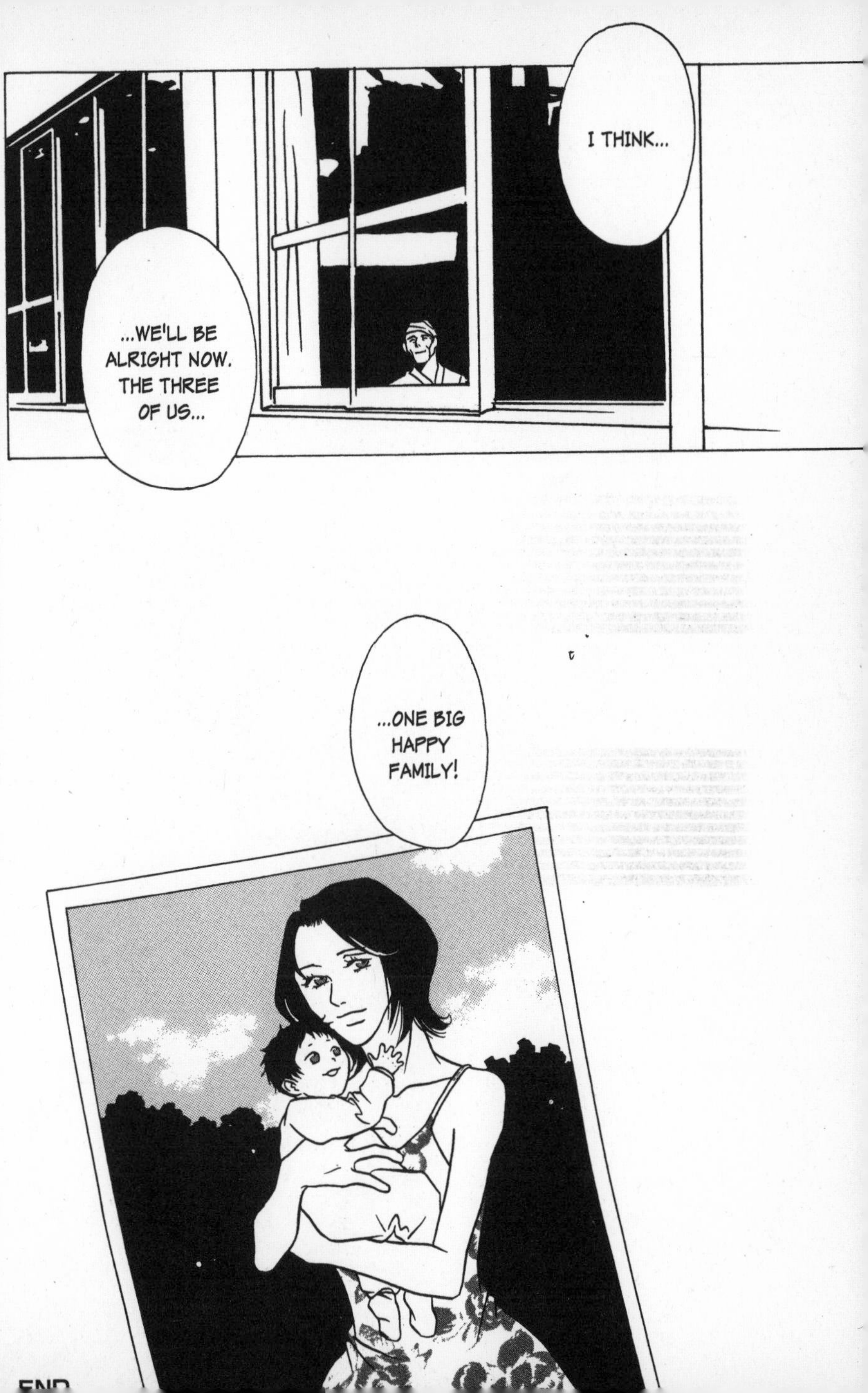
I THINK...
...WE'LL BE ALRIGHT NOW. THE THREE OF US...
...ONE BIG HAPPY FAMILY!
END

LIST 6

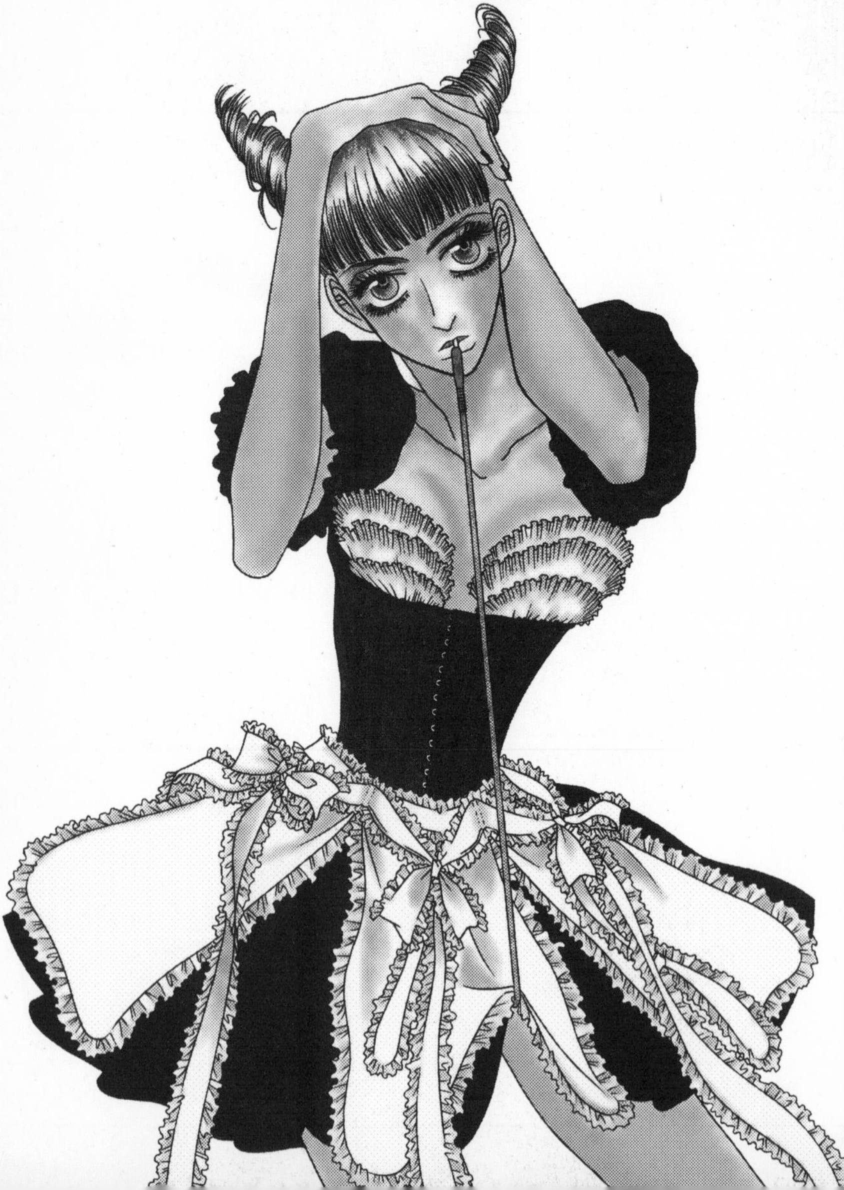

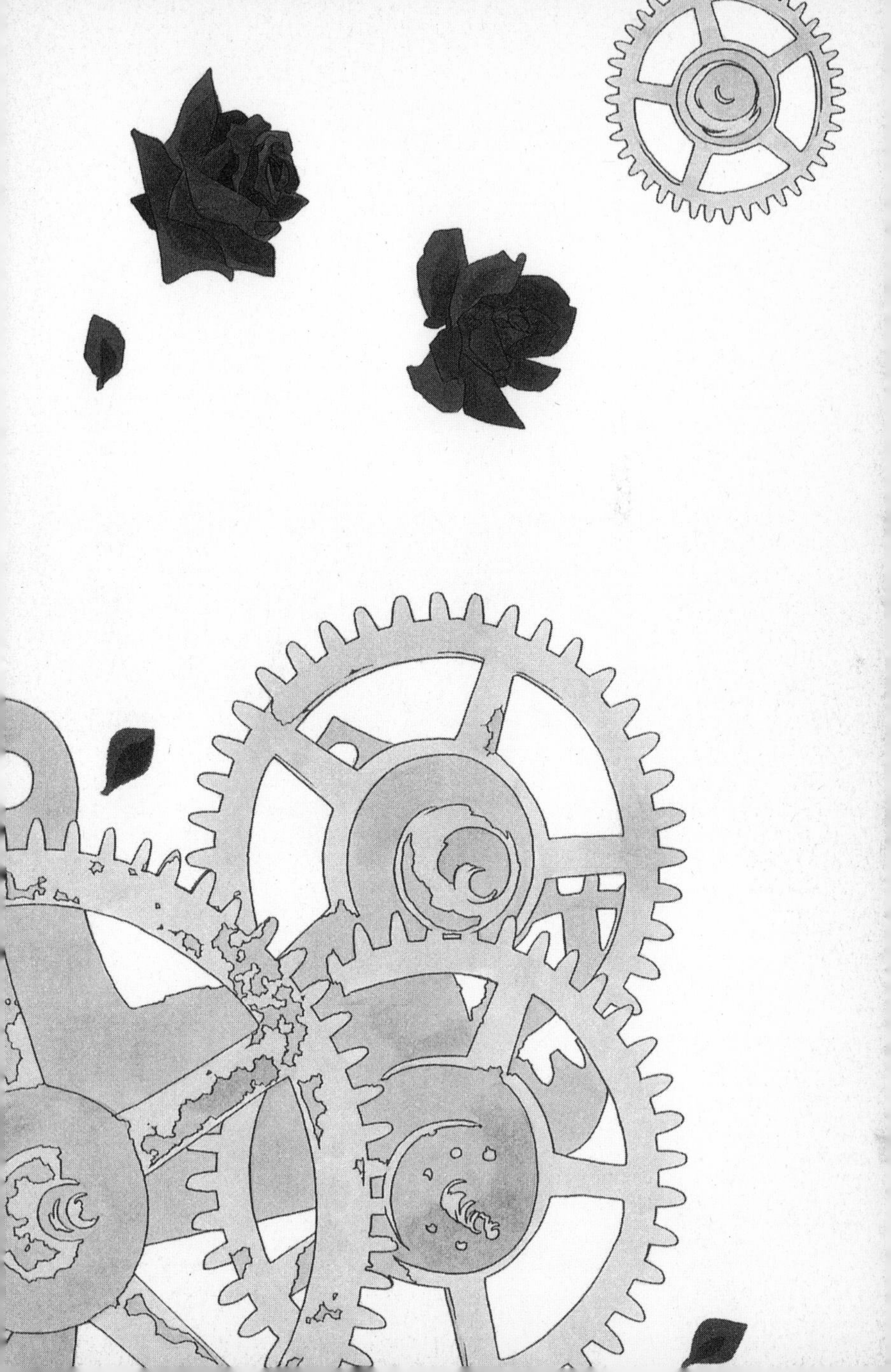

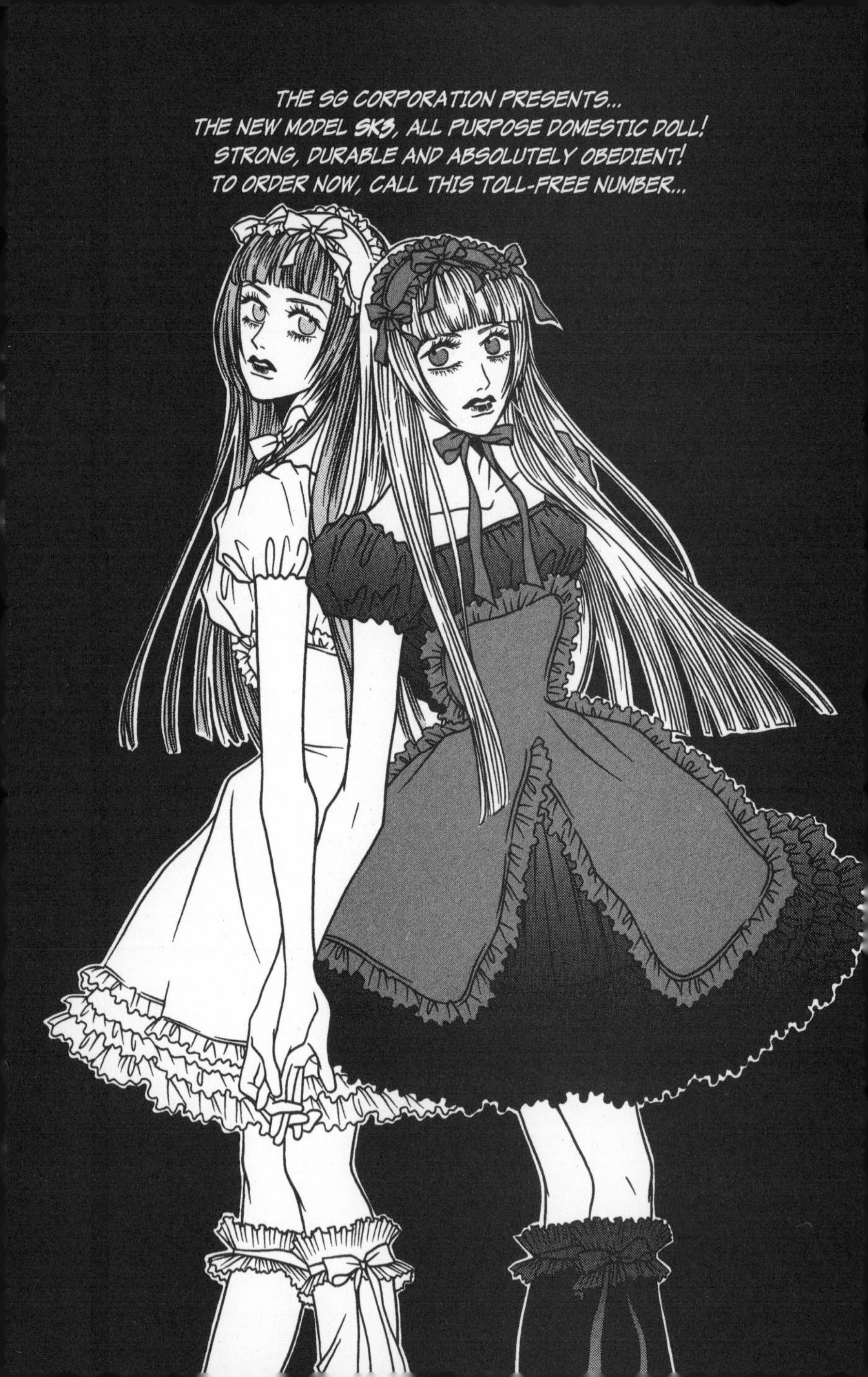
THE SG CORPORATION PRESENTS...
THE NEW MODEL SK3, ALL PURPOSE DOMESTIC DOLL!
STRONG, DURABLE AND ABSOLUTELY OBEDIENT!
TO ORDER NOW, CALL THIS TOLL-FREE NUMBER...

6. a maid servant

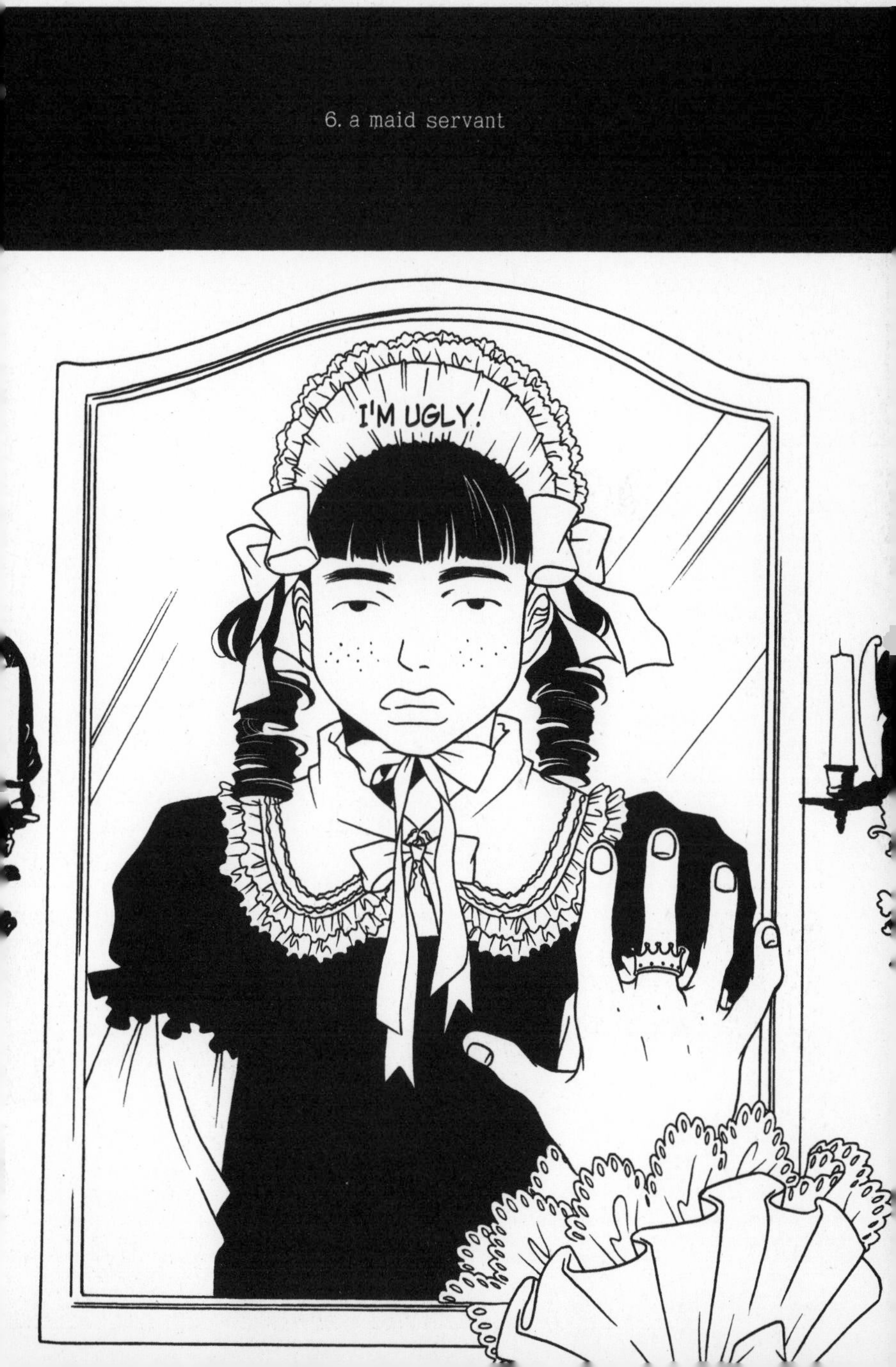
I'M UGLY.

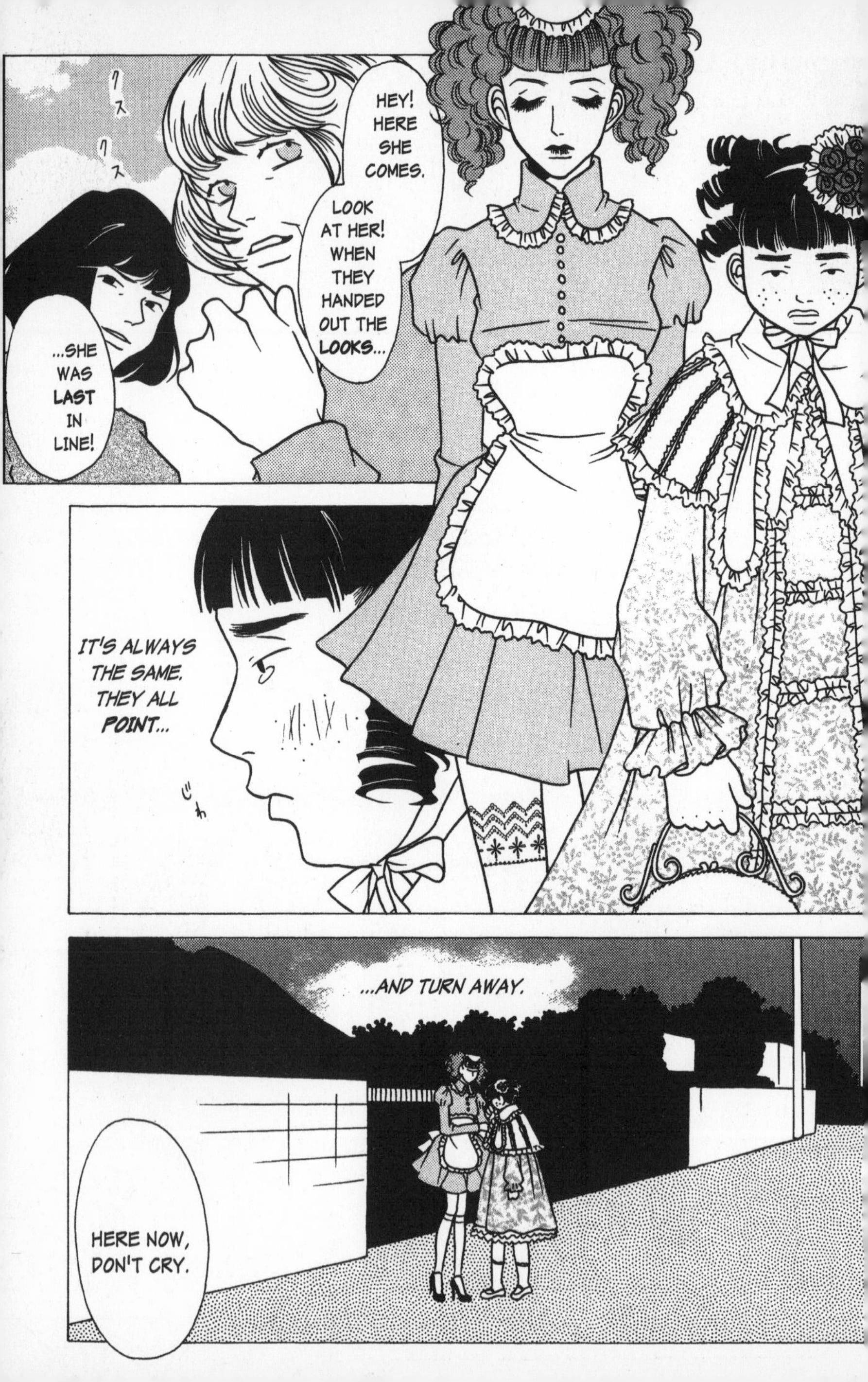
HEY! HERE SHE COMES.
LOOK AT HER! WHEN THEY HANDED OUT THE LOOKS...
...SHE WAS LAST IN LINE!
クス クス
IT'S ALWAYS THE SAME. THEY ALL POINT...
じわ
...AND TURN AWAY.
HERE NOW, DON'T CRY.

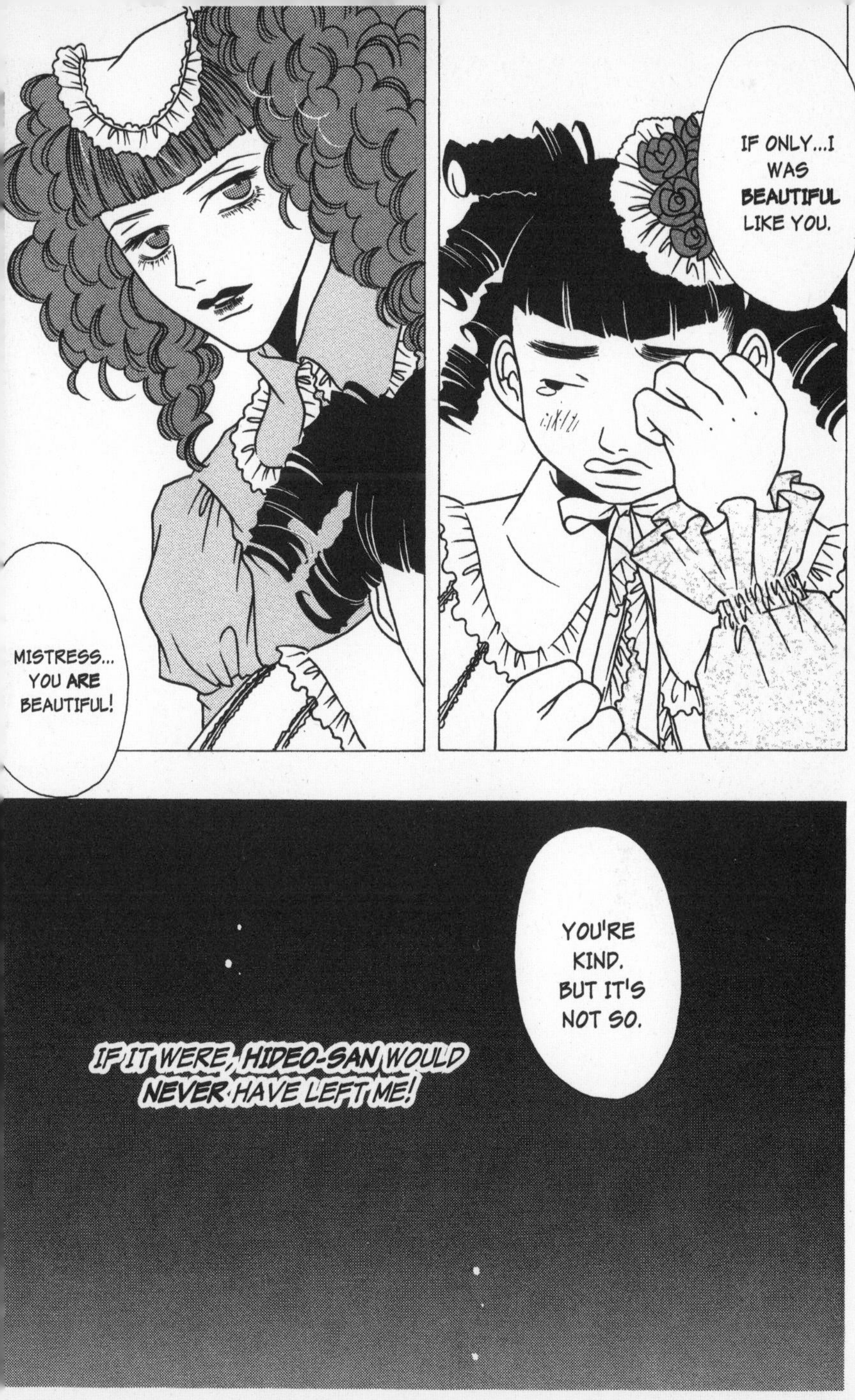
IF ONLY...I WAS BEAUTIFUL LIKE YOU.
MISTRESS... YOU ARE BEAUTIFUL!
YOU'RE KIND. BUT IT'S NOT SO.
IF IT WERE, HIDEO-SAN WOULD NEVER HAVE LEFT ME!

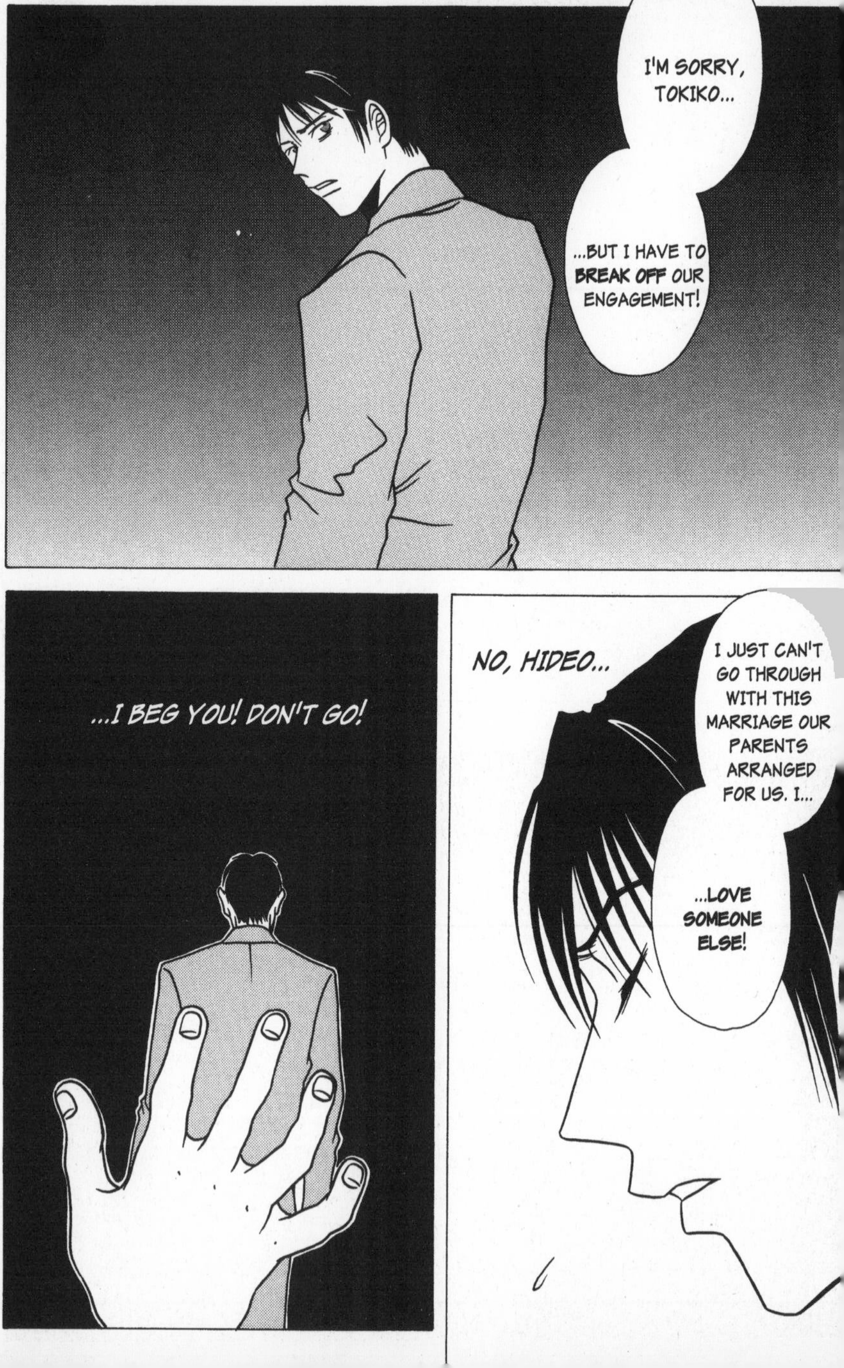
I'M SORRY, TOKIKO...
...BUT I HAVE TO BREAK OFF OUR ENGAGEMENT!
I JUST CAN'T GO THROUGH WITH THIS MARRIAGE OUR PARENTS ARRANGED FOR US. I...
...LOVE SOMEONE ELSE!
NO, HIDEO...
...I BEG YOU! DON'T GO!

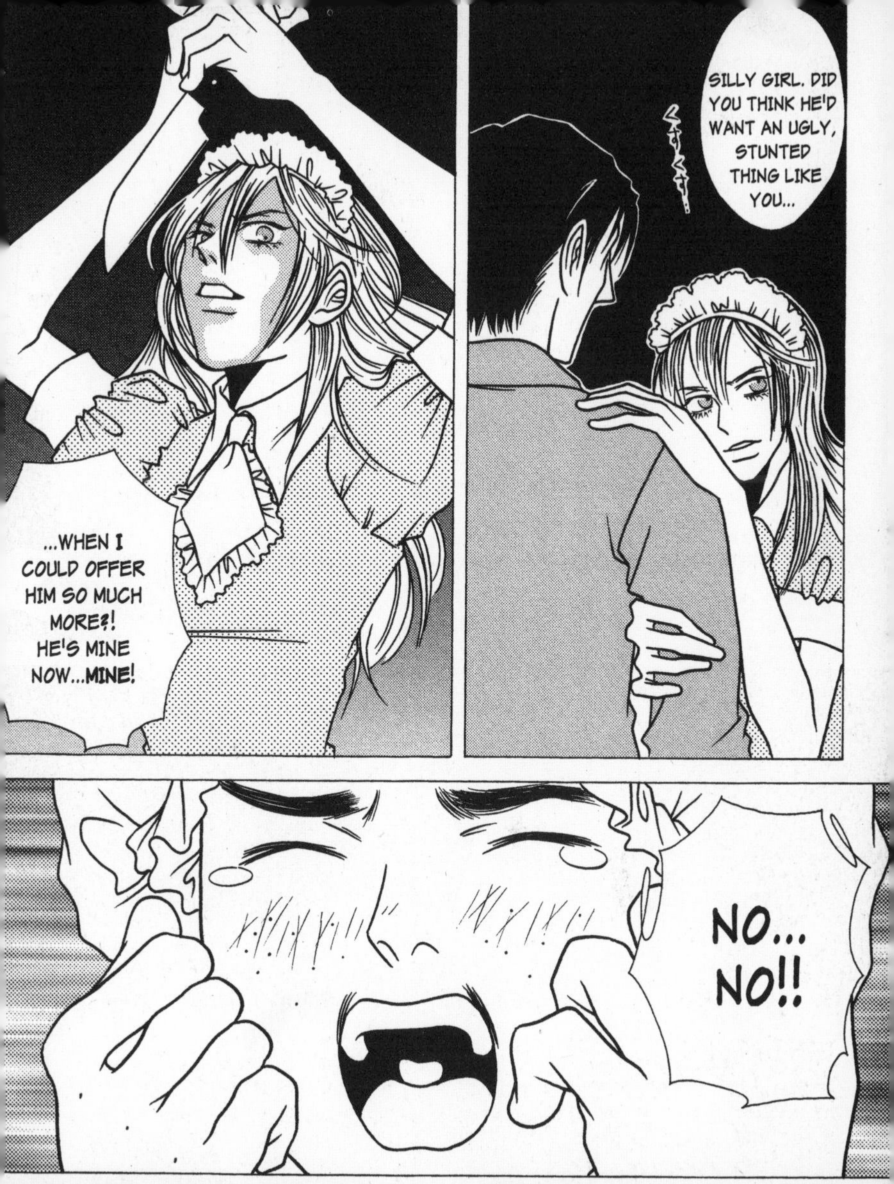
SILLY GIRL. DID YOU THINK HE'D WANT AN UGLY, STUNTED THING LIKE YOU...
くすくす…
...WHEN I COULD OFFER HIM SO MUCH MORE?! HE'S MINE NOW...MINE!
NO... NO!!

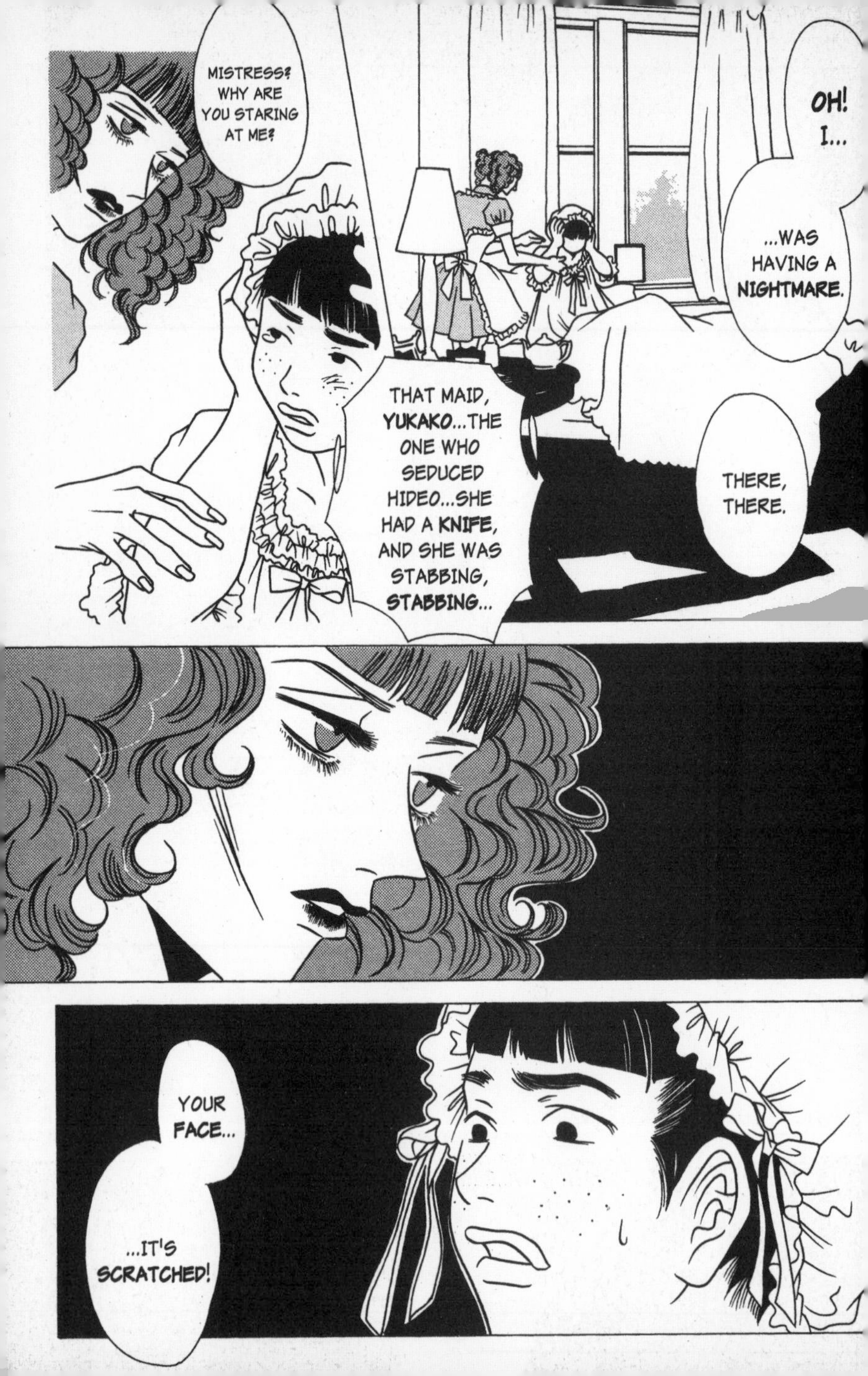
OH! I...
...WAS HAVING A NIGHTMARE.
THAT MAID, YUKAKO...THE ONE WHO SEDUCED HIDEO...SHE HAD A KNIFE, AND SHE WAS STABBING, STABBING...
THERE, THERE.
MISTRESS? WHY ARE YOU STARING AT ME?
YOUR FACE...
...IT'S SCRATCHED!

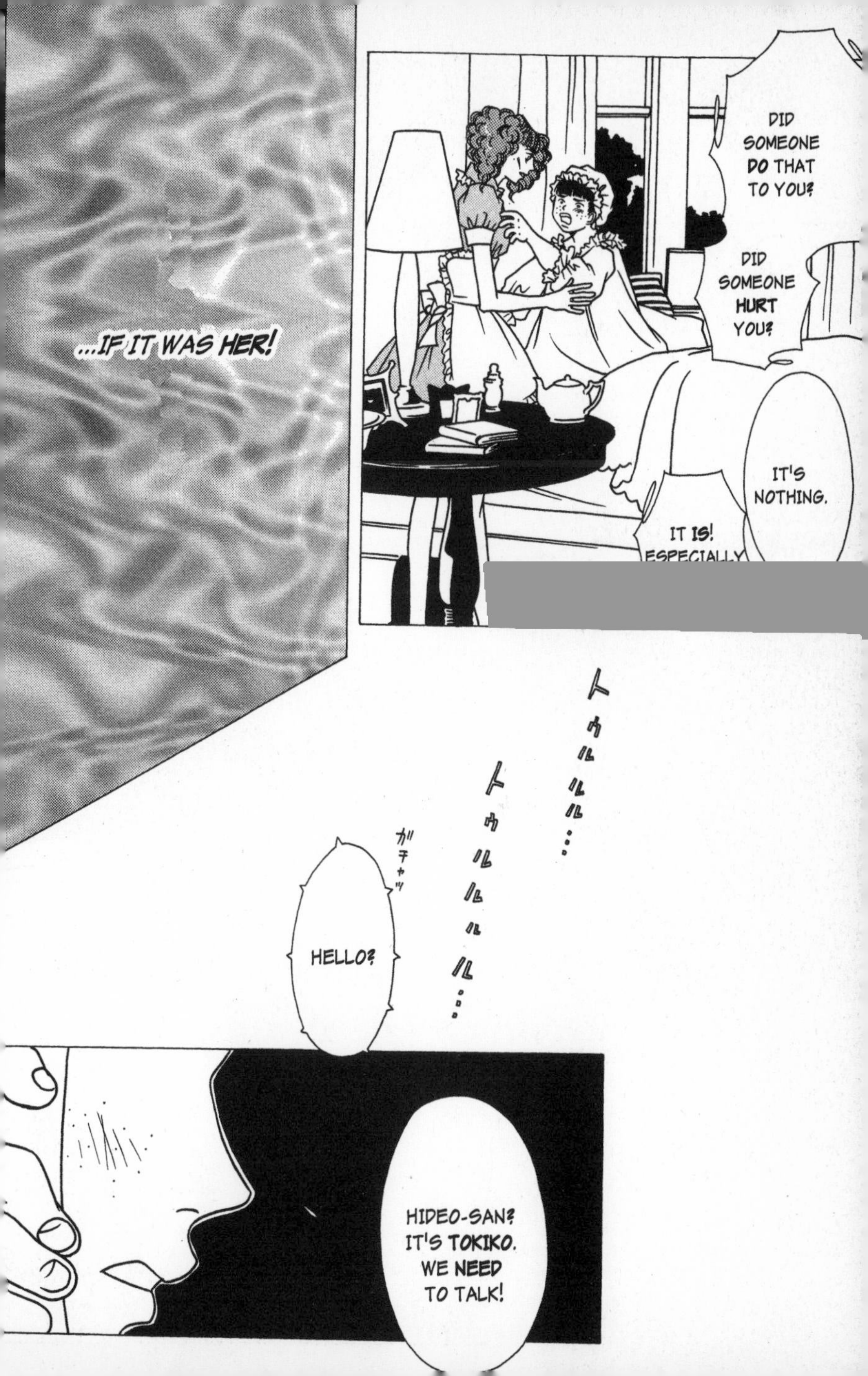
DID SOMEONE DO THAT TO YOU?
DID SOMEONE HURT YOU?
IT'S NOTHING.
IT IS! ESPECIALLY
...IF IT WAS HER!
トゥルル...
トゥルルルル...
ガチャッ
HELLO?
HIDEO-SAN? IT'S TOKIKO. WE NEED TO TALK!

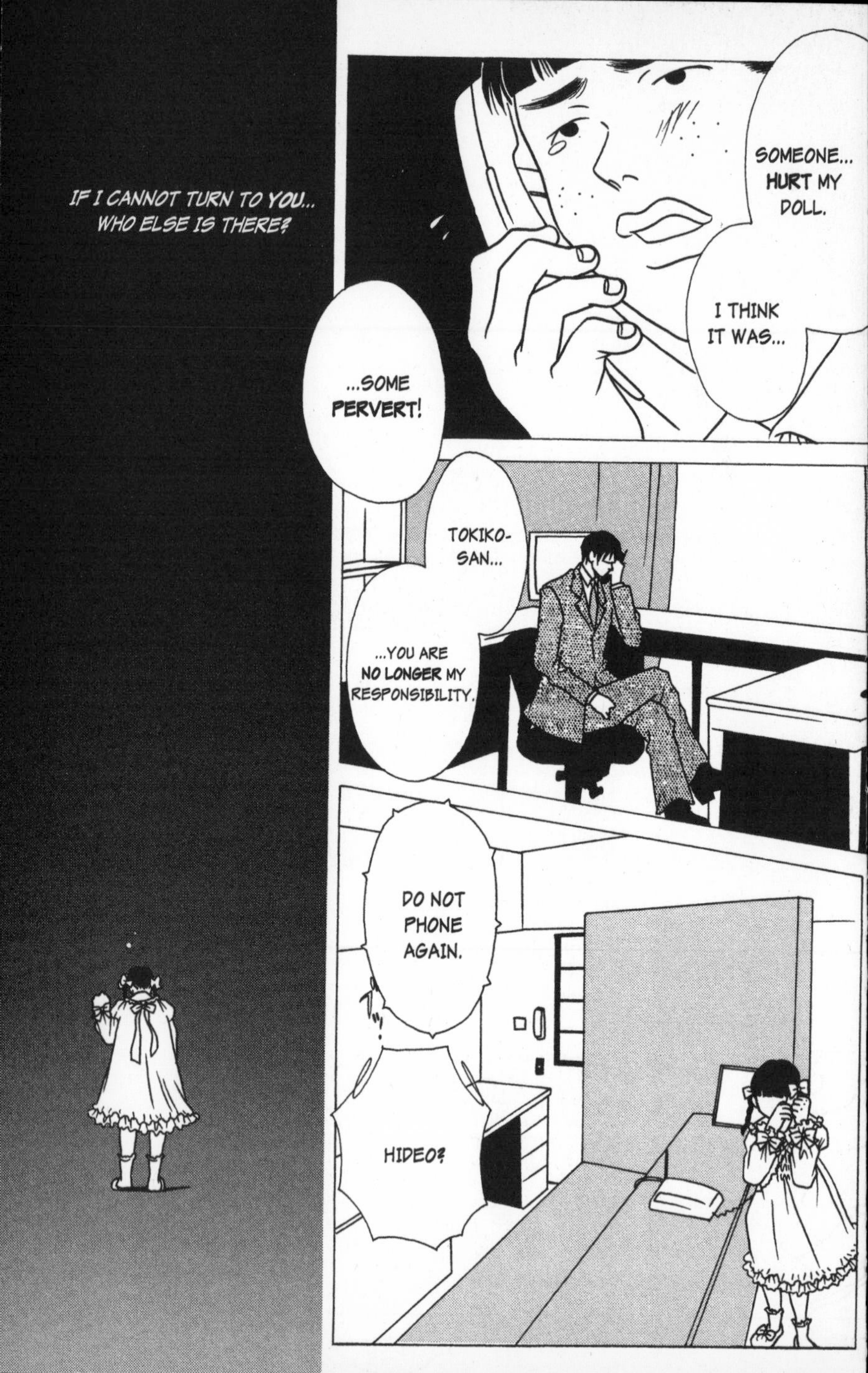
IF I CANNOT TURN TO YOU... WHO ELSE IS THERE?
SOMEONE... HURT MY DOLL.
I THINK IT WAS...
...SOME PERVERT!
TOKIKO-SAN...
...YOU ARE NO LONGER MY RESPONSIBILITY.
DO NOT PHONE AGAIN.
HIDEO?

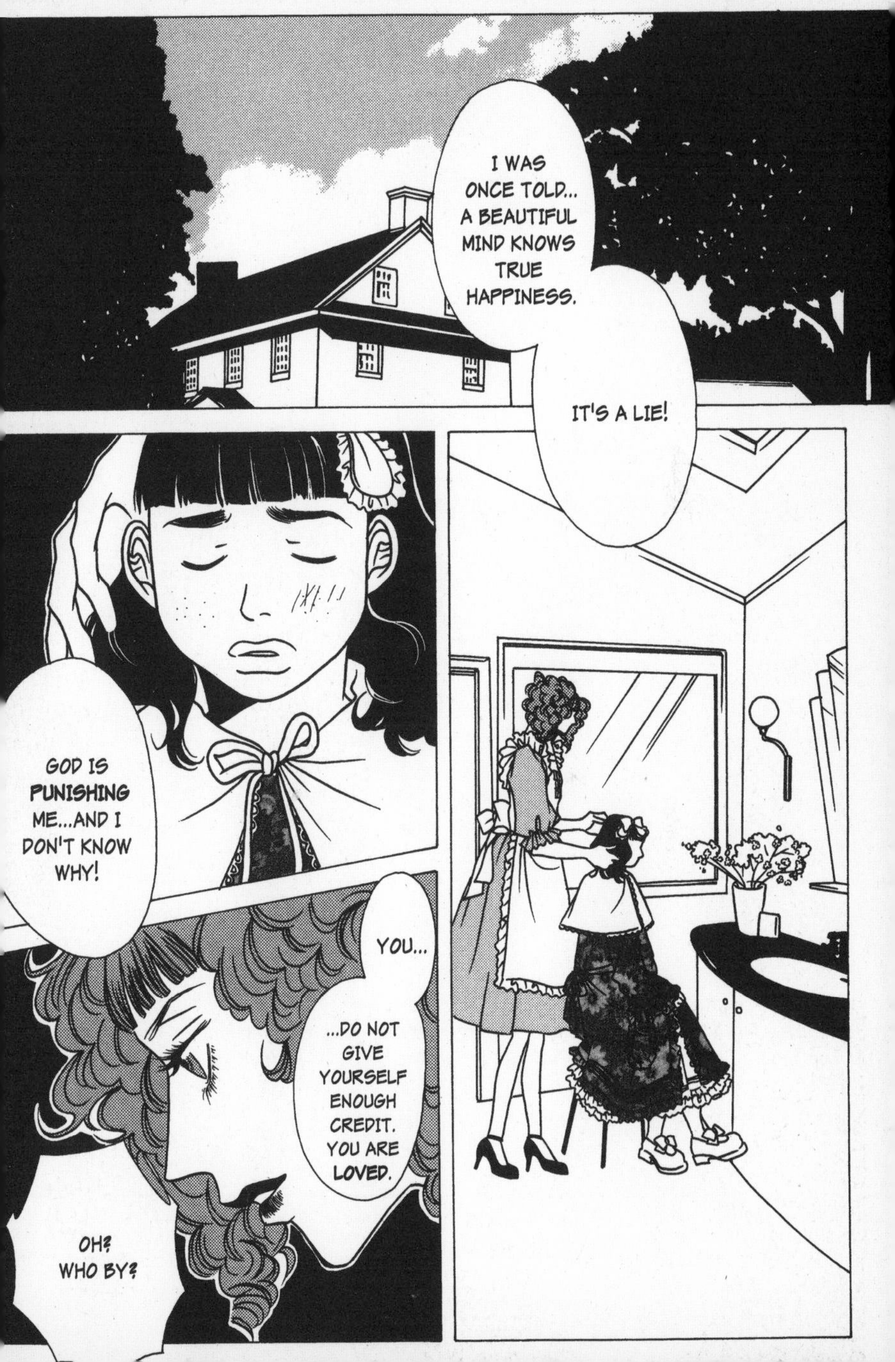
I WAS ONCE TOLD... A BEAUTIFUL MIND KNOWS TRUE HAPPINESS.
IT'S A LIE!
GOD IS PUNISHING ME...AND I DON'T KNOW WHY!
YOU...
...DO NOT GIVE YOURSELF ENOUGH CREDIT. YOU ARE LOVED.
OH? WHO BY?

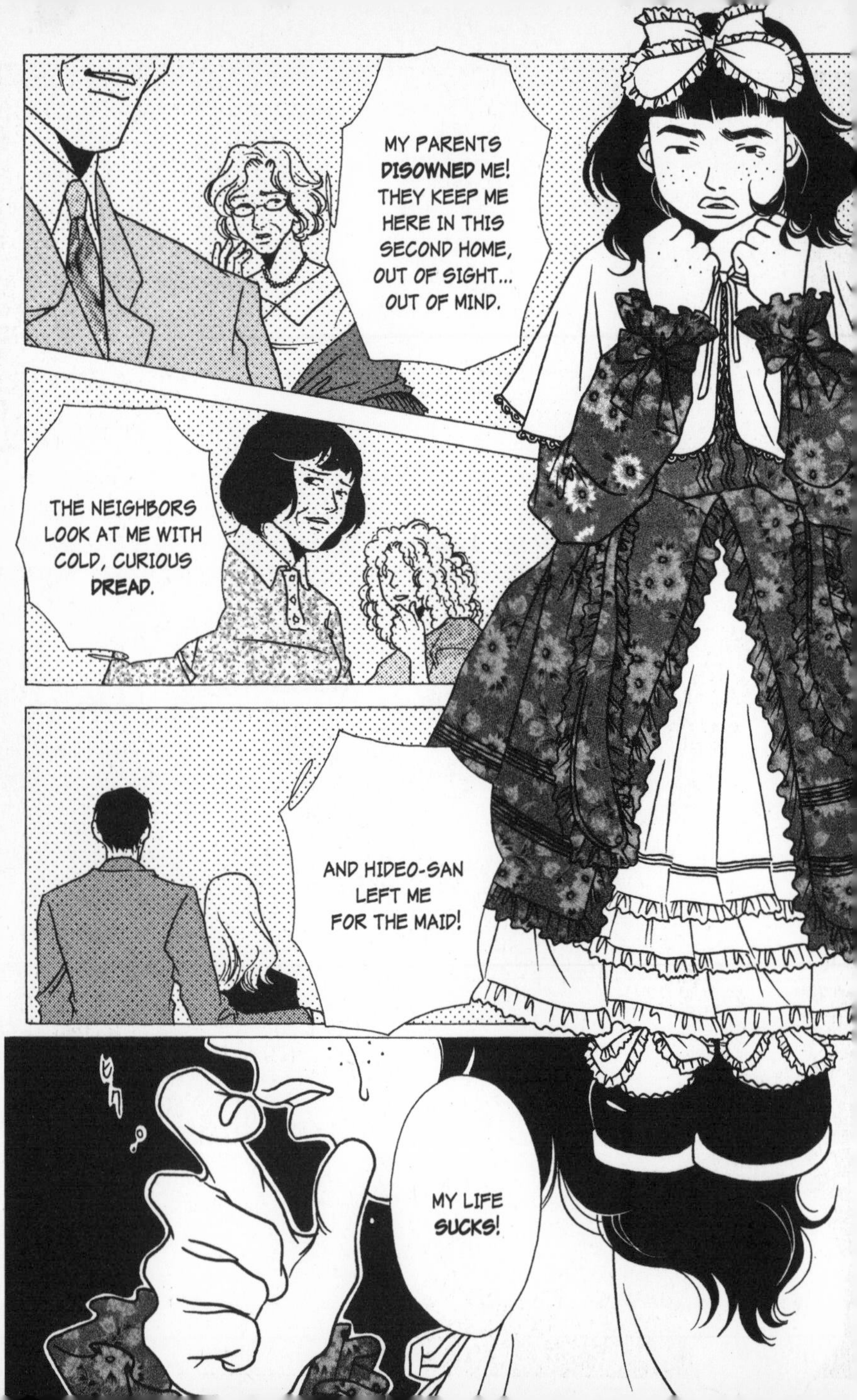
MY PARENTS DISOWNED ME! THEY KEEP ME HERE IN THIS SECOND HOME, OUT OF SIGHT... OUT OF MIND.
THE NEIGHBORS LOOK AT ME WITH COLD, CURIOUS DREAD.
AND HIDEO-SAN LEFT ME FOR THE MAID!
MY LIFE SUCKS!

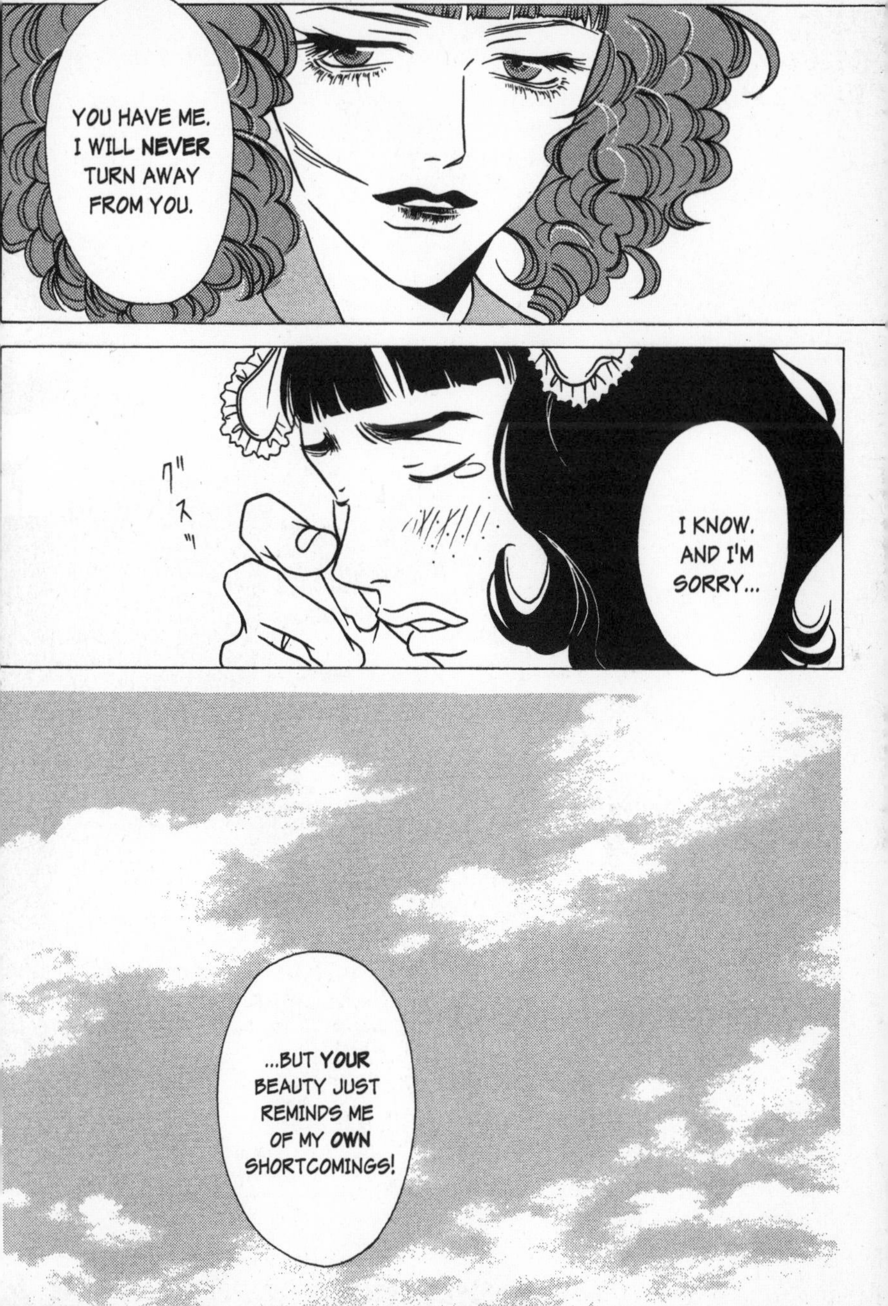
YOU HAVE ME. I WILL **NEVER** TURN AWAY FROM YOU.
I KNOW. AND I'M SORRY...
グスッ
...BUT **YOUR** BEAUTY JUST REMINDS ME OF MY **OWN** SHORTCOMINGS!

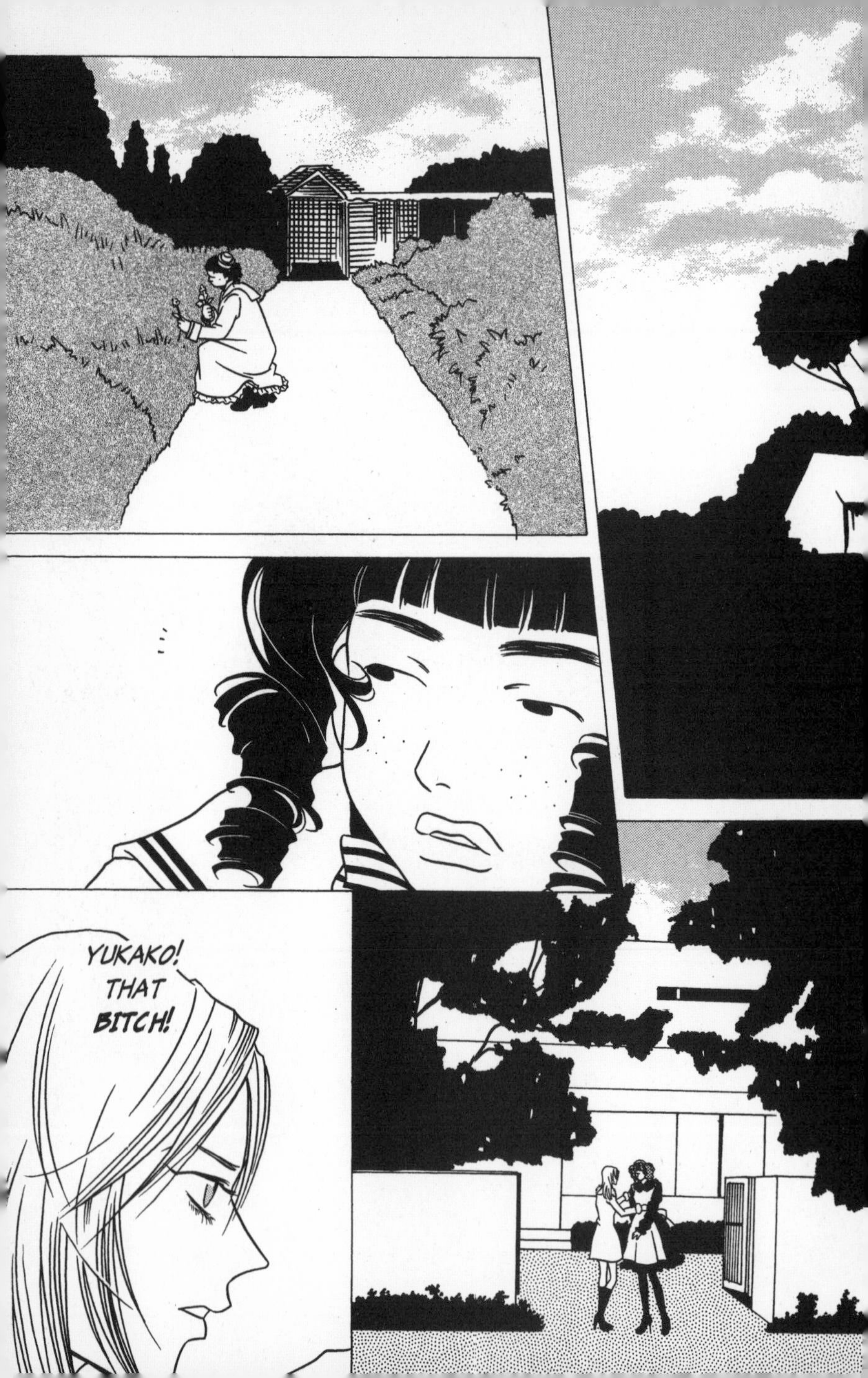
...
YUKAKO! THAT BITCH!

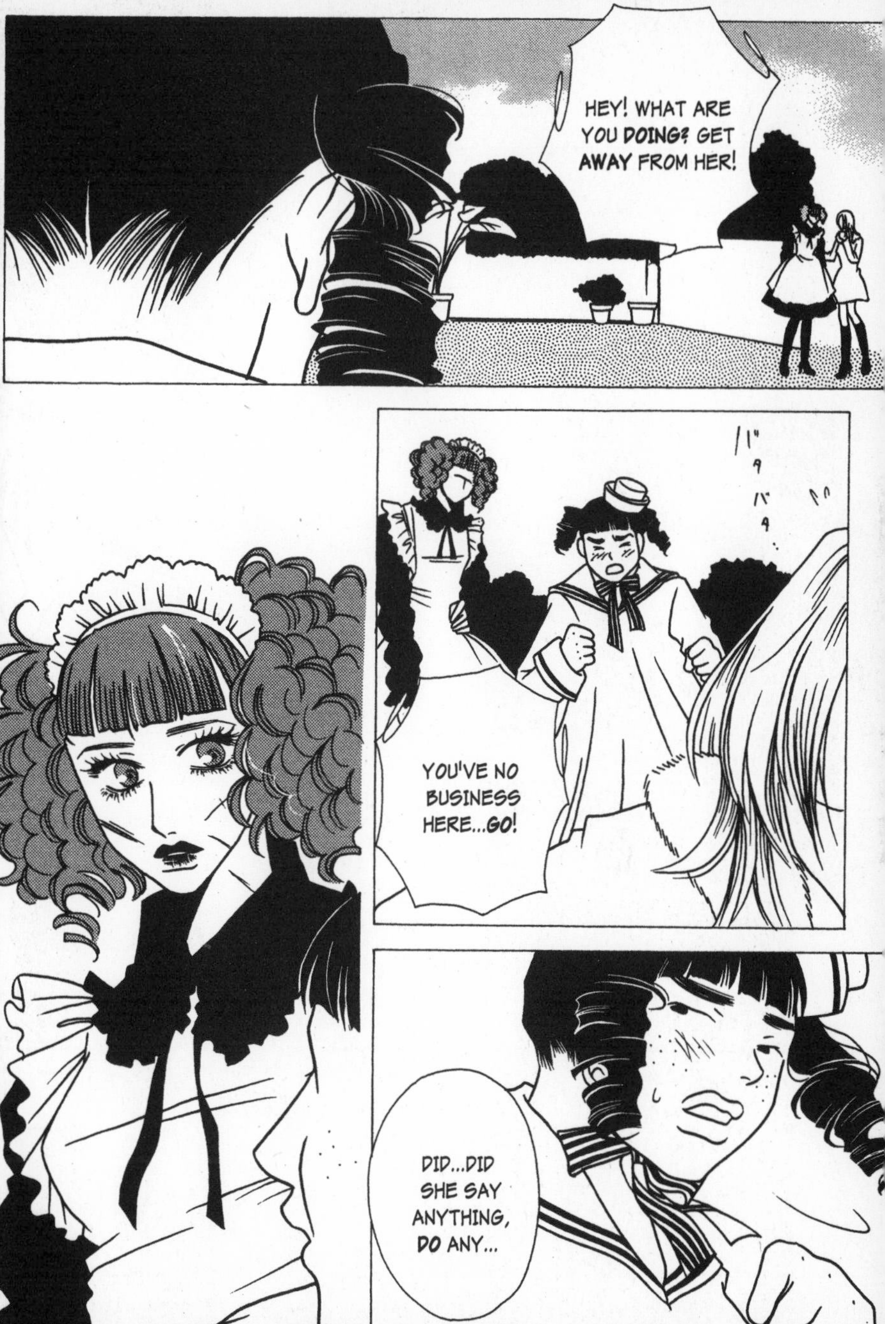
HEY! WHAT ARE YOU DOING? GET AWAY FROM HER!
バタバタ
YOU'VE NO BUSINESS HERE...GO!
DID...DID SHE SAY ANYTHING, DO ANY...

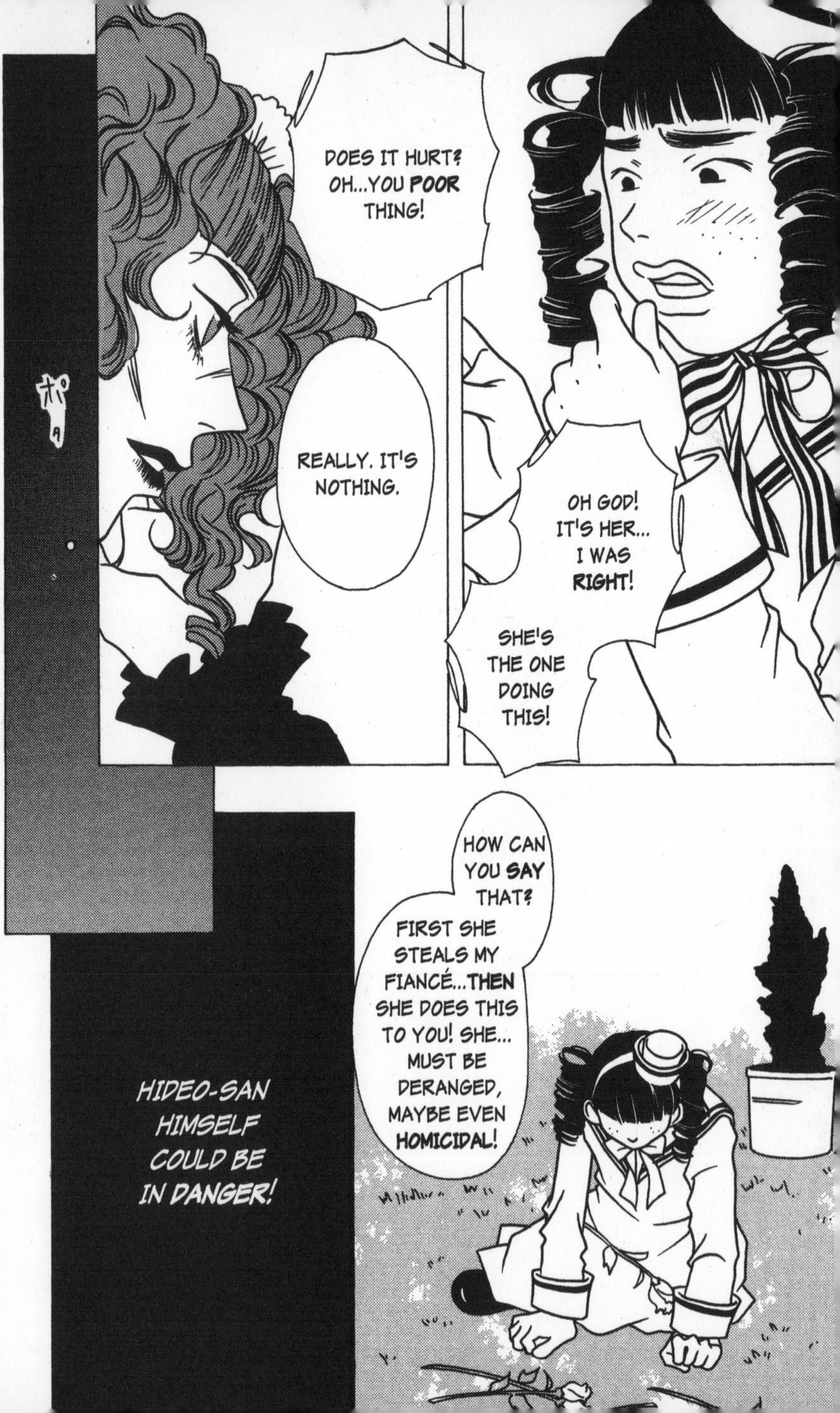
OH GOD! IT'S HER... I WAS RIGHT!
SHE'S THE ONE DOING THIS!
DOES IT HURT? OH...YOU POOR THING!
REALLY. IT'S NOTHING.
ポ
HOW CAN YOU SAY THAT? FIRST SHE STEALS MY FIANCÉ...THEN SHE DOES THIS TO YOU! SHE... MUST BE DERANGED, MAYBE EVEN HOMICIDAL!
HIDEO-SAN HIMSELF COULD BE IN DANGER!

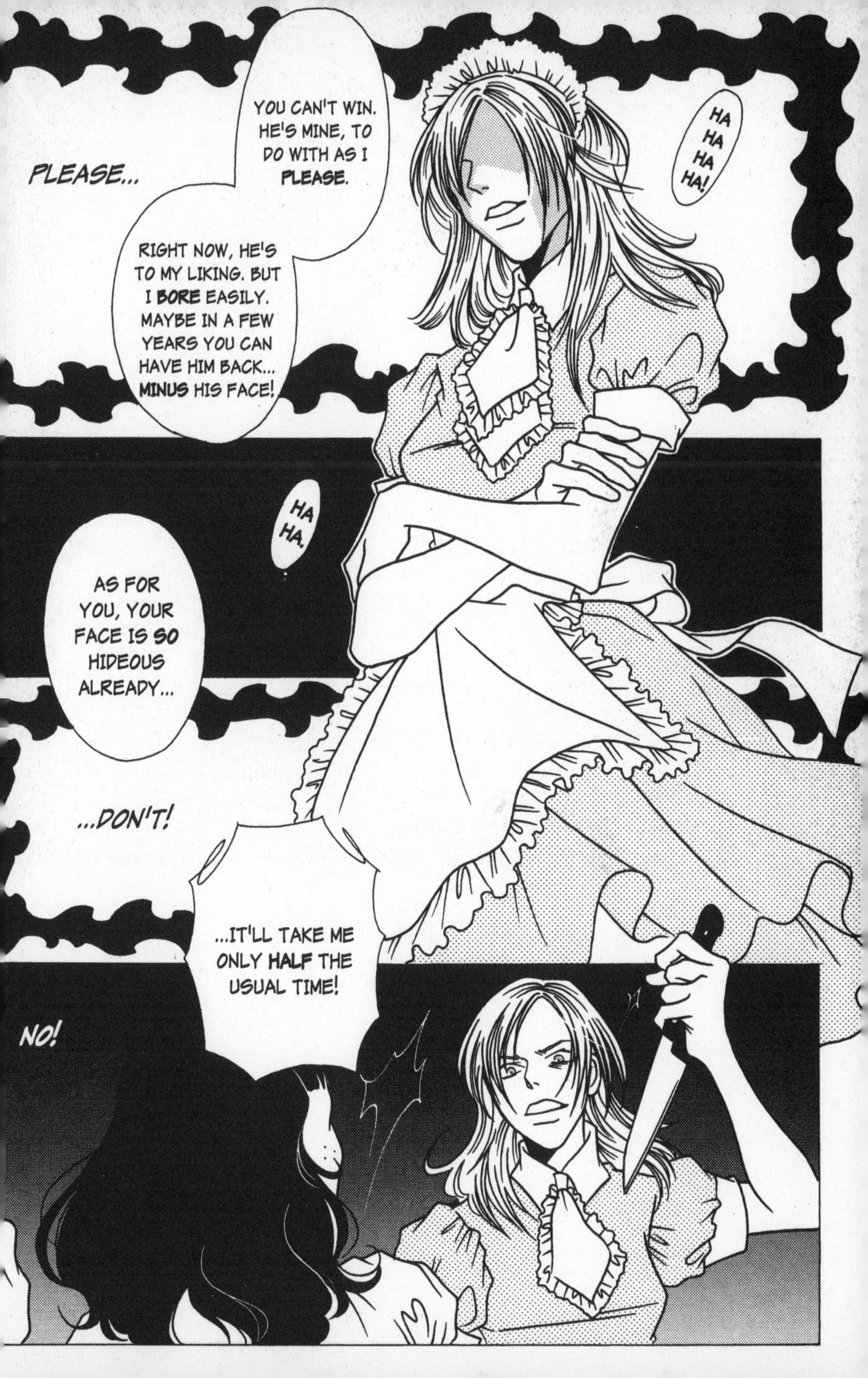
HA HA HA HA!
YOU CAN'T WIN. HE'S MINE, TO DO WITH AS I PLEASE.
RIGHT NOW, HE'S TO MY LIKING. BUT I BORE EASILY. MAYBE IN A FEW YEARS YOU CAN HAVE HIM BACK... MINUS HIS FACE!
PLEASE...
HA HA.
AS FOR YOU, YOUR FACE IS SO HIDEOUS ALREADY...
...DON'T!
...IT'LL TAKE ME ONLY HALF THE USUAL TIME!
NO!

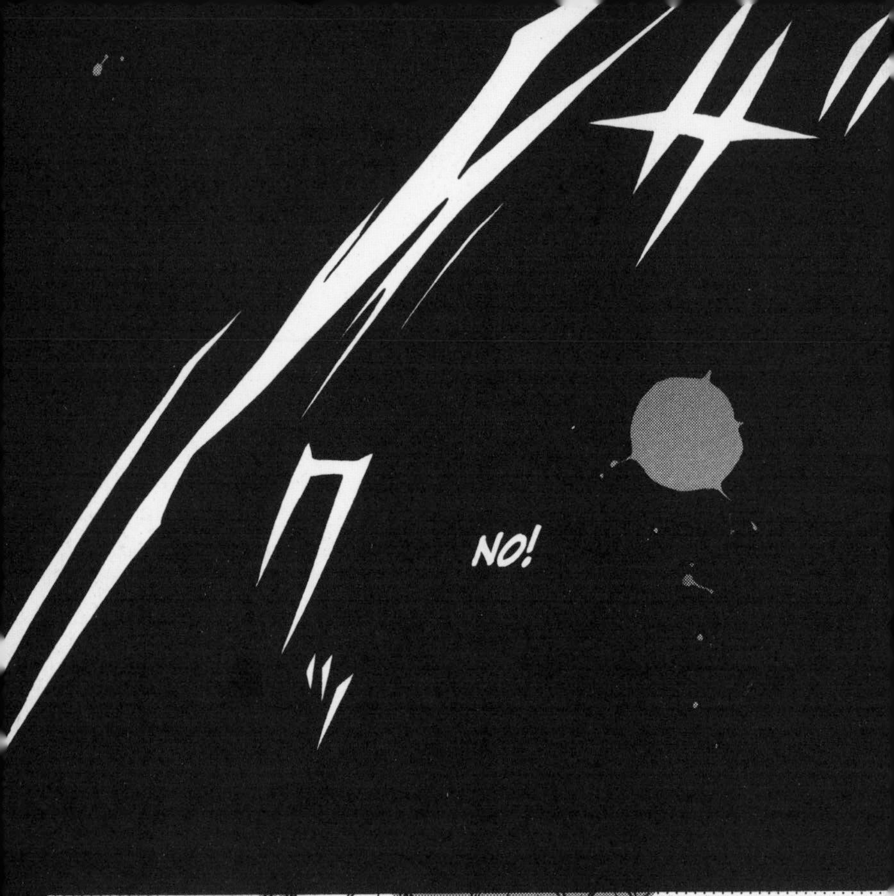
NO!
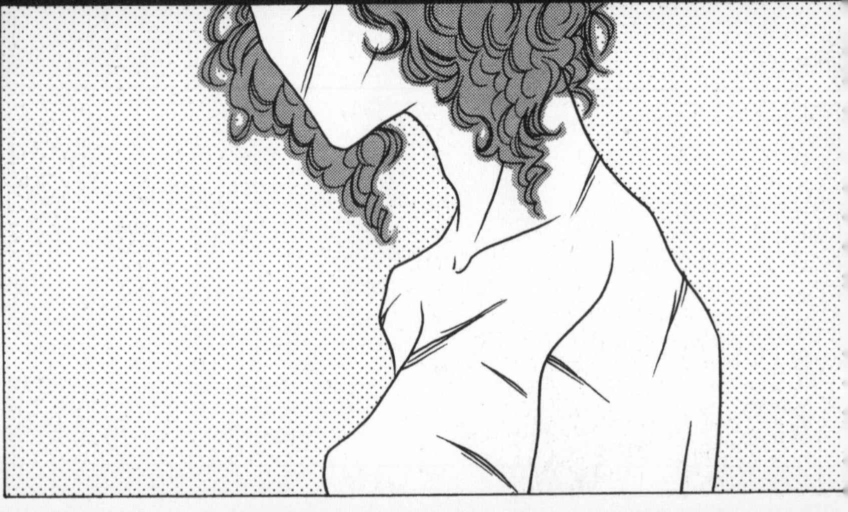

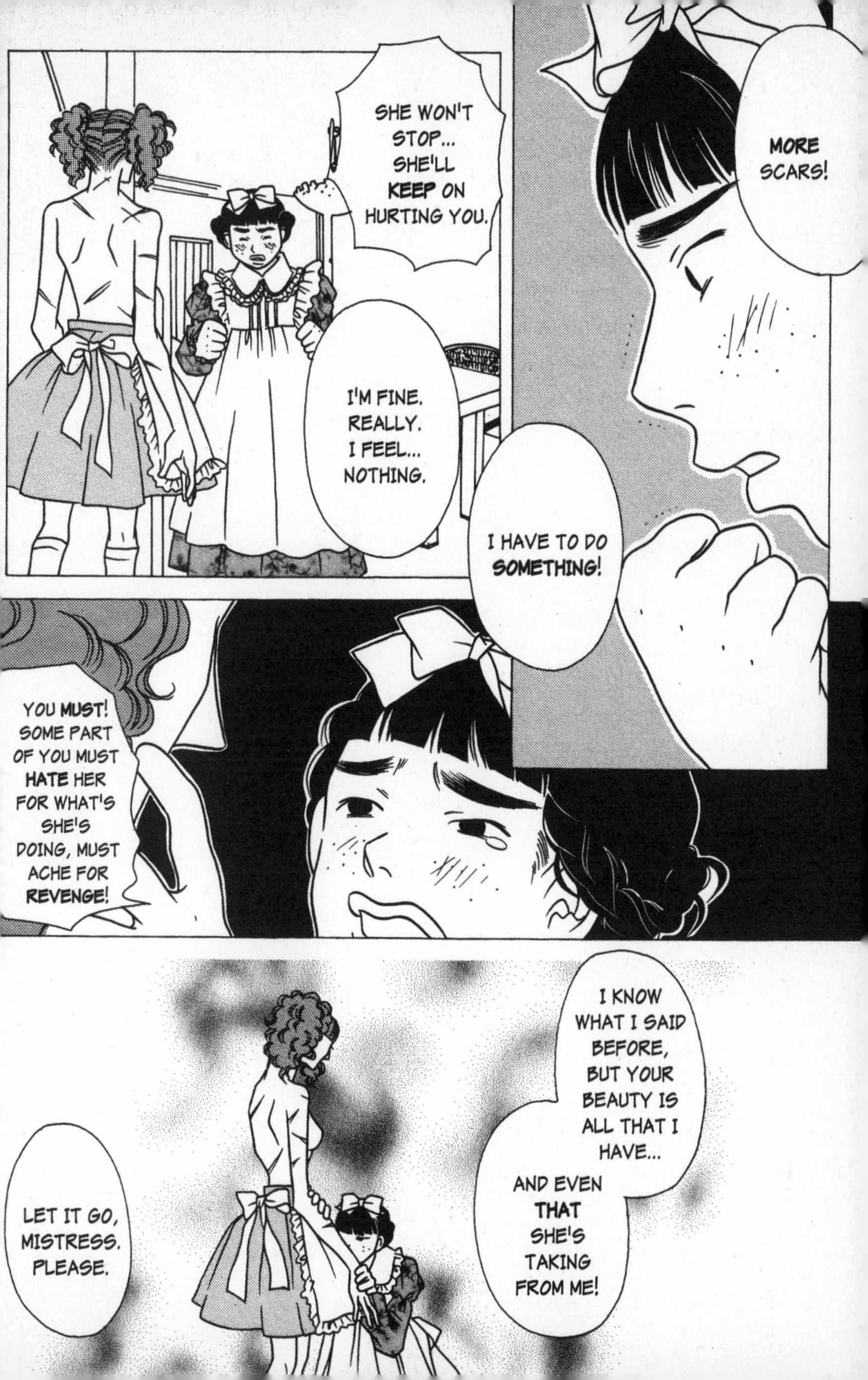
MORE SCARS!
I HAVE TO DO SOMETHING!
SHE WON'T STOP... SHE'LL KEEP ON HURTING YOU.
I'M FINE. REALLY. I FEEL... NOTHING.
YOU MUST! SOME PART OF YOU MUST HATE HER FOR WHAT'S SHE'S DOING, MUST ACHE FOR REVENGE!
I KNOW WHAT I SAID BEFORE, BUT YOUR BEAUTY IS ALL THAT I HAVE...
AND EVEN THAT SHE'S TAKING FROM ME!
LET IT GO, MISTRESS. PLEASE.

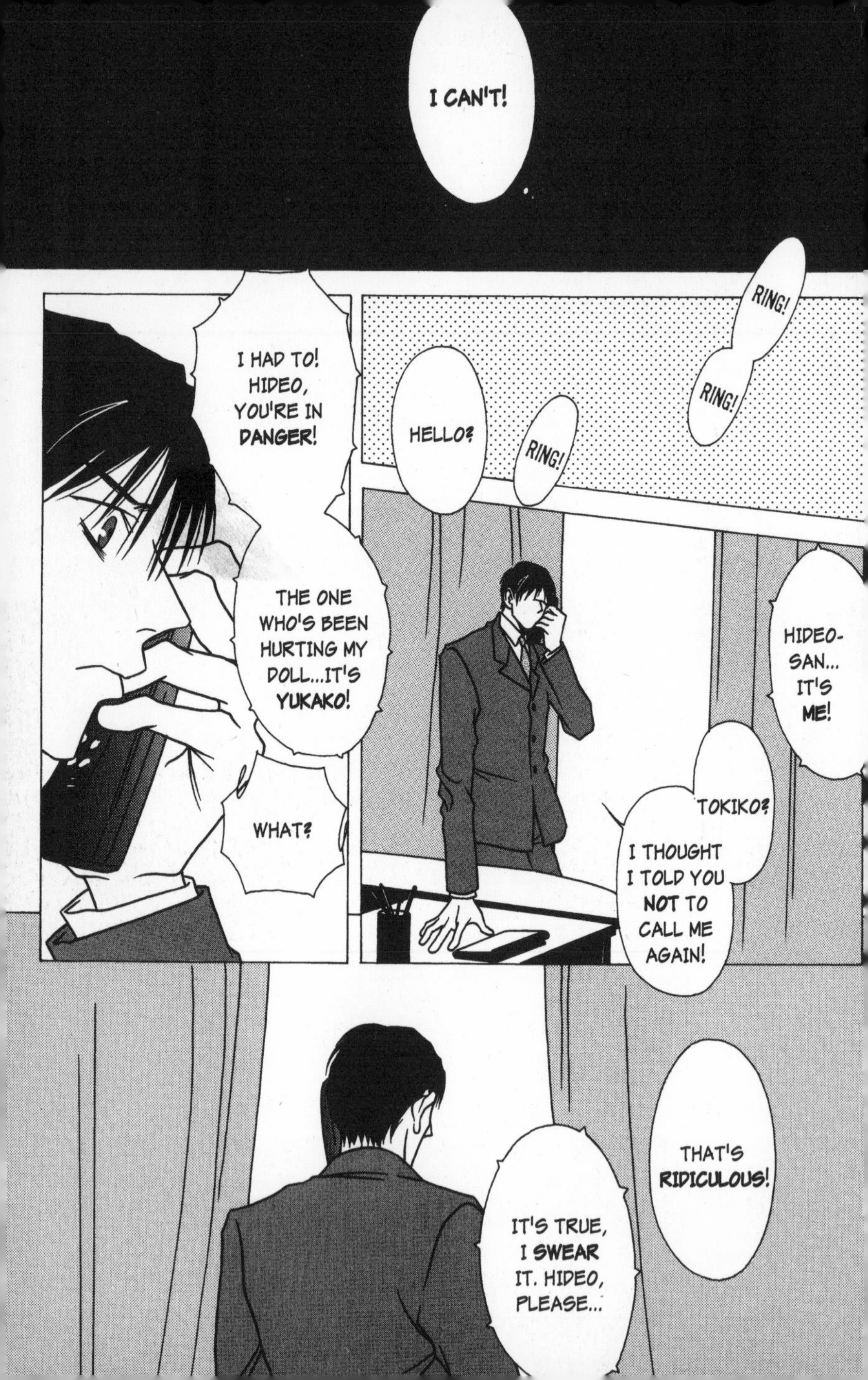
I CAN'T!
RING!
RING!
RING!
HELLO?
HIDEO-SAN... IT'S ME!
TOKIKO?
I THOUGHT I TOLD YOU NOT TO CALL ME AGAIN!
I HAD TO! HIDEO, YOU'RE IN DANGER!
THE ONE WHO'S BEEN HURTING MY DOLL...IT'S YUKAKO!
WHAT?
THAT'S RIDICULOUS!
IT'S TRUE, I SWEAR IT. HIDEO, PLEASE...

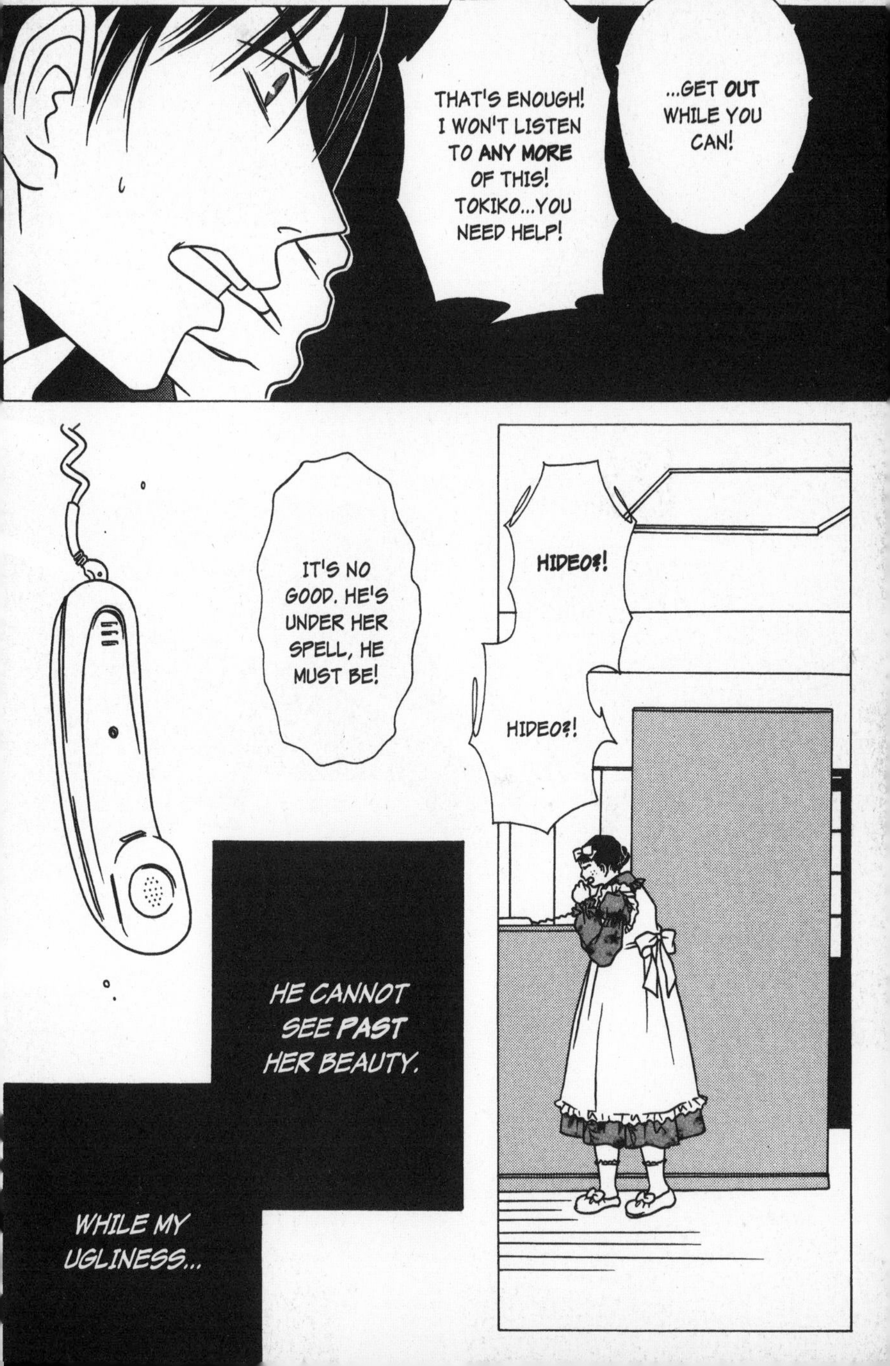
...GET OUT WHILE YOU CAN!
THAT'S ENOUGH! I WON'T LISTEN TO ANY MORE OF THIS! TOKIKO...YOU NEED HELP!
HIDEO?!
HIDEO?!
IT'S NO GOOD. HE'S UNDER HER SPELL, HE MUST BE!
HE CANNOT SEE PAST HER BEAUTY.
WHILE MY UGLINESS...

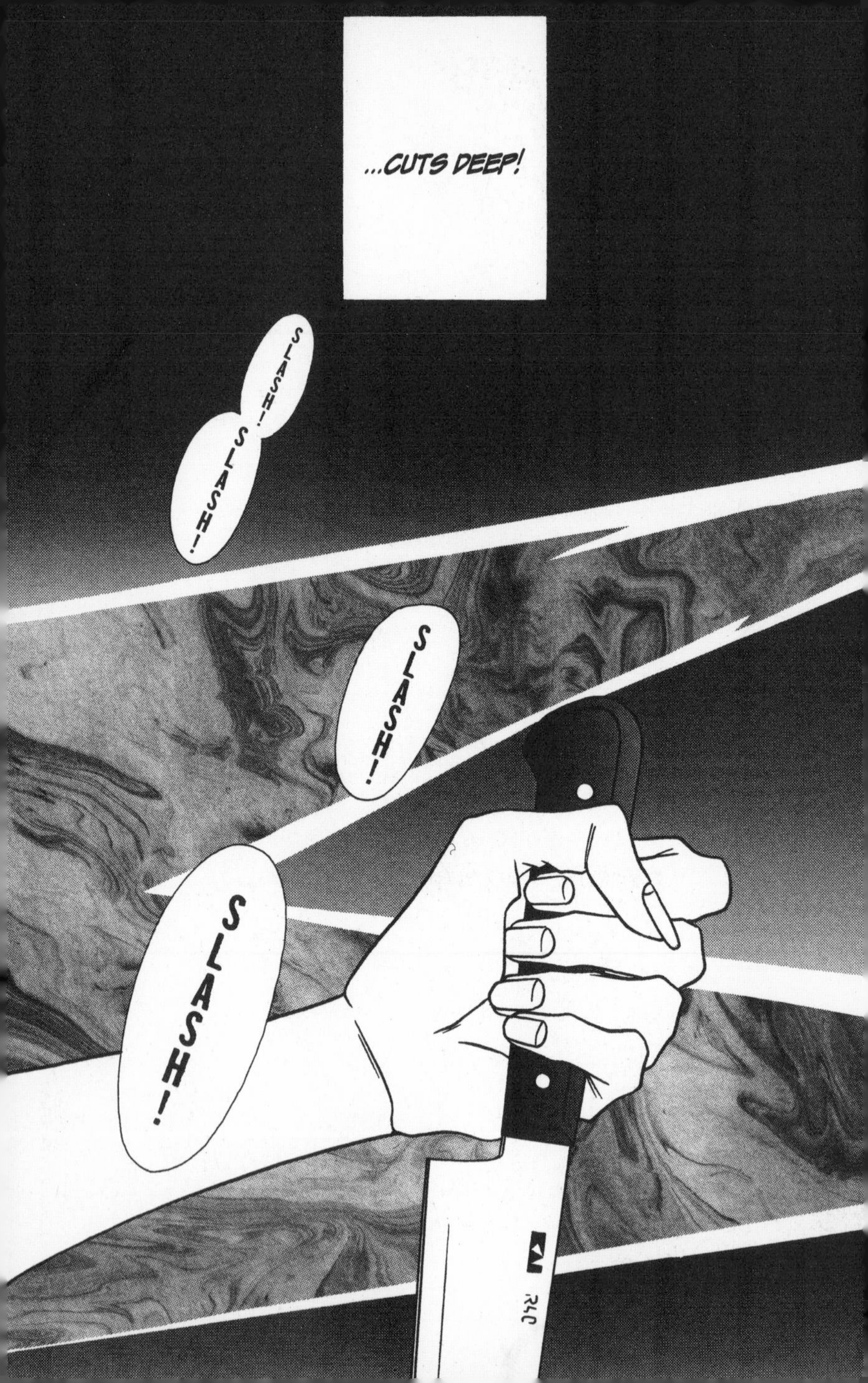
...CUTS DEEP!
SLASH!
SLASH!
SLASH!
SLASH!

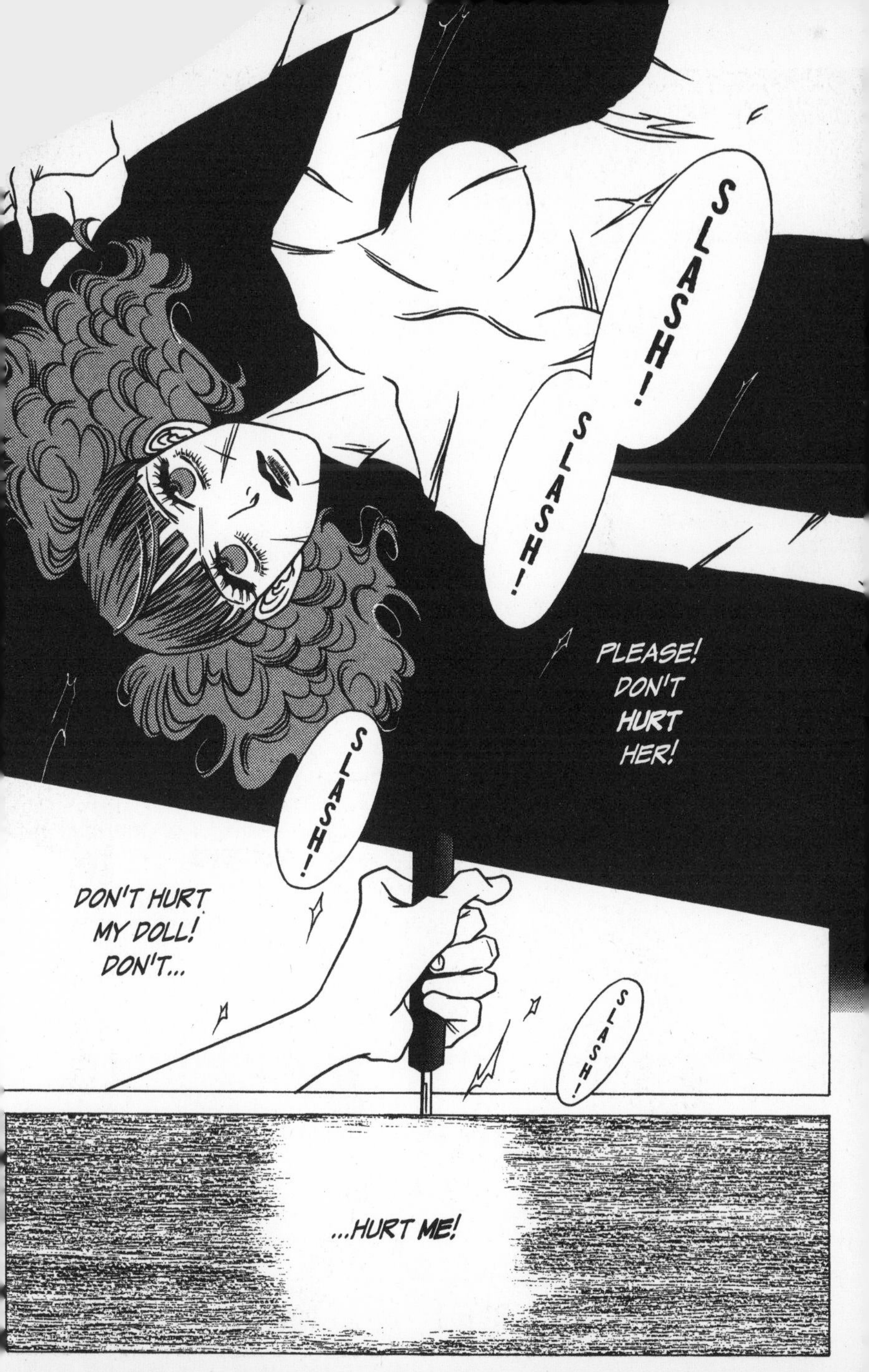
SLASH!
SLASH!
PLEASE! DON'T HURT HER!
SLASH!
DON'T HURT MY DOLL! DON'T...
SLASH!
...HURT ME!

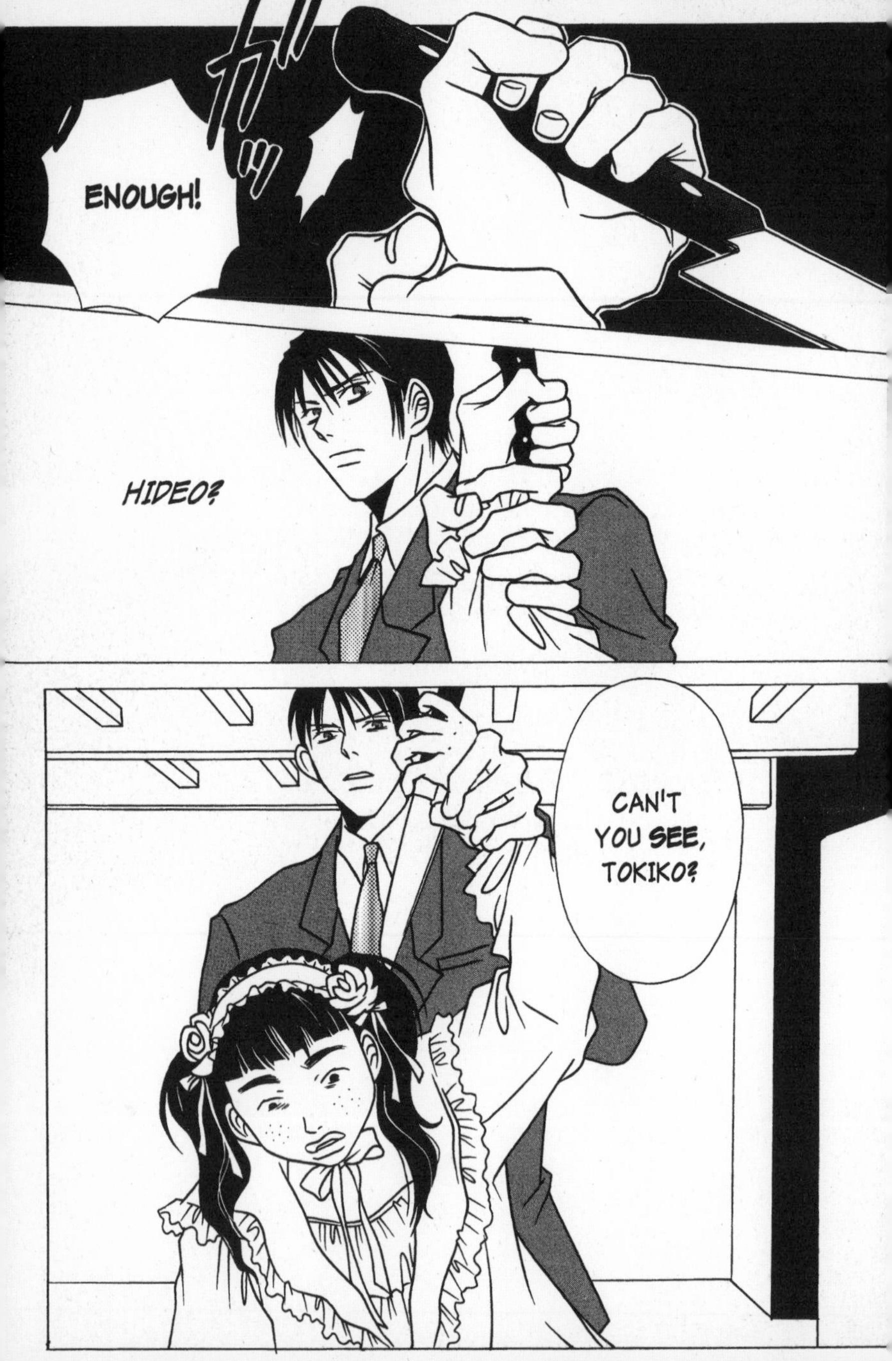
ガッ
ENOUGH!
HIDEO?
CAN'T YOU SEE, TOKIKO?

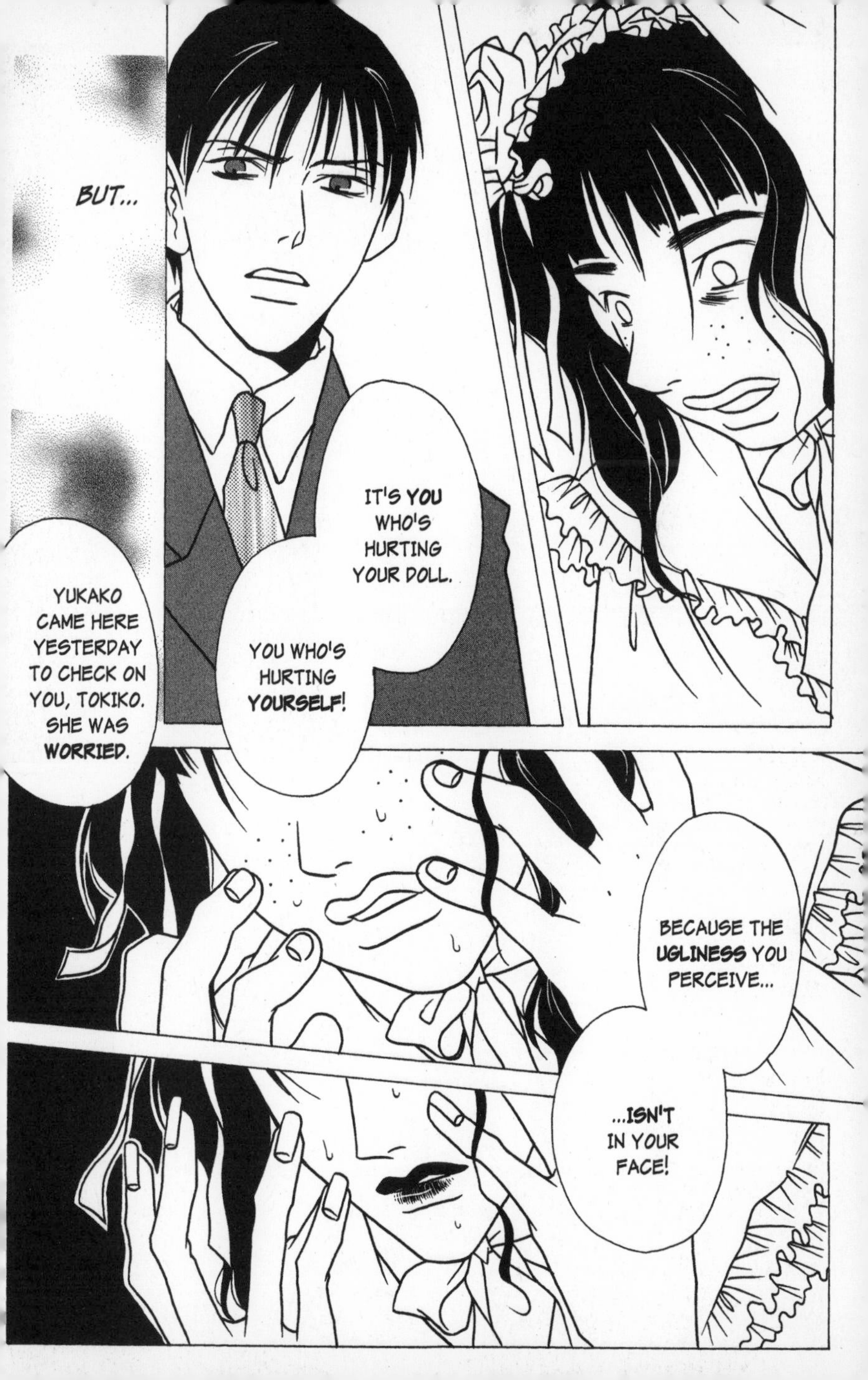
IT'S YOU WHO'S HURTING YOUR DOLL.
YOU WHO'S HURTING YOURSELF!
BUT...
YUKAKO CAME HERE YESTERDAY TO CHECK ON YOU, TOKIKO. SHE WAS WORRIED.
BECAUSE THE UGLINESS YOU PERCEIVE...
...ISN'T IN YOUR FACE!

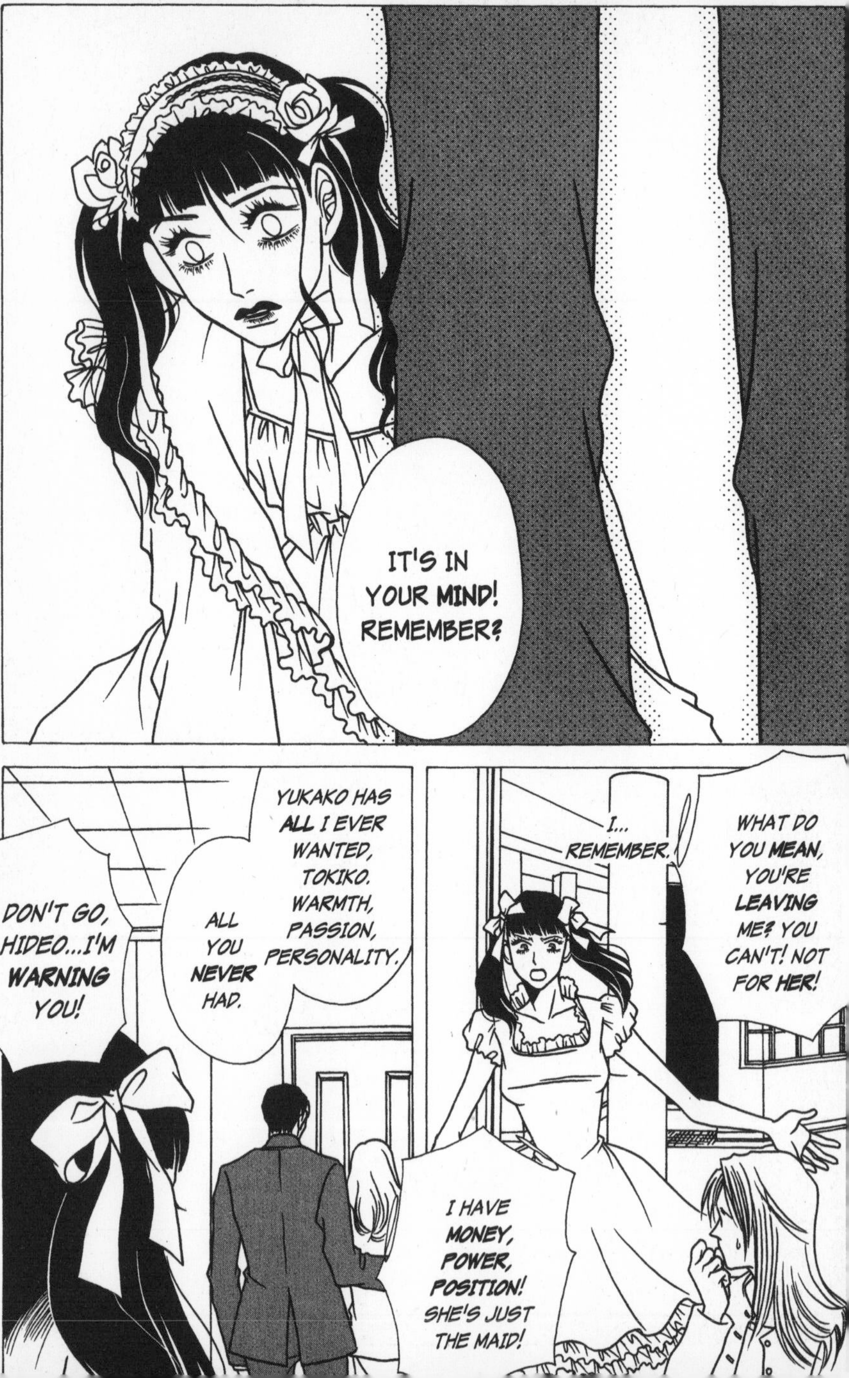
IT'S IN YOUR MIND! REMEMBER?
WHAT DO YOU MEAN, YOU'RE LEAVING ME? YOU CAN'T! NOT FOR HER!
I... REMEMBER.
I HAVE MONEY, POWER, POSITION! SHE'S JUST THE MAID!
YUKAKO HAS ALL I EVER WANTED, TOKIKO. WARMTH, PASSION, PERSONALITY.
ALL YOU NEVER HAD.
DON'T GO, HIDEO...I'M WARNING YOU!

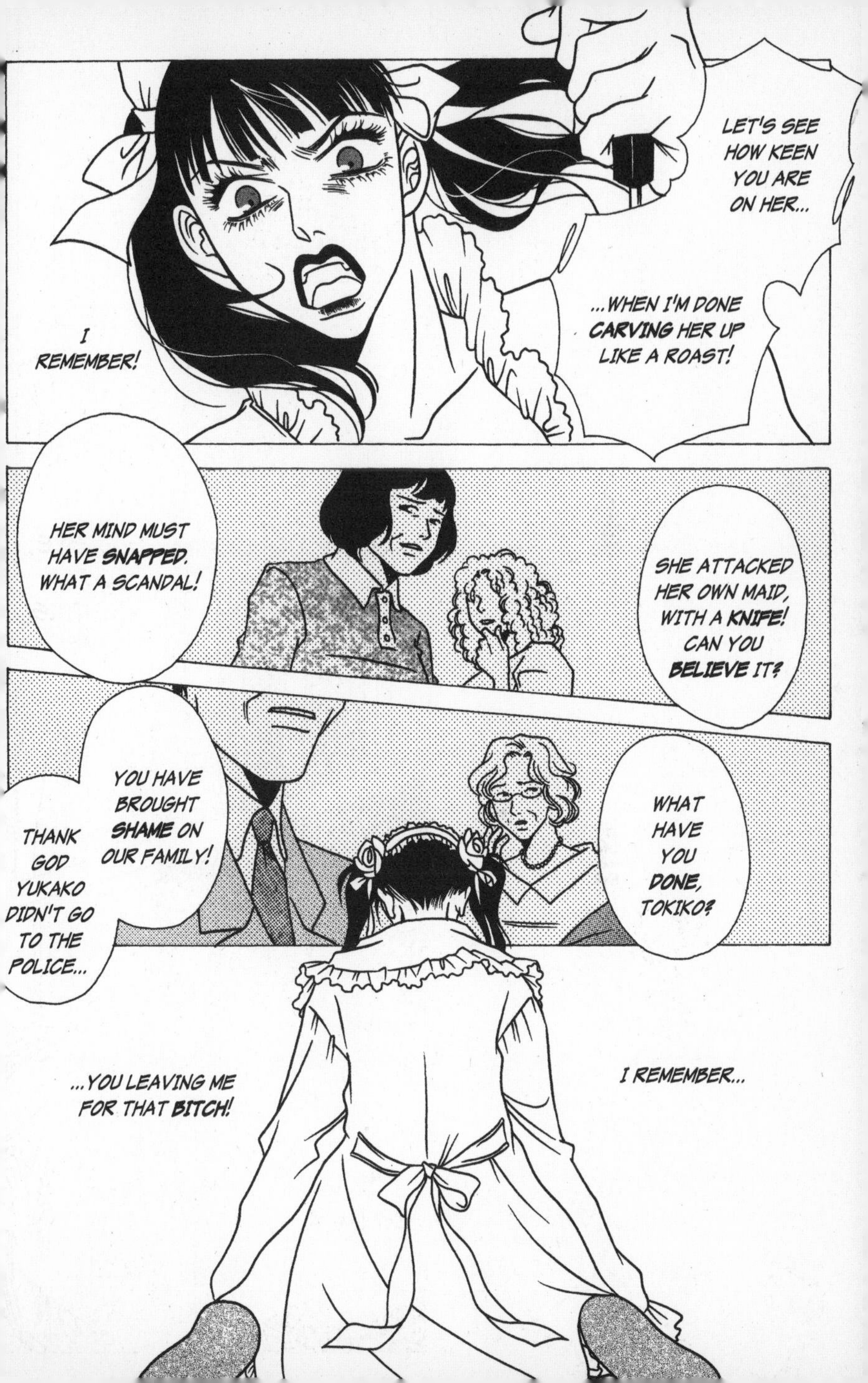
LET'S SEE HOW KEEN YOU ARE ON HER...
...WHEN I'M DONE CARVING HER UP LIKE A ROAST!
I REMEMBER!
SHE ATTACKED HER OWN MAID, WITH A KNIFE! CAN YOU BELIEVE IT?
HER MIND MUST HAVE SNAPPED. WHAT A SCANDAL!
WHAT HAVE YOU DONE, TOKIKO?
YOU HAVE BROUGHT SHAME ON OUR FAMILY!
THANK GOD YUKAKO DIDN'T GO TO THE POLICE...
I REMEMBER...
...YOU LEAVING ME FOR THAT BITCH!

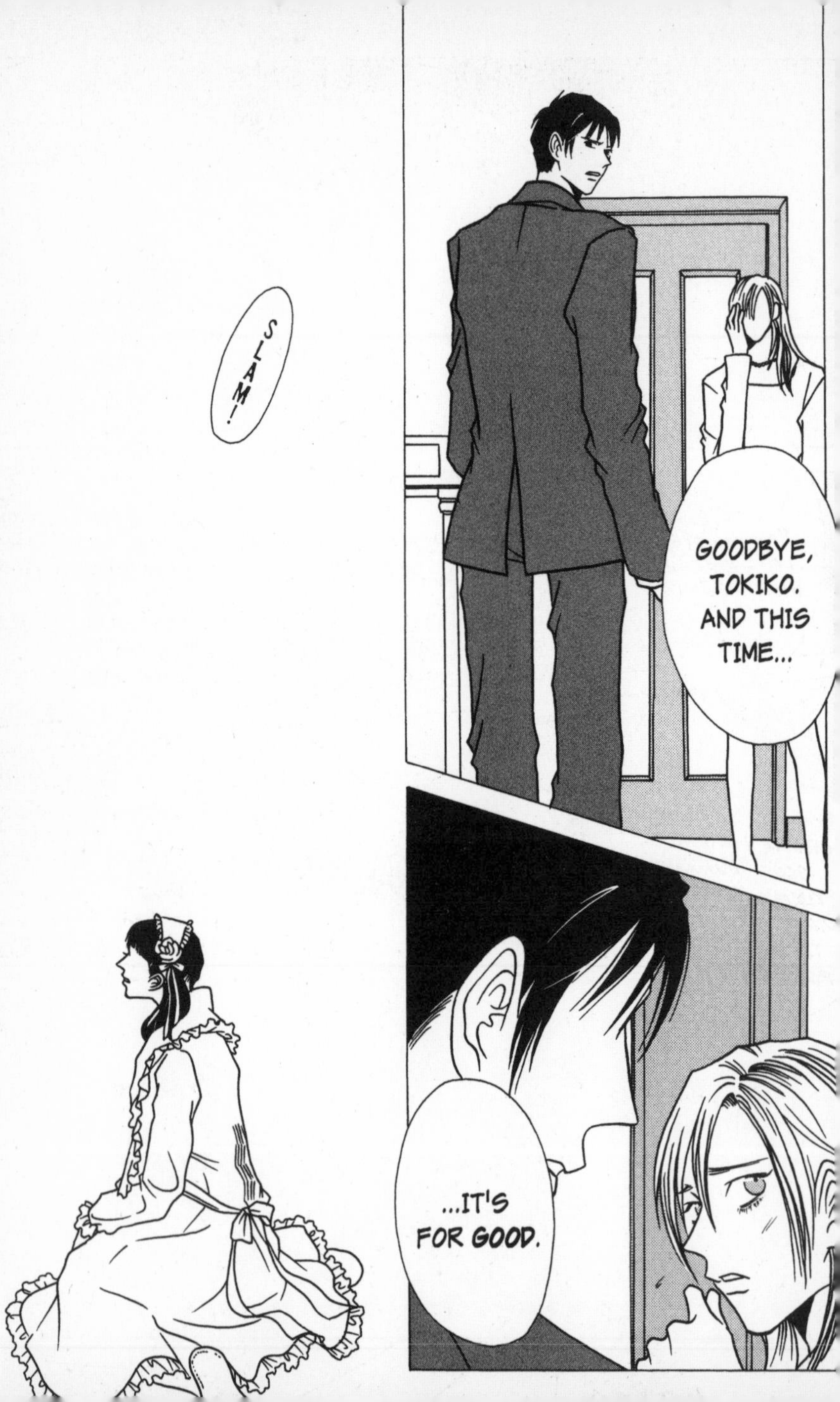
GOODBYE, TOKIKO. AND THIS TIME...
...IT'S FOR GOOD.
SLAM!

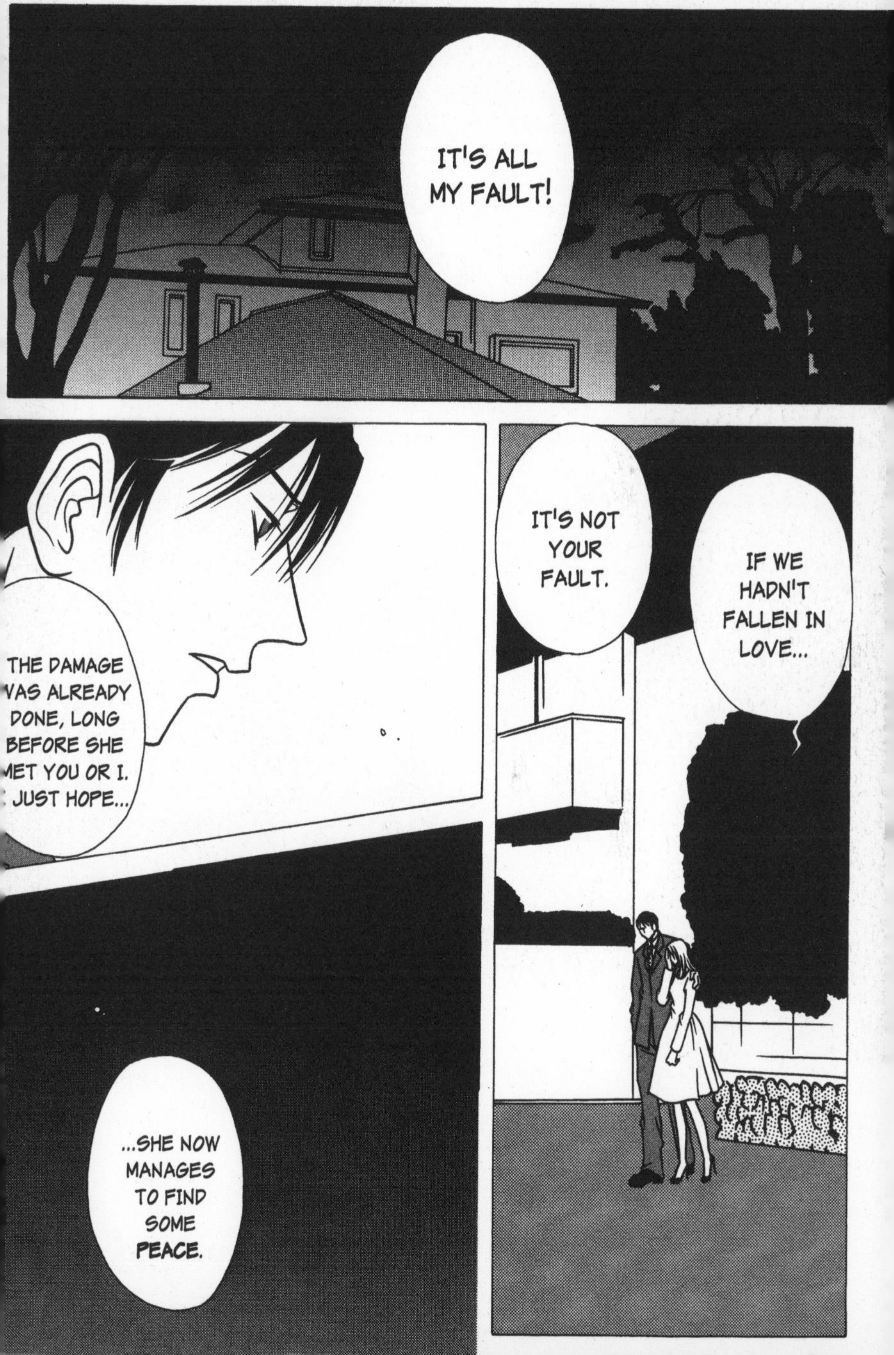
IT'S ALL MY FAULT!
IF WE HADN'T FALLEN IN LOVE...
IT'S NOT YOUR FAULT.
THE DAMAGE VAS ALREADY DONE, LONG BEFORE SHE MET YOU OR I. JUST HOPE...
...SHE NOW MANAGES TO FIND SOME PEACE.

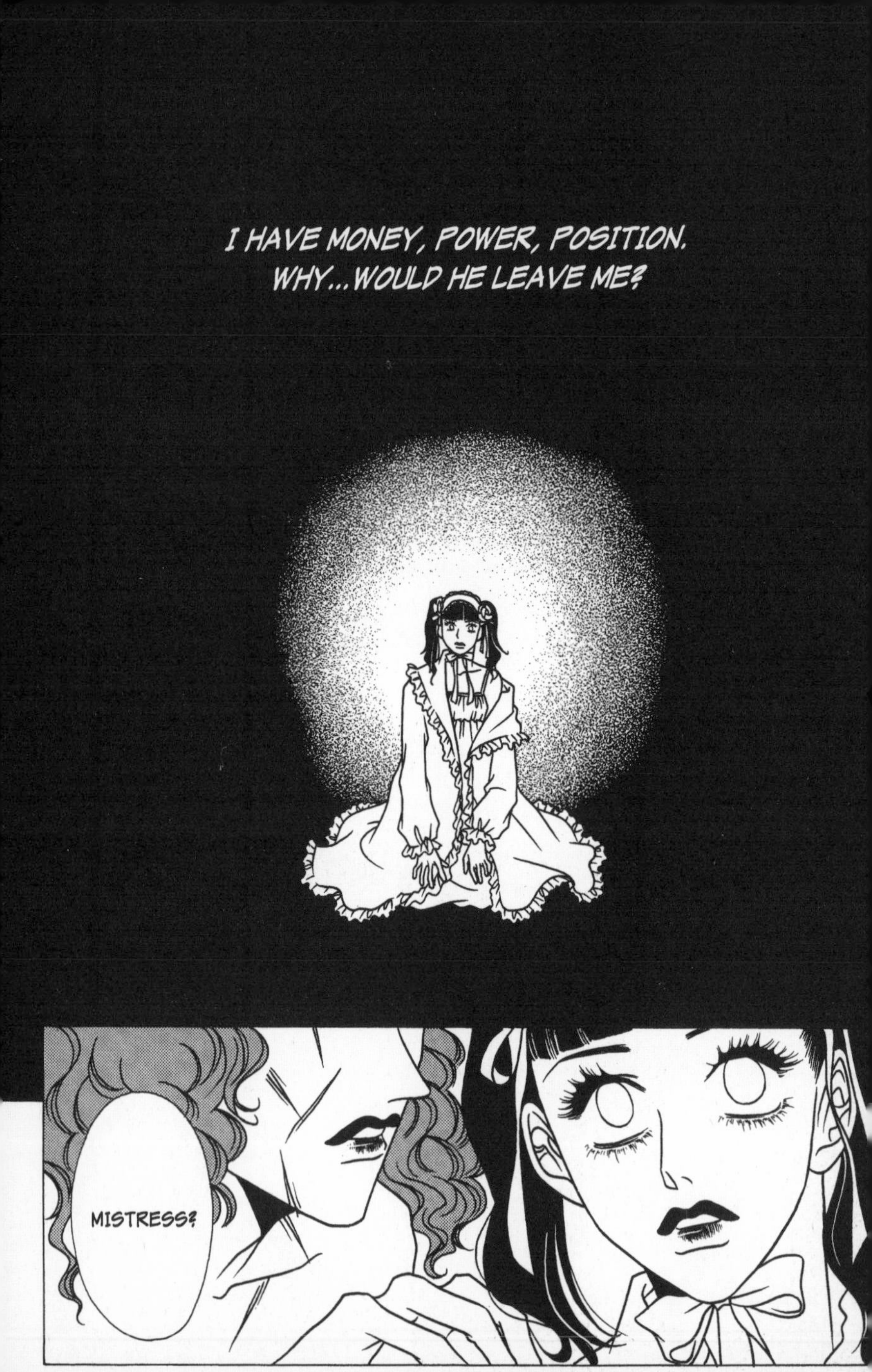
I HAVE MONEY, POWER, POSITION.
WHY...WOULD HE LEAVE ME?
MISTRESS?

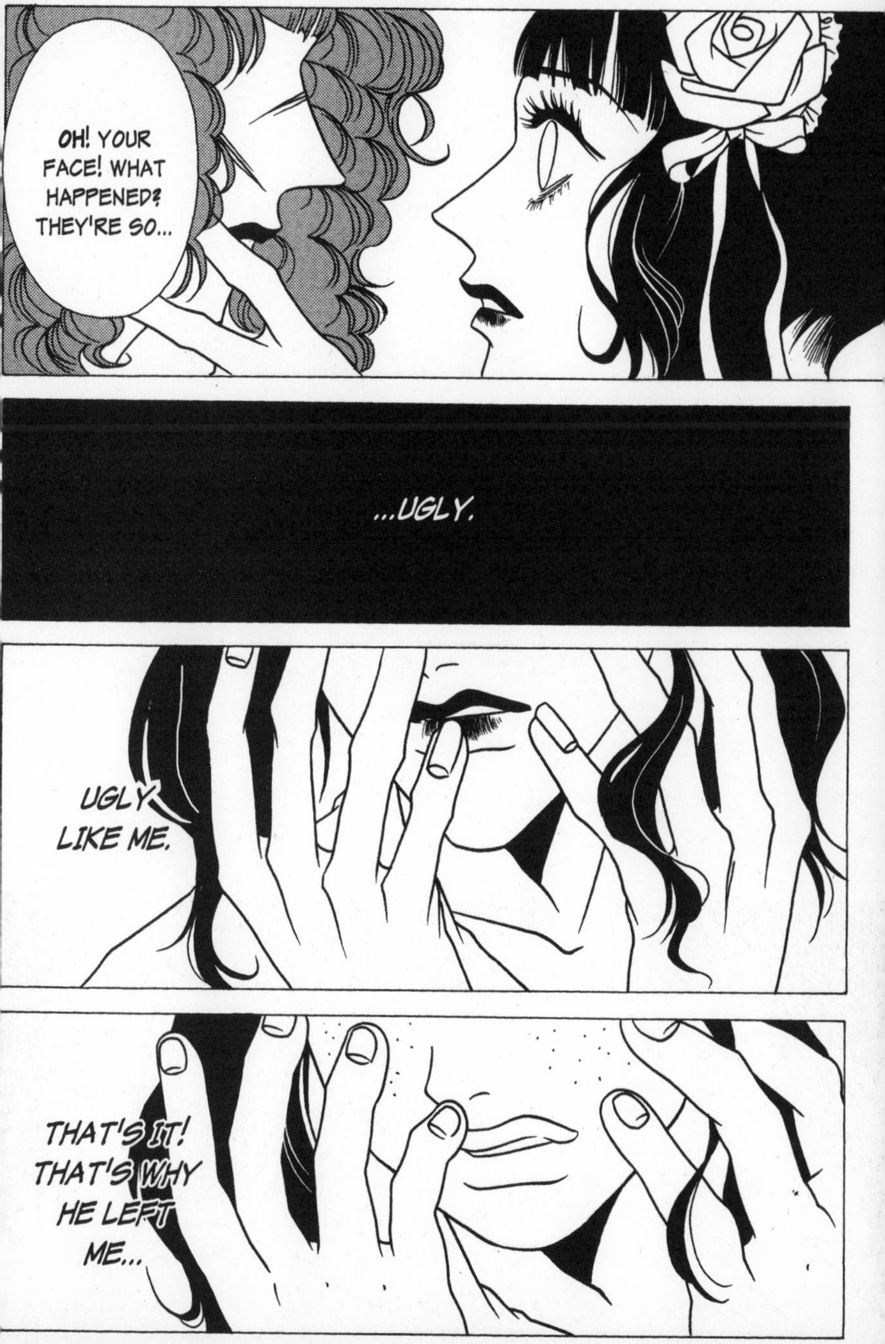
OH! YOUR FACE! WHAT HAPPENED? THEY'RE SO...
...UGLY.
UGLY LIKE ME.
THAT'S IT! THAT'S WHY HE LEFT ME...

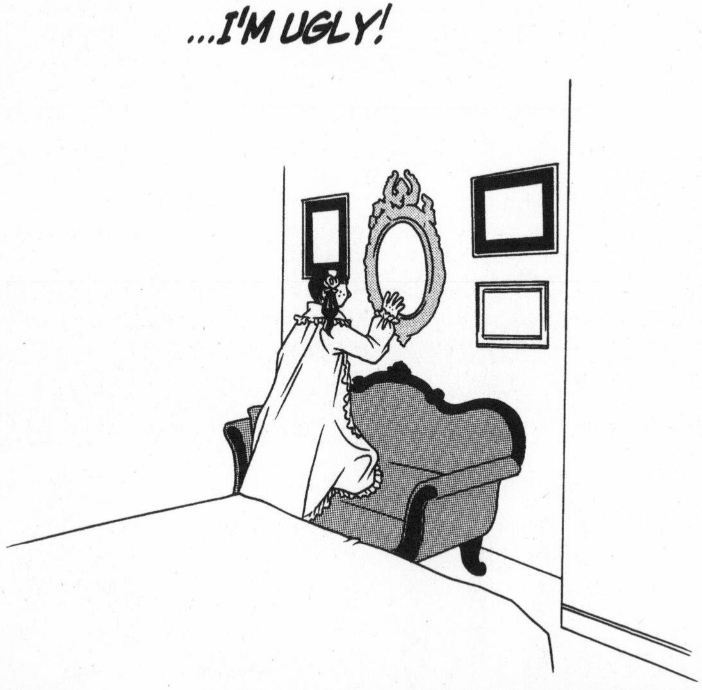
...I'M UGLY!

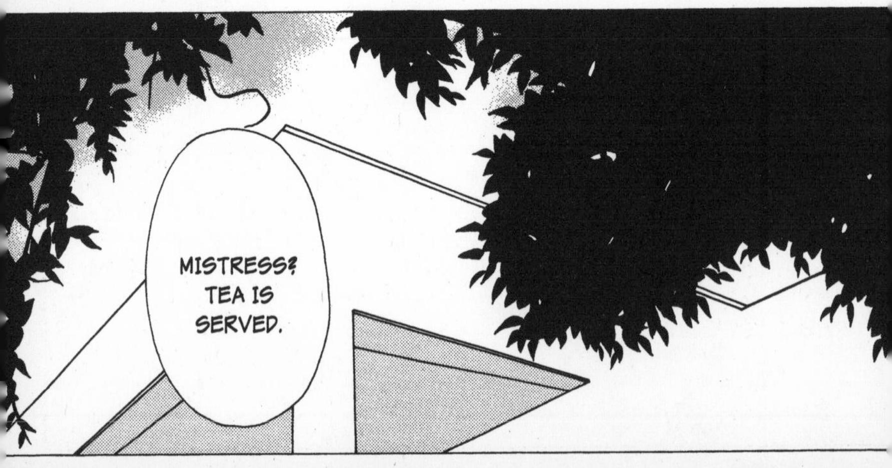
MISTRESS? TEA IS SERVED.

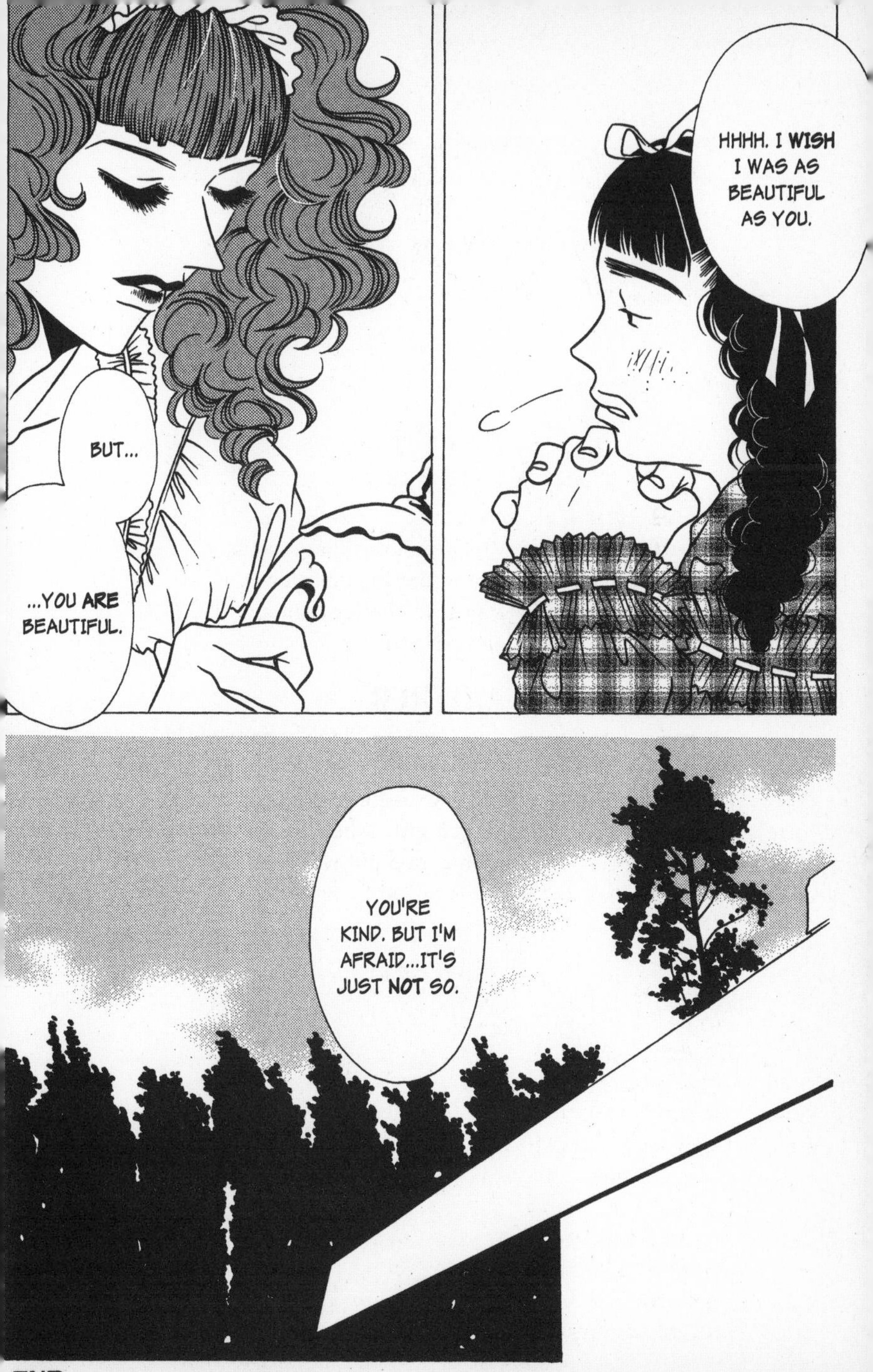
HHHH. I WISH I WAS AS BEAUTIFUL AS YOU.
BUT...
...YOU ARE BEAUTIFUL.
YOU'RE KIND. BUT I'M AFRAID...IT'S JUST NOT SO.

END

IN THE NEXT VOLUME OF

DOLL

SIX NEW TALES OF
ANDROIDS AND ANGST, INCLUDING:

MIKA

Machines are meant to do jobs that are too dangerous,
dirty or distasteful for humans...but there are some
unpleasant tasks even they cannot manage. At her
workplace, Mika picks up where the dolls leave off.
What can one mousy woman do better than any doll...
and how long can she keep it up?

MOTHER

Meet the Remodeler, someone who illegally alters dolls
for money. The Remodeler's neighbors are a single mom
and her young son, who believes that--if he's good--
Santa Claus will bring him a gift. When the law shows
up at the Remodeler's home, find out what comes to
those who have been naughty and those who have been
nice!

MAKOTO

Makoto can see people's past and future. Her special
ability is accompanied by special treatment and special
limitations...and she hates every minute of it. How does
the introduction of a boy doll affect this fortune-teller's
vision of her own future?

S

When the doll manufacturing SG Corporation is threat-
ened by an anti-doll terrorist group, they call upon a
very special doll known only as S...which was originally
created to assassinate illegally remodeled dolls!

ALSO AVAILABLE FROM TOKYOPOP®

**For more
information visit
www.TOKYOPOP.com**

ALSO AVAILABLE FROM TOKYOPOP

MANGA

.HACK//LEGEND OF THE TWILIGHT
@LARGE
ABENOBASHI: MAGICAL SHOPPING ARCADE
A.I. LOVE YOU
AI YORI AOSHI
ANGELIC LAYER
ARM OF KANNON
BABY BIRTH
BATTLE ROYALE
BATTLE VIXENS
BRAIN POWERED
BRIGADOON
B'TX
CANDIDATE FOR GODDESS, THE
CARDCAPTOR SAKURA
CARDCAPTOR SAKURA - MASTER OF THE CLOW
CHOBITS
CHRONICLES OF THE CURSED SWORD
CLAMP SCHOOL DETECTIVES
CLOVER
COMIC PARTY
CONFIDENTIAL CONFESSIONS
CORRECTOR YUI
COWBOY BEBOP
COWBOY BEBOP: SHOOTING STAR
CRAZY LOVE STORY
CRESCENT MOON
CULDCEPT
CYBORG 009
D•N•ANGEL
DEMON DIARY
DEMON ORORON, THE
DEUS VITAE
DIGIMON
DIGIMON TAMERS
DIGIMON ZERO TWO
DOLL
DRAGON HUNTER
DRAGON KNIGHTS
DRAGON VOICE
DREAM SAGA
DUKLYON: CLAMP SCHOOL DEFENDERS
EERIE QUEERIE!
ERICA SAKURAZAWA: COLLECTED WORKS
ET CETERA
ETERNITY
EVIL'S RETURN
FAERIES' LANDING
FAKE
FLCL
FORBIDDEN DANCE
FRUITS BASKET
G GUNDAM
GATEKEEPERS
GETBACKERS

GIRL GOT GAME
GRAVITATION
GTO
GUNDAM BLUE DESTINY
GUNDAM SEED ASTRAY
GUNDAM WING
GUNDAM WING: BATTLEFIELD OF PACIFISTS
GUNDAM WING: ENDLESS WALTZ
GUNDAM WING: THE LAST OUTPOST (G-UNIT)
HANDS OFF!
HAPPY MANIA
HARLEM BEAT
I.N.V.U.
IMMORTAL RAIN
INITIAL D
INSTANT TEEN: JUST ADD NUTS
ISLAND
JING: KING OF BANDITS
JING: KING OF BANDITS - TWILIGHT TALES
JULINE
KARE KANO
KILL ME, KISS ME
KINDAICHI CASE FILES, THE
KING OF HELL
KODOCHA: SANA'S STAGE
LAMENT OF THE LAMB
LEGAL DRUG
LEGEND OF CHUN HYANG, THE
LES BIJOUX
LOVE HINA
LUPIN III
LUPIN III: WORLD'S MOST WANTED
MAGIC KNIGHT RAYEARTH I
MAGIC KNIGHT RAYEARTH II
MAHOROMATIC: AUTOMATIC MAIDEN
MAN OF MANY FACES
MARMALADE BOY
MARS
MARS: HORSE WITH NO NAME
METROID
MINK
MIRACLE GIRLS
MIYUKI-CHAN IN WONDERLAND
MODEL
ONE
ONE I LOVE, THE
PARADISE KISS
PARASYTE
PASSION FRUIT
PEACH GIRL
PEACH GIRL: CHANGE OF HEART
PET SHOP OF HORRORS
PITA-TEN
PLANET LADDER
PLANETES
PRIEST

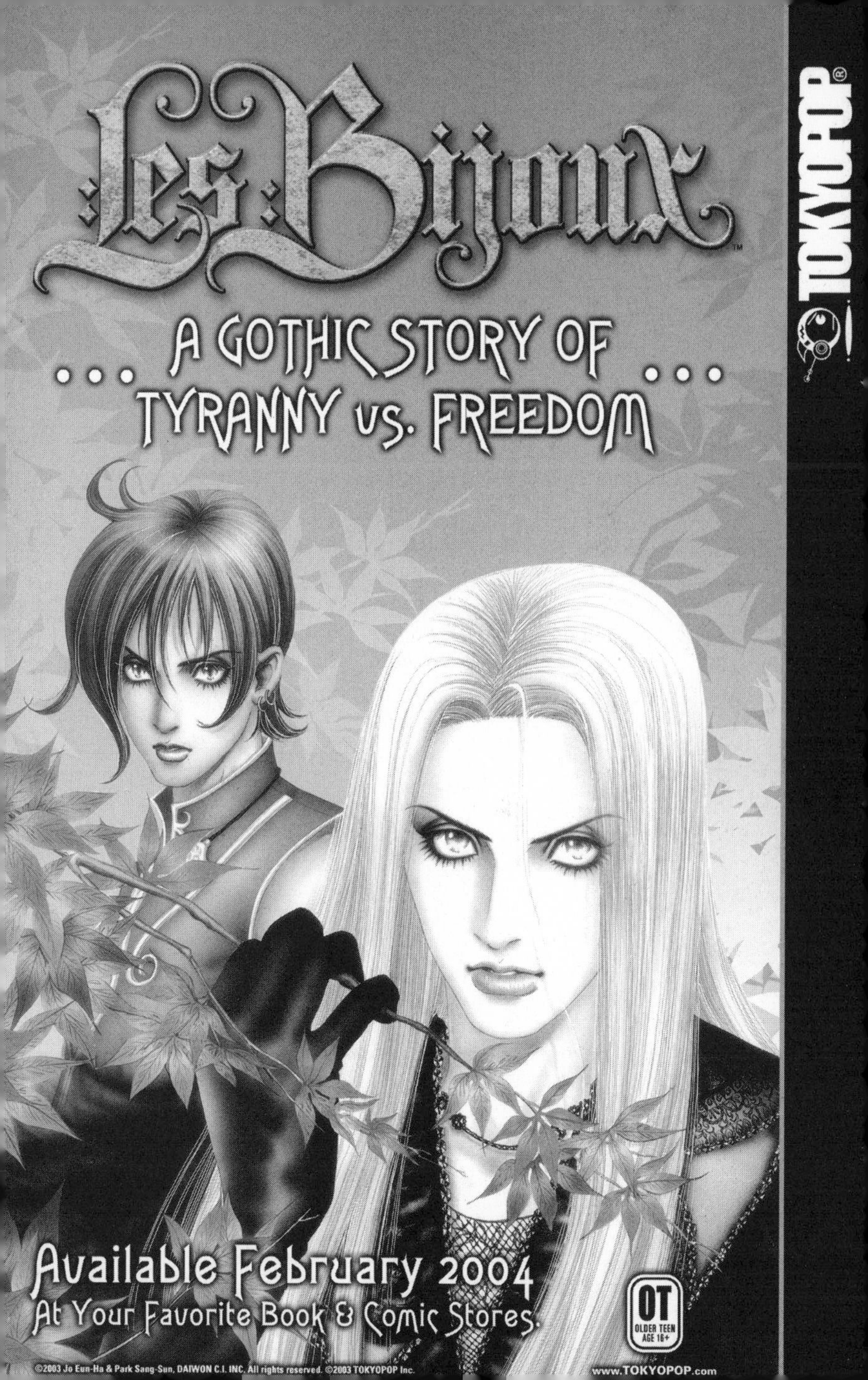
TOKYOPOP®
Les Bijoux™
... A GOTHIC STORY OF TYRANNY vs. FREEDOM ...
Available February 2004
At Your Favorite Book & Comic Stores.
OT
OLDER TEEN AGE 16+
©2003 Jo Eun-Ha & Park Sang-Sun, DAIWON C.I. INC. All rights reserved. ©2003 TOKYOPOP Inc.
www.TOKYOPOP.com

LAMENT of the LAMB ™

SHE CAN PROTECT HER BROTHER FROM THE WORLD.
CAN SHE PROTECT THE WORLD FROM HER BROTHER?

OT
OLDER TEEN
AGE 16+

Princess ai

Courtney Love & D.J. Milky put their spin on celebrity and fantasy.

TOKYOPOP

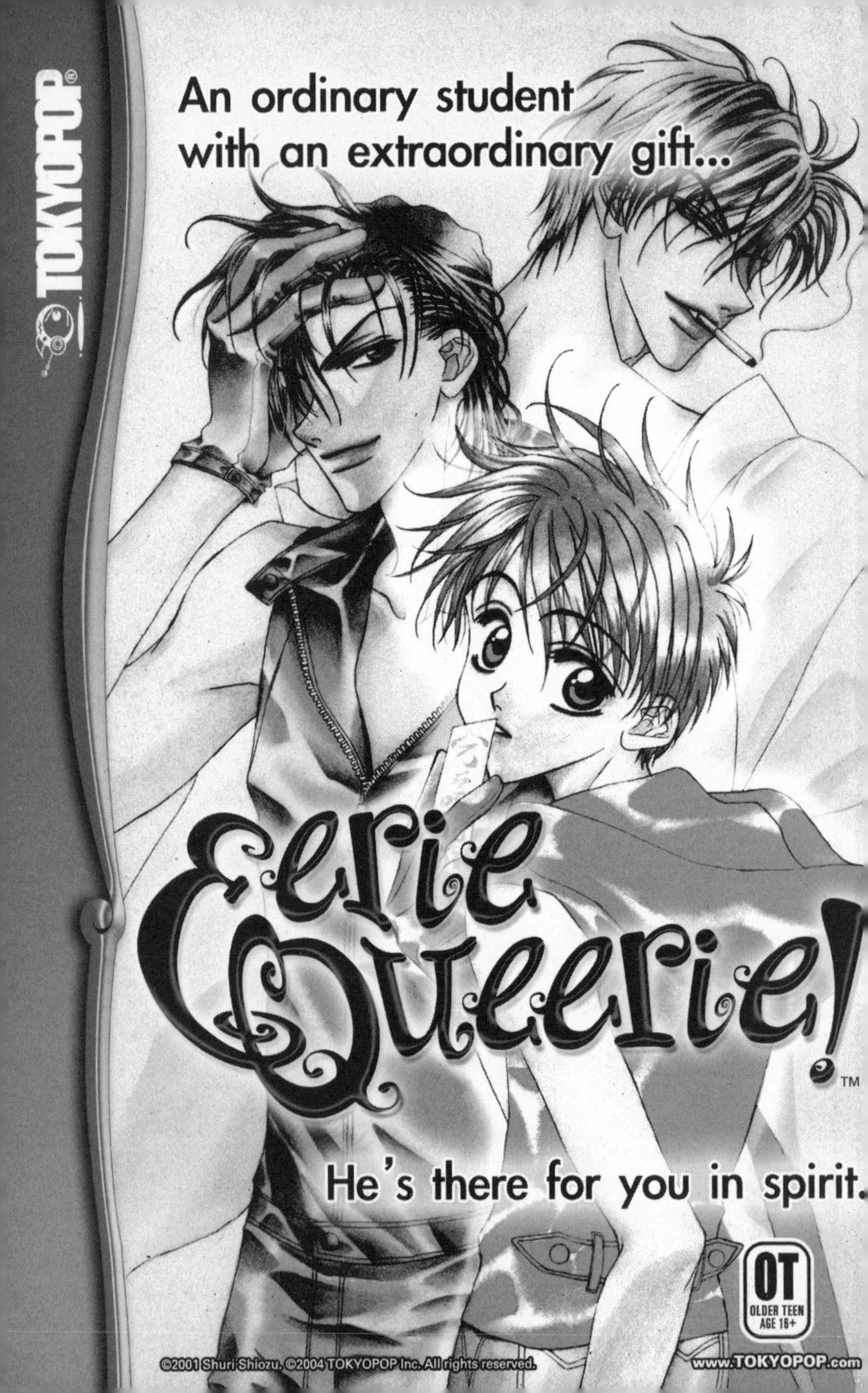
TOKYOPOP®
An ordinary student
with an extraordinary gift...
Eerie Queerie!™
He's there for you in spirit.
OT
OLDER TEEN
AGE 16+
©2001 Shuri Shiozu. ©2004 TOKYOPOP Inc. All rights reserved.
www.TOKYOPOP.com

STOP!

This is the back of the book.
You wouldn't want to spoil a great ending!

This book is printed "manga-style," in the authentic Japanese right-to-left format. Since none of the artwork has been flipped or altered, readers get to experience the story just as the creator intended. You've been asking for it, so TOKYOPOP® delivered: authentic, hot-off-the-press, and far more fun!

DIRECTIONS

If this is your first time reading manga-style, here's a quick guide to help you understand how it works.

It's easy... just start in the top right panel and follow the numbers. Have fun, and look for more 100% authentic manga from TOKYOPOP®!